CONSTRUCTIVE GUIDANCE AND DISCIPLINE

Preschool and Primary Education

Custom Edition

Marjorie V. Fields • Cindy Boesser

Taken from:
Constructive Guidance and Discipline: Preschool and Primary Education,
Third Edition
By Marjorie V. Fields and Cindy Boesser

Taken from:

Constructive Guidance and Discipline: Preschool and Primary Education, Third Edition
by Marjorie V. Fields and Cindy Boesser

Published by Merrill Prentice Hall
Upper Saddle River, New Jersey 07458

This special edition published in cooperation with Pearson Custom Publishing.

Printed in the United States of America

10

Please visit our web site at www.pearsoncustom.com

ISBN 0–536–70468–6

BA 995948

PEARSON CUSTOM PUBLISHING
75 Arlington Street, Suite 300, Boston, MA 02116
A Pearson Education Company

For the cause of
worldwide peace and harmony.
May it begin in the
hearts of children
and spread.
And may teachers
be sowers of the seeds
of peace and harmony.

Foreword

This is a practical book with many examples and contrasts. It is not, however, a mere collection of recipes, but a book full of instructive examples based on sound theoretical reasons. It also communicates a way of thinking about young children and attitudes of empathy.

The approach the authors recommend is good because it solves problems in positive ways and promotes the development of healthy personalities. In addition, though, the authors have a vision of autonomy as the aim of education that goes far beyond the development of healthy personalities. Since this vision may not have been articulated as forcefully as it could have been, I would like to take this opportunity to discuss autonomy as intended by Jean Piaget as the aim of education.

Autonomy in Piaget's theory means something different from its common meaning. Autonomy usually means the *right* to make decisions for oneself, and many people mistakenly think that it means the *right* to do whatever one pleases. In Piaget's theory, autonomy does not mean the right, but instead the *ability* to make decisions for oneself about right and wrong, independent of reward and punishment, by taking relevant factors into account. When one takes relevant factors into account, one is not free to lie, steal, break promises, disturb other people, or be irresponsible.

Parents and teachers have traditionally tried to teach right and wrong by using reward and/or punishment. Reward and punishment give the appearance of working but the result in the long run is either blind conformity or susceptibility to manipulation through reward and/or punishment. The Watergate coverup affair, for example, happened because the men under President Nixon expected to be rewarded for doing what they knew to be morally wrong. As far as the effects of punishment are concerned, we all know how the possibility of punishment leads to the calculation of risks.

A clear example of moral autonomy is Martin Luther King's struggle for civil rights. He took relevant factors into account, concluded that the laws discriminating against African Americans were unjust, and fought to put an end to these laws. Many people tried to stop him with incarceration, dogs, water hoses, and threats of assassination, but he could not be manipulated by reward or punishment.

The important question for parents and teachers is: How can we raise children to become morally autonomous adults who make decisions based on what is right, rather than on what is rewarded or punished? Piaget's answer to this question was that we foster the development of autonomy first by refraining from using reward and punishment. By giving stickers to children for completing worksheets, for example, we unwittingly teach them to become susceptible to manipulation by reward. If we punish children for lying, to cite another example, children can learn only to avoid being punished. Piaget would suggest that, instead of punishing a child for telling a lie, we might look him or her straight in the eye and say with affection and skepticism, "I can't believe what you are saying because . . . . I want you to sit down and think about what you might do next time if you want me to believe you." This appeal to the human relationship between the child and the adult and to the direct consequence of the act has the effect of motivating the child to construct *from within,* over time, the value of honesty. Children who are thus supported in building their own convictions about the importance of honesty cannot tell lies, even for a president who might dangle rewards.

A discussion of specific techniques is beyond the scope of the present context, and the reader is urged to read this book. I also recommend *The Moral Judgment of the Child* (Chapters 2 and 3) by Piaget.

Today's children live with many serious potential problems, such as drug abuse, AIDS, teenage pregnancies, and guns in schools. Although these may all look like separate problems, they are actually all symptoms of the inability to make decisions for oneself by taking relevant factors into account. Children who can take relevant factors into account do not take drugs, for example.

The belief that rules and values must be put into children from the outside through lectures, rewards, and punishment is outdated. Rules and values must be constructed (made) by children *from the inside* if they are to become the children's own. Only when children have convictions of their own do they have the moral courage to say "No" to drugs, sex, and violence. Children need the same strength of internal conviction Martin Luther King had when he stood up to the punishment heaped upon him.

The time to start fostering the development of autonomy is at an early age. Through building strong human relationships, exchanging points of view with children, and allowing them to learn from their own mistakes, we can help them develop the capacity to take relevant factors into account. Autonomy is a complicated goal, and I congratulate the authors for going beyond the perspective of what seems to work in the short run. What seems to work in the short run often defeats our long-range goal of turning out adults who can decide for themselves between right and wrong.

Constance Kamii
Birmingham, Alabama

Preface

Constructive Guidance and Discipline: Preschool and Primary Education attempts to bring together the best of what is known about helping young children become happy, responsible, and productive people. We present guidance and discipline concepts within a framework of child development, developmentally appropriate practices, and Constructivist education. Thus, only discipline approaches that are consistent with all three aspects of this framework are recommended here. We take a stand about what is best for young children, rather than merely presenting an impartial overview of various approaches. We are convinced that adults cannot effectively assist children's moral development through the coercive approaches of behavior modification.

Major Theoretical Influences

The information and ideas presented in this text come from a number of respected sources. We see four theorists as having major influences on child guidance concepts in this century: Alfred Adler, Carl Rogers, B.F. Skinner, and Jean Piaget. Rudolf Dreikurs' recommendations of logical and natural consequences extended Adler's concepts, Thomas Gordon popularized Rogers' ideas through his Parent Effectiveness Training work, Skinner's work founded the widespread behavior modification techniques, and Piagetian scholars such as Constance Kamii and Rheta DeVries are spreading the word about Piaget's views on the development of morality. Though we reject Skinner's approach for the reasons explained in Chapter 9, we believe that the other three theorists have compatible views. Adler, Rogers, and Piaget all perceive the child as actively seeking understanding. This is in contrast with the Skinnerian view, which sees education as something that happens to a child from outside sources. Adler and Rogers, as well as Piaget, respect the child's personal rate and style of developing social understanding. All three perceive the proper adult role as facilitating rather than controlling the child's gradual development as a constructive member of society. Piaget's theoretical framework is much broader than that of Rogers or Adler, including all moral development as well as intellectual development. Thus, Adlerian and Rogerian concepts can be included as part of a Piagetian perspective, though the reverse is not true.

The research and writing of Jean Piaget and Constructivist scholars regarding intellectual and moral autonomy are central to the message in this book. We have adapted Thomas Gordon's recommendations for effective communication and interpreted Rudolf Dreikurs' concept of logical and natural consequences into our discussion of a Constructivist approach to discipline. We have also drawn on Erik Erikson's emotional development studies, referred to guidelines from the National Association for the Education of Young Children, and quoted Rheta DeVries. Many other sources used in this book are listed at the end of the chapters.

We look at guidance and discipline as teaching activities; therefore, the principles of effective early childhood education apply as much to guidance and discipline as to academics. In addition, we discuss the ways in which effective early childhood education practices prevent or alleviate many common discipline problems.

Like any other aspect of teaching, guidance must acknowledge diversity among youngsters. In our recommendations, we have considered individual differences due to innate temperament, or individual physical and intellectual capabilities. We also discuss the implications of culture, class, family problems, and gender.

We increasingly recognize that teaching must deal with youngsters whose lives are in crisis. These youngsters create major new challenges in guidance and discipline. Two chapters are devoted to providing background and support to teachers whose classrooms include youngsters with special physical and emotional needs or learning difficulties. Though parent involvement is crucial to all aspects of education and for all children, we emphasize the home-school link most in these chapters.

Changes in the Third Edition

This edition continues and strengthens the approach of the previous editions. We have continued to work at making the message of the book clear and understandable. Since behavior modification is so pervasive in our society, the recommendations in this book require most readers to radically alter their thinking. Assisting students in a major paradigm shift requires that principles be carefully documented and clearly explained. We have found that the examples of classroom practice are most effective in helping students understand the concepts; therefore, we have carefully reviewed the classroom vignettes, adding more and better examples.

This edition brings on the expertise of Dr. Lory Britain and Sierra Freeman for the chapter on children with serious emotional problems. Both Lory and Sierra have been working in the "trenches" with at-risk children and their families and have first-hand insights to share as well as a solid research base. Dr. Eileen Hughes, author of the chapter on children with disabilities from the second edition, has added to and strengthened that chapter for the third edition.

This edition adds a "test bank" for instructor convenience. These are not test items requiring mere rote memory; they simulate actual classroom situations where problem solving is required for effective discipline. This approach to testing is congruent with a Constructivist approach to education, allowing the college teacher to model the principles recommended.

Organization of the Text

The first three chapters of the book constitute the foundations section. Chapter 1 begins to explain a view of discipline as a way of teaching autonomy and self-discipline while promoting self-esteem. Concepts introduced in Chapter 1 are more fully addressed throughout the book. Chapters 2 and 3 consider stages in children's physical, emotional, intellectual, and social development as they relate to discipline problems and solutions. We consider a clear definition of discipline and its goals, plus knowledge of child development, to be the basic understandings for a discussion of discipline.

Part II presents various approaches to discipline in descending order from most positive to negative. This sequence can also be considered as an ascending order from least intrusive to most intrusive. Chapter 4 discusses how to prevent behavior problems by matching the child environment to developmental stages. Chapter 5 explains the role of developmentally appropriate programs in preventing discipline problems. Chapters 6 and 7 emphasize both the prevention of problems and intervention when problems do occur. Chapter 6 explains how the adult example influences child behavior and shows how to help children use those examples during conflict situations. Chapter 7 presents effective ways to communicate with children both to prevent conflict and to address problems that arise. This subject of effective communication includes how to negotiate solutions to existing problems. Chapter 8 explains changing unproductive behaviors by using related consequences to help children understand why certain behaviors are unacceptable. Chapter 9 analyzes behavior modification approaches, and explains why rewards and even praise are counterproductive to goals of self-discipline. The dangers of punishment are presented in Chapter 10.

Chapters 11 through 15 constitute Part III, which builds on the previous two parts. Child development knowledge from Part I is used as part of determining the cause of behavior problems. Then information about guidance approaches from Part II is used to select an appropriate response. Part III analyzes typical causes of discipline problems and relates them to the approaches relevant to each. These chapters emphasize the necessity of dealing with the cause of problems rather than just the symptoms. Chapter 11 discusses the relationship between maturational level and acceptable behavior, and Chapter 12 looks at how unmet emotional needs cause problem behavior. Chapters 13 and 14 explore serious problems with causes outside of the classroom and suggest help for the teacher or caregiver. Chapter 15 presents an overview of possible discipline problem causes and provides assistance in identifying which causes pertain to a particular situation. This chapter also provides a guide for matching causes with the approaches to discipline that are most likely to be effective for each.

Providing Examples

Because we wanted to balance theoretical explanations with real-life examples, we use typical scenarios to illustrate ways of facilitating self-discipline and moral autonomy through approaches to discipline. Many of these examples are quite long to provide the context surrounding the situation. This is congruent with our message that teachers must not respond just to the behavior, but rather consider the many factors that might relate to the cause of the behavior. These "stories" have proven extremely useful to college students trying to visualize the practical applications of text material and struggling with abstract concepts.

Meet the cast of characters: Dennis, Maureen, Sheri, and the rest of the staff of the Midway Children's Center, a composite of typical preschool/child-care centers in the suburbs, provide examples of discipline with three- and four-year-olds. Mrs. Jensen, her first-grade students, and the staff of a typical city school demonstrate the same concepts with primary grade children. Second-grade teacher Mr. Davis and his student teacher, Beth, have joined us for the third edition. Mrs. Jensen and Mr. Davis represent all the caring and effective public school teachers we have known. Because contrasting the desirable with undesirable practices often helps us define the desirable, we have also provided examples of common practices that we do not recommend. For this purpose the mythical teachers, preschool teacher Joanne and first-grade teacher Miss Wheeler, are described in some very real situations. All teachers are fictional, but the good and bad situations described are real. We use first names for the child-care staff and last names for public school staff, not to imply more respect for the latter, but only as a reflection of common practice.

Though the examples refer to preschoolers and to first or second graders, we emphasize that the guidance concepts refer to preschool, kindergarten, and all primary grades. Using fewer grade levels was intended merely to simplify the cast of characters for the book.

Examples from readers' own experience will be the most instructive. We believe that significant time with youngsters, preferably enough to establish an authentic relationship with them, is necessary for internalizing theories about guidance and discipline. We believe that personal observation and experience are crucial to learning, whether in preschool or adulthood.

We use the term *teacher* throughout the book to refer to caregivers as well as other teachers. Any adults guiding children through their day are teaching them. We firmly believe that adults working with children in child care must be as knowledgeable about child development as any other teachers. Since youngsters are so profoundly influenced by the adults in their lives, it is essential that all teachers have a solid understanding of how to influence youngsters in positive directions.

Discover the Companion Website Accompanying This Book

The Prentice Hall Companion Website: A Virtual Learning Environment

Technology is a constantly growing and changing aspect of our field that is creating a need for content and resources. To address this emerging need, Prentice Hall has developed an online learning environment for students and professors alike—Companion Websites—to support our textbooks.

In creating a Companion Website, our goal is to build on and enhance what the textbook already offers. For this reason, the content for each user-friendly website is organized by topic and provides the professor and student with a variety of meaningful resources. Common features of a Companion Website include:

For the Professor

Every Companion Website integrates **Syllabus Manager™**, an online syllabus creation and management utility.

- **Syllabus Manager™** provides you, with an easy, step-by-step process to create and revise syllabi, with direct links into Companion Website and other online content without having to learn HTML.
- Students may log on to your syllabus during any study session. All they need to know is the web address for the Companion Website and the password you've assigned to your syllabus.
- After you have created a syllabus using **Syllabus Manager™**, students

may enter the syllabus for their course section from any point in the Companion Website.

- Clicking on a date, the student is shown the list of activities for the assignment. The activities for each assignment are linked directly to actual content, saving time for students.
- Adding assignments consists of clicking on the desired due date, then filling in the details of the assignment—name of the assignment, instructions, and whether or not it is a one-time or repeating assignment.
- In addition, links to other activities can be created easily. If the activity is online, a URL can be entered in the space provided, and it will be linked automatically in the final syllabus.
- Your completed syllabus is hosted on our servers, allowing convenient updates from any computer on the Internet. Changes you make to your syllabus are immediately available to your students at their next logon.

For the Student

Topic Overviews—outline key concepts in topic areas.

Web Links—general websites related to topic areas as well as associations and professional organizations.

Read About It—timely articles that enable you to become more aware of important issues in early childhood education.

Learn by Doing—put concepts into action, participate in activities, complete lesson plans, examine strategies, and more.

For Teachers—access information that you will need to know as an inservice teacher, including information on materials, activities, lessons, curriculum, and state standards.

Visit a School—visit a school's website to see concepts, theories, and strategies in action.

Electronic Bluebook—send homework or essays directly to your instructor's e-mail with this paperless form.

Message Board—serves as a virtual bulletin board to post—or respond to—questions or comments to/from a national audience.

Chat—real-time chat with anyone who is using the text anywhere in the country—ideal for discussion and study groups, class projects, etc.

To take advantage of these and other resources, please visit the *Constructive Guidance and Discipline: Preschool and Primary Education,* Third Edition, Companion Website at

www.prenhall.com/fields

Acknowledgments

We thank the following reviewers of this edition for their insight:

Patricia A. Cantor, Plymouth State College; Susan Culpepper, University of Montevallo; Elaine Goldsmith, Texas Women's University; and Janet Sawyer, Virginia Tech.

MARJORIE FIELDS:
I wish to thank Constance Kamii for her continued patience and guidance in my quest to better understand Constructivism and moral autonomy. Thanks also to all the teachers whose classrooms I have visited and who have provided models of kind and constructive discipline. These include my sister, Deborah Hillstead, a wonderful kindergarten teacher who keeps me in touch with classroom reality. I have learned the most from children themselves, however. All the youngsters in all the classrooms where I have spent time over the last two decades helped me to understand child development and guidance. Raising my own two sons also taught me a lot, and I must thank them for being the subjects of my longitudinal research. Now I have a granddaughter who will teach me even more about child development.

I am deeply indebted to the many teachers who allowed me to take photographs in their classrooms and then assisted with parental permission forms. I appreciate the guidance of our editor, Ann Davis, and I am grateful for the hard work of Sheryl Langner, the production editor. I wish to acknowledge Margaret Grogan and Yana Polyakova, whose support at work makes my writing possible. And many, many thanks to my dear husband for his patience and help.

CINDY BOESSER:
I owe the fullest measure of thanks to my mother, Mildred, for filling my formative years with genuine positive guidance. Each moment of understanding, each act of respect, and each word of encouragement helped me to grow in the belief that I was a capable, responsible, accepted human being. I have benefited from observing my sister, Kate Boesser, raise my beautiful nieces. She is obviously using the guidance skills she learned in childhood, and is building upon them with her own constantly growing

awarenesses. And I am exceedingly thankful for the hundreds of teachers I have worked with in my career: the children. No one could have taught me better about their needs, their struggles, and their unique ways of learning. Co-workers Lauren Gallagher and Nettie Lessman were most helpful in the sharing of ideas, honest feedback, brainstorming, and caring enough to try and try and try again, in one of the most demanding and rewarding of occupations: early childhood education. Also I sincerely appreciate the parents of children in my care, who have brought the theories of parents as partners to reality. As a stepmom, I am very grateful to my delightful stepchild, Shalom Schrader, and to both her mother, Penny Schrader, and her father, my husband, Steve Krall, for patiently helping to "raise the parent" in me for the past decade. And last, but certainly not least, to my beloved son, Benjamin Krall, who through the blessing of his openness and strong verbal skills daily opens windows for me into the exciting, frustrating, hopeful, challenging, and complex process of a human being busily constructing himself every moment of every day!

About the Authors

Dr. Marjorie Fields has been teaching in the field of early childhood education for over 30 years. She first taught kindergarten, then first grade, then began teaching teachers. Thanks to her own children, she was also actively involved in cooperative preschools and various types of child care.

She has a doctorate in early childhood education with research in parent involvement. She is active in early childhood professional organizations at the national and local levels and has served as vice-president of the National Association of Early Childhood Educators. She has also served on the national governing board for the National Association for the Education of Young Children. She has published extensively in the field of emergent literacy as well as child guidance.

This book is the outgrowth of over 25 years' reading and thinking in conjunction with developing and teaching an early discipline course. Dr. Fields credits her two sons with helping her learn what is most important about child guidance and discipline.

Cindy Boesser has a wide experience in the field of early childhood education. She held a variety of positions in a private, nonprofit preschool/child care-center: aide, teacher, co-director, and program administrator. She has also worked in a university-sponsored child-care center and as a teacher's aide in public school. She ran a quality child-care program in her home for five years that was the first in her region to receive NAFCC Accreditation. She currently works for the Public Library Youth Services, sharing her love for children's literature through story-times and class visits.

CONTRIBUTING AUTHORS

Dr. Eileen Hughes coordinates the Early Childhood Development Program at the University of Alaska, Anchorage. She teaches both undergraduates and graduate students working in child care or public school settings. Dr. Hughes' background in early intervention has led her to the study of quality care and education for all children. For the past twelve years, she has studied principles underlying the Reggio Emilia approach to support teachers in their own study of young children to plan meaningful curriculum. Dr. Hughes is the author of Chapter 13.

Dr. Lory Britain has 30 years of experience developing curriculum materials and teaching children, parents, student teachers, and professionals in a variety of settings, including the university, community college, and private sector. She has been published internationally and her works include *The Young Child as Scientist* (co-author Christine Chaille) and *It's My Body* and *Loving Touches* (under the name of Lory Freeman). Dr. Britain is Director of Evaluation and Training for the Relief Nursery of Lane County, a nationally recognized and replicated therapeutic and family support program for families and children from high risk environments.

Sierra Freeman is a special education inclusion teacher in Dedham, Massachusetts for elementary school children. She received her Masters degree from Wheelock College after completing the Teaching Students with Special Needs program. Ms. Freeman has worked in early intervention with children with special emotional needs at both the Relief Nursery of Lane County and Head Start. She has extensive experience providing family support and service coordination for the parents of young children.

Dr. Britain and Ms. Freeman collaborated on Chapter 14.

Contents

PART TWO

7. *Effective Discipline Through Effective Communication* 144

8. *Helping Children Understand and Accept Limits* 166

Constructive Guidance and Discipline

Preschool and Primary Education

Part One

DISCIPLINE FOUNDATIONS

The first three chapters of this book provide the basic information necessary to study the topic of discipline. In Chapter 1, we define discipline as discussed in this text, comparing the concept of constructivist discipline with authoritarian and permissive discipline. As part of this definition, we examine discipline in terms of the goals or outcomes desired. Chapter 1 also introduces the two basic premises of the book. One of these is working toward long-term discipline goals rather than only immediate concerns. The other is matching the discipline approach to the cause of the problem behavior.

Chapters 2 and 3 focus on child development issues that directly affect discipline in preschools and primary grades. Understanding how children grow, learn, and think helps adults to live more harmoniously with youngsters. This understanding not only creates more tolerance for normal childish behaviors, but it also reduces inappropriate adult expectations. Adults who lack this understanding often unknowingly create discipline problems by putting children in situations where they are sure to have problems. Adults who understand child development are able to use that knowledge to determine what skills are appropriate to teach children at various ages. We believe that effective discipline approaches must be based on knowledge of child development.

1

THINKING ABOUT GUIDANCE AND DISCIPLINE

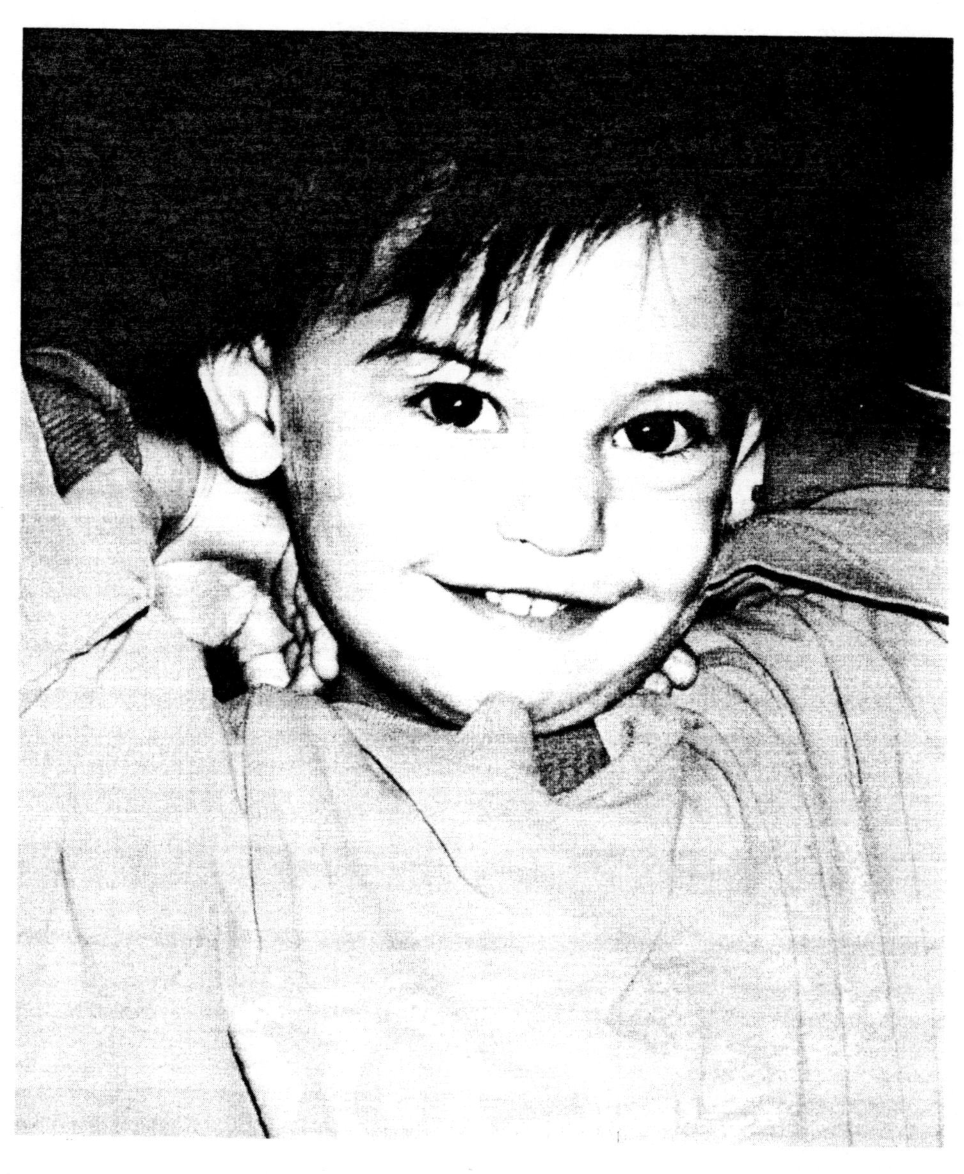

This first chapter is supposed to help you understand everything else in this book and give you our definitions for the terminology used throughout subsequent chapters. Ideally, as you read this chapter, you will begin to understand the differences between internal regulations and external controls for behavior. There are big differences in the outcomes and in the processes leading to each.

DEFINING DISCIPLINE

Notice that the title of this book includes both guidance and discipline. The term *guidance* is usually associated with helping youngsters deal with problems (as in *guidance counselor*) and the term *discipline* is too often associated with punishing children for doing things adults don't like. As you read, you will see that the term *discipline* is used broadly in this book, and that it includes what people generally think of as guidance but does not include punishment. The first definition of discipline in the *American Heritage Dictionary* refers to training that develops moral or mental improvement; the second definition refers to self-control. Both of these definitions are similar to ours. However, we totally disagree with the third and fourth definitions, which refer to control by enforcing, order based on submission to rules and authority, and punishment intended to correct or train (Soukhanov, 1992). This book will explain why we are convinced that external controls, such as punishment, counteract the behavior and attitudes our society so desperately needs.

What is your view of discipline? Have you always thought of it as punishing a child for doing something wrong? Many people think that discipline is a smack on a child's bottom. You may have heard a (sick) joke that refers to a paddle as the "board of education." This book defines discipline differently: *helping children learn personal responsibility for their behavior and to judge between right and wrong for themselves.* The emphasis is on teaching as we help youngsters learn responsible behaviors, rather than merely stopping unproductive actions. Instead of just enforcing rules about what not to do, we want to help children learn to make wise choices about what they should do. Note that learning to make wise choices for themselves is very different from just doing whatever they want. We are not advocating a lack of behavior controls or permissive approaches. Instead, we are advocating approaches that help children understand why certain behaviors are better than others, and that help children choose to act in a desirable manner, whether or not an adult is there to "catch" them at it.

We view discipline as teaching, not merely controlling, and therefore recommend that school discipline be planned at least as carefully as other aspects of the curriculum. Schools long ago gave up punishing students for not knowing how to read or do a math problem (Butchart & McEwan, 1998). Instead of punishing children for missing skills and understanding, teachers now teach what is missing. This is the same process we advocate for helping children with missing social skills, and for teaching them understanding related to behavior.

HIGH STAKES

Can we afford to spend school time teaching social skills and caring attitudes? Evidence shows that we can't afford *not* to. Experienced teachers know that other areas of the curriculum won't get covered if discipline is not taught appropriately. But more importantly, observers of human nature and human development researchers (Eisenberg & Fabes, 1998; Coie & Dodge, 1998; Williams & Shaps, 1999) know that it doesn't really matter what else people learn if they don't learn to become caring, principled, and responsible; their lives will be lived in shambles. In addition, it is becoming increasingly clear that schools must teach caring, communication, negotiation, and other violence prevention lessons in an effort to make schools and neighborhoods safe (Bebeau, Rest, & Narvaez, 1999).

Discipline is a hot topic. Teachers, parents, politicians, ministers, and the media all express great interest in the topic of discipline. Better discipline is seen as the cure for a number of educational and societal ills—from poor test scores to increasing juvenile crime. People often seem to believe that they are experts on discipline simply because they have experienced it. Many advocate simplistic views of how to reach complex goals—methods that usually focus on how to force young people into compliance. These recommendations ignore evidence about the results of such efforts. Statistics on delinquency, dropouts, and pervasive violence suggest that much discipline is missing its mark (National Association for the Education of Young Children, 2000; Bebeau, Rest, & Narvaez, 1999). With more than 3 percent of American adults either in prison or on probation, we have proof that punishment doesn't work (Levinthal, 2000).

Most adults have strong ideas about how children should be disciplined. These ideas are often based on adults' own experiences of discipline as children. You may have heard someone say, "My dad beat me when I did

It doesn't matter what else people learn if they don't learn to become caring, principled, and responsible.

wrong, and I turned out fine." Another person might report a total lack of adult controls, expressing either resentment or pleasure at the memory. Rarely do people start from scratch and think about discipline on an analytical, rather than emotional, basis. We invite you to begin this exploration.

THE GOALS OF DISCIPLINE

Discipline approaches must be determined by our goals. As Butchart says, "The ends and means are inseparable" (1998, p. 2). Start by asking yourself, "What is the purpose of discipline?" It may be tempting to look at discipline merely as a means to keep control so you can teach other things, but children and society need so much more.

LONG-TERM GOALS

Whenever you teach something, you need to start by clarifying your long-term educational goals. Teaching discipline or anything else without long-term goals is like trying to plan a trip route without knowing where you are headed. In order to examine long-term goals, you may find it useful to ask yourself what kind of people you value. Notice that the word is *people,* not *children.* Is there a difference? If you are thinking about children, you might be attracted to the goal *obedient;* however, you are not likely to choose that label for an adult characteristic. Keep in mind that early discipline influences character for a lifetime; therefore, it is essential to think about what kind of people function best in society rather than merely considering what kind of children are easiest to manage. What traits will make the best contribution to a democratic society?

Adults commonly choose goals such as confident, kind, and happy. Some see caring as the foundation for building a better world (Noddings, 1995). Parents may choose *assertive* and *curious* for their children, too. It is helpful to be aware that some combinations such as these may not be compatible. For example, some adults might unthinkingly choose both *assertive* and *obedient,* or both *curious* and *cautious.* What do they really want? How can they best help children develop the skills and attitudes for happy, responsible, and productive lives? What character traits will best serve the person and society?

POSITIVE SELF-CONCEPT

There is general agreement that we want youngsters to grow up with a positive self-concept (see Hyson, 1994; Harter, 1998). Although almost everyone voices this goal, many still use discipline methods that damage self-esteem. Children are routinely treated with much less respect than adults are. They are lectured, ignored, bullied, and bribed in ways no adult would ever put up with. Children often aren't really listened to, either. Later chapters will discuss how punishment and other coercive tactics—even praise and other rewards—can damage a person's self-esteem.

SELF-DISCIPLINE

Nearly everyone also agrees that self-discipline is a goal for children (Albert, 1996; Teaching Tolerance, 1997; Coloroso, 1994). Most approaches to discipline describe themselves as promoting self-discipline (Beane, 1999; Glasser, 1992). Disagreements center around what leads to this goal. Many believe that rewards for acceptable behavior, and punishments for unacceptable behavior, will lead to self-discipline. Such viewpoints do not recognize that being manipulated by reward and punishment is vastly different from learning about what is right and how to make wise, caring decisions (Kohn, 1993). In contrast, this book is based on the view that children can't learn to regulate their own behavior as long as others are regulating it for them.

MORAL AUTONOMY

A more sophisticated and little known version of self-discipline is called *moral autonomy.* This is a concept presented in Jean Piaget's *The Moral*

Judgment of the Child (1932/1965), and elaborated for modern audiences by Piagetian scholars DeVries (e.g., DeVries, Hildebrandt, & Zan, 2000) and Kamii (e.g., Kamii & Ewing, 1996). According to these sources, *autonomy* means being governed and guided by your *own* beliefs and understanding. The morally autonomous person is kind to others out of personal feelings of respect for other human beings. The opposite is *heteronomy,* which means being governed or ruled by someone else. The heteronomous person would be kind to others only if that behavior would be rewarded, or if its absence would be caught and punished.

Some people misinterpret this concept and get worried when they hear about autonomy. They think that being governed by yourself means doing whatever you want. However, Kamii points out in the foreword to this book that Piaget's theory of autonomy doesn't mean just the *right* to make decisions for yourself but the "ability to make decisions for oneself about right and wrong, independent of reward or punishment, by taking relevant factors into account." If you think about the meaning of that statement, you see that a merely self-serving decision would be excluded because it wouldn't take into consideration the "relevant factors" of other people's needs. It is important to note that being governed internally also means that children are not so susceptible to peer pressure; therefore, morally autonomous persons wouldn't join in inappropriate group activities for fear of being rejected by their peers.

Therefore, it is a person *without* moral autonomy or self-discipline who is likely to act irresponsibly when there are no external controls. In fact, that description fits some young college students away from home for the first time. College dormitory life testifies to the fact that some well-meaning parents and teachers deny young people an adequate opportunity to develop inner controls. Inexperienced at self-regulating their work, play, and sleep, some first-year college students find themselves unable to achieve a workable balance.

Autonomy does not mean lack of control; rather, it refers to the *source* of control. Autonomous people carry those controls within themselves. They are never without them, even when alone. Heteronomous people, by contrast, experience control only when someone else is present. They depend on an external judge to reward or punish their behavior. When you help youngsters develop moral autonomy, you affect how they behave, even when misbehavior isn't likely to be caught. Autonomous people don't need policing to keep them on the right path.

LONG-TERM VERSUS QUICK-FIX SOLUTIONS

Are teachers responsible for keeping children safe and orderly and also for helping them develop positive self-esteem, self-discipline, and moral autonomy? That's a tall order! Don't forget that teachers have to teach, too. Can they really be blamed if they have a hard time thinking about long-range discipline goals? After all, teachers usually have a student for just one year. Parents, however, are generally aware that they will be dealing with this child

Skillful teachers know they don't have to choose between protecting children's self-esteem and keeping order.

through the teen years and beyond. One mother reports that she was powerfully motivated to help her son Michael learn self-discipline when she thought about his getting a driver's license in ten years. While Michael was little, she could protect him from harm by watching over him herself, but she doubted that she could ride along to make sure he was driving safely when he was 16. She knew that inner controls would stay with Michael long after she couldn't. Therefore, she focused on discipline approaches that foster inner control rather than obedience.

Nevertheless, even parents are sometimes tempted to ignore the future and concentrate on making their lives easier for now. Teachers may be under the added pressure to present a "well-disciplined" class, in the old sense of appearing quiet and controlled. This can make a difference at evaluation time with principals who don't understand how young children learn best. As a result, discipline methods that boast quick, short-term results at the expense of children's self-esteem and autonomy remain popular. You will read about some of these methods in Chapter 9.

Fortunately, many teachers care too much about children to give in to temptation. They resist quick-fix approaches and work on positive alternatives. They know that helping children live together peacefully now and preparing them for the future can be compatible goals. Skillful teachers know how to work toward long-term discipline goals while maintaining a peaceful and productive learning environment. They know they don't have to make a choice between protecting children's self-esteem and keeping order. With the guidance of these knowledgeable and dedicated teachers, children can learn from experience to make wise decisions. In the process, they can also develop the positive self-esteem and moral autonomy necessary for becoming "competent, caring, loving and lovable people" (Noddings, 1995, p. 366).

DISCIPLINE MODELS COMPARED

Common approaches to discipline vary—from the very authoritarian, in which the adult makes all the rules and punishes any deviation, to the very permissive, in which the child makes all the decisions. Too many people think they have to choose one or the other of those models. One teacher says she plays the "heavy" until she can't stand herself; then she switches to the opposite until she can't stand the kids. Too few adults (teachers as well as parents) are even aware of any other options. We do not recommend trying to combine permissive and authoritarian styles in an attempt at a middle ground, but there are alternatives that balance the power of adult and child. You don't have to choose between either the adult or the child having all the power. A shared power model best meets the needs of all. The needs and views of both the adult and the child can be accommodated when discipline is viewed as teaching.

DISCIPLINE THEORY TERMS

Many terms have been used to describe the different approaches to discipline. *Authoritarian* and *permissive* are commonly understood terms and concepts. Alternatives to these extremes have been harder to define and to understand. Baumerind (1967) wrote about authoritative discipline and explained how it differed from the authoritarian model through a focus on teaching rather than punishment. However, many people get confused by the similarities between the words *authoritarian* and *authoritative.*

Greenberg (1992b) compares forms of discipline with forms of government. The *autocratic* holding of power by the adult is compared to a dictatorship, and *anarchy* is the label for the overly permissive style that grants too much power to the child. In contrast, Greenberg describes a shared power approach that she labels *democratic.*

DeVries and Zan (1994) use yet another way of explaining discipline styles. They contrast three classroom situations and label them: (1) the *boot camp,* (2) the *factory,* and (3) the *community.* The boot camp uses reward and punishment to enforce obedience. The factory model has the same controlling goals as the boot camp, relying heavily on reward and punishment, but with a kinder and gentler touch. The factory model describes the majority of classrooms we have seen. The community, in contrast, uses the constructivist model to assist children's development of

The following list categorizes the various models of teaching and guidance discussed previously, and shows their relationship to one another.

Comparing Discipline Terminology

Obedience models	Respect models	Neglect models
Authoritarian	Authoritative	Permissive
Behaviorist	Constructivist	Maturationist
Boot camp	Community	
Autocratic	Democratic	Anarchy

moral autonomy. Fortunately, few teachers are as harsh as those in the boot camp model, but unfortunately too few have the skills to create a true community of learners.

Because we view discipline as teaching, we believe it makes sense to compare discipline models to learning theories: behaviorist, maturationist, and constructivist. The authoritarian style is consistent with the *behaviorist* philosophy of education, with its emphasis on molding behavior via reward and punishment. The permissive style is compatible with the *maturationist* philosophy of education, with its belief in time as the best teacher. The best alternative to these extremes of too much and too little adult intervention is the *constructivist* approach to education. Constructivism does not reflect a "middle ground" between behaviorism and maturationism; rather, it is a whole different view of learning and of guidance and discipline. It is not a "nicer" way to get obedience; instead, it strives for much more than obedience. Constructivism helps children learn from their experiences and from reflecting on those experiences (DeVries, Hildebrandt, & Zan, 2000; Duckworth & Cleary, 1990; Kamii & Ewing, 1996; Piaget, 1965). Through this process, the learner is assisted in gaining increasingly sophisticated levels of understanding. Thus, children gradually develop the ability to take many relevant factors into consideration when deciding what action is best for all concerned.

DISCIPLINE GOALS COMPARED

In essence, each discipline style has the same motive: love and/or concern for the child. However, each has very different goals. Obedience is the target behavior in the authoritarian model, preferably unquestioning and immediate obedience (Kohn, 1993). The permissive model overemphasizes individual freedom (Baumerind, 1967). The constructivist model works toward self-determined, responsible behavior, reflecting concern for the good of others and for oneself as well (Kamii, 1984). The constructivist approach acknowledges the complexity of the ever-changing world; therefore, it teaches children to think for themselves about desirable or undesirable actions rather than telling them predetermined answers to current dilemmas. "When we simply tell children how they must behave, reward their good behavior and punish their bad, we fail to build their understanding of moral concepts that can guide their behavior when they encounter new situations to which these values might apply" (Williams & Sshaps, 1999, p. 28).

DIFFERENCES IN DISCIPLINE FORMS

Not surprisingly, each model uses very different forms of discipline (Bronson, 2000). Punishment and reward are used almost exclusively in the authoritarian model (Dobson, 1970; Canter & Canter, 1992). Lack of any discipline is the distinguishing feature of the permissive model. Between these two clear-cut extremes, but not a blend of them, the constructivist model offers a multifaceted set of discipline options that will be explained in this book. These options focus on teaching and, like all good teaching, begin with good human relationships. Mutually caring and respectful relationships with adults and peers encourage youngsters to think about the effects of their behavior on other people. Teaching children to think critically is an essential aspect of constructivist teaching about discipline, and about other topics as well. Constructivist discipline strategies are aimed at helping children construct socially productive behavior rules and values for themselves. As Pritchard (1996) says, "We hope the result is that children become better able to reason, and thus more reasonable human beings."

DIFFERENCES IN RESULTS

Which model is best? What are the results of each? We can never be certain about research findings concerning human beings because we cannot ethically control the variables in a person's life. Each person is a unique blend of genetics, family dynamics, societal influences, and individual experiences. However, certain trends occur frequently enough to suggest a relationship. The authoritarian model is associated with anger and depression, as well as low self-esteem and the inability to make self-directed choices (e.g., Straus, 1991; Robinson, Mandleco, Olsen & Hart, 1995; DeVries, 1999). Likewise, those people with an overly permissive background demonstrate low self-esteem and difficulty getting along with others. The shared power model results in high self-esteem, good social skills, general competence, and self-discipline (DeVries, 1999; Butchart & McEwan, 1998; Ramsey, 1991).

Research provides evidence that youngsters who have the opportunity for choice and self-direction in preschool are more able to make wise choices as teenagers. They are less likely to use drugs, to become pregnant, or to drop out of school (Schweinhart, Weikart, & Larner, 1986). You don't have to wait for ten years, however, to see the results of helping children become morally autonomous.

THREE PHILOSOPHIES OF DISCIPLINE

Behaviorist: Molds behavior via reward and punishment
Constructivist: Helps children learn from experience
Maturationist: Believes that time is the best teacher

Constructivist discipline approaches help most children quickly learn to negotiate solutions to problems, to resolve their own conflicts (e.g., Gordon, 1989; Kreidler, 1994; Siccone & Lopez, 2000) and to self-direct their learning activity (DeVries & Zan, 1994).

TEACHING FOR MORAL AUTONOMY: THE CONSTRUCTIVIST APPROACH

Certain basic ideas are central to a constructivist approach to discipline:

1. A relationship of mutual respect between adult and child is the foundation for development of moral autonomy (Kamii, 1982). Mutual respect means that it is just as important for you to treat the child with respect as it is for the child to treat you with respect.
2. Constructivist teachers always strive to help children understand *why* a behavior is desirable or undesirable.
3. Providing age-appropriate choices for youngsters and supporting them in solving their own problems is a way of showing respect for children and also a way of teaching thinking and assisting understanding.
4. When undesirable behavior occurs, your discipline efforts must address the cause of the behavior for effective teaching to take place.

Now let's examine these concepts in more detail.

MUTUAL RESPECT

Constructive discipline involves respect and affection for the child. The quality of the relationship between child and adult is crucial to the success of any discipline approach. Unless a child knows you care about him or her, and unless that child is concerned about maintaining a relationship with you, there is really no reason for the child to pay attention to what you ask. Having a relationship with a child requires investing time in getting to know children as individuals and attempting to understand them. If you are going to be effective during a behavior crisis, you need to first build a relationship by spending time on pleasant interaction. Spending time with a youngster and listening to that child not only helps an adult understand the child but also demonstrates respect. Too often adults expect youngsters to listen to them but don't reciprocate. Respecting children and their viewpoints helps them to respect our viewpoints (Kamii, 1984; Riley, 1984). According to DeVries and Zan (1994), "Children do not develop respect for others unless they are respected" (p. 76).

Mutual respect is an essential ingredient of effective discipline (Dill, 1998). Any discipline response can turn into punishment if accompanied by put-downs, which, of course, are inherently disrespectful. For instance, to call a child "sloppy" for spilling something, or "mean" for knocking down some blocks, would destroy the educational value of your discipline teaching. The child would focus on self-defense rather than on the problem

To be effective during a behavior crisis, you need to first build a relationship by spending time in pleasant interaction.

behavior. It is also important to be aware of how your attitude is projected. Anger or disgust in your tone of voice can override even the most carefully chosen words. Listen to yourself as you talk to the children in your care: Are your words something they would want to listen to? Or are you teaching them to tune you out by a steady stream of commands and criticism?

HELPING CHILDREN UNDERSTAND

Often it seems obvious to an adult why a certain behavior is inappropriate. But young children have little experience in the world and don't automatically know all that seems obvious to you; therefore, you need to help youngsters learn the reasons behind rules and requests. Sometimes words are helpful teaching tools, but usually young children need experiences to help them understand the explanations. You can teach without punishing by asking Aaron to mop up the puddle he made when he splashed water on the floor during exuberant water play. Similarly, you can help Kenji learn a better way of showing he wants to play than by knocking over other children's buildings. The teacher's role in developing moral autonomy is to help children figure out why their behavior is causing a problem and provide them with the opportunity to help resolve the problem.

Mrs. Jensen discovered one day that she had not helped Lesa to understand why she was asked to leave group time: Lesa came up to Mrs. Jensen after the group meeting and said, "I'm sorry. I won't do it again." Mrs. Jensen asked her, "Won't do what again?" She was astounded at the child's honest reply, "I don't know." Too often, youngsters learn to mouth meaningless words of apology or appreciation with no idea about what they mean or why they would be appropriate.

Perhaps the most crucial understanding for young children is that other people have needs and wishes different than their own. Dennis' approach to the following doll bed dilemma was aimed at helping Sara and Christie begin to think about a viewpoint other than their own. Learning to consider the viewpoints of others in making decisions is part of learning moral autonomy. According to Piaget, we also teach moral autonomy and the necessary understanding of others' views when we help children realize the effects of their behavior rather than merely punishing it.

Teaching Problem Solving: An Example

When preschoolers Sara and Christie were tugging on the same doll bed, each screaming, "I had it first!" Dennis, their teacher, resisted coming over and immediately taking the toy away, although it might have been simple to say, "If you can't play nicely, I'll have to put this away." Nor did he start the usual inquisition trying to determine which child had it first so that he could make the fairest decision. Those approaches are common where the teacher's goal is simply to solve the problem for now and where the discipline approach is authoritarian.

Because Dennis' goals are long-term, he wanted to help children learn to think about their behavior and to develop skills for solving their own conflicts. His discipline approach is constructivist. Therefore, he facilitated decision making on the part of the children instead of making the decisions himself. He helped the girls to clarify the problem by stating what it appeared to be: "You both want a bed for your dolls." He further identified the dilemma: "There's only one of these beds and two sleepy babies." Then Dennis asked them what they thought they could do to solve their problem. In this way, he helped the girls learn to think about fairness for both sides.

Problem solving takes practice, just as other complex skills do. It is also dependent on levels of maturity. Young children have limited reasoning ability, but they become more capable when encouraged to discuss their different views. The teacher works with children at their levels of maturation, demonstrating ways of expressing their feelings and suggesting possible approaches to solutions. The teacher may ask questions, such as, "Where else could a baby doll sleep in this house?" This method still leaves the children in charge of a search for alternatives. Even if they aren't immediately successful, Dennis doesn't take over. However, if the children's frustration and anger appear to be getting beyond their ability to control, he might resort to taking the doll bed and putting it out of reach until they cool down. He then would assure the girls that they could have it as soon as they come up with a solution.

GUIDING CHOICES

Constructive discipline encourages children to make as many of their own decisions and choices as possible. This helps children to learn from their mistakes as well as their successes. In other words, your job is to help children learn how to make wise choices, not to make all the choices for them. In the process of learning to regulate their own behavior, children make both good and bad choices for themselves. It is hard, but necessary, to let youngsters make some poor choices as well as good ones. No matter what their age, people tend to learn best the lessons learned through their own experience—especially from analyzing their mistakes. Think about your own mistakes: Probably someone older and wiser warned you, but you had to find out for yourself, didn't you?

Of course, adults must monitor the choices; not all choices are safe or appropriate. For instance, children don't have the choice of putting their fingers in an electrical socket to experience a shock. But they do have the choice of not eating their snack and getting a little hungry, or the choice of not cooperating in play and subsequently being rejected by peers. Teachers whose goal is helping children learn to think for themselves don't help by thinking and acting for their students. They do not instantly step in and solve conflicts for youngsters. Instead, conflicts and problems are seen as potential learning situations and opportunities for you to offer meaningful teaching (Bronson, 2000). The children work at problem solving. The teacher's job is to facilitate the process as needed.

TREATING THE CAUSE RATHER THAN THE SYMPTOM

No amount of respect, teaching, or choice will make discipline effective *unless your approach deals with the reason why the behavior occurred.* If you only stop the behavior without treating the cause, the behavior problem will probably continue to be repeated (Kaiser & Rasminsky, 1999). Discipline is like weeding a garden: If you don't get the roots out with the weeds, the weeds will be back in a few days. Effective approaches to discipline work to get at the root of the problem. A main focus of this text is matching guidance and discipline approaches to the cause of the behavior problems.

It isn't easy to figure out why children do the things they do. You certainly can't determine the cause simply by seeing the behavior. For instance, there

No discipline approach will be effective unless it works on the *cause* of the behavior problem.

are several reasons for why Aaron might have spilled water during water play. Perhaps he was just having such a good time that he didn't think about where the water was going. It is also possible that he spilled because of immature coordination, which made it hard for him to pour the water where he intended. Then again, maybe he knew what he was doing and did it on purpose. He might have spilled to get attention or to alleviate boredom.

A useful way to think about the cause of undesirable behavior is to think about what the child needs in order to act in more appropriate ways. You may find it useful to ask yourself the questions in the box *Discovering Causes of Behavior Problems* as you work toward helpful interventions for each youngster.

Each different cause of behavior problems points to a different solution. Yet there are many teachers and caregivers who have one solution for any and all infractions of the rules. Think about the commonly used time-out bench as it would affect Aaron in the case of each suggested cause for the spilt water. How would the time-out bench affect his feelings about preschool fun if the spill was caused by his eagerness to explore? How would time-out affect his feelings about himself if the spill was caused by poor coordination? If attention-getting or boredom was the cause, would time-out keep Aaron from spilling again? As you read future chapters, you will find

DISCOVERING CAUSES OF BEHAVIOR PROBLEMS

Ask yourself the following questions as a guide toward discovering the cause of a behavior problem:

Is the environment meeting this child's needs?
Is the program meeting this child's needs?
Are behavioral expectations appropriate for this child?
Does the child have unmet physical or emotional needs?
Is this child missing some social skill?
Does this child need help with communication skills?
Does this child understand why a behavior is important?
Has this child learned inappropriate ways of getting needs met?

suggestions of appropriate responses to each of these and other causes of undesirable behavior.

Observing to Discover the Cause The best way to determine the cause of a child's behavior is to observe the child carefully and record your observations. You need to know a lot about a child to plan effective discipline. You need to know whether this is usual or unusual behavior, and also under what circumstances it occurs. Are certain activities likely to trigger it? Is there a pattern of when, where, or with whom behavior problems are most likely? What do you know about the child's home routine, health, or family situation that might provide some clues? Communicating with parents and keeping careful records of child behavior are both indispensable parts of determining the cause of problems. You assess the child's social learning needs through this process of finding causes for behavior problems. This assessment is an essential guide for effective teaching.

Never overlook the possibility that you may have caused a discipline problem. Chapters 2 and 3 illustrate how a mismatch between child development and teacher expectations can cause discipline problems. Chapters 4 and 5 discuss how inappropriate school environments and programs often cause behavior problems. Chapters 6 and 7 raise the issue of undesirable adult examples and communication styles as sources of undesirable child behavior. Chapters 9 and 10 explain how coercive and punitive discipline approaches backfire and create worse behavior problems. Chapters 11 and 12 examine various situations, looking for the cause. Chapters 13 and 14 explore causes outside the realm of the classroom. Chapter 15 helps you keep it all together.

As you read this text, you will be guided to match probable causes of behavior with appropriate approaches to discipline. Selecting the right approach requires that you understand many different approaches, and also that you understand children and the many different reasons for their actions.

CONCLUSION

This chapter has attempted to stimulate your thinking about your values as they relate to guidance and discipline. Our discussion and comparison of definitions and goals of discipline resulted in the recommendation of constructivist discipline, rather than an authoritarian or a permissive approach. We began an introduction to ways of implementing constructivist approaches to discipline, with more complete explanations to come in the following chapters. If you are now saying to yourself, "But don't kids need limits?" or "I know people who grew up with complete freedom and they felt their parents didn't care," then go back and re-read the chapter. If these are new ideas for you, it will take careful reading and thought to understand that there are helpful alternatives to forcing obedience. The choice isn't just between power-tripping children and letting them run wild.

This chapter offers an overview of ideas presented in the rest of the book. If you can't visualize how all this works yet, don't worry; that's what the rest of the chapters are for. We hope that you will supplement what you read here with further reading from the recommended reading list at the end of the chapter. We also hope that you will spend significant time with young children, proving guidance and discipline concepts to yourself through your own observation and experience. If you haven't read the foreword and preface to this book, we suggest you do so. Constance Kamii's discussion of moral autonomy in the foreword should help you better understand the idea. The preface should provide further explanation about the theory-base and intent of the book. The preface also gives an overview of the three-part organization of the text: (1) discipline foundations, (2) discipline approaches, and (3) matching discipline causes to discipline approaches. Be sure to read the introductions to each section of the text.

As you continue to read and think, remember that going to school represents the child's entry into our society (Watson, 1999). For the first time, young children may be encountering the necessity of following basic rules and of respecting the rights of others. The skills of problem solving, predicting consequences, and planning ahead are vital for children to escape the culture of violence (Dill, 1998).

FOR FURTHER THOUGHT

1. Create your list of desirable goals for discipline. Compare your list with those of others. Select the three characteristics you would most want to encourage through child guidance. Explain your choices and compare them with a friend's.
2. Think about your own parents' approach to child rearing. What characteristics do you think they most valued? How did those values influence your own childhood? Do your choices reflect those of your parents or are they different?
3. How would you rate yourself on a continuum from heteronomy to autonomy? How does this rating reflect the discipline approaches of your parents and teachers? If you are

heteronomous, can you help children become autonomous?

4. A problem to solve: Carlos is using the doll buggy. Betsy wants it and grabs it away. Carlos hits Betsy, and the battle is on.
   a. Describe a response that solves the problem without teaching autonomy or self-discipline.
   b. Describe a response that solves the problem and does teach autonomy and self-discipline.

RECOMMENDED READINGS

Butchart, R. E., & McEwan, B.(1998).*Classroom discipline in American schools: problems and possibilities for democratic education.* Albany, NY: State University of New York Press.

DeVries, R., & Zan, B. (1994). *Moral classrooms, moral children.* New York: Teachers College Press.

Kamii, C. (1982). Autonomy as the aim of education: Implications of Piaget's theory. In C. Kamii (Ed.), *Number in preschool and kindergarten* (pp. 73–87). Washington, DC: National Association for the Education of Young Children.

Noddings, N. (January 1995). A morally defensible mission for schools in the 21st century. *Phi Delta Kappan,* 365–368.

Piaget, J. (1965). *The moral judgment of the child.* New York: Free Press. (Originally published in 1932.)

2

PHYSICAL AND EMOTIONAL DEVELOPMENT AFFECT CHILD BEHAVIOR

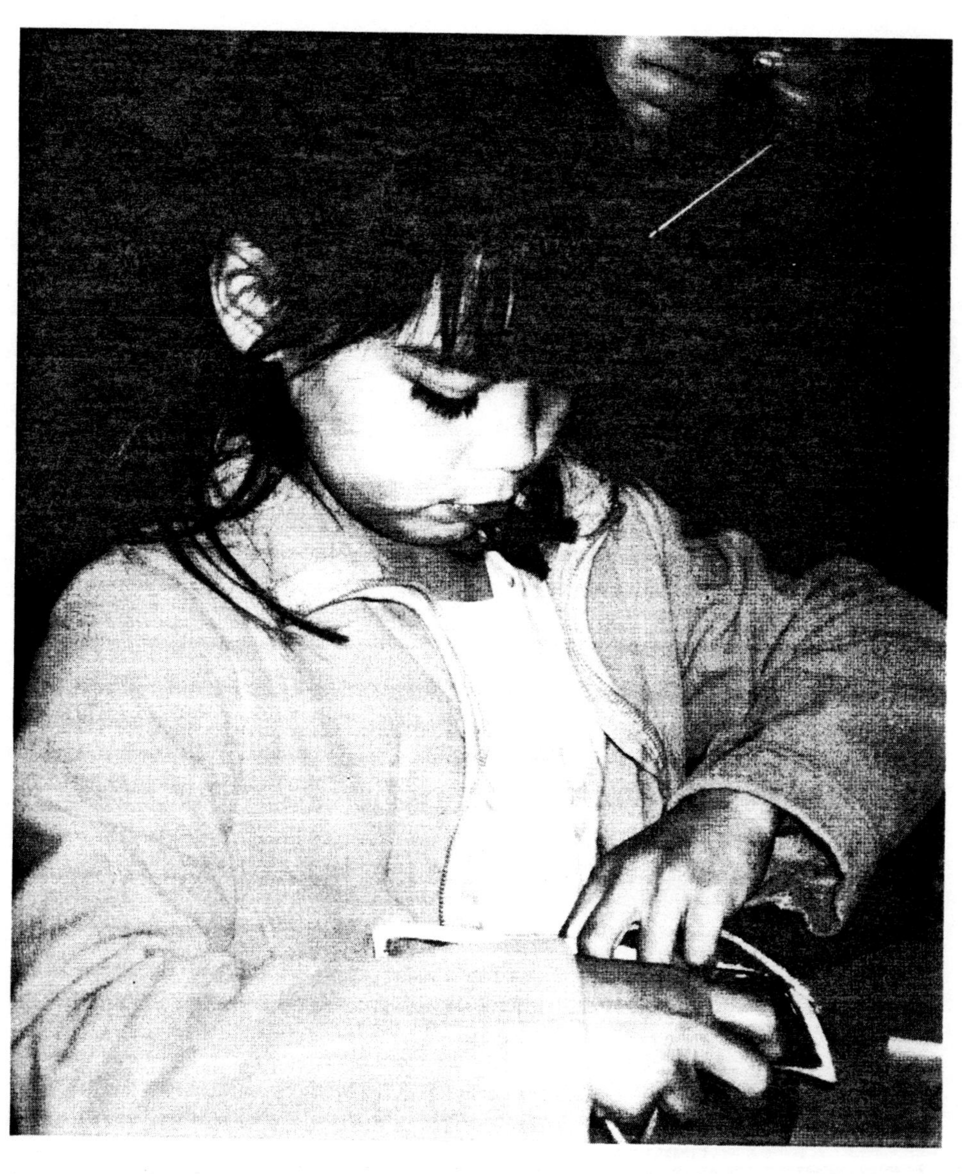

Child care and teaching become much easier when you are knowledgeable about child development and can match your expectations of children to their individual maturation levels. Each stage of child development brings its own set of needs, abilities, and perspectives. Your knowledge of children's physical, emotional, intellectual, and social development will help you guard against adult-caused behavior problems. Knowledge of child development will also help you to understand when inappropriate behavior occurs because a child is still working on a developmental task and does not mean to be "naughty" at all. Child guidance and discipline also require knowledge of basic human needs that can create behavior problems if unmet. Such information will provide useful guidelines for discipline interventions.

In this chapter and the next, we examine some aspects of child development as they pertain to discipline issues. These chapters are not intended to be a comprehensive coverage of child development. Please refer to the recommended readings at the end of each chapter for more comprehensive coverage sources.

SAMPLE PHYSICAL DEVELOPMENT ISSUES

It is obvious that young children's physical needs and abilities are different from those of adults. Young children are not as strong or well-coordinated as adults or older children; they also require more rest and more frequent nourishment. Additionally, they are unable to sit still for very long. Teachers sometimes forget this last fact and cause trouble for themselves and their students.

NEED TO MOVE AROUND

Devon and several of his classmates in Miss Wheeler's first-grade class routinely upset their teacher's day. They simply won't sit still and listen during group time.

They are always getting up and wandering around when they are supposed to be working in their seats. Miss Wheeler constantly reminds them to sit still or to go back to their seats. She just doesn't understand that most young children have difficulty sitting still for very long. Next door, in Mrs. Jensen's first-grade room, children are free to move around between learning centers. There is very little enforced sitting in that room, and very little need for the teacher to reprimand anyone. Miss Wheeler feels like a police officer instead of a teacher, but she thinks it is the children who are at fault. Matching her expectations to the children's level of development would make her life much easier, as well as eliminate a lot of needless tension for her students.

Children need to move, not only for their physical development, but also for their intellectual development (Leppo, et al., 2000). Brain research shows that physical movement stimulates the myelinization process critical to neural pathways in the brain. The process of myelinization allows young children to gain control over their muscles and their sensory abilities; it also facilitates their cognitive processes (Berger, 1998). Physical movement also assists the delivery of oxygen and glucose to the brain, optimizing its performance (Leppo et al., 2000). Some children with little physical movement experience are delayed in both body and space awareness. The spatial confusions can contribute to reading and writing difficulties (Corso, 1993; Hannaford, 1995), as well as to behavior problems. Some young children are continually getting into trouble because they are not aware of where their body is in relation to other people.

Physical activity is necessary for productive behavior, as well as for good health and intellectual development.

Rather than trying to keep children still, adults help children better by promoting physical activity (Pica, 1997). Physically active children are healthier and eventually grow up to be more active, healthy adults. Increased child activity is needed to counteract the problem of childhood obesity in the United States. In addition, physically competent children tend to have higher self-esteem than less-competent peers. Competence in performing motor skills boosts children's confidence. Success and enjoyment associated with physical activity affects how children feel about themselves and how they interact with peers. Having good agility, balance, coordination, power, and speed can promote social interaction and peer acceptance. Children with physical disabilities that affect their gross-motor development often share their classmates' interest in physical activities. Therefore, playgrounds and outdoor equipment should be accessible for children with disabilities (Bredekamp & Copple, 1997).

SMALL-MUSCLE COORDINATION TAKES TIME

Not only do young children have a need to exercise their large muscles regularly, but they are also not very adept at small-muscle work (Bredekamp & Copple, 1997). Both of these attributes create problems in classrooms where children are expected to sit at their seats and do paperwork much of the day. Such a schedule focuses on the children's areas of weakness and, therefore, puts a huge pressure on them.

Individual differences and gender play a role in the development of dexterity. Girls tend to be more advanced than boys in fine-motor skills and in gross-motor skills requiring precision, such as hopping and skipping. Boys generally excel in skills that require force and power, such as running and jumping (Berk, 1996). For most children, it is a fact of physical development that fine-motor coordination lags behind gross-motor coordination. Beau, who is a fast runner and a great climber, may not be able to tie his shoes yet; and Tera, the best rope jumper in kindergarten, may not be able to make a pencil do her bidding. Placing pressure on these children to perform above their current level of development will result in frustration and feelings of failure. Negative behaviors will surely follow. Matching your expectations to the children's abilities will avert some potential discipline struggles.

> One sad example of a teacher's lack of understanding has left a permanent scar on the young woman who shared her story. When May was in the first grade, she and her classmates were to copy the homework assignment from the chalkboard and then take it home to do it. Writing was still a slow and laborious process for May, so it took her a long time to copy from the board. Unfortunately, the teacher decided everyone had had enough time to copy the assignment and erased the board. May felt panicky and tried to find another child whose paper she could copy from. The girl she asked covered her paper, and so May gave up. The next day, May and several other children who showed up without their homework were publicly humiliated by having to go up to the front of the room to be chastised. Whether May's recollection of being told she

was stupid is accurate or not, her perception of feeling stupid is clear and ongoing. She reports lasting feelings of incompetence.

Although you want to be careful not to push fine-motor tasks too early, fine-motor development can be encouraged appropriately (Bredekamp & Copple, 1997). Ample opportunities for practice, appropriate tools (scissors that actually cut, for instance), and adult support assist children's fine-motor dexterity. Children with certain kinds of identified disabilities may require adaptations or assistive technologies for activities such as writing and drawing. By the time they enter the primary grades, children are usually much more capable of fine-motor work than when they were preschool age, when it often generates neurological fatigue.

NEEDS FOR FOOD AND REST

Young children also have a need for adequate food and rest in order to work and play cooperatively at school. Children need these energy boosters at more frequent intervals than adults do. Sometimes Kelsey can't play cooperatively in the morning preschool session, and Dennis, her teacher, figures that she didn't eat much breakfast that day. When this happens, he allows her to have her mid-morning snack a little early. Dennis is taking into consideration Kelsey's individual needs as well as the group's needs. The standard practice of snack time acknowledges the fact that little people in general can't eat much at one time and can't go as long between meals as older people can.

Scheduled rest time at the preschool level acknowledges a need at that age, but formal rest periods tend to disappear once children enter the public schools. Yaisa attends the before- and after-school child care program at Lincoln Elementary. She gets to school at 7:30 in the morning and doesn't go home until 5:30 in the evening. Sometimes she gets crabby and picks a fight or bursts into tears for no apparent reason. Fortunately, her teacher understands that when Yaisa acts that way, she needs a break, not a punishment for being difficult. Mrs. Jensen sees Yaisa's need and encourages her to find a comfortable pillow and a good book in the secluded classroom book nook. After a short rest, Yaisa is able to participate with the group again. Mrs. Jensen is trying to teach Yaisa and others with similar needs how to take a break when they need it, rather than push themselves beyond their limits. Her classroom offers several soft, seclusive spots, and her schedule offers the flexibility to use them.

EMOTIONAL DEVELOPMENT AND GUIDANCE

Children come into this world with unique characteristics and then encounter a unique set of people and influences. Each child experiences the world in different ways. The combination of biological and experiential factors work together to form individual personalities and ways of reacting to others (Saarni, Mumme, & Campos, 1998).

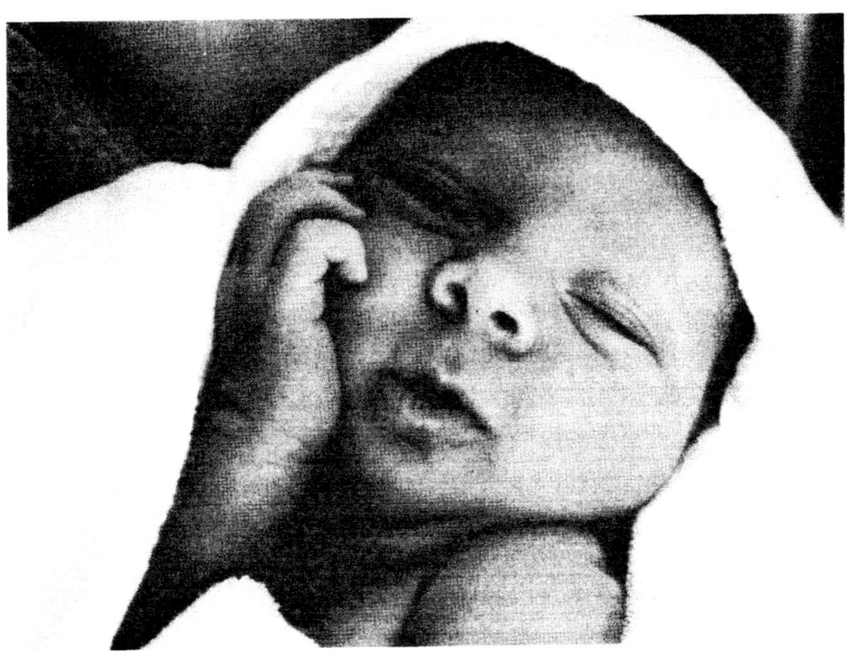

Some personality characteristics are apparent at birth.

TEMPERAMENT

Temperament is defined as the "constitutionally based individual differences in emotional, motor, and attentional reactivity and self-regulation" (Rothbart & Bates, 1998, p. 109). The temperament a child is born with is a primary influence on emotional development. It not only determines much about how the child behaves, but also about how others react to the child (Reinsberg, 1999). This interactive process between youngsters and those around them shapes emotional development and self-concept in positive or negative directions. The challenge for the caring adult is to respond positively to the more difficult child.

Research has identified distinct differences in several personality characteristics that are apparent from birth (e.g.: Sansom, Smart, Prior, Oberklaid, & Pedlow, 1994; Thomas & Chess, 1977). Some of these characteristics make children easier to live with than others do. Those children who are more regular in their patterns of eating and sleeping obviously make life easier for their caregivers. Those who are most responsive can be more fun to interact with; however, negative responses may also be more intense with more responsive children. Those who easily adapt to new situations and respond favorably to a new toy or new people are likely to elicit more favorable responses from others (Wieder & Greenspan, 1993). Some youngsters seem to be born friendly, pleasant, and joyful, but others seem to start out life as the opposite. These individual differences influence the child's interactions throughout life, and certainly are a factor in behavior and discipline (Hyson, 1994).

Some temperament differences appear to have underlying biological roots. For instance, one study demonstrated that shy children have different heart rhythms than others (Kagan, Reznick, Clarke, Snidman, & Garcia-Coll, 1984). Another study found that "irritable" children may have different levels of certain hormones than more even-tempered children (Gunnar, Mangelsdorf, Larson, & Hertsgaard, 1989). Research on the behavior genetics of temperament indicates that heredity plays a significant role (Caspi, 1998). Studies tracing twins and siblings who were adopted and raised apart provide further evidence that certain personality tendencies may be inherited (Buss & Plomin, 1984).

Some of these innate temperament and personality characteristics have a direct bearing on school behaviors. Children seem to be born with a certain level of activity, with the more active infant becoming the more active child. Individual attention span and distractibility factors are also evident from birth. Children who are born with a high energy level and a low attention span, and who are easily distracted, are often in trouble in school settings. Children who are outgoing and even-tempered by nature will be easy to have in class while children with the opposite traits will need significant support with social skills and emotion regulation. Teachers will find it more productive to help children channel their traits positively instead of trying to change the child's nature. This is part of making school fit the child, as opposed to trying to make the child fit the school.

DEVELOPMENTAL STAGES

Though individual differences and family dynamics (Eisenberg & McNally, 1993) play a significant role, children nonetheless seem to progress through the various stages in their emotional development. Erikson's (1963) theory of personality encompasses the entire lifespan and attempts to explain patterns of behavior throughout every stage of life.

According to Erikson's widely respected theory, each of these stages has a particular focus, or developmental task, that influences the child's responses at this time. We find Erikson's explanation of emotional development especially relevant to discipline issues. Understanding child behavior in terms of the stages that Erikson describes can help us prevent discipline problems; this understanding also can be used to guide intervention when problems do occur (Gordon & Browne, 1996). We will discuss only the stages relevant to early childhood, although Erikson's stage theory continues through adolescence, adulthood, and old age.

These stages are roughly correlated to ages, but individual differences and diversity of experiences create variations from this norm. Theoretically, a child completes one stage and goes on to the next, but in actuality people seem to continually work on all previous stages while they proceed along the continuum. Teachers and parents also may notice a child under duress

ERIKSON'S STAGES OF CHILD DEVELOPMENT

- Trust versus mistrust: Babies learn whether or not the world around them is safe and nurturant.
- Autonomy versus shame: Toddlers learn to define themselves as individuals or feel shame about their independent urges.
- Initiative versus guilt: Children learn to test their individual powers and abilities or feel guilty about making "mistakes."
- Industry versus inferiority: Children extend their ideas of themselves as successful workers or learn to feel inferior and incapable.

regressing to a former stage. Some serious problems, such as family crises and how they affect learning, will be discussed in Chapter 14.

Trust versus Mistrust Even if you never plan to work with babies, you need to know about the trust versus mistrust stage of development, which Erikson relates to infancy. This is the time when babies are making their first discoveries about what kind of a world they have entered. Many are welcomed into homes where they are the center of attention, and their slightest protest is met with efforts to alleviate distress. These babies begin early to trust that they are important and that the world is a safe and friendly place. Some babies aren't so lucky, however. Their parents may be overwhelmed with personal problems, and a baby is just one more worry, or their caregivers may be overworked and untrained. These babies may cry from hunger or other discomfort without any response. What a different image of themselves and their world these babies get!

About sixty years ago, parents were told that picking up babies when they cried would spoil them. Dutiful mothers and fathers fought their natural urges to respond to the cries of their infants. Instead, they attended to feeding and changing needs on a set schedule, to which the child was expected to conform. Remnants of this theory persist in American society today, threatening the healthy development of trust in infancy. Parents and caregivers need to know how important it is to respond to a baby's cries. Children's early efforts to communicate their needs deserve a response. Responsive adults are essential to a child's trust development.

Children continue to actively work on trust during preschool and beyond, especially if they had a problem with it earlier. They are looking for evidence that they can count on people in their larger world. The reassurance of caring and consistent adults in their daily lives helps youngsters develop trust. Some have had negative past experiences that led them to expect continued disappointments from people they encounter (Thompson, 1998). You may see some of these children constantly checking to see if someone is still their friend. They may also frequently seek the

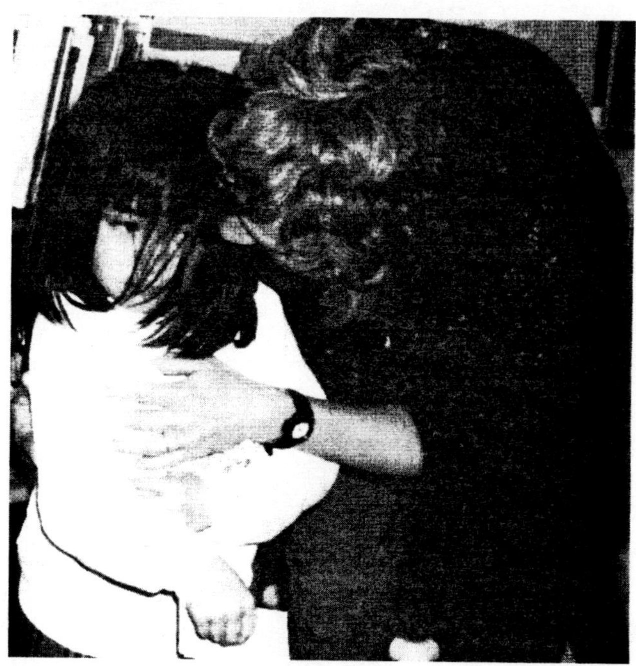

The reassurance of caring and consistent adults in their daily lives helps youngsters develop trust.

reassurance of the teacher's attention. Others just expect rejection, as in the example below:

> September 29th was the first child's birthday in her class. However, Mrs. Jensen didn't see Eli's mother put party invitations into six of the children's cubbies. As the first child discovered hers, a mad rush of others hopefully checked their cubbies. There were a few shouts of delight and many disappointed faces. "Oh Dear!" Mrs. Jensen thought. "I should have made it clear that party invitations should not be distributed at school unless all children were included." Mrs. Jensen noticed that Kurt didn't even bother looking. He didn't expect to be invited, just as he couldn't believe anyone would let him join in their play.
>
> Kurt's life hadn't made him feel secure or wanted. He had been in four foster homes in two years. Mrs. Jensen wondered what *his* birthdays had been like. Mrs. Jensen reached for her circle time basket and removed the story she'd planned to read, replacing it with A. A. Milne's *The World of Pooh*. She put her bookmark on page 70, "In which Eeyore has a birthday party and gets two presents." She also changed her plans for the topic of the group discussion, deciding to discuss feelings of being left out.
>
> Mrs. Jensen begins group time by sharing a short, humorous but sad, personal story of a time she remembers feeling left out as a child. Two children share similar experiences. When Mrs. Jensen reads the part of the story where Piglet wishes Eeyore "Many happy returns of the day" and Eeyore can hardly

believe that his friends remembered his birthday and even gave him presents, Kurt giggles especially loudly.

After the story, the group discusses how Eeyore felt and they come up with a list of ways to help him trust his friends next year. Mrs. Jensen then points out how she put paper candles on her calendar to mark all the children's birthdays. She ends with an explanation about most homes not being big enough to invite a whole class, so they will have birthday celebrations in the classroom for everyone. She mentions the birthdays coming up during the next few months, and Kurt beams as she ends with, "And December 6th we'll celebrate Kurt's birthday!"

Class parties are acceptable this year because she doesn't have any children in her class from families who don't celebrate birthdays or holidays.

If a child's experiences lead to a lesson in mistrust rather than trust, that child's whole life can be affected. Future friendships, and even marriages, may suffer from this lack of trust. It first appears as insecurity with friends and excessive demands on teachers. Later in life, an inability to trust co-workers and the suspicion of spouses can undermine relationships. As relationships fail to withstand the pressure, a vicious cycle of self-fulfilling prophecy is perpetuated. We have all known children and adults who fit this pattern: They expect others to reject them, so they behave in ways that invite rejection. Your challenge is to help children have experiences that will reverse this cycle before it is too late.

Autonomy versus Shame Erikson's autonomy stage is the period when youngsters work at defining themselves as separate from the adults they have, until now, completely depended on. (Erikson's use of the term *autonomy* to describe emotional development is different from Piaget's concepts of intellectual and moral autonomy, which were discussed in Chapter 1.) The toddler years are the time for development of autonomy, as Erikson defines it. As infants, children are so dependent that they actually consider themselves a part of their parents or caregivers. But toddlers suddenly begin to see that they are separate people, with ideas and wills of their own. They need to test this new revelation to make sure it is true and to convince themselves of their independence. This period is known as the "terrible twos" and can create serious discipline problems for the unwary adult. It doesn't necessarily disappear at age three, so beware. The formerly docile child suddenly says an emphatic "No!" to all suggestions and tests the limits that are set.

For instance, Andrew is so caught up in his ability to say "No!" that he sometimes says "No!" to things he really wants. "Do you want some ice cream?" his mother asks. "No," says Andrew proudly. Because Andrew is her sixth child, Debbie has been through this behavior before. She knows that right now her two-year-old is focusing on his power to say "Yes" or "No," not on whether or not he really wants some ice cream. When Andrew inevitably changes his mind and does decide to have ice cream, Debbie doesn't lecture him about the fact that saying "No" means he doesn't get any. Instead, she encourages his new independence by respecting his decisions, either way.

Children who don't get ample opportunities for making choices can be incredibly stubborn.

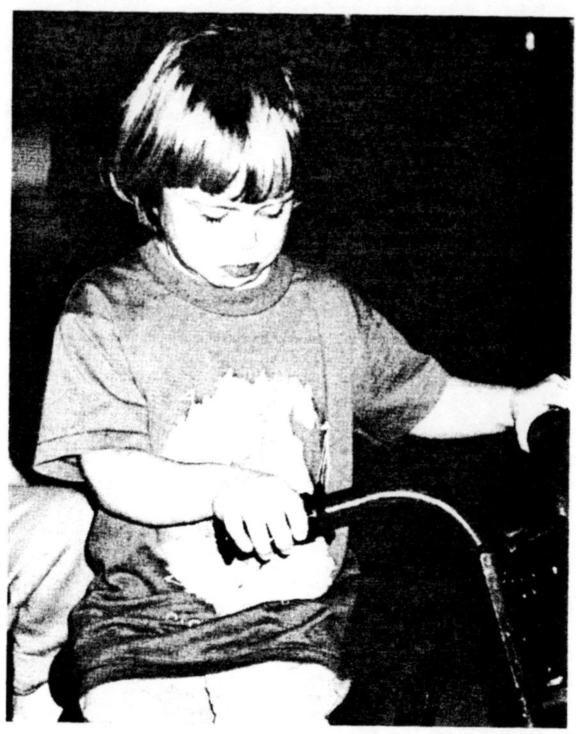

Additionally, Debbie gives Andrew as many opportunities as possible to make decisions and choices. These opportunities not only help him feel proud of his independence, but they also help him cooperate during times when there is no choice. Children who routinely have a chance to exercise their personal power are more able to accept times when adults must make the decisions. Conversely, children who don't get ample opportunities for making choices can be incredibly stubborn. In other words, Debbie knows that letting Andrew make decisions such as whether or not to have ice cream or which shirt to wear will make it easier when he *doesn't* get to decide what time he goes to bed. The following example also demonstrates how giving children choices helps them to accept adult limits when they are required:

> Out for a fall cranberry hunt, Jeffrey bounded along the trail ahead of the group. He squealed with delight as he came upon the first icy puddles of the season. What an inviting challenge! His teacher resisted warning him and the other youngsters away from the adventure. Dennis, an experienced teacher of young children, reminded himself of the extra little socks tucked in his daypack, just in case. Besides, the children were sure to come across hundreds of puddles this winter. No amount of adult warnings about hidden depths and wet feet would discourage any naturally inquisitive child from testing that ever-so-thin layer of brittle, frozen skin. If denied, they would probably just sneak ahead and try it once they were safely out of sight. So Dennis let the children choose which

puddles to test. He enjoyed watching the individual youngsters pounce from one shattering splash to the next. Soon the inevitable happened, and Jeffrey yelped! He had almost lost his boot to an ice-hidden mud's sucking grip. Impressed by its strength, he investigated the next puddle with a bit more respect. He was learning! Later that afternoon, a cloud bank stole the sun's warmth. The teacher approached Jeffrey matter-of-factly and said, "It's time to put your knit hat on." Because he had made plenty of his own choices already, Jeffrey easily accepted that this one was not his.

Preschool, and even primary grade, children still have the need to assert themselves. If you understand this need and learn to give lots of choices, it is often incredibly easy to get children to cooperate. Kimberly's child-care teacher, Dennis, used this understanding to solve a problem that Kimberly was having at her child-care center. It seemed that Kimberly was asserting herself by refusing to cooperate when getting ready to go home, antagonizing her tired and hurried father. Dennis didn't give any attention to the undesirable behavior by wheedling and bribing her to get her boots and coat on, nor did he take away her independence by forcing her to put them on. Instead, he gave Kimberly some choices. The choice was not *whether* to get ready to go home, but rather *how* to get ready. "Do you want to put on your boots first or your coat first?" asked Dennis. "Would you like me or your daddy to help you with your zipper?" was the next question. "Can you put on your own boots, or would you like help?" was another. In no time at all, Kimberly was ready to go *and* feeling proud of herself.

Erikson's theory says that when children do not develop emotional autonomy, they develop a sense of shame instead. Shame can be caused by their experiences with adults who don't understand what is happening when children assert themselves; these adults think that their job is to stamp out "naughtiness." Unfortunately, they may only be successful at making children believe they are being bad, when really the children are just working at being grown-up. As a result, the children develop feelings of shame about the natural urges of independence.

Initiative versus Guilt Erikson's next stage of emotional development is called initiative versus guilt. Most preschool children are in this stage. You will see them further testing their individual powers and abilities. Their physical and intellectual abilities increase rapidly as they joyfully try out their new skills.

Developmental tasks now include the need to participate in real work. Megan is always right there when it is time to prepare the afternoon snack. She takes great satisfaction in setting the table or spreading peanut butter on celery sticks. She practices small motor coordination, and even math skills, as she meticulously places five raisins on each celery stick. Her feelings of accomplishment and confidence are also growing. Megan and her classmates are invited to assist with many necessary jobs in the afternoon session of preschool. They care for the guinea pig, cleaning her cage and feeding her. They water the plants, sweep up under the sand table, and organize the dress-up clothes on hooks. They take pride in this work because the afternoon teachers, Dennis and Nancy, communicate their belief in the children's abilities. The teachers accept the children's ability levels and don't make a fuss if a job isn't done perfectly, or if a little something is spilled in the process.

Whenever the afternoon staff thinks about developing a new learning center, they first discuss the plan with the students. Dennis knows from his classes in early childhood education, as Nancy knows from raising four children, that children will learn much from the planning process and that their involvement will help ensure that the new materials are used appropriately. After a field trip to a bank, the children want to play bank in the pretend play area. Instead of looking all weekend for materials, Dennis and Nancy invite children to bring things from home that could be used in a bank. The weekly newsletter explains the plan to parents and asks them to contribute. On Monday, the children arrive with old checkbooks, deposit slips, canceled checks, a real cash box, and play money. Aaron's mom works in a bank, so she contributes a pad of loan application forms.

As the interested youngsters work to arrange these materials in a way meaningful to them, they cooperate in problem solving and planning. They are willing to invest effort to resolve disagreements in *their* bank. Before long, things are set up to their satisfaction, and several youngsters are busily scribbling on the checks, making important banking transactions. These children are feeling good about the work they have done, and it shows in their behavior.

In the morning session at Midway Children's Center, the teacher makes the snack in advance and pours juice for each child. Joanne discourages the children's offers to help, telling them that they will only spill if they try to pour their own juice. Joanne spends long hours after school and on weekends preparing materials and rearranging the classroom. She prides herself on always having everything ready for her students when they arrive. She wouldn't dream of using class time to set up a new activity; everything is strictly preplanned and scheduled. She doesn't have pets in her class because she doesn't have time to care for them, and the children "are too young to do it properly." Everything is under control: hers.

In spite of all her careful planning, Joanne has many more discipline problems than the afternoon staff does. The students often seem disinterested in what Joanne has planned for them. They frequently "misuse" the materials, pursuing their own ideas instead of copying the model at the art table. When the children don't follow Joanne's plans, she tells them how disappointed she is.

Josh and his friends feel ashamed when they disappoint their teacher. They don't understand that it is their healthy curiosity and energy that is getting them into trouble. They only know that what they are interested in doing is "bad." They assume that they are bad children. Because Joanne's training is with older children, she isn't familiar with this stage of child development. Thus, she often misinterprets the children's actions. What a different kind of experience this teacher and her young students would have if Joanne only knew how to harness their constructive energy into activities that would develop their sense of initiative.

When children are feeling good about the work they have done, it shows in their behavior.

Feeling successful at real work can even help to heal a child's damaged emotional development, as in this story about Robert:

> Robert's behavior had become progressively more aggressive as the school year continued, and Mrs. Jensen was very concerned. In fact, things were getting out of control. Last week, when she had to remove Robert from the block area where he was hitting other children with blocks, he had hit and kicked her uncontrollably. She tried to hold him soothingly, but his outburst didn't stop until he was exhausted. He refused to be comforted by her.
>
> Mrs. Jensen planned an activity she thought Robert would enjoy. The class had enjoyed the book *Philomena,* which made them want to have a lemonade stand, so they were going to all help make lemonade. Mrs. Jensen brought the lemons and other ingredients to school and set them out. When Robert arrived, she encouraged him to come and make some lemonade. She modeled how to push down hard on the lemon to make the juice come out, commenting that she could feel the muscles in her arms get harder as she pushed on the lemon. Robert looked interested and then pointed out his big muscles in his arms as he squeezed a lemon. "You can feel my muscle if you want," he said proudly.

Since Robert had been the first to start making lemonade, the other children allowed him to tell them how to do it. Robert had a great time, and even cheerfully helped with the cleanup. Mrs. Jensen told him, "I enjoyed working with you today, you really know a lot about making lemonade."

Robert was feeling so good about himself, he was friendly and cooperative at storytime and saved the teacher a place to sit next to him at snacktime, giving her a hug as she did so.

Of course, one day doesn't undo years of problems, but each step toward meeting a child's emotional development needs is a step in the right direction.

Industry versus Inferiority School-age youngsters are working through an emotional development stage that builds on the preschool stage of initiative versus guilt. Erikson calls this next stage industry versus inferiority. During this phase, children are extending their ideas of themselves as workers and contributing members of society. If they feel successful, their behavior mirrors their good feelings about themselves; negative behaviors go along with negative feelings about themselves. Their tasks now focus on earning recognition by producing things and mastering the tools to do so. In a subsistence society, this stage means learning to hunt, fish, cure skins, gather berries, and preserve food. For mainstream society, it means learning to read, write, think quantitatively, and work cooperatively. Feeling successful at this age means seeing yourself as a capable person. Once again, children need to have opportunities for real work that is meaningful to them and that they are allowed to do on their own.

Mrs. Jensen's first graders were planting seeds this morning as part of their study to learn how things grow. They had read about what plants need to grow and now they were reading the specific directions on the seed packets. They had a variety of fast-growing seeds available: beans, radishes, lettuce, and alfalfa. They also had access to a variety of planting materials and containers.

Some were interested in the idea of watching bean sprouts grow in a jar of water. Others liked the idea of growing an alfalfa crop in a paper cup filled with dirt. The prospect of actually growing a radish to eat was attractive to many. The youngsters had the opportunity to explore as many of the options as they wished. They also had the freedom to do their planting in their own way. The parent helper was worried because some of the seeds weren't being planted at the recommended depth. Mrs. Jensen reassured him that the variety of planting approaches and the varying results were an educational experience. The children certainly weren't worried. They felt very important to know that they were starting the process of making something grow.

When the seeds were planted, the youngsters began making journals for recording the growth of their plants. The children made the books themselves, counting out the agreed-on number of pages, choosing a cover color, and then folding and stapling the pages into booklet form. The parent helper noticed that the children could not keep the pages lined up as they stapled. He offered to help with folding and stapling. Mrs. Jensen explained to the well-meaning

When children feel successful, their behavior mirrors their good feelings about themselves. Negative behaviors go along with bad feelings about themselves.

father that the children took pride in doing this work themselves. Sure enough, the children all *loved* their books, crooked and crumpled as they were. Everyone felt like a success.

Too many children are labeled as failures at this stage. You certainly have seen the devastating consequences for the child who fails to begin reading on society's schedule. This is the child whom others shun for being dumb. This is the child who disrupts class out of frustration and anger. This is the child the teachers are eager to send off to the reading specialist. Many students who eventually become school dropouts begin dropping out in first grade (Schorr, 1989). Lifelong inferiority complexes begin early. The children in the following examples were spared:

> Shelley had a narrow escape. She came home in tears, saying, "I'm dumb now." Her teacher had said she wanted Shelley to go to the reading specialist for help on her phonics skills. Fortunately, this step couldn't be taken without a parent conference. Miss Wheeler explained to Shelley's mom that Shelley didn't seem able to do the daily phonics worksheets; therefore, she obviously needed special help. Shelley's mother was puzzled by this report, because her daughter was already reading at home and wrote wonderful stories, too. Her teacher was

surprised to hear about Shelley's success at home. She couldn't figure out how a child could read and write but not be able to do phonics sheets. Miss Wheeler was new to first grade after teaching in the upper grades and wasn't knowledgeable about beginning reading. She didn't realize that phonics sheets are much more abstract than actual writing is, and that most children learn phonics through meaningful writing experiences. Miss Wheeler listened to the child's mother, however, and did not further damage Shelley's belief in herself as a learner.

Blake not only couldn't do worksheets, but also really wasn't interested in writing when he was a first grader. Mrs. Jensen met with his parents and decided that Blake just wasn't ready yet. They knew he was a bright child and would become a reader and writer in time. They made sure that he had plenty of opportunities to experience books and many purposes for writing, but they made no demands for a certain level of performance from him. Most of all, they made sure that he never felt like a failure. They knew that not reading in first grade wasn't fatal, but that feeling like a failure could endanger his self-esteem and his future ability to learn. This child was supported as he negotiated the *industry versus inferiority* stage in his own time.

EMOTION REGULATION

The ability to control, or regulate, emotions plays a big role in acceptable behavior (Katz & McClellan, 1997). There is a lot for young children to learn: how to deal with frustration, cope with fear and anxiety, and express pleasure are just parts of developing emotion regulation. When Danny throws himself on the floor, kicking and screaming, he demonstrates that he cannot control his emotions. When Meadow puts her thumb in her mouth instead of crying after her mother drops her off, she demonstrates progress in emotion regulation. When Desmond is able to wait his turn on the slide, he shows the progress he has made. Min Ho's nonexpressive style is evidence that he has learned his family's cultural standards for emotion regulation.

With adult assistance, children become more able to behave in socially acceptable ways as they mature. They learn not to cry at minor disappointments, and how to comfort themselves when upset. They also gain the ability to control impulsive behavior. Impulse control is needed for a social skill such as taking turns, which requires that a child be able to postpone the immediate gratification of desires. Adults who become impatient with very young children's lack of such control need to know that it is partly dependent on physical maturation of the brain and central nervous system (Hyson, 1994). Of course, the way a child reacts to emotional situations depends on a complex interaction of biological differences in experiences, temperament, family, and culture. The early childhood years are the crucial period for the development of emotion regulation (Katz & McClellan, 1997). Like other kinds of learning, it is assisted by good teaching, as Mr. Davis shows here:

The second grade classroom is abuzz with activity as children work on their electricity projects. Chris is trying to build a working flashlight, but it only works

The ability to control, or regulate, emotions plays a big role in acceptable behavior.

some of the time, and Chris is getting more frustrated by the minute. Chris finally reaches the end of his patience and begins to pound the table with his materials and rip his flashlight apart. His face gets red and he looks as if he might cry.

Mr. Davis sees what is happening and goes over to Chris, kneeling down next to him. He talks in a low, calm voice, and suggests that maybe Chris should take a break from working on the flashlight. He proposes that he and Chris work on it together either during lunch recess or choice time later on. Chris stares at the table, blinking back his tears. Mr. Davis disperses the crowd of children who have been attracted by the banging, saying, "Let's give Chris some room right now." Chris gets the privacy he needs as he works on cooling down and getting his feelings under control.

At lunch time, Mr. Davis and Chris work together rebuilding the flashlight. They are relaxed and laughing together when Mr. Davis says to Chris, "Boy, it's a lot easier working on this now when we aren't upset, isn't it?" Chris smiles and agrees as they continue to work, laughing at their mistakes along the way. With the support of Mr. Davis, Chris is learning about how to deal with frustration.

Generally, young children's emotional development involves growth in several areas that directly relate to guidance issues:

1. Children learn varied and effective ways of expressing their emotions.
2. They learn better control of their emotions.
3. They gain in their ability to understand their own feelings, as well as those of others (Hyson, 1994).

Chapter 3 includes these issues as they relate to social development, Chapter 6 will discuss the influence of adult models on this process, and Chapter 7 presents ways of effectively expressing feelings.

HUMAN NEEDS

Adler (1927) proposed the existence of basic human needs for personal significance, including social recognition and belonging. When these needs are met, people feel good about themselves and tend to interact with others in positive ways. This creates a cycle of positive interaction that further convinces them that they are significant in their world. When these needs are not met, the reverse is true: Human nature leads people who feel insignificant to behave in ways that further alienate them from the acceptance and approval they desire.

Power A need for being in charge of your own actions, also known as personal power, is central to feeling significant (Adler, 1917). Children and adults who experience too much external control over their behaviors have unmet power needs. This may make them bossy and controlling of others, or it may overwhelm them to frustration and anger. Sometimes temper tantrums are a result of feeling powerless. You may have seen situations when children began screaming and crying when told they had to do something that seemed insignificant.

If you have spent much time with young children, you will recognize these statements as common: "I don't have to!" "My Mom said!" "You're not the boss of me!" These are clear evidence of children's attempts to get personal power.

Young children are especially vulnerable to unmet power needs because they are able to make so few actual decisions for themselves. This is another reason why it is important to give them choices as often as possible and say "No" as seldom as possible. Youngsters whose power needs are met are definitely easier to get along with.

Attention A major indicator of significance and social recognition is having other people pay attention to you. Being ignored is painful because it makes you feel unimportant. Having someone listen to what you have to say, or be interested in what you are doing, is incredibly validating. Unfortunately, many adults unwittingly teach children to misbehave in order to get the attention they crave. They pay no attention to children who are getting along well or who are working productively; they only give attention when there is a problem. This means that many children have no idea how to get attention in positive ways; therefore, they strive to get it in negative ways. Interestingly, the drive for attention is so strong that people would rather have others mad at them than ignoring them.

> Jarod has been sitting in group time waving his hand wildly, hoping to get a turn answering a question. He knows all the answers, but never gets a chance to show it. He is getting very disgusted at listening to other kids who don't know the right answer. Why won't Miss Wheeler call on *him?* He could tell her the right answer. Jarod decides not to wait to be called on anymore; he yells out the answer to the next question. Miss Wheeler instantly reprimands him for breaking the rule about raising his hand and sends him to the time-out bench. As he sits there all alone, he sees the plants that the class planted last week. Some are starting to sprout. Jarod systematically breaks the tender shoots off the plants.

Acceptance Being accepted by others, having friends and playmates, is an essential human need. Some people behave in ways that makes others want to be with them, and others do the opposite. Young children generally lack understanding of others' feelings; this often causes them to act in ways that get rejection. Teachers of young children see variations of the following situation over and over again. Social skill problems such as this will be discussed in Chapter 3:

> Adam wanted to play with Shaun, an older, admired playmate, so he ran up to him and exuberantly banged into him. Shaun didn't see this as a friendly gesture, so he shoved Adam away—hard. Adam fell against the wall and cried brokenheartedly, not just from the bump but also from the rejection.

MOTIVES OF MISBEHAVIOR

Dreikurs (1964) added on to Adler's theory of basic human needs by describing a set of unconscious motives for misbehavior that result from not having the basic needs met: power, attention, revenge, and avoidance of failure. We have addressed power and attention previously and also described Jarod's revenge. "Avoidance of failure" means a child or adult has totally quit trying. This is the result of experiencing too much failure and becoming convinced there is no hope of success.

CONCLUSION

Some lucky kids have parents and teachers who help them feel successful and important. These children are accepted for who they are and encouraged to work and grow in their own way. Some lucky kids have parents and teachers who help them develop trust in others and belief in their own abilities. Some youngsters are born with difficult temperaments, and yet encounter acceptance for who they are. These children do not develop poor self-concepts or develop discipline problems that worsen each year. Some children are not so lucky. Their healthy emotional development is thwarted by parents or teachers who do not understand child development or human needs.

FOR FURTHER THOUGHT

1. Observe an early childhood setting, watching for examples of young children's inability to sit still for very long. What problems do you see when adults forget this aspect of child development?
2. As you observe young children, try to identify different temperaments as described in this chapter. What is the difference between a person's current mood and that person's temperament?
3. Think about people you know well. Do any of them exhibit signs suggesting they may not have developed trust as described in this chapter? How does that problem affect their social interactions?
4. Observe toddlers, watching for expressions of developing emotional autonomy as described in this chapter. How do adults respond? Do you recommend any different responses based on your understanding of this aspect of emotional development?
5. Observe preschoolers, watching for expressions of their desire for real work. Does their environment meet this need? What changes could be made to assist their development of initiative?
6. Observe young children in public schools, looking for the difference between those who are succeeding with school tasks and those who are not. In what ways do the youngsters express their feelings about their abilities?
7. A problem to solve: Jeremy isn't working on his writing assignment. He is fooling around and bothering others instead.
    a. What are some possible causes of this behavior?
    b. How would you address the various causes?
    c. How might the problem have been avoided?

RECOMMENDED READINGS

Erikson, E. (1963). *Childhood and society* (2nd ed.). New York: Norton.

Greenspan, S. I., & Greenspan, N. T. (1985). *First feelings: Milestones in the emotional development of your baby and child.* New York: Viking.

Hyson, M. C. (1994). *The emotional development of young children: Building an emotion-centered curriculum.* New York: Teachers College Press.

Katz, L. G., & McClellan, D. E. (1997). *Fostering children's social competence: The teacher's role.* Washington, DC: National Association for the Education of Young Children.

Pica, R. (1997). Beyond physical development: Why young children need to move. *Young Children, 52* (6), 4–11.

Schorr, L. (1989). *Within our reach: Breaking the cycle of disadvantage.* New York: Anchor Books/Doubleday.

3

INTELLECTUAL AND SOCIAL DEVELOPMENT AFFECT DISCIPLINE

Young children are not miniature adults. That idea is central to early childhood education and basic to the constructivist view of learning. It reminds us that children have unique needs that must be considered in their care and education. The statement also cautions us against adult egocentricity in assuming that children's thinking is the same as ours. In this chapter we examine some ways in which children's ways of thinking influence their behavior and affect your discipline decisions. Information about young children's intellectual and social development will not only help you immeasurably in the areas of guidance and discipline, but it will also help you be a more effective teacher in general.

INTELLECTUAL DEVELOPMENT ISSUES

Lev Vygotsky and Jean Piaget, both born in 1896, are two major contributors to the understanding of intellectual development. They are both considered *constructivists* because they emphasized that knowledge is actively constructed by the learner rather than passively received from others. However, neither suggested that input from others is not necessary; both writers acknowledged the essential role of social interaction for the development of understanding. Vygotsky wrote convincingly of social experience shaping how people think and interpret their world (Berk, 1994). Piaget's work frequently discusses the role of social interaction with adults and with peers, as learners exchange viewpoints to construct understanding. Piaget (1932/1965) explained that social interactions between children are necessary for the development of intelligence, morality, and personality.

Both Piaget and Vygotsky also described processes of organizing information as central to learning. Vygotsky's work (1934/1962, 1978) describes young children moving from randomly categorizing information in "heaps" to an increasingly more sophisticated classification system based on analysis of the relationship between pieces of information. Piaget's work focused extensively on the significance of individually created logico-mathematical frameworks for classifying relationships between ideas and information (Gruber & Voneche, 1977).

What is commonly known about the work of either Piaget or Vygotsky is only the tip of the iceberg, and their most significant contributions are widely ignored due to their complexity. Piaget and Vygotsky are each best known for the one aspect of their work that is easiest to understand: Vygotsky is best known for the idea of the *zone of proximal development* (Dixon-Krauss, 1996), which will be discussed later in this chapter. Piaget is known for his *stage theory,* indicating a sequence of maturation in understanding and thinking. Vygotsky agreed with Piaget that young children's thinking differs from that of older children, and that abstract thought is a later development (Berk, 1994). Due to Piaget's life and career lasting much longer than Vygotsky's, Piaget and his associate researchers at the Geneva Institute were able to amass huge quantities of research data about the learning process. Because children were the subjects of the studies, they provided excellent views of children's thinking.

YOUNG CHILDREN'S THINKING IS DIFFERENT

The work of Piaget and his colleagues clearly shows that a child's view of the world and reality is different from an adult's. Children's limited reasoning ability, coupled with their limited experience, often bring them to conclusions inconsistent with adult logic. This situation often gets children into trouble. Teachers and parents get angry at youngsters for what adults perceive as disobeying rules, telling lies, being selfish or inconsiderate, and behaving in totally irrational ways. To make matters worse, the children don't realize that they have done anything wrong. For a parent or teacher who doesn't understand what Piaget (1964) has explained about intellectual development, this behavior can be totally infuriating. However, it is often just normal behavior for a young child.

BREAKING RULES

Part of Piaget's (1965) famous and extensive studies of children's thinking involved their understanding of rules in games. He focused on rules in the game of marbles, finding out that children's views of rules differ with age. The younger children weren't able to follow the rules but believed that they were quite sacred and imposed by adults. Piaget pointed out that these youngsters nevertheless seemed unconcerned about following the rules. Older children felt free to change the rules by mutual consent, but then felt bound by them. Piaget related this concept to the difference between guidelines for life that are imposed by others and those that children reason for themselves. The latter situation signals moral autonomy.

The way children deal with the rules of a game can help adults understand how children deal with societal rules and expectations (Piaget,

It is important for adults to realize that children who break rules, whether in play or elsewhere, may not understand that they have done so.

1965). As you watch youngsters playing games, you can see for yourself that their ideas about rules vary with their ages.

Dennis is amused at how his three-year-old students think about rules for their games. When they play hide-and-seek, they tend to yell out, "Here I am! Come find me!" If some adult sets up a race, the children don't wait for "ready, set, go." After the race, if someone asks who won, they all say with conviction, "I won! I won!" It is clear that young children respond according to their perceptions of what is important, not according to adult rules.

Most preschool youngsters don't understand, or can't cope with, the competitive aspect of games. The first time Dennis set up a game of musical chairs with four-year-olds, he quickly learned a better way of structuring the game. He was faced with torrents of tears when youngsters were "out" after not finding a chair. Dennis immediately changed the rules so that there was a chair for everyone; the challenge was simply to find a seat quickly when the music stopped. The important thing was that no one was forced out of the game.

Primary-grade children become concerned about rules and about winning. The desire to win often colors the interpretation of rules, and each child wants to change the rules in his or her favor. Mrs. Jensen values the arguments and discussions that are an inevitable part of board games among her first graders. She recognizes that learning to resolve their own disputes about rules helps children learn to reason. She appreciates that young children can learn about cooperation from these opportunities to consider each other's position (e.g., DeVries & Zan, 1995; Siccone & Lopez, 2000). By learning to consider the viewpoint of others, children learn about behaving in ways that are compatible with the needs of others. This lesson takes time and careful adult assistance, but it is an important part of the long-term goals of discipline.

It is important for adults to realize that children who break rules, whether in play or elsewhere, may not understand that they have done so. Much of what adults take for granted is unknown to children. Piaget's (1965) studies of moral development indicate that young children are not capable of understanding why certain behaviors are acceptable or unacceptable; therefore, many behavior problems are caused by a lack of understanding, and the child truly has no idea of wrongdoing.

BEING SELFISH

It is normal for young children to see things only from their own viewpoint. This aspect of their intellectual development affects their interactions with others. They are not necessarily being inconsiderate when they overlook a playmate's feelings; a very young child is often not even aware that someone else *has* feelings (DeVries & Zan, 1996). It's not surprising, then, that young children have many conflicts and that their teachers spend a great deal of time dealing with those conflicts. Teachers who understand child development don't get upset at these normal misunderstandings. Instead, they use the situation as a teachable moment, as Dennis does in this next example:

> Juan is playing by himself in the sandbox, carefully filling a dump truck with sand and emptying it, creating a hill. Celeste is playing next to him with a toy bulldozer. She suddenly drives her bulldozer over Juan's hill to flatten it out for a road. Juan immediately starts to cry and to hit Celeste.
>
> Dennis arrives on the scene and comforts both children. He has observed enough from across the room to say to Juan, "I don't think Celeste knows why are upset; can you use your words and tell her?" But Juan is too upset to talk yet, and so Dennis gives him more time by rephrasing the question. By then Juan is able to say that he didn't want Celeste to touch his hill.
>
> Dennis realizes that neither child had considered the intentions of the other. Juan thought Celeste was being mean, and Celeste was shocked that he was mad at her. Having encouraged Juan to express his view, he then asks Celeste to explain what she was doing. It turns out that she was trying to be helpful in building a road, not understanding what Juan was doing. With help from Dennis, Juan is able to say, "I don't want a road, I'm making a hill." With this information, Celeste is happy to work on her road in another part of the sandbox and all is peaceful, for the moment.

Conflict is an opportunity for an alert teacher to help youngsters tune in to the feelings and viewpoints of their playmates. Knowledgeable teachers do not blame the children or make anyone feel guilty for being thoughtless of others; they understand that this behavior is normal for young children.

Mrs. Jensen also works at helping her young students grow beyond their egocentricity by encouraging them to tell one another how they feel. Often she needs to help children find the words to express themselves; they learn from her example as she walks them through the process of communicating their feelings in a constructive way. (Effective communication of these useful *I messages* is discussed further in Chapter 7.) This is part of effective guidance, which teaches lifelong interpersonal skills. As children's intellectual ability to understand the views of others develops, their social development is enhanced as well. Learning to think about how others feel, called *perspective taking,* is discussed further in the Social Skills section of this chapter.

The goal is voluntary unselfishness, but many adults force children to share instead. Few adults would be as generous with their prized possessions as parents and teachers often insist youngsters must be. Would you turn your new car over to someone you barely know because "she doesn't have one"? Why should Rosa let Samantha ride her new bike? Rosa's right of ownership and right to decide whether or not to share must first be respected in order to prepare her to voluntarily share. Only when sharing is a real choice and not coerced can a child make the choice to be generous. Even with classroom materials not owned by any individual, the rights of possession must be respected. Youngsters should also be encouraged to stand up to aggressors who attempt to take things by force (Slaby, Roedell, Arezzo, & Hendrix, 1995). Of course, we need to teach them how to do this assertively rather than aggressively.

TELLING LIES

As a child, seeing things from your own viewpoint may mean that something is true because you *want* it to be true. This belief causes children to tell "lies" that they genuinely consider truths. An adult who understands how children think can help a youngster learn from this situation. When Christie tells her teacher that she is going with Kimberly to Disneyland next week, Dennis understands and is able to respond with empathy: "You really *wish* you could go to Disneyland." This response helps Christie separate her wishes from reality without making her feel bad about herself. The following example presented an actual problem of disappearing preschool material:

> Maggie was in her favorite dress-up outfit from the playhouse. She announced to Sheri that the outfit she was wearing was her own and that she was going to wear it home and even to bed. Sheri said, "Dressing up is one of your favorite things to do at school, isn't it?" Maggie agreed and then repeated that the outfit was hers.
>
> Sheri tried again, "I recognize those clothes as preschool dress-up clothes. It sounds like you wish they were your very own. You want to be able to take them home with you." Maggie held her ground, and Sheri tried explaining, "If everyone took their favorite clothes home, we wouldn't have any dress-up clothes to play with at school." Finally, Maggie seemed to be listening.
>
> Yet Maggie still insisted that the clothes were hers, but she was very attentive as Sheri continued to discuss the problem. "I remember a few times when you went home with the dress-up clothes you were wearing. When I

found out, I felt bad. I was worried that there would not be enough dress-up clothes at preschool anymore."

After listening carefully, Maggie put her arms around Sheri's neck and whispered in her ear, "Sheri, I know they are preschooler clothes." Then she smiled and danced away.

Maggie's struggle with fact and fantasy is not unusual. Piaget (1965) found that young children really do not understand the nature of a lie. Even six-year-olds in his study could not differentiate between an honest mistake and a purposeful mistruth. Additionally, they tended to judge how bad it was to tell a mistruth in relation to how likely it was to be found out and therefore punished. Thus, with this line of reasoning, a believable lie is acceptable, yet a lie that stretches the truth too far is bad. Piaget's research about children's thinking should help teachers and parents understand why explaining their adult logic to youngsters doesn't work. Instead, children need to experience the problems that come from trying to deceive others. As they get older, they can be helped to realize the impact of deceit on relationships. For this to be effective, children must have caring relationships with others (DeVries, 1999).

SCHOOLWORK PROBLEMS

Intellectual development stages determine what kinds of materials and activities best help children learn. If you don't match the experiences and materials to the children, you are sure to have behavior problems as well as academic problems. Piaget's (1960) work explains the importance of young children having real experiences with real materials to construct their knowledge about the world. The term *concrete* is often used to describe the type of materials children need for productive explorations. They include the water in the water table, the hammer and nails in the woodworking center, and the blocks in the block center.

Some teachers present letters, numbers, and other symbols to children who cannot yet make sense of them. This developmentally inappropriate instruction can create discipline problems. When children are not capable of doing what they are asked to do, they are likely to behave in ways adults dislike. Certainly they are not likely to complete the work on schedule. Often youngsters who are frustrated and discouraged by school tasks that are beyond them are then punished for not doing the work. It is common to see these children sitting dejectedly at their desks during recess, staring helplessly at a worksheet. Is it any wonder that they are tempted to be less than cooperative or even to lash out in anger?

Some people get confused and think that plastic magnet letters or wooden letters that fit into puzzles are concrete. These letters can be touched and moved around, but they are still only *representational* symbols. Some representational materials are more easily recognized than letters or numbers are. For instance, a doll is more recognizable as a symbol for a baby than are the letters in the word *baby*. Pictures of real things are not concrete either, but they may be useful symbolic representations.

Sometimes teachers are striving for developmentally appropriate education but don't realize that none of their teaching materials are concrete. Not everything that a child can touch and manipulate is concrete. Clocks and quarters are examples of apparently concrete materials that are actually representational rather than concrete. Young children can't construct knowledge of time or money through manipulation or observation of clocks or coins. No wonder lessons in telling time and making change are such difficult activities for young children. They involve both *symbolic representation* and arbitrary *social knowledge*. As such, they cannot be learned through an exploration of materials.

Teachers who understand how young children learn have fewer problems with child behavior because they provide age-appropriate learning activities and materials for children. They provide many real-life experiences and choices. (See Chapter 5 for further discussion of this topic.) A classroom that provides choices for children allows them to decide for themselves what type of materials and activities make sense. Mrs. Jensen's first grade has a wide assortment of concrete and representational materials accessible on open shelves for children to make selections. Miss Wheeler next door keeps everything but the worksheets in closed cupboards and rarely brings out anything else. She doesn't realize that the worksheets are entirely representational and meaningless to many of the children in her classroom.

> Desmond was in Mrs. Jensen's room, and his identical twin brother, Devon, was in Miss Wheeler's class. Devon tried to pretend he was Desmond so he could get into the room with all the interesting things, but he was sent back. Desmond was having a happy and productive year while Devon was in trouble constantly. One day Devon took matters into his own hands and got out an armload of special things from the teacher's cupboard, placing them enticingly on the tables as he had seen them in Mrs. Jensen's room. Now his room was a nice place to be, just like his brother's. But Miss Wheeler didn't appreciate his efforts. She was upset that he would dare to get into the cupboard without permission. How sad that she missed the important message Devon was sending about his learning needs.

SOCIAL SKILLS AND GUIDANCE

Missing social skills are the single most common cause of discipline problems. Children's squabbles over materials and their unskilled efforts to make friends cause frequent disruptions to both preschool and primary classrooms. Social skills are discussed last because we see them as an outgrowth of the previously discussed aspects of development. Physical abilities, emotional development, and levels of intellectual understanding all combine to determine current levels of social skill and understanding.

The early years are crucial for social development. Youngsters who do not develop social competence in the early childhood years typically continue to experience difficulty with peer acceptance throughout the school years (Katz

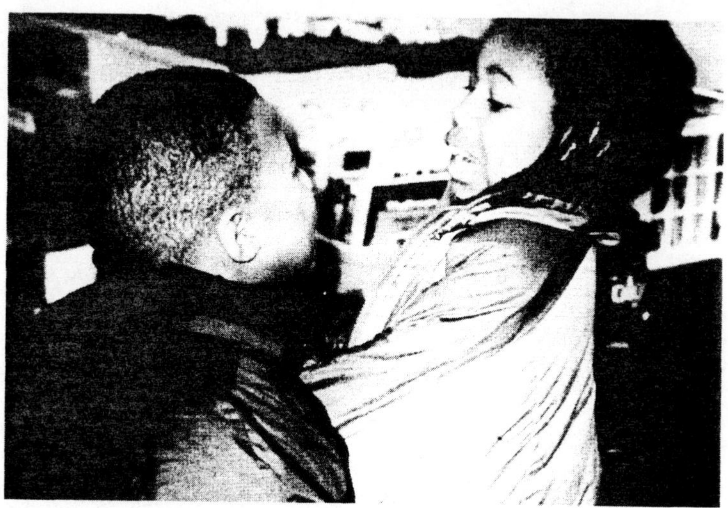

As youngsters experiment with different ways of interacting with others, they observe the results of various approaches.

& McClellan, 1997; Johnson, Ironsmith, Snow, & Poteat, 2000). Not surprisingly, these children are at risk as adults for social and emotional problems (Kupersmidt, Coie, & Dodge, 1990; Miller, 1993). Helping youngsters learn how to make a friend and be a friend is crucial to their life-long happiness. It's also a big help to teacher happiness when children learn how to get along.

CONSTRUCTING KNOWLEDGE FOR SOCIAL SKILLS

Children construct knowledge as a result of reflecting on their experiences. As they experiment with blocks, for instance, they observe the results of trying to stack, balance, and bridge structures. Thinking about the results helps children revise erroneous ideas. This process helps them construct understanding about such concepts as gravity, balance, and measurement. Children construct their theories of how the social world works in the same sort of trial and error situations.

As youngsters experiment with different ways of interacting with others, they observe the results of various approaches. Reflecting on the results of their social overtures can help children figure out how to play with others successfully and how to make friends. We have remarked previously on the value of peer conflicts as teaching situations. You may be surprised to hear that children's fights are useful teaching tools. Conflicts tend to challenge children's assumptions and encourage an exchange of viewpoints. They help youngsters realize that not everyone sees things their way. Thus, conflicts provide the necessary experience for learning and they provide the teachable moments. Helping children deal with their disputes gives the teacher an opportunity to guide children's thinking about the experience. The adult role varies, depending on the child's individual levels of emotional, intellectual, and social development.

Teaching children to think critically about their behavior and to use reasoning abilities to learn to solve interpersonal problems is consistent with current recommended approaches to teaching other subjects. National guidelines in every area of the curriculum urge teaching for critical thinking and problem solving instead of old approaches of memorized learning (National Research Council, 1994; National Council of Teachers of Mathematics, 1995). These curriculum guidelines also require greater sensitivity to individual differences, which is equally applicable to helping children learn social skills. Some adults think it is enough to simply tell children how they are expected to behave and then punish them if they do not. That approach would be the same as a teacher merely demanding mastery of mathematics without instruction, assessment, and reteaching (Butchart & McEwan, 1998).

Like any other learning, the ability to successfully master social skills requires that children's physical and emotional needs are met. A child who lacks security and confidence has difficulty working on anything else. Children are most likely to be secure, confident, and socially competent if their parents are warm and attentive and also help them understand limits (e.g., Hart, Olsen, Robinson, & Mandleco, 1997; Putallaz & Heflin, 1990). If these needs cannot be met adequately at home, schools must try to fill the gaps.

Have you noticed that we are not talking about social skills as learning to say *please, thank you,* and *I'm sorry?* These are polite ways of speaking, but they are only superficial behaviors and do not necessarily reflect true feelings. Some adults and children confuse these memorized phrases with the understanding needed for true social competence. You have certainly seen children who are caught doing something wrong and who automatically say, "I'm sorry," yet show no signs of remorse. These children have merely learned the magic words for getting out of punishment. Too many adults focus on teaching socially acceptable words instead of helping children understand others and develop caring feelings.

> Mrs. Jensen realized the uselessness of teaching words instead of understanding several years ago when she rescued Stephanie from Jason's physical aggression. Jason was angry at Stephanie and was gripping her wrists very hard, hurting her. After Mrs. Jensen pried his hands off Stephanie and helped Stephanie to tell Jason how she felt, she asked Jason what he could do to make Stephanie feel better.
>
> Jason said "Thank you," and Mrs. Jensen asked Stephanie if that made her feel better. Stephanie replied in a distainful voice, "No. Jason, you have to say 'sorry.' " So Jason said, "Sorry." However, Mrs. Jensen could tell that one platitude was as meaningless as the next.

HOW CHILDREN DEVELOP SOCIAL COMPETENCE

As in other teaching topics, we need to start with the "basics" when we teach social skills. First, we need to think about a child's motivation for prosocial

BASICS OF PROSOCIAL BEHAVIOR

1. Successfully "entering play," which leads to
2. Having friends, which leads to
3. Caring how your actions affect others, which leads to
4. Willingness to work at "perspective–taking," which leads to
5. Prosocial behavior

Consider the alternative:

1. Being *un*successful at entering play, which leads to
2. Not having friends, which leads to
3. Not caring how your actions affect others, which leads to
4. Unwillingness to work at perspective–taking, which leads to
5. Antisocial behavior

behaviors, such as sharing or otherwise compromising. You have surely seen youngsters who don't care one bit whether they hurt other children or make them mad. These are usually the children who feel rejected by others, and who reject others in return. If a child doesn't care about others, you aren't going to have much luck with lessons about getting along. Being able to consider another person's feelings is a different issue than wanting to (Pritchard, 1996). It really isn't until children have something to lose, such as a playmate, that they have reason to consider how their actions affect others.

Therefore, the first "basic" for learning social skills is having friends, which for children means having playmates. In order to have playmates, children must be able to successfully enter into play with others, which may be the most "basic" part of developing social skills. The process of playing with others not only provides motivation for learning social skills, it also provides excellent practice (Lillard & Curenton, 1999). Play provides many opportunities for conflict and negotiation, which help children learn to consider the needs and feelings of others. Considering the needs and feelings of others is called *perspective-taking,* and is also basic to developing social skills.

Though each piece contributes to the other, we see a necessary initial sequence to the components of learning social competence: first comes the ability to enter play successfully, which creates feelings of being accepted by others, which leads to friendships and to caring about others. These relationships make youngsters more willing to consider the perspective of others instead of just their own. When these pieces are in place, a child is generally open to teacher assistance with social skills and behaves in a fairly socially acceptable manner. Let's look now at how to help get these pieces into place.

Learning How to Enter Play How many times have you seen a child crying because of not being allowed into a play situation? Asking "Can I play?" is often ineffective and can even invite rejection because it offers the power to say "no." Instead, children can be helped to learn more productive strategies for being accepted as a playmate.

Children first must be helped to avoid advances that disrupt the ongoing play. Too often a child will barge into a play situation like a bull in a china shop and be totally surprised and crushed when the other children get mad. It may be useful in these cases to teach a beginning strategy that does not interrupt: simply playing alongside a potential playmate, doing a similar activity (Ramsey, 1991). Five-year-old Seanne expressed this idea clearly. She

Helping children learn how to be accepted by others may be one of the most important things you teach.

told her teacher, "I learned how to play with a boy today." When her teacher asked her what she did, Seanne explained, "I just watched what he was doing with Legos and then I played like him."

Another useful approach is to first observe what the desired playmate is doing; in other words, to work at seeing things from the other child's viewpoint. This observation provides information that the child can use by offering a way to contribute or fit into the existing play. When the child's goal is to join a group at play, it is worth the effort to figure out what the others are doing first. The child who joins a group with a contribution to ongoing play is most likely to be accepted. Six-year-old Ray explained this very well to his five-year-old brother, Phil.

> Phil was complaining to his mother that Ray wouldn't let him play with his group at recess that day. Ray quickly defended himself, saying, "You could have played with us if you had just started playing what we were playing. But instead you tried to make us stop our game and listen to what you wanted to do. Next time, Phil, just start doing what we are already doing, OK?"

It is important to help youngsters experience success in these efforts and so develop confidence that they will be accepted. A child who approaches playmates with confidence is more likely to gain entry to play. Conversely, the unsure child is more likely to experience rejection. Rejection starts a cycle of unproductive behaviors that lead to increased rejection (Kemple, David, & Hysmith, 1997). Teachers can make a difference with careful teaching and coaching, as in the example below:

> Peter and Sasha are deeply engrossed in their play. They have created elaborate boat replicas with Legos and have made pretend spears and spear throwers out of unifix cubes. More unifix cubes have been used to represent the seals they are now playing at hunting with their spears. Their cries of "ya ya ya" accurately capture the tone used by their fathers when they pursue seals on the Yukon River by their village.
>
> Joe comes over and wants to play with Peter and Sasha. He picks up one of the "seals" and starts adding unifix cubes to it, saying "Look how long a road I can make with this." Sasha grabs back the pretend seal that he was about to spear and tells Joe to stop. Joe starts to cry, saying, "I wanna play too!" Peter and Sasha ignore him as they continue with their seal hunt.
>
> Mrs. Akaran, their first-grade teacher, sees there is a problem and comes to help. She has been admiring the quality and complexity of Peter's and Sasha's pretend play, and doesn't want to disturb them. She realizes that the problem is caused by Joe's inept attempts to join the two more socially adept boys. Therefore, she focuses her attention on helping Joe begin to learn some important missing skills. The teacher goes to Joe, puts her arm around him comfortingly, and whispers conspiratorily to him as she pulls him aside. "Come over here and let's figure out what you can do." Joe stops crying and listens as Mrs. Akaran urges him to watch what Sasha and Peter are doing.
>
> "What are they using those unifix cubes for?" asks his teacher as she assists Joe's observation of his desired playmates. She gets Joe to think about what others want instead of just considering his own desires. Then Mrs. Akaran asks Joe what he could do to help with the seal hunt; she is proposing a strategy for entering play that is often successful. With a little help, Joe decides that he could make a seal and a spear for himself out of the unifix cubes not currently in use. He makes his own pretend play props, and then his teacher encourages Joe to go over where Sasha and Peter are playing and try them out. She watches to see what happens, noting with satisfaction that the other boys allow Joe to join in on the hunt.

Notice that the teacher didn't use her adult power to get Joe accepted as a playmate. Well-meaning teachers often insist that no child be rejected (Paley, 1999), but such intervention overlooks a teachable moment and may actually make things worse for that child. There is usually a reason for a child not being allowed to play, and it is the teacher's job to assess the situation and figure out that reason. Usually there is a missing skill or understanding on one side or the other; the teacher needs to identify what needs to be

HOW TO HELP CHILDREN DEVELOP SOCIAL COMPETENCE

1. Coach youngsters in successful play–entry strategies.
2. Encourage close friendships and caring relationships.
3. Use children's disputes to help them exchange viewpoints and learn perspective–taking.
4. Teach negotiation skills for conflict resolution.

learned and then teach it. Insisting that a child be allowed to play just covers up the problem, teaches no skills or understanding, and may make other children more resentful of the child forced upon them. You may also want to consider how you feel when you are having a meaningful conversation with a best friend and an uninvited acquaintance joins you. Is it perhaps reasonable at times for children to ask not to be disturbed by others?

ENCOURAGING FRIENDSHIPS Teachers and parents also help children become socially competent by encouraging friendships. Friendships are important for a variety of reasons. Children are more likely to be successful when initiating contact with friends, thus increasing their confidence (Kemple, David, & Hysmith, 1997). Children's play is more sophisticated and mature when they are playing with friends, which improves their competence. Children care more about the feelings of friends than about those of other people (e.g., Eisenberg, 1992), thereby encouraging them to practice perspective–taking. By early elementary school, many children have established a best friend. These relationships are important because they offer the best opportunities for developing the interpersonal understandings needed for socialized behavior.

LEARNING PERSPECTIVE–TAKING Once children experience the joy of friendships, they are motivated to work at keeping them. As stated previously, this gives a reason for trying to understand another child's viewpoint in a conflict.

The ability to see things from another's viewpoint, *perspective–taking,* is essential to social competence. Without this ability, youngsters remain self-centered and unable to relate to the interests, needs, and rights of others. Until children can take into consideration the viewpoint of another person, they cannot make progress in reasoning about fairness. When they can only see their own views, their idea of justice consists of that which they desire for themselves. Obviously, this perception will not endear them to playmates.

There is considerable difference of opinion about how early children are able to understand and empathize with another person's feelings (e.g., Lillard & Curenton, 1999). We agree that certain forms of empathy appear early, such as sympathizing with another child who is sad. However, the ability to take another person's view into consideration when it conflicts with your own is entirely another matter. A three-year-old who gives a cookie to a hungry child when there are plenty of cookies is not likely to do so when there is only one cookie, especially if that two-year-old wants the cookie for himself or herself. Though very young children have been observed sharing and helping others (Eisenberg, 1992), it is not clear that these are demonstrations of true perspective-taking. Positive social behaviors may be motivated from other sources.

Young children need adult assistance as they learn perspective-taking and realize that other children also have feelings.

Despite differences in the research, there is agreement that awareness develops gradually from an egocentric perspective to the ability to respond to and even predict how others will feel. According to Selman (DeVries, Hildebrandt, & Zan, 2000; Selman 1980), with experience and guidance, people move through five levels of perspective taking as follows: Level 0, not recognizing that others have feelings or ideas different from your own, is common during preschool and even kindergarten. During the primary grades, most children operate at level 1. At this point, young children realize that others have their own feelings, but can't consider someone else's feelings while thinking about their own. Our observation shows that this is particularly true when their own feelings are in opposition to the other person's. As they move into upper elementary school, level 2 thinking is more common. This brings the ability to consider another person's views as well as their own. Levels 3 and 4 bring increasing decentering and the ability to coordinate mutual perspectives. However, these generally do not emerge until adolescence and adulthood.

This information about children's thinking should help you to be more accepting of how they behave. You will respond differently when you realize that young children probably aren't being mean when they disregard another child's feelings; they're just being young. This information about levels of intellectual development also offers essential guidance for helping children move to higher levels. The message is not to just accept the child's lack of perspective-taking, but to aim your teaching one level higher than what the child is doing (DeVries, Hildebrandt, & Zan, 2000).

Working with young children, you will often see situations like the following:

> Jessie is working on a drawing, using the only yellow marker at the table. Jeremy reaches over and grabs the marker out of Jessie's hand. He seems somewhat startled when Jessie yells at him and tries to grab the marker back. Soon the two are in a tug-of-war, with both sides claiming they need the marker.
>
> Dennis stops the struggle and calms the children with his gentle presence. He works at getting each child to explain his or her feelings, trying to get them to use the "I messages" he consistently models. (See Chapter 7 for more detail on "I messages.") Then Dennis shows Jeremy where he can get another yellow marker.

When Jeremy grabbed Jessie's marker, he demonstrated that his perspective taking was at level 0. Therefore, Dennis aimed at helping Jeremy realize that Jessie has wishes and feelings, too. It probably wouldn't be worthwhile trying to teach higher level cooperative negotiation to Jeremy because it would be too far above his level of understanding.

Children can make better than normal progress through these levels of understanding with the support of understanding teachers (DeVries & Zan, 1994). And, as Vygotsky (1962/1934) reminds us, children can perform at higher levels with assistance than they can alone. Vygotsky's writings about the *zone of proximal development* and *scaffolding* refer to how adults help children to do things, and thus teach them to perform independently. Storybooks may also provide assistance to children as they learn to think about the feelings of others. In *Jamaica's Blue Marker* (Havill, 1995), Jamaica comes to understand why Russell was acting mean; this type of story may help your young students think about how others feel.

The ability to understand and empathize with others is crucial to adult society as well as children's interactions. "Children are less likely to behave aggressively toward someone if they can put themselves in the other person's place and imagine that person's thoughts and feelings" (Slaby, Roedell, Arezzo, & Hendrix, 1995, p. 145). This statement seems equally true for adults.

Learning Conflict Resolution Children who have some perspective-taking ability can be helped to learn conflict resolution skills. The ability to avoid and resolve conflicts constitutes another essential aspect of social competence. It involves the ability to communicate personal needs and to listen to others expressing theirs. It also involves willingness to compromise as well as the capacity to manage aggression (Siccone & Lopez, 2000). All these aspects of negotiation require the child to take into consideration the viewpoint of others. These sophisticated abilities require significant practice.

> "You dummy!" yells Megan as Sam pours rice into the funnel at the rice table. Her teacher calmly walks over and asks Megan, "You don't like something Sam is doing?" Then the teacher guides Megan's words from merely expressing anger to clear communication of what is upsetting her. Sam needs help hearing this

Conflict resolution combines several social and communication skills and requires significant practice.

message and deciding what to do about it. The teacher is there to make this a valuable learning experience for both children.

As mentioned in Chapter 1, children do not get this practice if adults solve problems for them. Instead, adults must guide youngsters in age-appropriate ways and help them to resolve their own differences. For very young children with limited language ability, the teacher may do the talking for both parties in providing the two viewpoints. As children mature, they can gradually take a more active role in the expression of their different views. The goal is for the teacher or parent to intervene as little as possible. Effective communication for conflict resolution is discussed further in Chapter 7. In the following example, Stephen seems to have learned a lot:

> Darren had grabbed a truck from Stephen and wouldn't give it back. Then he took a larger truck and hit Stephen with it. The first impulse of the teacher, Maureen, was to go to Stephen and see if he was all right. But the chain of events that happened next kept her out of it.
>
> Stephen stood up, looked at Darren with an angry face, and said, "What's my face telling you? I'm mad and if you hit me again or won't play nice I'm going someplace else to play!" Then Stephen sat down and began to play again. Darren looked surprised, gave back the truck, and they were off playing together again. Maureen caught Stephen's eye, smiled, and winked a congratulatory message. She felt wonderful to see the results of the teaching she had been doing.

THE TEACHER AS COACH

A variety of teaching methods are useful in helping children develop social competence. The teacher who respectfully considers children's viewpoints is teaching by example. When children are involved in a dispute, the teacher's appropriate role might be more of a coach, providing encouragement, critiquing the performance, and recommending strategies for improvement. Sometimes the most helpful adult role is to stand back and let children experience the social consequence of their actions. Mathew might need to learn from experience that other kids don't want to play with him when he grabs things from them. Chapters 6, 7, and 8 in part two of the text explain these teacher roles more fully.

Although it is important not to intervene more than necessary, it is also important to be there as needed, both for safety and support. Therefore, when Dennis sends Yaisa over to the playhouse with a suggestion for joining in play there, he also tells her to come back and talk to him if it doesn't work. Dennis helps Yaisa to watch what Kelsey and Megan are playing and to think of how she can help. He helps her plan her entry into the play activity, and stays nearby to lend her confidence while she carries out the plan. Dennis could simply tell Kelsey and Megan they have to let Yaisa play, but that wouldn't teach Yaisa useful social skills. It certainly wouldn't make her more popular with her peers, either.

The playground at recess definitely offers the richest opportunity to help children learn social skills. Yet, in most schools, teachers are given recess time as part of their preparation time, leaving playground supervision to aides. The problems with this situation are many: the ratio of children to adults is likely to be at least 100 to 1, making it impossible to do any teaching. Even mere crowd control is a challenge with those numbers. Even if the numbers were appropriate, the aides can't know the children well enough to provide guidance aimed at the needs of individuals. In addition, very few aides have adequate background and training to provide the kind of guidance that will be beneficial. No wonder kids just get sent to the principal when a fight breaks out. The opportunity for on-the-spot problem solving is lost. For this reason, more and more teachers are choosing to go out to recess with their students. They report that they come to know their students much better as a result.

DISCIPLINE APPROACHES

The type of discipline techniques used by teachers and parents also relate to children's social skills (e.g., McNeilly-Choque, Hart, Robinson, Nelson, & Olsen, 1996; Butchart & McEwan, 1998). Children who are disciplined through punishment tend to show aggression and hostility toward peers. Children who are helped to understand the harmful effects of their behavior on others exhibit more positive social behaviors. Children who are aggressive to others are generally rejected, but those who show consideration for others are sought-after playmates. Therefore, teaching why certain behaviors are acceptable or not, instead of just punishing undesirable behavior, can lead to better social skills and better relationships with peers.

TEACHING LEADS DEVELOPMENT

Though young children are not maturationally capable of functioning at high levels of interpersonal understanding (Selman & Schultz, 1990), they grow toward higher levels with adult assistance. As Vygotsky says, "The only good kind of instruction is that which marches ahead of development and leads it" (1962/1934, p. 104). This can be compared to how we help babies learn to talk: Just because they can't talk yet doesn't mean we don't talk to them. Just because their early efforts aren't very good doesn't mean we don't respond and encourage further effort. In these ways, we effectively teach oral language. Similarly, we can effectively teach higher levels of thinking by modeling and scaffolding more advanced levels than the child is capable of independently.

ACCOMMODATING INDIVIDUAL DIFFERENCES

There are some basic developmental accomplishments that apparently transcend cultural differences (Bowman & Stott, 1994). These include learning how to make friends, learning language, learning to organize and integrate perceptions, and how to think, imagine, and create. But these accomplishments vary according to the cultural context in which they occur (Lillard & Curenton, 1999). Therefore, it is important to remember that appropriate social behavior varies from group to group. The child's culture, family background, economic status, and gender generate different views of social competence. The teacher who holds all children to one standard of behavior is actually being unfair to some.

CULTURAL DIFFERENCES The culture of school reflects the dominant culture of the setting. Those children whose homes and family expectations are most similar to school have the least adjustment to make. Cultural differences affect communication due to differing ideas about such things as when and how speech is used, what body language means, and whether it is polite to look directly at the speaker. Culture differences affect relationships, too. Different groups hold varying ideas about the proper relationship between children and adults and about whether it is better for children to be cooperative or competitive. Teachers who hold all youngsters to one standard inadvertently cause some to fail socially and academically.

For instance, white middle-class preschoolers tend to exhibit very different interaction styles from African American and Latino children observed in Head Start (Rizzo & Corsaro, 1991). The Head Start youngsters teased each other and used competitive and oppositional talk without being upset by it. On the contrary, this interaction style seemed to cement friendships within the group. In contrast, the white middle-class preschoolers were very concerned about hurt feelings and were easily upset by negative

Teachers who accept cultural and individual differences help prevent school failure.

comments. Rizzo and Corsaro concluded from their research that interaction perceived as friendly among one group would be perceived as aggressive and intimidating by the other. Many white middle-class teachers would misunderstand and squelch the social interactions of a child who used teasing as a friendly overture.

Another study compared a Head Start program for African American children with a preschool program for middle-class white children (Lubeck, 1985). The teachers in each school were from the same culture as their students, apparently extending parental assumptions about child rearing into the school setting. The beliefs about how children learn were very different in these two schools: The Head Start teachers believed children learn by listening and repeating what they were told. The preschool teachers emphasized learning through experimentation. The Head Start teachers in the study used language to reinforce the authority of adults. The preschool teachers in the study used language to get children to think for themselves.

Not surprisingly, these differences result in quite different ways of thinking and viewing the world. Each approach is an adaptation to, and preparation for, the experiences expected by that cultural group. For many people, fitting in with their own culture and succeeding in the dominant culture are not compatible. Sensitive teachers will help children bridge the gap by being explicit about expectations, instead of assuming that everyone knows what is expected and being upset when some don't conform (Lubeck, 1994). Teachers who respect all cultures will also educate themselves about their students' cultures and modify expectations to assist all children in feeling comfortable.

Socioeconomic Differences Class differences based on family income, jobs, and educational background also result in different behavioral goals and patterns. Like cultural differences, these style differences are neither good nor bad. However, they may cause children from different backgrounds to be less comfortable with each other (Ramsey, 1991). Like other people, teachers are often less comfortable with those from different backgrounds.

Teachers who remember that different is neither better nor worse will help more children succeed in school. The youngsters whose background values are different from teachers' are most at risk for school failure and dropping out (Schorr, 1989). As Ramsey (1991) says, "We must be sure that we do not exacerbate economic disadvantage by undermining the social skills and styles that children have developed, even though they may be less compatible with the current structure of the classroom" (p. 61).

Gender The fact that a child is a boy or a girl also affects acceptable behavior. Although we acknowledge that sex-role stereotyping contributes greatly to behavior differences between boys and girls, we also believe that some innate differences may be unavoidable. Buying dolls for boys and trucks for girls has had limited success. Boys generally prefer to play with boys, and girls generally prefer to play with girls (Powlishta, 1995).

This gender segregation appears to be a result of different styles of play. More boys tend to engage in rough-and-tumble play, and girls may congregate in the playhouse. Gilligan's (Gilligan & Wiggens, 1987) research links these different styles with different developmental goals, each with its own set of social interaction problems. Girls seem to focus on relationships, forming exclusive cliques that create hurt feelings. Boys focus on establishing their importance through games of power that cause physical injuries. The separation of males and females begins during the toddler years and increases from preschool into the elementary grades. Youngsters' preference for same-sex playmates may be a result of expecting someone of their gender to be more like themselves, therefore more likely to behave in predictable and compatible ways (Maccoby, 1986).

Many researchers have studied this phenomenon and recorded efforts to redirect youngsters. However, coercing cross-gender contact has made little difference in free-choice preference (Maccoby, 1986). When boys and girls do play together, the boys tend to dominate and the girls may become tentative (Powlishta & Maccoby, 1990). By the time they reach kindergarten, youngsters who engage in play activities associated with the opposite sex are likely to be ridiculed by their peers (Damon, 1983).

Not only do children separate themselves by gender, but adults also interact with boys and girls very differently (Beal, 1994). Usually girls are treated in ways that encourage compliance and dependence, and boys are treated in ways that encourage assertiveness. As a result of being essentially segregated and treated differently, boys and girls tend to belong to separate cultures. Due to these differences, boys may fit less well into a quiet and controlled school environment. For this reason, most teachers would rather have more girls than boys in their classrooms.

Is there a reason to try to change this pattern? It seems that boys and girls may benefit from interacting with one another (Feiring & Lewis, 1991). Children with at least one playmate of the opposite sex demonstrate higher levels of social competence (Howes, 1988). Interacting with male friends may help girls become more independent and assertive (Powlishta, 1995), and interacting with girls may help boys become more caring, cooperative, and less aggressive.

You can do something to minimize the segregation and make an effort to treat boys and girls the same. Group projects that interest both boys and girls can encourage cooperative interaction between them. In contrast, organizing games as "girls against boys" emphasizes gender distinctions. Being aware of typical differences in adult interventions with boys and girls can help you avoid them. Beal's (1994) research found that girls get more teacher attention when they are playing quietly. If a girl misbehaves, the teacher usually reprimands her quietly and privately. Boys traditionally get more teacher attention than girls. Teachers keep a constant eye on them, watching for signs of misbehavior. When there is a problem, teachers are more likely to give a public reprimand. Interestingly, many boys seem to enjoy this attention and therefore are more likely to misbehave in the future. As we will explain in Chapter 9, behaviors that get attention are most likely to be repeated.

CONCLUSION

This chapter and Chapter 2 examine some aspects of child development only as they directly pertain to discipline issues. Knowledge about children's thinking can help you distinguish between immature thinking and purposeful misbehavior. Information about the development of social competency will help you intervene in more productive ways. When teachers understand child development and match their expectations to what individual children can comfortably do, teachers are happier with their work and they have more cooperative students. Matching your expectations to child development can make the difference between dreading to go to school and looking forward to each new day.

Social development tends to be the primary content for teaching discipline. Children who have trouble getting along with peers and cooperating in a group create common discipline problems. Therefore, the topic of social development leads us into our next section, which discusses approaches to discipline. See the sources in recommended readings at the end of the chapter for more comprehensive coverage of child development.

FOR FURTHER THOUGHT

1. Observe young children playing games. What evidence do you see of their unique perception of rules?
2. As you interact with young children, watch for examples of their inability to think about another person's viewpoint. Try to help youngsters learn to express their views and to hear those of another child. Analyze this experience and discuss with your peers how you might improve your approach.
3. Listen to young children. Do you hear them confusing personal fantasy with fact? What is the best adult response?
4. Do you know a youngster who has difficulty being accepted into play with other children? Practice the coaching techniques described in this chapter. What are the results? What did you learn?
5. Have you or someone you know experienced difficulty in school because of a mismatch with the culture of the school? How did you or your friend respond? What were the long-term effects?
6. A problem to solve: Paul accidentally spilled the paint at the easel, but he denies that he did it.
   a. What is the probable cause of this "lie"?
   b. What is the best adult response to the situation?

RECOMMENDED READINGS

Asher, S. R., & Coie, J. D. (Eds.). (1990). *Peer rejection in childhood.* New York: Cambridge University Press.

Edwards, C. P. (1986). *Promoting social and moral development in young children: Creative approaches for the classroom.* New York: Teachers College Press.

Gilligan, C. (1982). *In a different voice: Psychological theory and women's development.* Cambridge, MA: Harvard University Press.

Johnson, C., Ironsmith, M., Snow, C. W., & Poteat, G. M. (2000). Peer acceptance and social adjustment in preschool and kindergarten. *Early Childhood Education Journal, 27*(4), 207–212.

Kagan, J., & Lamb, S. (Eds.) (1987). *The emergence of morality in young children.* Chicago: University of Chicago Press.

Kemple, K. M. (1991). Research in review: Preschool children's peer acceptance and social interaction. *Young Children, 46*(5), 47–54.

Lillard, A., & Curenton, S. (1999). Research in review: Do young children understand what others feel, want and know? *Young Children, 54*(5), 53–57.

Piaget, J. (1965). *The moral judgment of the child.* New York: Free Press. (Originally published in 1932.)

Ramsey, P. G. (1991). *Making friends in school: Promoting peer relationships in early childhood.* New York: Teachers College Press.

Slaby, R. G., Roedell, W. C., Arezzo, D., & Hendrix, K. (1995). *Early violence prevention: Tools for teachers of young children.* Washington, DC: National Association for the Education of Young Children.

Part Two

DISCIPLINE APPROACHES

Chapters 4 through 10 present an overview of approaches to discipline. We present these approaches in sequence, from most to least positive; this presentation also moves in sequence from least intrusive to most intrusive.

Chapters 4 and 5 examine ways to prevent discipline problems from occurring—the most pleasant discipline option. Chapter 4 looks at the interpersonal environment as well as the physical setting of the classroom. Chapter 5 explores prevention of behavior problems through the school program: its content and implementation. Chapter 6 shows how adult examples can teach children desirable behaviors, including how to accept and regulate their emotions. Chapter 7 explains how to teach communication and negotiation skills so that youngsters can manage potential behavior problems for themselves. Chapter 8 presents ways to enforce limits while helping children learn why certain behaviors are more desirable than others. Chapter 9 discusses the problems of behavior modification, an approach we do not recommend but that is widely used. In Chapter 10, we explain why punishment is damaging to the discipline goals of most people in society.

We do not believe that any one discipline approach holds all the answers for all children at all times. Determining the cause of the behavior is essential to selecting the appropriate discipline approach. We have confidence that teachers and caregivers with a wide knowledge of possible discipline approaches and a good understanding of child development are best prepared to respond appropriately in a given situation. However, we do not believe that all approaches are good ones. This section warns against counterproductive approaches as well as recommends productive ones.

4

CREATING ENVIRONMENTS THAT PREVENT DISCIPLINE PROBLEMS

Some people think of discipline as just dealing with misbehavior. It is much more productive to think about how to avoid behavior problems in the first place. You may have visited a classroom where things went so smoothly that you envied the teacher for having such a well-behaved group of students. Chances are that the children were normal, but the teacher was very skilled at creating an environment that made it easier for kids to cooperate. This skill is a much more sophisticated approach to discipline than simply reacting to problems. In this chapter we will look at ways you can prevent the cause of many behavior problems by creating a classroom emotional environment and physical environment that helps children get their needs met.

THE EMOTIONAL ENVIRONMENT

The adults set the tone in school and determine whether it is a "caring community" (Watson, 1999) or a "dog-eat-dog" society. As part of a caring community, children acquire the judgment, sensitivity, self-control, and skills to be able to treat others well (Watson, 1999 p. 25). Teaching children caring and kindness may be the most important mission of our schools (Noddings, 1995). This chapter begins the description of how to create a caring community through respect and concern for children's needs. Future chapters will discuss other aspects of the caring community.

POSITIVE TEACHER EXPECTATIONS

The teacher's attitude can create an environment that encourages either positive or negative behavior (DeVries & Zan, 1994). Naturally, no teacher would deliberately encourage negative behavior, yet it is possible to send messages unconsciously that are better not sent. Nonverbal communication is especially likely to reveal your inner feelings. Body language, tone of voice, and intensity often speak louder than words (Gordon & Browne, 1996).

If you are convinced that children want to work and play constructively, your whole manner of relating to them communicates that expectation. However, you may be convinced that children want to get away with whatever they can and have no interest in learning. This expectation, too, will be communicated by your tone of voice as you speak to children and by the amount of freedom you give them. You can pretty well count on children to behave according to your expectations.

> Mrs. Jensen's first-grade class has just come in from recess, and the youngsters are moving purposefully around the room as they prepare for their next activity. They have the freedom to choose among the classroom centers and to decide individually whether to eat a snack now or later. The classroom is alive with the sounds of decision making as children refocus their energies. Some go first to wash up before a snack and find a comfortable spot to relax and eat. Beau and Desmond are hungry but want to finish the block structure they were working on before recess. Food isn't allowed in the block area, so they postpone their snack. Yaisa and Shantae take their snack into the playhouse, where eating is allowed, and happily incorporate snack time into their dramatic play. Now that the youngsters have learned the routines and the classroom rules, Mrs. Jensen sometimes feels she really isn't needed. She is able to use this time for observing and recording children's progress.
>
> Mrs. Jensen has trusted her children to self-direct their free-choice time, and they have lived up to her expectations. This makes school more pleasant for her and for her students. Contrast Mrs. Jensen's room with Miss Wheeler's.
>
> Next door, Miss Wheeler has no time for observing. She is busy directing and controlling everyone's behavior. In her first-grade class, all the children must eat their snack as soon as they come in from recess, whether they are hungry or not. This schedule makes a long wait in line for handwashing, with lots of pushing and shoving during the wait. It isn't easy, but Miss Wheeler makes the children all sit still until everyone is finished eating before they are excused for the next activity. Then she assigns them by table to specific centers, where they must stay until she flashes the lights signaling rotation to the next center. Jimmie is a constant problem, always trying to sneak out of his assigned center to the blocks. Lydia cries a lot, saying she doesn't want to play with those "mean kids" from her table. Miss Wheeler is in constant demand to settle disputes and make children stay where they are supposed to be. She sees this situation as clear evidence that these young children aren't capable of self-direction. Actually, *she* is getting in the way of their self-direction.

Unfortunately, many teachers run their classrooms like Miss Wheeler does, and they create discipline problems for themselves. Their lack of trust in children to make good choices makes them over-controlling, which means individual children don't get their needs met.

You probably remember those teachers you really liked and those you didn't. You probably were much more cooperative with the ones you liked. They were undoubtedly the ones who let you know they had faith in you and gave you the opportunity to prove they were right. They probably also were the ones who made the effort to get to know their students as individuals,

When teachers take time to build relationships with their students, they have better behaved classes.

building a *relationship* with each. We know teachers who go to great lengths to build relationships with their students, even inviting small groups to the teacher's house for dinner. Establishing this rapport lets the teacher tune in to what is special about each child.

CLEAR GUIDELINES

It is essential that children understand exactly what behaviors are acceptable in school. Your positive outlook is not enough if children are confused about what they are to do. Young children often do not have the experience to know what is and what is not acceptable. Social norms are not self-evident.

> Mrs. Jensen started the school year by reading a book called *Little Monster Goes to School.* Little Monster does a lot of bad things, like sticking his arm out of the bus, tripping other kids, and getting into their lunches. Mrs. Jensen's first graders were properly horrified at this behavior. The story provided a good start for a discussion about how to act at school. Then the class was invited to brainstorm behavior limits. Mrs. Jensen helped them to combine their ideas into a few main ideas and to phrase them in positive instead of negative terms. "Don't run" became "Be careful." "Don't hit, don't shove, and don't spit" became "Be kind and talk things over." Mrs. Jensen wrote these as the children watched. They were displayed on a bulletin board that the children decorated with monster pictures they created at the paint easel. Most of the children learned to read the guidelines and referred to them when a classmate didn't follow one.

Children will more likely follow guidelines they themselves have helped to determine. They will also actively remind other children to do the same. Did you notice that we aren't talking about making *rules,* but instead use the terms *guidelines* and *limits?* Reynolds (1996) points out the differences between limits and rules: Limits and guidelines are flexible, taking circumstances into consideration; rules are rigid and tend to apply regardless of circumstances. Limits or guidelines encourage thinking and decision making; rules allow neither. Therefore, limits and guidelines foster moral autonomy, and rules foster heteronomy. Consider the difference between "Be careful" and "Don't run." The rule "Don't run" or even "Always walk" encourages children to test it and see what happens. Obviously there are times when kids can run, and even times when they should. The limit of being careful encourages children to reflect on what it means to be careful; "Being careful" becomes a topic of discussion to encourage children to self-evaluate their behavior according to that standard.

> Blake was driving a toy car on the block road he and Raymond had built. The car zoomed faster and faster as Blake began a fantasy about a jet car. Raymond was absorbed in building a bridge over his part of the road and wasn't paying attention to the jet car. He had finally gotten the right combination of blocks and the right balance to make his bridge stay up when Blake's jet car crashed into it. Mrs. Jensen heard the heated exchange of words between the boys and managed to get to them before the disagreement escalated to blows. "He knocked down my bridge!" complained Raymond. "I didn't mean to!" exclaimed Blake.
>
> What a perfect opportunity for important teaching. Mrs. Jensen could use this situation to help Blake, and also Raymond, to think about the effects of their actions. Her question, "Were you being careful of Raymond's bridge when you drove your car so fast?" is designed to encourage thought. So is the question, "How could you make your car go fast and still be careful of what other children are doing?"

Notice, Mrs. Jensen doesn't give answers, she helps kids think. Children also need help understanding the difference between accidents and carelessness. As explained in Chapter 3, young children tend to judge the act by the consequence. The big mess in the following example made Jessica think she had done something terrible.

> Jessica was trying to mix up some powdered paint. Maureen had gotten it out and meant to work with Jessica on the project, but Maureen got distracted for a few minutes by Mathew's untied shoelace and then by Kelsey's need for a band-aid. Jessica thought she could surprise Maureen and have the paint all mixed when she got back. Oops! A huge glop of blue powder came out all at once, overwhelming the paint jar and spilling onto the table top. By the time Maureen returned, Jessica was in tears and sobbing, "I didn't mean to. I beed careful." Maureen was able to reassure Jessica that sometimes accidents do happen, even when you are being careful. Maureen admitted that she had had a similar problem when she tried to pour the paint powder, and that's how she learned to use a scoop instead. Jessica calmed down as Maureen helped her scoop the blue powder back into the paint can.

All people have needs for friendship, success in worthwhile endeavors, and recognition for their efforts.

Young children have much to learn, but you might assume that they should at least know better than to sit up on their knees during story time. Surely they realize that sitting that way blocks the person's view behind them, and that means they are not following the guideline "Be kind." But remember that young children think about their own needs and have trouble considering someone else's position. Mrs. Jensen doesn't constantly remind children to sit down in the front rows; instead of nagging, she structures a learning experience to help them begin to understand consideration for others. She assigns each table of children to a specific row during the first group meeting of each day. During other group sessions, they are allowed to choose their own places, but for this one group time they take turns experiencing how it feels to be in the back rows with other children in their way. Mrs. Jensen encourages the children who can't see to remind the others politely when they are thoughtlessly blocking the view. This experience provides an important lesson in seeing things from another person's perspective and in communicating a problem. The children soon take responsibility for reminding one another to be considerate, and eventually remember most of the time not to kneel in front of someone.

MUTUAL RESPECT

Children are more likely to go along with what you want if you are also willing to go along with what they want sometimes. In other words, you encourage children to respect your wishes by showing respect for theirs

(Miller, 1996). As DeVries and Zan (1994) say, "Children do not develop respect for others unless they are respected" (p. 76). Most adults are pretty clear about why they want kids to respect adults, but perhaps you haven't thought about respect between youngsters. Learning to respect the needs and rights of others is basic to treating others well. Treating others well is central to what our society views as acceptable behavior. The construction of moral values is widely believed to be based on learning respect for others (DeVries, Hildebrandt, & Zan, 2000).

Respectful Communication You teach children about mutual respect by your example of showing respect for them. What does it mean to respect children? An obvious indicator of respect is how we talk to children. Too often adults speak to children in ways they would never consider speaking to an adult. Respecting children also involves accepting them for who they are instead of trying to make them into what you want. Chapter 3 explains some ways in which young children's thinking differs from adults'. Many adults have trouble accepting children's reasoning; they try to get youngsters to parrot adult reasoning instead. Respectful interaction involves listening to children to understand their viewpoints and asking them honest questions about their thinking.

How does an honest question differ from a "dishonest" one? An honest question is one you don't already know the answer to. "What color is your dress/shirt?" is a dishonest and patronizing question from any adult who is not color blind. "Why do you think that happened?" is an honest question unless you have a preconceived "right" answer in mind. If we ask others what they think, we need to accept their answer. What they think may not be what *you* think, but certainly it correctly describes their thinking.

Respecting Children's Needs Chapter 2 describes how young children's physical development needs affect their behavior. Adults demonstrate respect for children by allowing for these needs. Matching the physical environment to children's needs will be discussed further in the second part of this chapter. Chapter 2 also explains children's emotional development and needs in terms of their behavior. Respect for youngsters means accepting their strong needs to be "big": important, successful, and contributing members of the group. Endless shouts of "Watch me!" demonstrate how important it is to be big when you are small.

The human need to be significant is one reason why respect for children involves letting them have choices and be decision makers. In Chapter 1, we discuss choice as crucial to the development of moral and intellectual autonomy, as described by Piaget. In Chapter 2, we discuss the role of choice in the emotional autonomy stage, as described by Erikson, and in the need for power, as described by Adler. Choices are essential for feeling good about life and about your position in it (DeVries, Hildebrandt, & Zan, 2000).

Teachers who make all the decisions in their classrooms have more rebellious students. Teachers who involve children in deciding how best to accomplish goals have a much easier time. Occasionally, even the most enlightened teachers find themselves in a power struggle. Power struggles occur when you give an ultimatum and a child decides not to go along with it.

Dennis learned a lesson on the day he said, "No one eats lunch until your mess is cleaned up." Amy flatly refused to pick up the dress-up clothes she had been trying on. Now what? Dennis didn't really intend to deprive anyone of lunch; his remark had just been thoughtless. But the other children had picked up on it and were telling Amy she wasn't going to get any lunch. Amy was wailing over the thought of missing lunch, but she was not picking up any dress-up clothes.

Would the children ever believe him again if he let Amy have lunch without picking up? He couldn't in good conscience actually deny her food. What could he do?

He decided that he could teach a really valuable lesson to his young students. He could demonstrate how to admit an error graciously and to remedy it. This social skill is pertinent to the lives of preschoolers as they work at getting along. Dennis congratulated himself on modeling something much better than the "might makes right" concept, which his threat of missing lunch had perpetuated. So he went over to Amy and gently touched her shoulder to get her attention. He sat down on the floor beside her and explained that he had spoken without thinking. He assured Amy that she would not miss lunch.

Feeling calmer, Amy was able to listen as Dennis clarified his intent: to get the playthings out of the way so there would be space for eating lunch. With the ultimatum removed, Amy was able to problem-solve and reason. She proposed to move her dress-up clothes out of the way for now and finish putting them away after lunch when she wasn't so terribly hungry. Dennis was pleased to accept the compromise, realizing that it was not only logical but also a mutually face-saving solution.

Later, as he thought about the incident, Dennis examined the issue of saving face as it relates to power struggles. He acknowledged that his own pride was involved and thought about children's pride. He decided that if he got himself into a similar situation again, he would not hesitate to back off. He analyzed his reasons for going against the common assumption that adults must not lose in a battle of wills with a child. Dennis' conclusion was that losing such a battle meant damaged pride and therefore damaged self-esteem. Were his own pride and self-esteem more important than the child's? Because enhancing children's self-esteem was one of his major educational goals, Dennis was clear about the answer. He didn't want to make himself feel important at the expense of a little child. His was a respectful solution and one that took courage on his part.

CHILDREN'S EMOTIONAL NEEDS

Damage to pride or self-esteem generally is expressed in some undesirable behavior. In fact, bad feelings of any kind are likely to show up as "bad" actions. Conversely, a classroom that nurtures children's good feelings will encourage "good" behavior (Siccone & Lopez, 2000). Helping children in your classroom feel good about themselves and their school experience is an important part of effective classroom management and harmonious group dynamics.

It's Okay to Be Different Feeling good about yourself requires that you be accepted for who you are. In Chapter 3 we discuss the danger of teachers not understanding and accepting behavior patterns from a culture other than their own. Classrooms that accept and honor cultural differences meet the needs of minority students while teaching other children concepts of cultural pluralism (Mallory & New, 1994; Hunt, 1999). In respecting the cultural background of the child, it is also important to see the child as an individual and not just as a member of a certain group (McCracken, 1993). Seeing children as individuals helps guard against stereotyping them according to their culture. The teacher's attitudes can affect the attitudes of children and may counteract prejudiced ideas (Derman-Sparks, 1999).

Most teachers find that they have a lot to learn to avoid common, well-intentioned, but generally counterproductive efforts toward multiculturalism. Boutte and McCormick (1992) explain the mistaken and limited assumptions that most teachers demonstrate. Teachers find that it requires significant study for learning how to achieve true cultural plurality, as opposed to "pseudomulticulturalism."

> Mrs. Jensen is working within her school to help her colleagues move away from pseudomulticulturalism. Her school as a whole is very proud of its annual Multicultural Fair. For this event, each grade level represents a different country or culture. Each group makes costumes to wear and learns songs and dances to perform. They form a huge parade, winding through the school and into the multipurpose room for the songs and dances. Though this is quite spectacular, Mrs. Jensen is convinced that the way it is done teaches nothing helpful and probably creates stereotypical thinking.
>
> What do the kindergartners think or understand as they are instructed in making "mukluks" from paper bags as part of their Eskimo costumes? Do they realize that mukluks are made from animal skins, not paper bags? Do they understand why people living in cold climates, without access to shoe stores, would make and wear mukluks? Do they realize that their classmate Sasha, who wears velcro-fastened sneakers, is half Eskimo? When they join the school parade right behind the Chinese dragon created by the third graders, what connections do they make between dragons and mukluks?

Remember, young children are not capable of understanding abstract issues involving different time periods and faraway places. They create their theories based on what they see and experience. More on this topic in Chapter 5.

Cultural stereotyping is not limited to minority groups. One of the common misconceptions is that all white children are from a common culture, a perception that overlooks different backgrounds among them. No matter what skin color or ethnicity a child has, family patterns, religious beliefs, and class differences create unique cultural backgrounds for each (Gordon & Browne, 1996). In addition, Caucasian children may be recent immigrants from a variety of countries: Russia, Romania, and now Croatia are represented in Mrs. Jensen's school, in addition to children with Asian, Native American, and Latino backgrounds.

Each child comes to school with a unique set of prior experiences that include a set of family values. Many of these values relate to guidance issues. Different families have different ideas about acceptable and unacceptable behavior; they also have different ideas about how to teach children to be better behaved. Teachers need to get acquainted with parents in order to understand these differences (Gonzalez-Mena, 1993). Getting acquainted is also essential for dialogue about how to deal with differing expectations between home and school.

Some of these children speak languages other than English at home and come to school with limited English proficiency. Not only does a language difference complicate communication between teacher and child, it puts the child at great risk for social isolation. Lack of a mutual language certainly gets in the way of play and other interaction with peers, often leading to frustration and/or withdrawal for the child unfamiliar with the dominant language. Tabors points out that these children are caught in a "double bind of second language learning: To learn a new language, you have to be socially accepted by those who speak the language; but to be socially accepted you have to be able to speak the new language" (Tabors, 1998 p. 22). Group play that requires little verbalization is essential for counteracting the social isolation that inhibits language learning. Mrs. Jensen notices that block play offers an ideal opportunity for second language learning. Other helpful teacher strategies include having a predictable schedule and using repetitious songs and rhymes; these strategies help the preschool and primary grade children learning English as a second language just as they help younger children learning English as their first language.

Including Children With Special Needs Children with special needs who are included in regular classrooms add another dimension of diversity. The teacher's example will help counteract children's fears of this and other kinds of differentness. When you focus on the child and not the disability, you will more easily integrate the child with special needs into your group (Bredekamp & Copple, 1997). You can help your other students become comfortable with a wheelchair, prosthesis, or whatever special assistance a child requires. Then your students, too, can focus on the child as a person. Children with special needs often are rejected by peers because they are different (Ramsey, 1991). Sensitive teachers can help with this problem. The mother of a child with Down syndrome spoke with tears of joy about the friends her son had found after he was included in a first-grade classroom with a helpful teacher. The little boy just couldn't stop talking about his friends.

All people have needs for friendship, success in worthwhile endeavors, and recognition for their efforts. It is unacceptable for any child to be excluded on the basis of disability or skin color, and it is the teacher's responsibility to make sure such exclusion does not occur (Elswood, 1999). Children spend a large part of their day in the school setting and must be able to find friends, success, and recognition at school. It is essential that a teacher understand these needs and know how to provide for them. Books such as *Creative Resources for the Anti-bias Classroom* (Hall, 1999) may offer ideas for activities to counteract stereotypical thinking; however, we caution you to be selective and avoid substituting paper and crafts activities for real experiences.

FRIENDSHIP Classrooms and child-care centers where friendship and socializing are encouraged tend to be happy and harmonious places. Important social studies lessons occur constantly as the teacher assists youngsters in their efforts to work cooperatively. Disagreements are viewed as teaching opportunities instead of reasons to keep kids apart. These classrooms are places where the teacher isn't continually telling children to be quiet. The teacher's energy is directed into more useful ways of helping children use their time productively.

With building community as a goal, the children's energy isn't wasted by trying not to talk to one another. Teachers who understand the need for friendship and the value of peer interaction don't go around being mad at kids for doing what comes naturally. And kids don't end up feeling bad about wanting to communicate with their peers. Happier teachers and children create a friendly, relaxed atmosphere more conducive to learning of all kinds.

In fact, schools truly committed to building caring communities schedule time for children to enjoy one another in a relaxed atmosphere (Watson, 1999). Mrs. Jensen's school encourages teachers to take their students on a two-day overnight outing to a nearby camp that offers cottages for sleeping and a lodge for group gatherings. She schedules this event for early in the school year to maximize its benefit. Many parents go along, helping to supervise the children, but also creating bonds among parents and between parents and the teacher. We also know teachers who schedule Saturday family hikes for their classes, contributing their own time to the important goal of building community.

Such events help children make individual friends as well as create group camaraderie. As we have stated before, having friends is essential to children's healthy social and emotional development. Children who have difficulty making a friend need the teacher's assistance. Sometimes missing skills are the problem, and other times it is a lack of contact due to shyness. You can encourage the interaction of shy children by setting up small groups for cooperative learning activities (Phillipsen, Bridges, McLemore, & Saponaro, 1999).

In spite of the importance of having a friend, you probably have seen situations when best friends have been separated in school so that they will not disturb one another's work. This well-intentioned intervention ignores the importance of friendship for the child's intellectual and emotional development (DeVries & Zan, 1994; Bhavnagri & Samuels, 1996). Youngsters learn a great deal as they strive to get along with a friend: They learn to think about another person's views (Burk, 1996), they learn much about compromise and problem solving, and they learn about caring and being cared for (Noddings, 1995). They also practice emotion regulation (Katz &

McClellan, 1997). These things don't happen with just any peers; they require someone who is special to the child (Azmitia & Montgomery, 1993). As we have said before, a child must care enough about another child to be willing to examine egocentric views and work out disagreements.

> Mrs. Jensen works to ensure that children in her first-grade classroom find friends. She doesn't have a seating chart at first. Instead, she encourages youngsters to try different places for a couple of weeks. After they have had a chance to get acquainted, the children are asked to choose a place to sit for a while; Mrs. Jensen puts their names at those places for the time being. There is always an opportunity to make new choices as new relationships blossom. Mrs. Jensen says, "The most important thing you can do for some kids in a school year is to make sure they have friends."
>
> Some teachers are not tuned in to friendship as a legitimate need and overlook its educational value. Miss Wheeler is not only unaware of the importance of friendship, but she also doesn't know that children need to interact with their peers as a part of learning. She spends much of her energy each day in futile efforts to keep children from socializing. Her attempts to enforce an unnatural quiet in her classroom are counterproductive to academic and emotional development.
>
> Mrs. Jensen, however, enjoys the busy hum of children sharing ideas and discussing experiences. In this environment, the several children who came to her class speaking a language other than English are fast becoming fluent in English. The interactive learning style of this classroom is perfect for their language-learning needs. Sometimes individual children need to be reminded to talk more softly, but they are not told to be silent in Mrs. Jensen's classroom. She notices that adults talk while they work and wonders why so many try to impose silence on children.

Recognition If most teacher interaction with students is as part of a group, many children will feel lost or invisible. When the teacher interacts with children as individuals, they know that they have the teacher's attention. Communicating on an individual basis also makes it easier for the teacher to interact appropriately with children of various cultures. Mrs. Jensen makes sure to notice and comment to each child about his or her activity during free-choice time. Her comments and questions help each child feel important and valued. Her students don't need to engage in inappropriate attention-getting behaviors to get her to notice them. Because each child has her undivided attention at some time, they more easily share her attention during group times or when she is working with another child.

Getting to know students' families greatly enhances a teacher's ability to treat children as individuals (Powell, 1994). Home visits have been routine for Head Start teachers for years. Other preschool teachers, and even elementary teachers, have begun to adopt this valuable approach for getting to know their students. A home visit is a good chance to learn from parents. You can find out what the parents want from their child's educational

Getting to know students' families greatly enhances a teacher's ability to treat children as individuals.

experiences, and you can learn special information about the child. For instance, knowing the child's pet name at home and something about his or her favorite family activities will help you relate more personally to the child.

Conferences between teacher and child provide for both individual attention and focus on individual progress. Mrs. Jensen usually manages to meet with each of her students once a week for five or ten minutes. She is convinced that the weekly one-on-one time is much more valuable than meeting with all children daily in a group. Interacting with children individually in this way also assists in building the relationships with them that are crucial to the teaching-learning process.

> Mrs. Jensen found time to meet with Blake after making the rounds of the room during quiet reading time. Everyone seemed engrossed in a book, so she hoped that she and Blake wouldn't be interrupted too much. During their conference, Blake told Mrs. Jensen about the books he had read recently and showed her how long his list of books completed had become. Then he read a particularly funny part from a book about King Bidgood in the bathtub. He also showed his teacher the letter he was writing to his pen pal in the third grade. They discussed whether or not Blake's letter clearly explained the way the classroom snake shed its skin. A copy of the final polished version of the letter would go into Blake's writing portfolio. Mrs. Jensen suggested some books about snakes that Blake might be interested in. Blake went back to his work with confidence and a renewed sense of purpose. During the conference, Mrs. Jensen made brief notes about Blake's progress and what skills he was ready for next.

Conferences like the one between Mrs. Jensen and Blake are increasingly being used as an alternative to tests for assessment and diagnostic purposes (e.g., Fields & Spangler, 2000). Traditional, competitive ways of assessing children's progress make only the best students feel proud and accomplished. All except the top few feel just the opposite. Too many minority youngsters are evaluated without regard for cultural influences (Bloch et al., 1994). Evaluation systems that compare children to one another have a much different effect than systems that compare children's current work with their own work a few months earlier.

When a child competes with a past personal record instead of with classmates, each child can feel a sense of accomplishment. Each can feel motivated to keep trying. For instance, children who look at a folder containing their writing and drawing for the year can see for themselves how much progress they have made. New approaches to evaluation help youngsters to set personal goals for themselves and take pride in their progress toward those goals (Kamii, 1990; Genishi, 1992). The ways in which you assess children's educational progress can help each child feel individually important and can help each feel successful.

Success Children experience feelings of success or failure during many different kinds of activities in school, including playground games as well as teacher assignments. Staley and Portman (2000) urge us to look at the kinds of games we encourage, pointing out that games such as *Duck, Duck, Goose* and *Red Rover, Red Rover* may be games of waiting, rejection, failure, and humiliation for many children. Non-competitive games and those that don't require being "picked" are encouraged instead.

Competitive situations are a set-up for failure, since not everyone can win. Therefore, the others become losers. In addition, competition is incompatible with the goal of building a caring community. If you pit children against one another, you undermine the development of kindness and cooperation. In order to foster the caring community and help everyone feel successful, you will want to arrange for *cooperative* games, contests, and projects. Situations where children work as a team for a common goal are productive. If you can't do without competition, have children try to "beat the clock" instead of one another (Clayton, 1997).

When all children are required to complete the same assignment in the same way, comparisons are inevitable, with results similar to those of competition. Open-ended activities allow for individual differences and discourage comparison by allowing children to use their creativity in how they complete a task. Open-ended activities are those with no one right outcome, and therefore no possibility of failure. Success is ensured because children can choose to work at their own appropriate level of challenge. Some children will easily succeed at almost any task the teacher comes up with, but they may not be sufficiently challenged to feel good about succeeding. Other youngsters are more vulnerable to failure. In both cases, open-ended activities can help all children experience feelings of success. Open-ended activities do not have set limits and they allow for extension

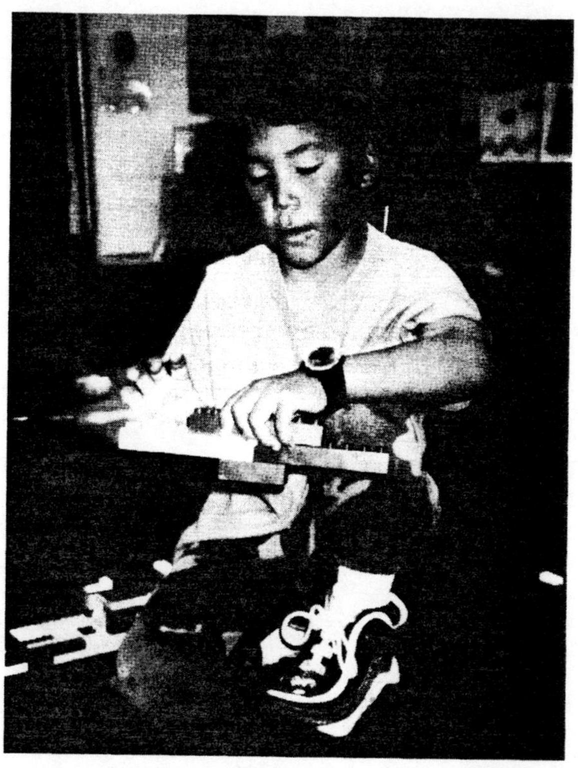

Open-ended activities can help all children experience feelings of success.

beyond the expected levels, creating an additional challenge where needed. In this case, youngsters can make a project as challenging as they wish. Open-ended activities are also an important aspect of inclusion. Often children with special needs require open-ended activities in order to participate with the other children. Feelings of success do not result from easy schoolwork; they result from the appropriate match between the challenge and the child's ability.

> The writing center in Mrs. Jensen's class provides for many levels of abilities and adapts to a variety of interests. It has a selection of paper in many sizes and colors, both with and without lines. There are also pencils and markers, staplers and hole punches. Children are free to use these materials as needed for their work and play. Nicole's "pretend" writing is as acceptable as Eric's invented spelling, and both children are able to use writing for their own purposes. Nicole uses writing for social purposes, putting a combination of pictures and symbols on a scrap of paper and giving it to a friend to establish contact. Eric shows an impressive literary background in the stories he creates and makes into books. Yaisa uses the writing center materials to enhance her dramatic play, making menus for her play restaurant, tickets to her puppet show, or shopping lists for the play store.

Contrast Mrs. Jensen's open-ended options with Miss Wheeler's closed-ended activity described next. She thought it would be fun for children, but trying to make a bear like the teacher's can be stressful.

Miss Wheeler showed her students how to cut out a teddy bear's head, belly, feet, and arms from the construction paper. The parts were already outlined, all the youngsters had to do was to cut along the lines. Then they needed to glue them together properly to make the finished product. Each child got only one set of parts to cut out.

Several youngsters accidentally cut into the lines and became upset about ruining their bear. They wanted fresh paper to start over, but there weren't extras. Most accepted tape as the solution, but Melinda and Dominic were adamant that they didn't want theirs taped. "But it won't be pretty!" wailed Melinda. Finally she seemed to accept that she couldn't have a new head for her bear, but the parent-helper noticed her sneak over and take another one when she thought no one was watching. The parent sympathized with Melinda and said nothing. In the meantime, Dominic was getting more and more upset. When the parent-helper tried to talk to him about solutions, he tore his paper up and refused to do the project at all. Then he left the classroom and went out to sit by himself in the hallway.

Certainly, there is also a need for activities with just one correct response. You need to provide a balance of open and closed activities in your classroom to meet the needs of all youngsters. Sometimes Kelsey seeks the challenge of closed tasks in preschool, such as putting a puzzle together or learning how to weave paper mats at the arts and crafts table. As she challenges herself with the specific task and succeeds, she builds her feelings of competence. At other times she seeks the freedom to test what she can build with various manipulatives or to explore freely with art materials.

Choice How can you, as a teacher, possibly provide just the right activity and material for each child all the time? You can't. What you can do is allow children a freedom of choice among a wide variety of interesting educational activities. You can count on each child almost always choosing the appropriate level of challenge and the right type of activity for the moment. Here is another value of child choice: Not only does it enhance the development of autonomy, but it also is invaluable for matching the curriculum to the child. Obviously, providing choice for your students is an important teaching strategy.

Allowing children to match their level of personal challenge to a variety of open-ended activities is a good classroom management strategy (e.g., Bredekamp & Copple, 1997; Feeney et al., 1996). Self-selection of an academic challenge also provides an alternative to ability grouping, which is a less effective effort to match the task to the child's ability. Research has demonstrated the negative effect of ability grouping on self-esteem and classroom dynamics (Cunningham et al., 1998). It doesn't take much time in a classroom to notice that children in the "low" group are most likely to act out or quit trying academically.

INSTEAD OF CONTROLLING, YOU COULD BE TEACHING

- Encourage choices
- Allow talking
- Provide for movement
- Accept more than one right way

You can count on each child almost always choosing the appropriate level of challenge and the right type of activity for current needs.

If you follow youngsters onto the playground, you also see that children in the low group are frequently rejected as playmates by children from the other groups. This rejection creates a segregation effect among youngsters of different academic achievement levels. It is especially disconcerting in light of the fact that a disproportionate number of minority children tend to be placed in the low group (Bloch, Tabachnick, Espinosa-Dulanto, 1994; Murphy, 1986). Teachers need to take special care that being a child from a certain ethnic group doesn't disadvantage the child academically (for example, Genishi, Dyson, & Fassler, 1994; Spencer & Markstrom-Adams, 1990). Teachers also need to take care that children are not socially disadvantaged because of academic labels.

The purpose of ability grouping is for supposed efficiency when the teacher is giving information. Ability grouping, with its many negative side effects, is part of a teacher-centered classroom where the teacher makes most of the decisions about what happens. In contrast, child choice is basic to what is known as a *child-centered* classroom. The teacher moves among the youngsters as they work at their choice of activities with their choice of friends; the teacher's role is to ask questions and make comments to encourage thinking. There is no place for ability grouping here. Instead, children choose learning activities based on their interests, and children of various ability levels work together to contribute in their own ways.

FORMAL LESSONS

Many curriculum programs have been created to help promote the type of emotional environment just described. These programs are aimed at helping children value themselves and others, teaching them cooperative strategies, and changing the way school personnel react to student conflict (e.g., Gibbs, 1995; Siccone & Lopez, 2000). These programs are most successful when they are implemented schoolwide, so that not only the teachers, but also the playground and lunchroom aides, the principal, the librarian, and all adults in the school treat children respectfully and know how to encourage peaceful conflict resolution. When parents are brought onto the team, the benefits are much greater.

Even if your school doesn't adopt such a program, you will find that the materials offer helpful ideas for class discussions and activities to promote kindness, caring, and cooperation. Mrs. Jensen uses many of the esteem-boosting and appreciation expression activities from the *Tribes* curriculum as part of building her classsroom community (Gibbs, 1995). Some programs, such as *Peacemaking Skills for Little Kids* (Schmidt & Friedman, 1992), suggest children's literature to help teach ideals of the caring community; others, like *Teaching Conflict Resolution Through Children's Literature* (Kreidler, 1994), use children's stories as the main focus.

In some schools, the school counselor comes into classrooms weekly and presents lessons from one of these programs. One school counselor combines the best activities from several programs and also offers workshops to help teachers with carry-over to the regular school day. *Second Step: A Violence-Prevention Curriculum* (Committee for Children, 1991) offers highly attractive photographs with explicit teacher instructions on the back, making it easy for teachers to present the lessons.

Much of the current material about guidance and discipline was created for violence prevention, due to the recent tragic rate of school violence. Creating a caring classroom reduces violence by addressing most major causes of violent behavior: unmet emotional needs, values of exclusion rather than inclusion, and lack of skills for peaceful conflict resolution. *Safe Schools, Safe Students: A Guide to Violence-Prevention Strategies* (Drug Strategies, 1998), a review and critique of a wide-range of violence-prevention programs, offers helpful guidelines for selecting materials that meet your goals. (See Appendix A for criteria.)

THE PHYSICAL ENVIRONMENT

Did you realize that the decoration, furnishing, and arrangement of a classroom affect a child's behavior? Have you investigated what effect the room colors and lighting may have on children? (Cool tones are more calming and fluorescent lighting can cause a problem.) Have you considered whether the room's decor may be over-stimulating for some children? Have you thought about whether or not your classroom invites children to do what you want them to do? Have you noticed whether each child can find seating that is the right size? Have you considered the effect on behavior when a child is either physically or emotionally uncomfortable in a school setting? If a child is exhibiting a behavior problem, be sure to examine the physical environment for possible causes of the problem. Following are some examples of common problem areas.

The classroom arrangement must reflect the types of interactions the teacher expects.

ANALYZING FOR CONSISTENCY

Is the classroom arrangement consistent with teacher expectations for children? A teacher-centered classroom typically has desks or tables arranged so that children can see and hear the teacher. In this type of class, the source of information and center of attention is the teacher. Therefore, it is consistent to have the room arranged to help students focus on the teacher. In contrast, a child-centered class is arranged in activity areas, often called *centers.* This arrangement allows the children's focus to be on the activities and materials provided. Seating arrangements that allow for student interaction are consistent with programs that value peer exchange of ideas.

First-grade teacher Miss Wheeler doesn't realize that her arrangement of desks in small groups facing each other does not match her expectations for children. She knows that it is more modern to have desks arranged this way than in rows, but she hasn't thought about why. These groupings are designed to encourage peer interaction and cooperative learning. The problem is that Miss Wheeler doesn't want children to talk in school. Her room arrangement counteracts the behavior she desires. Mrs. Jensen has the same desk arrangement, but it works for her because it is completely consistent with her expectations for behavior. To avoid confusion and conflict, it is important to create an environment that sends clear, nonconflicting messages. Joanne learns this message from Nancy in the following example:

> As she called the children to story-time with the xylophone, Joanne dreaded the inevitable power struggle that was sure to follow. Morning story-time at her preschool just wasn't working for her. The only floor space big enough for story-time was surrounded by shelves of toys, and the children just couldn't keep their hands off them. It was impossible to keep their attention. Because the shelves were on wheels, she tried pushing them as far back as she could. But the children just inched their circle back to get to them. She repeatedly reminded them that it was time for a story, not for toys. Still, it was like trying to keep bees from flowers!
>
> Frustrated, Joanne asked the afternoon storyteller, Nancy, how she dealt with the problem. "Oh, I gave up long ago expecting them to ignore the shelves," Nancy explained. "When story-time is coming, I ask for volunteers to help turn those shelves around to face the wall. They love the powerful feeling of moving furniture. Other children see the change in the room happening and know it's time for a story. And it goes without saying that it's not time to play with shelf toys—they can't even see them!"

Joanne's story-time arrangement gave a mixed message to the children. The toys surrounding them had been purchased and arranged particularly to attract people their age. These materials invited play. Conflicting with this invitation was the person with the book, also requesting their attention. Chances were high that some children weren't interested in that book just then but were fascinated with one of the toys, which were so enticingly near. Placing children in this situation and then asking them to obey the teacher with undivided attention creates needless conflict.

Nancy's solution provides a clear message about the focus of the activity and what is expected during this time. If some children are not interested in the book she is currently reading, she tells them they may go to another area in the room, where shelf choices are still available, and play with the toys quietly at a table. She has clearly defined her story-time space with the turned shelves. The messages from the environment and the teacher are not contradictory. It is easy for the children to recognize what they are to do. If children are "misbehaving," check to see if the setting is leading them astray with mixed messages.

Many public school lunch rooms offer examples of environmental mixed-messages: Hundreds of children are crowded together at long tables, excited about planning their upcoming playground activities, and yet the supervising adults demand quiet. For whose benefit is the quiet? What is the rationale for demanding it? Why are children punished for talking while eating lunch? How quiet is it in the teachers' lunch room? Whenever she can spare the time during her lunch break, Mrs. Jensen invites small groups of her class to have lunch with her in the classroom. This way, at least periodically, they have a more pleasant and civilized lunch experience.

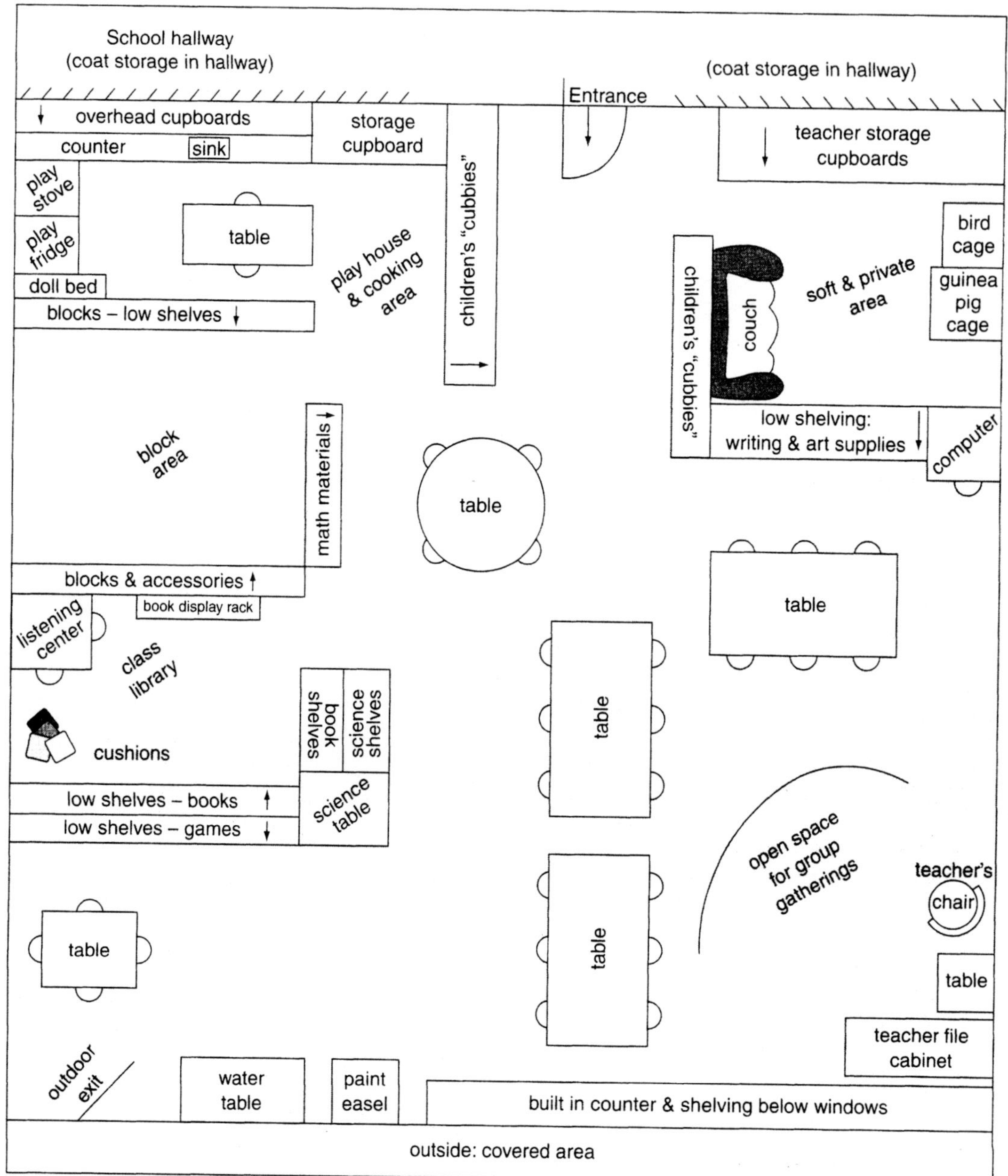

Figure 4–1
A sample primary grade classroom arrangement. The floorplan of this small classroom allows for student interaction and for privacy. It also provides protection for block constructions, a quiet spot for reading, and a group gathering spot without distractions. This plan could be adapted for younger children.

STUDYING TRAFFIC PATTERNS

The locations of learning centers can either make things run smoothly or can be a source of trouble (Kritchevsky et al., 1969). If the block-building center is not protected from people walking by, you can bet on frequent yelling, and even hitting, over ruined block creations. If the woodworking area is right next to the reading center, you can predict that quiet reading will be disrupted by noisy carpentry. You have already heard about Joanne's problem with the group gathering area surrounded by the toys.

Teachers work hard at planning their room arrangement. Even then, they are constantly monitoring how well it works and making adjustments as indicated. Mrs. Jensen originally had the blocks in a high activity part of the room, near the paint easels and the water table. The dramatic play area was in a quiet part of the room near the writing center to encourage writing as part of play. This arrangement seemed to make sense, except that her students tended to use the dramatic play materials as an integral part of their block creations. Children working at areas between the two centers were disturbed by others moving equipment back and forth. Mrs. Jensen valued the sophisticated play that was going on and didn't want to curtail the mix of materials. Instead, she decided to rearrange the room so that the blocks were adjacent to the dramatic play area. Naturally, she involved the children in planning and implementing the changes.

One day after school, the kindergarten teacher, Mrs. Taylor, stopped by Mrs. Jensen's room to talk. She had had a rough day. Eli's screeching as he defended his space in the block center had given her a headache—again. After chatting with Mrs. Jensen about the problem and hearing how similar problems were solved in the first grade, Mrs. Taylor made a plan. The next day, she asked her students if they had noticed there were lots of problems with people getting in each other's way in the block center. They had. So Mrs. Taylor and the kindergartners brainstormed about ways they could rearrange their classroom to make things better. The children thought of ways to use space that their teacher hadn't.

After school the next day, Mrs. Taylor and her aide were busy! They implemented the changes agreed on by the group and ended up with a much larger block area. In addition, the book nook was in a more secluded spot. The kids loved it all. In the enlarged block center, Eli was able to work alongside Scott and Darren without any conflict. A side effect was more children choosing to read in the book nook. Solving a discipline problem by making a change in the environment worked very well for Mrs. Taylor.

ALLOWING FOR MOVEMENT

Discipline problems can also be a result of keeping kids sitting too long. If youngsters are kept still and quiet most of the day, many will experience real discomfort. Have you ever found yourself simply unable to sit for another moment during a long meeting or a long airplane flight? If so, you probably know what kind of physical discomfort young children feel when they are asked to sit longer than they are able. The natural reaction to this discomfort

Children can work and learn more productively when their classroom offers opportunities for comfort and privacy.

is to get up and move around. In classrooms where moving is allowed and provided for, there is no problem. However, there are classrooms where children are supposed to stay in their seats until the scheduled recess provides relief. Sometimes a child can use a trip to the bathroom as an excuse to walk around, but this often leads to lots of playing around in the bathroom.

> Mrs. Jensen not only allows children to move around quite freely between activities in her classroom, but she also makes an attempt to provide high mobility activity choices when youngsters need them. Desmond, the lucky twin, is in her room. When he has a special need for activity, he can build with the big heavy blocks and exercise his arms and upper body. He can challenge himself with the balance beam or pound nails in the carpentry area. His twin brother, Devon, does not have these opportunities in Miss Wheeler's room.
>
> Devon squirmed in agony after sitting at his place endlessly doing worksheets. He was not allowed to get up for a book until he was finished, and he was always the last one done. Finally, unable to take it any longer, Devon stretched his leg and tripped another child passing by. Instantly, he was in big trouble and was sent to the principal's office. At least he got to walk on the way there.

PROVIDING FOR PRIVACY

Have you ever experienced strong antisocial feelings after extended periods of interacting with other people? Spending a full day in school, especially a long child-care day, can be extremely wearing psychologically. You will notice youngsters getting crabby as the day wears on. They are more than just tired; they are also tired of people. Some children make hiding places for themselves if given the chance. Abby built herself a little house in the block area, got inside, and covered the top with a doll blanket. She insisted that others keep out. Sometimes you will see a child simply taking refuge under a desk or a table. One little boy even got into a wastebasket to get away from it all.

Teachers are becoming more aware of children's need for a retreat from hubbub (Bredekamp, 1997). Many classrooms feature special places for being alone or visiting with a friend by yourself (Jones, 1977). Mrs. Jensen created a small space between two file cabinets and furnished it with cushions, books, and a reading lamp. Dennis found a spot under a stairway in the preschool that was perfect for one or two small children. It, too, has been cozily fitted with pillows and decorated with pictures. When the demand for the private spots becomes too great, children can either sign up on a waiting list or create their own spots. There is no reason why children can't do the same work in private that they can do in the middle of the room. In fact, sometimes children need a bit of privacy before they feel up to serious work. Some also need to have less stimulation from sights and sounds, as well as from people.

CONCLUSION

Teachers who understand and provide for privacy and mobility save themselves a lot of trouble and also save children from being "naughty." Teachers who plan the environment so that it doesn't create problems have smoother days. Adults who expect the best from children and communicate their expectations clearly find that children behave more positively. Adults who respect individual children, their families, and their cultures create caring classroom communities. Adults who provide choices and otherwise share power with children find them more eager and helpful. Teachers who help youngsters find friendship, success, and recognition help them to learn more effectively. When you meet children's needs in the physical and emotional classroom environment, many common discipline problems never arise.

FOR FURTHER THOUGHT

1. What are the behavior guidelines in an early childhood education program where you have spent time? How were these guidelines determined? Why do you think the youngsters either do or do not follow the guidelines?
2. In what ways have you seen teachers demonstrate respect for young children? In what ways have you seen teachers show lack of respect for youngsters? Which examples most closely match your own interaction with children?
3. How are friendships encouraged or discouraged in an early childhood program with which you are familiar? Would you recommend any changes to help children develop meaningful friendships?
4. Analyze an early childhood program for open-ended and closed activities. Is there a balance or does one type dominate? How do children's responses to the two types differ?

5. Observe teacher-child interaction, watching for the amount of individual attention provided. How do youngsters respond differently to individual interaction with the teacher than they do to interacting as part of a group?

6. Analyze the physical setting of a classroom. In what ways does the room arrangement prevent or create discipline problems? How are mobility needs met? How are privacy needs met?

RECOMMENDED READINGS

Bredekamp, S., & Copple, C. (Eds.). (1997). *Developmentally appropriate practice in early childhood programs serving children from birth through age 8.* Washington, DC: National Association for the Education of Young Children.

Burk, D. J. (1996). Understanding friendship and social interaction. *Childhood Education, 72* (5), 282–285.

Derman-Sparks, L., & ABC Task Force. (1989). *Anti-bias curriculum: Tools for empowering young children.* Washington, DC: National Association for the Education of Young Children.

Elswood, R. (1999). Really including diversity in early childhood classrooms. *Young Children, 54*(4), 62–66.

Harms, T., Clifford, R. M., & Cryer, D., (1998). *Early childhood environment rating scale.* New York: Teachers College Press.

Jones, E. (1977). *Dimensions of teaching learning environments: Handbook for teachers.* Pasadena, CA: Pacific Oaks.

Katz, L. G., & McClellan, D. E. (1997). *Fostering children's social competence: The teacher's role.* Washington, DC: National Association for the Education of Young Children.

Okagaki, L., & Diamond, K. E. (2000). Responding to cultural and linguistic differences in the beliefs and practices of families with young children. *Young Children, 55*(3), 74–80.

5

PLANNING PROGRAMS THAT PREVENT DISCIPLINE PROBLEMS

When children are interested and involved in learning, they don't have time for troublesome behavior. Which do you think would keep young learners involved better? Tracing and copying a different letter each day, or exploring print in books and signs that have an interesting message? Counting the number of dots on a worksheet or figuring out how to divide the raisins equally for snack time? The educational activities and objectives selected for a school or classroom are called its *curriculum*. It has been said that the best discipline is a well-planned curriculum (Greenberg, 1987). Prevention of problems is the idea behind that statement.

Young children are better able to cooperate in school when educational approaches match their developmental stages. Therefore, teacher expectations must be geared to the maturation level of the students, and curriculum must be appropriate to the children involved. When practices and materials created for older students are used for younger ones, many problems arise. Developmentally inappropriate teaching by adults results in inappropriate behavior from children.

Research shows that children in programs that are not developmentally appropriate exhibit more stress (Hart et al., 1998; Ruckman et al., 1999). Obviously, stress has negative effects on learning and on behavior. Therefore, it is no surprise that children in programs that are developmentally appropriate demonstrate higher levels of social skills than those in other kinds of programs (Jambunathan et al., 1999; Jones & Gullo, 1999). This chapter describes developmentally appropriate curriculum and program management; such practices will help to eliminate the causes of many behavior problems.

MAKING LEARNING MEANINGFUL

How do children act when they are bored or disinterested? Most likely you remember from your own childhood how you acted under those circumstances. Most youngsters will create some action when the teacher doesn't offer any. Often, however, these creative efforts do not conform to acceptable group behavior, and teachers call them discipline problems.

The National Association for the Education of Young Children (Bredekamp & Rosegrant, 1995) provides curriculum guidelines for preschool and primary grade youngsters (see Appendix B). These guidelines emphasize the characteristics of developmentally appropriate approaches to teaching young children. The following discussion explains how these guidelines can eliminate many potential discipline problems you might otherwise face as a teacher or caregiver.

RELEVANCE AND INTEREST

The National Association for the Education of Young Children (NAEYC) curriculum guidelines emphasize making curriculum relevant to children (Bredekamp & Rosegrant, 1995). Relevant curriculum allows children to investigate things that affect their lives, things they care about. Making snowflakes in Miami just because it is January would not be relevant. A unit on farming would not be relevant to youngsters in Nome. How the weather affects children's activities is relevant in both locations, as is how people get their food in each place. But kids themselves might be more concerned about the problem of the mudhole beneath the tire swing. That, too, offers an opportunity for meaningful study. Relevant learning helps keep youngsters engaged and on task—a classroom management challenge.

However, people get interested in things that are not part of their everyday life, too. Tapping into children's interests is also recommended in the NAEYC curriculum guidelines. Don't we all get more involved in things we are interested in? Mrs. Jensen is alert to questions and comments from youngsters that indicate their current interests (Jones & Nimmo, 1994). She encourages children to pursue these ideas and incorporates many child-generated topics into class activities. She is prepared for many of the ideas with collections of books and activity ideas for topics that frequently catch on in her classes. Mrs. Jensen knows from experience that kids are generally interested in dinosaurs, space, animals, and insects.

Ideas from individual youngsters often become a major curriculum focus in Mrs. Jensen's first grade. She knows that it doesn't really matter whether they are studying spaceships or turtles; children can practice the basic skills, broaden their knowledge base, and increase their feelings of competence with almost any topic. She uses children's various interests to provide a purpose for learning. For instance, reading to find out why turtles pull their heads inside their shells is a good way for children to practice reading and to learn to value reading skills. When children care about the work they are doing, they are less likely to be disruptive.

NAEYC Guideline #4: Curriculum addresses a broad range of content that is relevant, engaging, and meaningful to children.

NAEYC Guideline #6: Curriculum content reflects and is generated by the needs and interests of individual children within the group. . . . Making curriculum meaningful to children helps keep them engaged and on task.

Mrs. Jensen also knows how to help children become interested in subjects she is directed to cover. For instance, the topic of nutrition may sound pretty boring. It probably was when you had to memorize the food groups, but it isn't when you take a trip to the supermarket to buy items from each food group and use them for class cooking projects. Interest is sustained in the subject when a play store is set up next to the playhouse. Much thought and energy goes into writing grocery lists that reflect nutritious meal planning. These children are going far beyond mere memorized social knowledge; they are constructing logico-mathematical understanding about food and nutrition. When you channel children's energy constructively, they don't have so much excess to burn off inappropriately.

Dennis uses the same curriculum guidelines for preschoolers as Mrs. Jensen does for first graders. The principles are the same, although the expectations for children differ according to their developmental stage. He, too, ensures that the curriculum makes sense to kids. Instead of mindlessly reciting the alphabet, his students have frequent opportunities to see their names and the names of their friends used for labeling artwork and for keeping their place on a waiting list. Many children can recognize their own names and those of their closest friends. Some discuss how confusing it is when names start with the same letter, like the names Aaron and Amy or Kelsey and Kenji. The thinking that goes on during these discussions results in true construction of knowledge and genuine involvement in learning about letters.

INTEGRATED CURRICULUM

Both Dennis and Mrs. Jensen use *themes* and *projects* to organize their curriculum and help kids make sense of new information. Bredekamp and Rosegrant (1995) refer to themes, projects, and units as *conceptual organizers.* A theme, such as a study of birds, offers a variety of activities related to the topic of birds. However, the theme approach may not be as compelling a reason to learn about birds as a project, such as caring for the classroom finches who just laid eggs. Projects tend to have more immediate applicability to children's lives (Katz & Chard, 1993). Themes and project work are approaches to integrating the curriculum rather than offering disconnected pieces of information and isolated drills in basic skills. An *integrated curriculum* gives a context for learning and therefore makes learning more meaningful, as is recommended in the NAEYC curriculum guidelines. Any way of making learning meaningful increases student involvement and therefore decreases disruptive behaviors.

NAEYC Guideline #10: Curriculum allows for focus on a particular topic or content, while allowing for integration across traditional subject-matter divisions, by planning around themes and/or learning experiences that provide opportunities for rich conceptual development (Bredekamp & Rosegrant, 1995).

Children will learn more, and the school day will be smoother, if teaching is compatible with how children learn.

An integrated curriculum allows children to practice reading, writing, and math skills as they explore topics of interest. The topic itself usually involves social studies or science information. Art, music, and drama are incorporated as children express ideas about their learning. As we previously explained, children can learn in most subject areas using almost any topic. Dennis knows that actually using arithmetic to explore a subject is more useful than merely practicing arithmetic skills, so he helps children find the mathematics potential in the topics they are interested in.

> When the resident preschool expert on dinosaurs reported that a certain type of dinosaur had two hundred teeth, Dennis challenged the child and others who were interested to discover just how many two hundred is. They got out Unifix cubes and worked together as a group to identify two hundred; then they arranged them like top and bottom teeth to visualize the dinosaur's mouth. Danny commented, "I'll bet dinosaurs can eat faster than we can!"
>
> That remark led Dennis to suggest the idea of getting a partner and counting each other's teeth. Megan decided that they should count out the number of teeth in their mouths and make a display of them using the smallest Cuisenaire rods. Counting dinosaur teeth and their own teeth turned into quite a project, attracting different children over a period of several days. It led to further reading and further science information as a result.
>
> Kimberly was motivated to make pictures representing herself with her teeth and the dinosaur with its teeth. Several other children followed her example. Thus, artistic representation was added to mathematics, science, and reading as the curriculum was integrated around a dinosaur-teeth theme.

The play store in Mrs. Jensen's classroom is another example of a theme for an integrated curriculum. Children thought about foods for good nutrition while playing store. They practiced writing when they made their grocery lists, and they practiced reading both the lists and the labels on the food packages. They extended their mathematical thinking about counting and money as they made price tags and tried to figure out proper payment for each item. The class book in which each child contributed a drawing and a dictated message about the trip also helped children learn to read and write. The children learned more about their community during their field trip to the supermarket. Thus, the trip was part of the subject of *social studies*. There was also lots of social studies involved in resolving the inevitable disputes during these activities. Important negotiation skills were practiced while making group decisions also. Encountering others' points of view is an important learning experience (Hyson, 1994).

Second graders in Mr. Davis' classroom discovered a project during recess; they ended up using math and literacy in a study of science focused on environmental conservation.

> Fall rainstorms were eroding the steep hillside at the end of the playground. During recess, the playground aide told everyone to stay off it so it wouldn't get worse. But the hill was almost everyone's favorite place to play, and she had trouble enforcing the rule. She blew her whistle again and again, sending children inside who wouldn't obey her.
>
> Mr. Davis heard his students complaining about the loss and their doubts that it was really necessary to close the area. The conversation became a topic for a class meeting and Mr. Davis asked the class if they would like to go back outside and study the problem some more. Always eager for any reason to go outside, the children threw their coats back on and grabbed the notepads Mr. Davis handed out.
>
> Active debate ensued as they checked out the hillside, riddled by rivulets of water, with sloughing topsoil and gravel slides. Gradually, the observations became more critical. Mr. Davis encouraged them to write down what they saw and what they wondered about. He helped them focus on what might happen there and what they might be able to do to help the situation. Healthy disagreements arose, and Mr. Davis kept on saying, "Interesting idea. Write that down!"
>
> Regrouping in the classroom, the second graders shared what they'd seen and what they thought might help. Ideas included using rip-rap rock, staking burlap over the hill, putting in drainage, and even letting it slough away to a more stable slope. Some children cited their observations of city projects to stabilize slopes and a couple said one of their parents knew all about how to fix things like that.
>
> They decided they wanted to take on a "save the hill" project, but first they needed more information. Mr. Davis warned them that this project would take some serious planning, work, record keeping, and evaluating. The children were excited and wanted to get right to work. They planned walking field trips to observe some other sites, the children with expert parents said they would invite them as guest speakers, and Mr. Davis worked with the librarian to obtain relevant research materials.

Counting dinosaur teeth, playing store, and saving the trail are authentically integrated activities because the activities help children learn more about the topic they are studying (Fields & Spangler, 2000). Not everything labeled *integrated curriculum* fits this criteria. Too often, as John Nimmo says, "A pile of ideas is generated with a superficial connection to each other, and they're used to fill in slots in the weekly schedule" (Jones & Nimmo, 1994, p. 129). Poor Miss Wheeler does just that and wonders why her students don't act interested.

School needs to reflect the real world and children's own experiences in order for youngsters to perceive school as important.

RESULTS OF DEVELOPMENTALLY INAPPROPRIATE TEACHING

Developmentally inappropriate teaching by adults results in inappropriate behavior from children.

---

experience, never giving them any real experiences related to the topic. Of course, this approach leads to discipline problems because children don't pay much attention to a discussion they cannot understand.

Some teachers cover the same topics year after year without responding to the enthusiasms and questions of the children in *this* class *this* year. Then they follow up the meaningless lessons with developmentally inappropriate worksheets. Many youngsters will dutifully go along with the teacher and complete these purposeless tasks, but many others will cause classroom problems by trying to find something interesting to do.

Mrs. Jensen not only started with a topic of personal importance to her students when they studied birds, but she also provided opportunities for children to investigate at the concrete level. Examining real nests, collecting real material to make nests, and going through the process of creating their own models are the kinds of concrete experiences that match the way young children learn. They have the opportunity to construct their own understanding of birds' nests from the experience of creating replicas. The children engaged in these educational experiences are involved in the

NAEYC Guideline #13: Curriculum engages children actively, not passively, in the learning process. Children have opportunities to make meaningful choices.

business of learning and therefore aren't likely to disrupt anyone else's work. They are also building the base for thinking further about birds and will be better able to make sense of reading material on that subject.

Too often, teachers forget young children's need to focus on the real world of the here and now. Well-meaning teachers frequently lead youngsters into the totally unintelligible world of long ago or far away. Thanksgiving time is particularly likely to motivate teachers to explain the history of the original feast. Young children have notoriously inaccurate ideas about time and space. They may not understand the difference between something happening three hundred years ago and something happening last week. Ask a young child who has heard the story of the first Thanksgiving to tell you about it, and you will hear truly amazing misconceptions. Instead of wasting children's time with a presentation of incomprehensible historical facts, you would be wise to help them think about what they are thankful for in their own lives.

Efforts to offer multicultural education can also lead to developmentally inappropriate presentations (Clark, DeWolf, & Clark, 1992). Youngsters carry away distorted pictures of Native Americans as scary people in war paint who live in tepees (Billman, 1992). Some youngsters come to believe that African American people are currently slaves. Even efforts to build an appreciation for different cultures with displays of ethnic food and dress can backfire by emphasizing the differences rather than the commonalities among people (Greenberg, 1992a). Instead, teachers can enhance acceptance of cultural diversity in the children's own environment. The pictures on the bulletin board, the books in the library corner and at story-time, and the dolls in the playhouse can all reflect cultural and racial plurality. The messages that permeate their daily lives will have a positive effect on children's lifelong attitudes (e.g., Derman-Sparks, 1999; Hunt, 1999).

ACTIVE LEARNING

A related curriculum guideline has to do with encouraging children's active involvement in learning. Mrs. Jensen had a recent reminder of how important this is for her students' ability to pay attention to learning.

> The salmon run was still on when school started and many children had been fishing with their parents. Interest in fish was high, and Mrs. Jensen decided to capitalize on it. She planned a trip to the local fish hatchery so that her students could see the salmon fighting their way up the fish ladder. They also got to see the eggs being taken, fertilized, and put in tanks to grow. The field trip was just

Miss Wheeler has a different theme each week. This week it is rocks. She brought many different rocks to school for the children. (She thought it would take too much time for them to go outside and collect their own.) For writing time, each child is to write a letter to his or her rock. For art time, children are allowed to paint their rocks. For snack, they get a little piece of rock candy along with something more nutritious.

These activities may involve rocks, but they don't help children learn anything about rocks. This is a *correlated* rather than an *integrated* curriculum (Fields & Spangler, 2000).

REAL EXPERIENCES AND REAL MATERIALS

Both Dennis and Mrs. Jensen know that children will benefit more, and the school day will be smoother, if teaching is compatible with how children learn naturally. Integrating the curriculum is one way to match your teaching with children's learning. Children certainly don't separate the world into the categories *science, math,* and *social studies.* They just want to make sense of their world, with all its interrelationships, as they experience it. Therefore, school also needs to reflect the real world and children's own experiences in order for youngsters to perceive school as important. Teachers need to build on the experiences and knowledge that children bring to school with them (for further information, see NAEYC Guideline #8).

Eric brought a bird's nest for sharing time, and other children began talking about birds' nests they had seen. Mrs. Jensen encouraged the discussion by asking what they knew about birds and birds' nests. Most of the children in this suburban area had some sort of experience to share. Raymond told a story about when his mom had cut his hair outside on the patio; he had seen birds come and take the hair for their nests. Other children told about being careful of nests with eggs in them. The teacher decided to follow up on the children's experiences and build on the knowledge they already had.

Mrs. Jensen got out her own collection of birds' nests from past years for the children to examine. She had protected the nests by keeping them in clear plastic bags, which kept the nests from falling apart. A discussion about the kinds of things birds use to make nests was preparation for a field trip around the schoolyard to collect materials for making birds' nests. Each child had the opportunity to make a bird's nest model with the materials collected. Mrs. Jensen provided the "mud" to hold the material together; she had previously discovered that glue mixed with dirt and water allows for a successful nest-building experience.

As we explained in Chapter 3, children's way of learning starts with real experiences and real objects from which to make sense. Mrs. Jensen's students would not have made much sense out of a lesson on birds' nests without both their personal experience and the concrete materials the teacher provided. Some teachers don't understand this; they waste precious energy lecturing children about topics totally outside their realm of

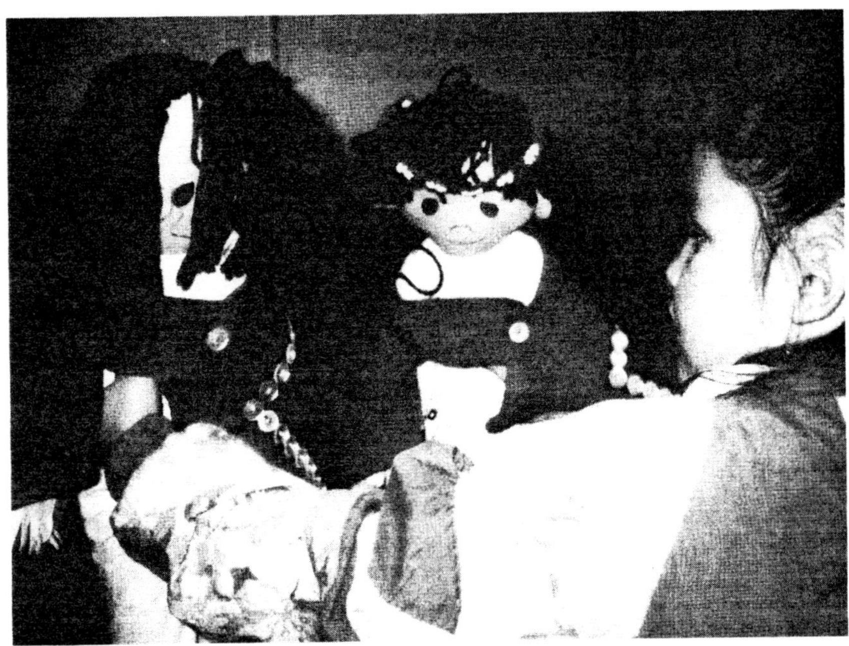

The pictures on the bulletin board, the books in the library, and the dolls in the playhouse should all reflect cultural and racial plurality.

right for young children: lots of action and the talking limited to answering some questions.

The follow-up portion of the plan went differently. The hatchery donated a few salmon for the children's closer study. One of the children's parents is a fish biologist who has offered to donate her time to help with this study. Back in the classroom, children crowd around a small table to watch the biologist cut open the fish and see what is inside. But first, the fish expert wants to tell the youngsters some things: how fish move through the water, the name and purpose of each fin, how fish breath, how the gills function, and how fish are marked for study.

Mrs. Jensen personally finds the lecture fascinating, though the Latin names for the various parts go over her head. She realizes, however, that a lecture appropriate for her is not appropriate for her students. Some children have started to talk among themselves, others are jockeying for position to see the fish better. One has wandered over to a table where other fish are displayed; he is engrossed in stroking their scales. A few youngsters are still interested in the biologist, but they want to tell her what *they* know about fish. The biologist sees that the children are restless and decides to get on with the dissecting. Unfortunately, most children have lost interest. Mrs. Jensen realizes she should have planned more specifically with the guest to ensure that the presentation would allow the children's active involvement rather than require only passive listening.

THE ROLE OF PLAY

Play is a perfect way to meet the guideline for engaging children actively and providing meaningful choices. Play also fits the guideline for emphasizing social interaction and learning from peers. In addition, it is an excellent way to encourage children's thinking, reasoning, decision making, and problem-solving abilities.

The play store project in Mrs. Jensen's classroom is not only an example of integrated curriculum (Chaille & Silvern, 1996) but also has many other benefits. Remember the social studies lessons about resolving disputes and negotiating group decisions? There are lots of important decisions to be made and problems to solve during play, whether it is pretend play, such as the play store, or games such as checkers or cards: Who gets to run the cash register? How do we resolve it when everyone wants to do it now? Which rules for Crazy Eights should we use today? Can Eric change the rules if he is losing? What an efficient use of time: Children are learning math and essential life skills at the same time.

Vygotsky (1978/1933) points out that play necessarily involves learning about rules and abiding by them. In this sense, play provides practice with controlling immediate impulses in the process of following the rules of the game or of a make-believe context. Rules in a game are pretty common, but you probably are wondering about rules in make-believe play. Think about children playing store: They follow the "rules" of shopping and paying for their purchases. If they are playing fire fighter, they follow the "rules" for putting out a fire. According to Vygotsky (1978/1933), "Whenever there is an imaginary situation, there are rules" (p. 95). Rules are necessary for guiding behavior in an imaginary situation because children have to agree on the "script" and the cast of characters (Bodrova & Leong, 1998). As children construct the rules necessary to keep their pretend play situation going, they develop logical reasoning skills and also both creative thinking and critical thinking abilities (Curran, 1999). Teachers can enhance children's cognitive and social development by encouraging pretend play.

It is interesting to note that as children get older their play increasingly emphasizes rules. Vygotsky described this development as moving from play that is obviously imaginary and subtly rule-bound (playing house) to play that focuses on rules but has subtle imaginary contexts (chess). Berk (1994) concludes that the rules involved in play help children understand expectations for desirable behavior and encourage children to act accordingly. This is another one of many reasons to include play in your curriculum.

USING TIME WISELY

Perhaps the most critical curriculum guideline has to do with making sure that what children are asked to learn is worth knowing. Respect for children should guide us away from the trivial and cute school activities that are all too common. Instead of wasting children's time having them all make identical red flowers for the bulletin board, let's think about what is truly

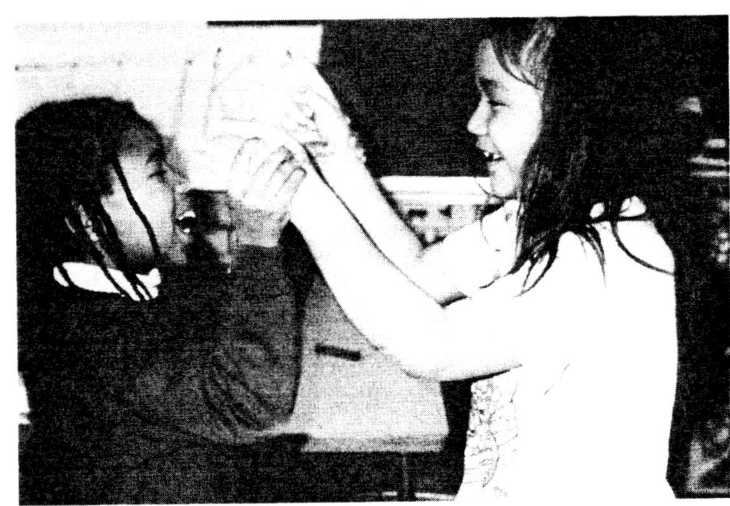

What's worth knowing? Perhaps learning to live peaceably together should be a curriculum basic.

important in their lives. Feeney puts things into perspective by reminding us that one of the most important things any of us can learn might be "how to find a friend when you're sad" (Feeney, Christensen, & Moravcik, 1996). Feeney makes this statement in the context of a broad view of what is worth knowing; it includes understanding the physical and social environment and yourself in order to better respect and care for the world and its people. She helps us evaluate the importance of colors and shapes in comparison to goals of becoming more human and helping our world survive. Respecting children involves respecting their time and using it wisely. Mrs. Jensen was surprised at how well the birds' nest activity met this goal.

> When the children finished making their birds' nests, Mrs. Jensen called them together for a group discussion. "What did you learn when you made the birds' nests?" she asked. Expecting answers about the way the mud felt and what ingredients worked best, the teacher was astounded to hear a whole different level of response: "Birds' nests are *really* hard to make!" "I'll never knock one down out of a tree," and "I won't ever shoot a bird" were the type of ideas generated. Making birds' nest models encouraged these youngsters to think about the bird's viewpoint, and it helped them develop an appreciation for birds and their struggle for survival. Certainly, these children will be better able to respect and care for the world they live in.

You also need to ask yourself whether what you are teaching is worth the effort at this time in children's lives. Many teachers have discovered the hard way that learning to tell time in kindergarten is *not* worth the effort. Others have decided that trying to teach everyone how to make change in first grade is wasted energy. Chapter 3 explained that telling time and making change are confusing to young children because they use arbitrarily designated representational symbols. Trying to teach these symbols too soon is about as productive as trying to teach a five-month-old baby to walk. Some topics are a waste of time because they are too easy and can be learned without specifically spending school time on them. For instance, directed instruction on colors is not necessary for most children. Colors are a part of life and are generally picked up as children decide which color crayon to use, which shirt to wear, or what color their favorite ice cream is. Talking with children about color as they engage in other activities is all the instruction most of them need.

However, some ideas are well worth the time and effort. We hope for greater emphasis on helping children learn to respect and protect the environment and to live peaceably together with respect for individual differences. These areas of study might be called science and social studies; they might also be called basics.

THREE KINDS OF KNOWLEDGE

Other curriculum guidelines can be derived from an understanding of the learning process. Any learner is more engaged and on-task when teaching approaches match the ways in which people learn. Different kinds of knowledge are best learned in different ways. Teachers who understand the differences between *physical knowledge, social knowledge,* and *logico-mathematical knowledge* are able to plan learning activities accordingly (Kamii, 2000).

Experimenting with objects and seeing what happens is the basis of physical knowledge. For example, what will sink and what will float is primarily learned by actually putting various objects in water and observing the result. Information from other people is the basis of social knowledge, also called *conventional arbitrary knowledge.* Information such as the days of the week, the names of the basic food groups, or the polite thing to say when someone sneezes are things we primarily learn from others. (Notice that these all vary from culture to culture; thus, they can be considered cultural conventions and are obviously arbitrary.)

Individual reflective thinking is the basis of logico-mathematical knowledge. This knowledge cannot be found in the objects explored, nor can it be "given" by a teacher. It is a system of relationships that must be constructed by each learner in a way that makes sense to him or her. Logico-mathematical thinking provides the framework for classifying, and therefore making sense of, any information. Physical knowledge and social knowledge are used in the construction of logico-mathematical knowledge, and logico-mathematical knowledge is necessary to construction of physical and social knowledge (Kamii, 1996). According to DeVries and Zan (1994), "Intelligence can be described as a framework of potential logico-mathematical relationships" (p. 194).

Therefore, in order to truly engage children's minds and help them be successful learners, teachers must ensure opportunities for experimentation

NAEYC Guideline #14: Curriculum values children's constructive errors and does not prematurely limit exploration and experimentation for the sake of ensuring "right" answers.

and reflection. Too many classrooms trivialize education by limiting teaching to transmitting social knowledge. Planning meaningful learning experiences for young children must take into consideration the three kinds of knowledge, as well as the developmental level of the students.

Several NAEYC curriculum guidelines relate to teaching for construction of knowledge: emphasizing thinking, reasoning, decision making and problem-solving (Guideline #15), providing experiences for children to succeed from their point of view (Guideline #19), building on what children already know and can do (Guideline #8), and encouraging conceptual frameworks for children's increasingly complex mental constructions (Guideline #9).

A crucial guideline for helping children learn to think is Guideline #14: valuing children's constructive errors, not prematurely limiting exploration and experimentation for the sake of ensuring "right" answers. This means you shouldn't tell Blake that his idea about why things sink or float is wrong; instead, you respectfully listen to his thinking. Then you ask some questions to get him to think further and possibly experiment further. You are willing to wait days or even years for the "right" answer; your goal is Blake's competence as a thinker. The answers that take years are for the type of questions that Blake will still be exploring in college physics classes; if you gave him your adult answer now, it wouldn't make sense anyway.

Teaching children to think is a component of many anti-violence curriculum programs (e.g., Gibbs, 1995). Creative thinking, intellectual problem solving, and reasoning all develop children's ability to manage social interaction challenges. Authoritarian approaches to academics, with an emphasis on memorizing answers given by authority figures, undermine children's ability to reason about moral issues as well as about academics (Dill, 1998). As you teach children to think critically, you create *intellectual autonomy,* the necessary partner to moral autonomy.

ORGANIZATIONAL STRATEGIES

Experienced teachers know when behavior problems are most likely to occur. They anticipate problem situations and plan ways to keep the day running smoothly. They use combinations of routines and novelty to avoid turmoil during transitions, waiting periods, and group times. They also use group time to prevent problems during other activities.

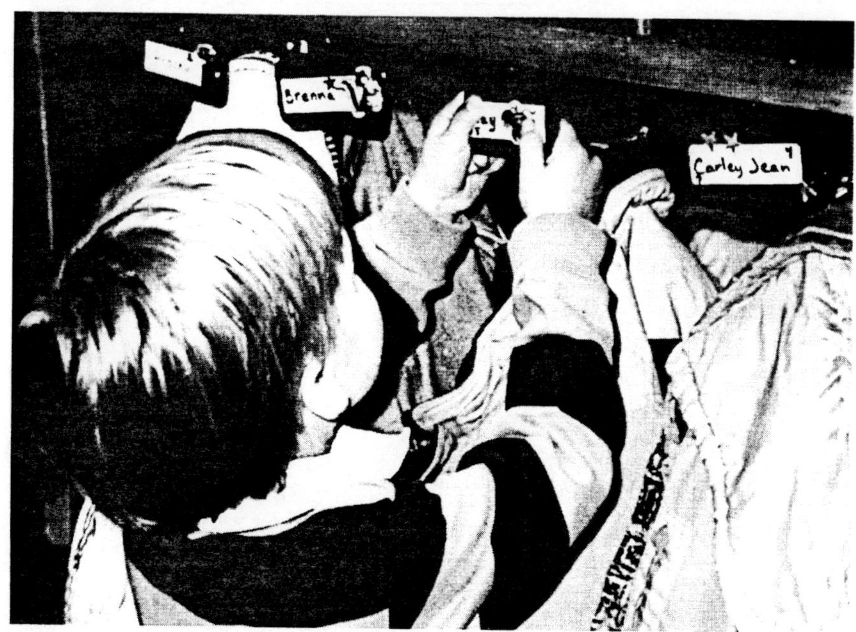

Routines help children know what to expect and assist them in being cooperative members of a group.

ROUTINES

Routines help children know what to expect and therefore assist them in being cooperative members of the group. Routines also provide emotional security through predictability (Hyson, 1994), which is especially important for children who are "at risk" because they come from homes where chaos is the norm (Dill, 1998). Because the children know the routine, it doesn't take any time at all for Mrs. Jensen's first graders to assemble for group time. They have a system for moving smoothly from their seats to the group area, and each child knows just what to do. Routines save the teacher from constantly having to tell the children what to do next; they know what comes next and what they are to do. It is important, however, that routines make sense (Gareau & Kennedy, 1991). Washing hands before snack time or hanging up coats after recess are routines that make sense. Washing your lunch spot even though it isn't sticky may not make sense. Just like adults, children more readily go along with regulations that make sense to them.

Having a routine does not mean being ruled by the clock. It doesn't mean that you stop whatever else is going on at exactly 11:15 each day and have story-time. But it is important that children have an idea of the sequence of events and what their role should be. Children in Dennis' preschool class know that they will get to work and play at their choice of activity when they first arrive at school and that there will be a time to gather together about mid-morning. They know where they can fix and eat their snack when they are ready for it. They know where to put their coats and belongings when they arrive, and they know where to find the materials they might need for a project.

Dennis plans his routines around children's needs; he alternates periods of active exploration with more quiet times and plans for outdoor play daily. The exact timing of transitions is based on his observations of the children in his preschool program; using these observations, he can determine when it is time for a change, such as gathering for a group time or going outside. He tries to be sensitive to children's needs for extended periods of uninterrupted concentration. He knows that they have long attention spans when they are doing something important to them. The myth of short attention spans is the result of giving children trivial activities that are not engrossing and not their choice. Unfortunately, many teachers do not know this fact, and they unwittingly reduce the children's ability to concentrate by making them constantly change activities (Nash, 1979).

When it appears that most of the youngsters may be winding down on their choice time activities and reaching closure, Dennis moves around the room telling each child that it will be group time in five minutes. This advance warning allows children to finish what they are doing and mentally prepare to move on. Occasionally a child will be too engrossed to quit and will ask to be excused from group or to join in a few minutes. Dennis' respect for children and their work comes through as he honors these requests.

MAKING TRANSITIONS

Many discipline problems occur during transition times, when children are moving from one activity or one place to another. Some children's temperaments can't handle the noise and movement associated with transitions in a child-centered classroom (Hyson, 1994). These youngsters need help figuring out how to cope. Most transition time behavior problems happen because teachers unrealistically expect children to wait patiently for too long while other children get ready to join them. Adults who respect children do not waste their time with prolonged periods of waiting. If they do, you can almost guarantee that children will be clever enough to find some way to alleviate their boredom. Unfortunately, this activity usually takes the form of poking or pushing the person in front of them. Few teachers appreciate these creative outlets.

> Mrs. Jensen dislikes having to line up her students and make them walk all together in a row. She knows that waiting in line is terribly boring for them and invites behavior problems. When her students go out for recess, she lets them leave individually or in small groups as they get ready. At the beginning of the school year, she spent time with her class discussing and practicing good manners when walking through the elementary school hallways. Her children generally remember to walk instead of run and to keep their voices down. When they forget, their classmates remind them. Not having lines is less trouble for Mrs. Jensen and her students and causes many fewer discipline problems.

Having children line up and wait will usually cause behavior problems.

The librarian, Mrs. Hill, insists on lines, so Mrs. Jensen's class gets practice in lining up when they go to the library. Instead of making the students who get ready quickly wait around and be bored while she gives her attention to the procrastinators, Mrs. Jensen creates some action of her own in the line. She leads the group in their favorite songs and finger plays to head off inappropriate kinds of activity. This approach also hurries the stragglers faster than nagging does; they are eager to join in the fun.

Mrs. Jensen uses a similar approach when she is gathering children together for group time. If it takes a while for everyone to arrive, she engages in a discussion with those who are there. She often uses this time to help children evaluate their activities, with questions such as, "What did you do special today at choosing time?" At other times, the children want to do their favorite finger play about the five little monkeys.

Getting to and from the mid-morning gathering are the only significant transition children must make in the morning preschool component of the Midway Children's Center day. An extra time-consuming transition is avoided by having outdoor play just before children go home at noon. That way, they are already in their coats when it is time to leave. Dennis' use of advance warning helps most children get prepared for a change of activity. When they are not interrupted in the middle of a project, they are much more agreeable. Keeping transitions to a minimum also keeps disruptions to a minimum. For most of the morning, youngsters are free to change learning activities as they are individually ready to do so.

When group time is over, Dennis avoids a stampede to the snack table by making a game out of sending a few children at a time. Sometimes he says, "Everyone wearing stripes today may go to the snack table." Next it might be those with plaid or print designs on their clothing. On other days, Dennis focuses on hair or eye color. Sometimes he holds up name cards to excuse the children one at a time; the youngsters practice reading their own and their friends' names to determine whose turn it is. These games keep children involved and learning during their short wait (Educational Productions, Inc., 2000). Those who arrive at the snack table first must also have something to do besides waiting. They either need to be allowed to begin eating immediately, or else another adult must be there to engage them in a song or activity.

Those children who remain at the center for the full-day program are faced with a number of transitions: lunch time, nap time, getting up from nap, going outside again, and parent arrival time. Each of these changes requires that children change gears and move from one mode of activity to another. Most also involve movement of groups from one place to another. Both aspects of transition are frequently upsetting to youngsters.

Tuning in to children as individuals will help remind you not to herd them into the next activity. One key to making smooth transitions lies in not unduly rushing children. As soon as you start to hurry kids, they immediately start to rebel. Respecting individual differences in youngsters is another important guideline for smooth transitions. Joshua is always hungry at lunchtime and eagerly gets going on his meal. Andrea makes slower transitions and has trouble tearing herself away from the dramatic play she is usually involved in. These two children require different treatment. Forcing Andrea into Joshua's schedule won't work for her.

Similarly, Amy, Jimmie, and Ahmed are ready for sleep at nap time, while Megan, Tory, and Kimberly rarely nap. The staff at the children's center solved their nap-time problems by separating sleepers from nonsleepers; the teachers allowed nonsleepers to play quietly after lying down with a book for fifteen minutes. It makes no more sense to attempt to force all children to sleep than to force them all to stay awake. There are real differences in the needs of children. A program with the flexibility to accommodate these differences greatly reduces its discipline problems.

Mrs. Jensen used increased flexibility to allow for differences and solve a problem at the end of daily choice time.

> Children in Mrs. Jensen's classroom were not being cooperative about cleaning up after choice time and getting ready to go out to recess. She wasn't interested in Miss Wheeler's approach of giving out candy as a reward to get children to clean up. Instead, she carefully watched to see what was happening instead of clean-up.
>
> What she noticed was that many children were just not ready to stop what they were doing because they hadn't had enough time. Many were bouncing

around for about ten minutes before they settled in to what they wanted to do with their choice time and then didn't really have enough time to complete anything before they were told to clean up. She decided to try something radical for a public school: a choice of staying in or going outside to play. Since the primary playground was just outside her back door, she could allow children to go out during recess if and when they were ready.

This plan worked very well, with clean-up coming after recess instead of before and going much more smoothly. On nice days, some of the indoor activity flowed outdoors and children didn't have to choose between their choice-time project and being outdoors.

GROUP TIME

Gathering together as a group is essential for building a sense of community in a classroom (e.g., Developmental Studies Center, 1998; Harris & Fuqua, 2000). This feeling of belonging and caring for one another is necessary for developing a social conscience. When youngsters meet together regularly, sharing rituals such as favorite songs and stories, they come to see themselves as a group. As a group, they can discuss mutual problems and create solutions that transcend the wishes of the individual (DeVries & Zan, 1994). This process promotes moral reasoning and decentering from an egocentric viewpoint. Children in classrooms with a sense of community tend to be more cooperative, supportive of one another, and empathetic (Noddings, 1995).

To get the most out of group time, teachers need to truly encourage student input, get children thinking about how to treat one another, and feel a sense of responsibility for their school environment (Watson, 1999). Some group times don't really engage children's minds, but instead drag them through a series of repetitive rote exercises (Harris & Fuqua, 2000). How engaged are children in merely reciting the responses to questions such as, "What day of the week is this?" "What is today's date?" and "How many days have we been in school?" We see lots of bored youngsters and frustrated teachers during this kind of group time. We also see children getting into trouble because they can't sit still and give the desired responses. Group time is much more productive when it is spent helping children work on moral issues they care about or helping them develop more appreciation for one another. The book *Ways We Want Our Class to Be* (Developmental Studies Center, 1998) offers many ideas for class meetings that build commitment to kindness and learning.

As important as group time can be, bringing young children together for a story or discussion time often creates trouble. Teachers complain about feeling like police officers as they continually remind children to sit down or pay attention at group time. Young children talk when they aren't supposed to; they wriggle and squirm and poke one another, and they even just walk away. Teachers with child-development knowledge realize that these behaviors are related to children's maturational stage. They understand that young children are not good at sitting still or being quiet, that they have trouble dealing with large groups, and that they aren't good at pretending to be interested when they are bored (Bredekamp, 1997). Many of these teachers seriously question the appropriateness of a group time at the preschool level; some question it in kindergarten as well. Yet these same teachers usually wish to have at least a brief period of togetherness.

Successful group times are not passive listening experiences for youngsters. They truly involve all children in the group activities and discussions. Some teachers find that a circle seating arrangement works best with this goal. A circle allows children to see one another during discussions and read body language as well as hear words. The group circle is consistent with a child-centered approach and with the purposes of group spirit; the teacher at the front of a group suggests a different purpose.

Some programs compromise on group time by having several small groups instead of one large group. Instead of two adults with twenty youngsters in a circle, each adult takes ten children for circle time. This method is a little closer to the guidelines for group size that Hymes (1996) discusses in his book, *Teaching the Child Under Six.* Hymes recommends the following guide for group size: The right number of children for a child to interact with is no more than the number of birthdays that child has had.

Another approach allows choice about participation in some group activities. Dennis is able to allow choice with his preschool group because there are other adults available to supervise children who do not choose to join. Dennis tries to make his circle time so attractive that youngsters will want to join in and stay involved. If he doesn't get much enthusiasm, he treats that response as useful feedback regarding the appropriateness or relevance of what he is offering at group time. For instance, if several children leave during the story he is reading, he might think twice about sharing that story again.

Dennis allows for a partly involved presence at group time as another way of meeting individual needs. Some youngsters can't seem to sit and listen without having something to occupy their hands. Therefore, children in his program are allowed to look at books or work on puzzles at the back of the group area. Only activities that are quiet and do not disturb the group discussion are allowed. Allowing quiet activities lets children who might not otherwise be able to cope with the enforced passivity benefit from the discussions and stories. Through this flexibility, Dennis provides a transition into group time for children who need it.

In other programs, teachers feel strongly about full participation but try hard to make group time more compatible with the needs of young children. They keep the time short and respond to signals from youngsters that they have reached their limit. Frequent opportunities to move and actively participate extend the amount of time children can cope with group times. Songs and rhymes that involve full-body movement provide useful breaks. Nevertheless, fifteen minutes may be long enough for most preschoolers to be involved in group time. This time period will gradually increase as children get older, but teachers need to take their cues from the children.

Many will argue that youngsters need to learn the social skills involved in a traditional group gathering because the next teacher will expect it. Others reject that argument on the grounds that children will more easily gain those skills when they are a little older. They believe there is no point in putting everyone through the misery of pushing the skills before youngsters are ready. This argument is similar to the prevailing view of toilet training: Wait until the child is ready, and it will happen quickly and painlessly.

WAITING TIME

This chapter previously addressed the issues of waiting in line and waiting for groups to start. They are a serious waste of children's time, as well as invitations to discipline problems (Davidson, 1980). However, there is another kind of waiting that causes just as many problems: when children must wait their turn.

Waiting for a turn is incredibly hard on young children for several reasons. One reason is that they don't have a sense of time. Because time is an abstraction, telling a child to wait five minutes for a turn with the tricycle is meaningless. Another problem is that young children don't understand why they must wait. They can't see things from another person's viewpoint, so they don't relate to another child's claim. Colin wants the tricycle. That desire is the only reality for him. The fact that Alex also wants it is irrelevant to Colin. With help from adults, youngsters gradually learn about the needs and feelings of others. With experience and maturation, they also learn to approximate time spans. While youngsters are in the process of learning, understanding teachers can help them cope.

> Kenji ran into the large-muscle room. He was eager to get onto the climbing tower, his favorite place to play. Suddenly a teacher came to tell him that he must get off and wait his turn. There were already four other children on the climbing tower. Four is the limit; that's the rule.
>
> Kenji looked confused and sad but climbed down. He gazed longingly at the children climbing and shouting. He kept asking Sheri, the adult in charge, when it would be his turn. Gradually, tears welled up in his eyes. Sheri realized that Kenji was in distress. She tried to explain to him that the other children were in the room first. Seeing that her explanations were getting nowhere, Sheri thought about other alternatives. Center rules allow youngsters to use equipment until they decide they are finished, so she couldn't even promise Kenji a certain time for his turn. She tried to distract him with suggestions about the block-building or woodworking centers. But Kenji was determined to be there to stake his claim as soon as someone got off the climbing tower.
>
> Then Sheri remembered the sign-up sheet that helped children wait their turn to hold the new pet rabbit last week. She asked Kenji if he would like to start a sign-up sheet to use the climbing tower. He agreed to this plan and helped Sheri locate paper, tape, and a marker. Kenji wrote his name four-

year-old style on the page and taped it to the wall near the climber. He seemed to feel better now that his claim to a turn was officially in writing. He said he would wait in the block center nearby. Sheri assured him she would call as soon as someone got off the climber. Without someone hovering nearby waiting for a turn, the pressure to stay on the climber eased. Soon there was a vacancy, and Sheri notified Kenji. He had been helped to cope with a hard situation. His feelings were respected even though he didn't immediately get his way. The experience helped him build understanding and trust in the waiting process.

Many teachers use sign-up sheets to ease turn taking and waiting. This approach fosters literacy development as well as social development. Of course, it works better if there aren't so many children in the group that it takes days for everyone to get a turn. When children are limited to a set amount of time for a turn, the sign-up sheet can be combined with an egg timer. Watching the timer ticking away or seeing the salt pour from one side to the other can help youngsters to experience the passage of time, making it a little less abstract. Of course, these timed waits must be short in order to be humane.

Much of the children's waiting involves waiting for help from an adult. Children have to wait less if there are more adults available to them. Public school classrooms generally not only have larger groups than recommended, but also have too few adults for the number of children. The maximum group size in kindergarten and the primary grades should be no more than fifteen to eighteen children with one teacher. If the group size is up to twenty-five, there should be two adults. For preschool age groups, it is necessary to have two adults responsible for no more than twenty youngsters (Bredekamp, 1997). We see much higher levels of social development and involvement in preschools where there is an adult for every five children and the group size is limited to twenty.

PARENT-HELPERS

Parent volunteers can make a major contribution to a smoothly running classroom. They can improve the ratio of adults to children, cutting down on the length of time children wait for adult assistance and being there to intervene when problems arise. When you involve parents in helping children learn, however, you accomplish more than a shorter waiting time for youngsters. A child whose parent spends time helping at school gets a clear message that the parent thinks school is important; therefore, the child also believes school is important. Additionally, when parents spend time helping, they tend to gain a better appreciation for the school program. Their increased understanding of the teacher's goals and methods makes parents more supportive of the teacher's efforts. Parental attitudes of support for school programs are also communicated to children, and those attitudes about school influence child attitudes and behavior.

PROGRAMS THAT PREVENT DISCIPLINE PROBLEMS

Avoid:

rushing
waiting
crowding
regimentation

Provide:

interesting activities
predictable routines
appropriate intellectual challenges
enough adults to help children

Kindergarten and primary-grade teachers generally ask for parent volunteers at the beginning of the school year. Many find that posting a list of specific jobs and asking parents to sign up is a good strategy. Parents whose work doesn't allow them to spend time at school may volunteer for something that can be done at home in the evening. Some preschools follow the same pattern, but cooperative preschools exhibit the ultimate in parent involvement. Cooperative preschools are run by parents who administer the budget, collect tuition, and hire the teacher. Parents take turns as teacher assistants to create appropriate adult-child ratios for their programs. Child-care programs generally exist because parents are not available during the day. However, with encouragement, parents may find it rewarding to visit during their lunch time and even to take occasional time off to be part of their youngster's child-care day.

CONCLUSION

Prevention of discipline problems has much to do with respecting children. When you respect youngsters, you make it easier for them to meet school expectations; you involve their parents in their education; you accept their emotional needs as valid; you plan programs carefully to fit their level of development; you help them learn to think about others; and you use their time and energy wisely. When you do these things, you will find that children are more cooperative, hardworking, and committed to learning.

FOR FURTHER THOUGHT

1. Conduct or observe a group meeting designed to build community. How effectively are children encouraged to think for themselves rather than repeat adult words? What activities are useful for building group bonds? What strategies are helpful for keeping children engaged and involved?

2. Think about curriculum topics you are familiar with. Identify those that are inappropriate for children too young to know the difference between a day and a week, let alone between one year and one hundred years. Identify those that are inappropriate for youngsters who have no idea of the difference between a town and a country.

3. Observe early childhood teachers' use of transition activities. Practice using some games for guiding children's movement in small groups from one place to another. Learn some finger plays and rhymes and practice using them to assist children during waiting time.

4. Try some techniques described in this chapter to help youngsters wait for a turn. Analyze the successes and the failures to learn from them.

5. A problem to solve: The kindergartners were lining up to go to the library. Tony got into line and immediately began pushing Tim, who was in front of him. Next, Tony grabbed Tim's arm and then began playing with his hair.

   a. What is the probable cause of this problem?
   b. How can you best deal with it now?
   c. How can you prevent similar situations in the future?

RECOMMENDED READINGS

Bergen, D. (1988). Designing play environments for elementary-age children. In D. Bergen (Ed.), *Play as a medium for learning and development.* Portsmouth, NH: Heinemann.

Bodrova, E., & Leong, D. J. (1998). Development of dramatic play in young children and its effects on self-regulation: The Vygotskian approach. *Journal of Early Childhood Teacher Education, 19*(2), 115–124.

Bredekamp, S., & Rosegrant, T. (Eds.). (1995). *Transforming early childhood curriculum and assessment* (Vol. 2). Washington, DC: National Association for the Education of Young Children.

Chaille, C., & Britain, L. (1997). *The young child as scientist: A constructivist approach to early childhood science education.* New York: Longman.

Charney, R. S. (1997). *Habits of goodness: Case studies in the social curriculum.* Greenfield, MA: Northeast Foundation for Children.

Davidson, J. (1980). Wasted time: The ignored dilemma. *Young Children, 35*(1), 13–21.

Developmental Studies Center. (1998). *Ways we want our class to be: Class meetings that build commitment to kindness and learning.* Oakland, CA: author.

Honig, A. S., & Wittmer, D. S. (1996). Helping children become more prosocial: Ideas for classrooms, families, schools, and communities. *Young Children, 51*(2), 62–70.

Hymes, J. (1996) *Teaching the Child Under Six.* West Greenwich: Rhode Island Consortium Publishers.

Jones, E., & Reynolds, G. (1992). *The play's the thing: Teachers' roles in children's play.* New York: Teachers College Press.

Kamii, C. (2000). *Young children reinvent arithmetic: Implications of Piaget's theory.* New York: Teachers College Press.

Katz, L. G., & Chard, S. C. (1993). *Engaging children's minds: The project approach.* Norwood, NJ: Ablex.

Rogers, C. S., & Sawyers, J. K. (1988). *Play in the lives of children.* Washington, DC: National Association for the Education of Young Children.

6

TEACHING DESIRABLE BEHAVIOR THROUGH EXAMPLE

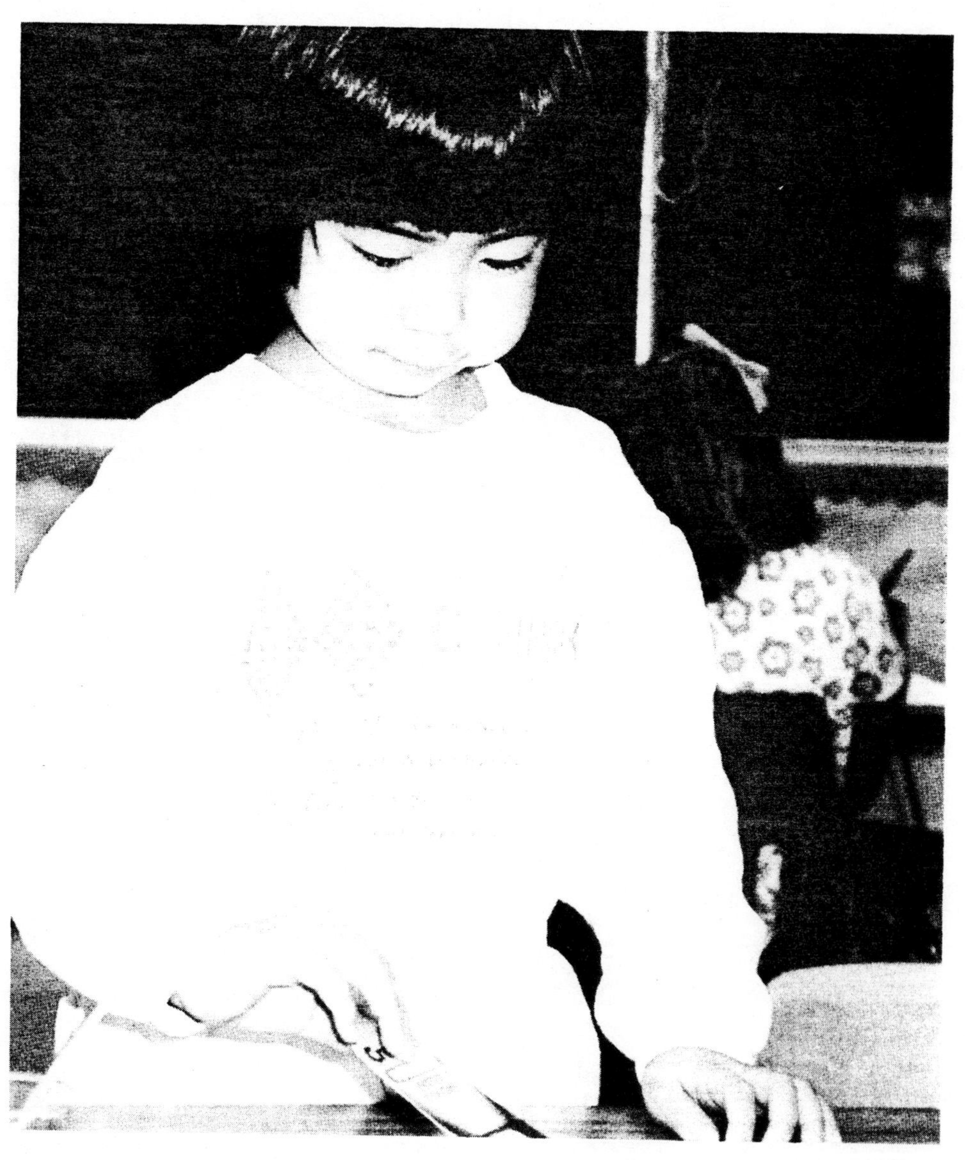

Discipline is a teaching activity, and teaching by example is a powerfully effective method (Katz & McClellan, 1991). Children use the examples of admired adults as they construct their own ideas of appropriate behavior. Therefore, teacher and parent examples are productive methods of guidance and discipline. This chapter will give examples of how models of desirable behavior help children learn to behave in socially acceptable ways. Sometimes the cause of inappropriate behavior is that children have learned from inappropriate role models.

If you doubt that children pick up the example of adults, watch them during pretend play. Parents and teachers are often embarrassed as they see children copying parts of adult behavior they'd rather not have repeated. Children also imitate the behavior they see on television and movies, with some extremely anti-social results (Horton & Zimmer, 1994). Positive adult models are crucial to counteracting such pervasive and violent influences.

Adults providing examples and children imitating them are both referred to as *modeling*. Let's look at how your positive modeling can help children learn desirable and useful ways of behaving.

INTERACTION STYLE

The way in which teachers and parents treat children greatly influences how children treat each other (e.g., Lickona, 1999; Putallaz & Heflin, 1990). A teacher who consistently speaks kindly and respectfully to students tends to have a classroom where children speak more kindly and respectfully to one another. However, a teacher who uses sarcasm and put-downs to keep kids under control will certainly generate more of that type of interaction among students.

Some classrooms and centers have a warm and friendly feeling as you walk into them, and others exude tension. The teacher usually sets the tone for the classroom, with children taking on the interaction style of the adult (DeVries & Zan, 1994). Research involving with the same message about adult role models reports that parents who are sensitive, responsive, and involved with their children have youngsters who behave in ways that make them more popular with their peers (Putallaz & Heflin, 1990). Children notice when adults respectfully consider children's ideas and feelings. From this example, they gain both attitudes and skills for getting along with other children and peacefully negotiating solutions to disagreements. Teachers and parents who exhibit very controlling behavior are setting an example of demanding their own way without regard for others. If that attitude is the adult example, then youngsters will learn to behave in the same way.

Children's literature is sometimes helpful for providing examples of behavior for discussion and analysis. For instance, *The Grouchy Ladybug* (Carle, 1977) or *Mufaro's Beautiful Daughter* (Steptoe, 1987) might spark discussion about how to treat others.

EXPRESSING FEELINGS

How do you deal with your emotions? Do you hold them in and try to hide the fact that you are upset? Or do you find yourself "flying off the handle," and yelling when things go wrong? The holding-in approach might sound like a more desirable model for kids, but we believe it is actually worse for them—and you—in the long run. Counselors often help clients learn to express their feelings because suppressed emotions will surface in some form and can cause physical problems, as well as further emotional problems. However, in some cultures, suppressing emotion is mandated.

Of course, throwing a tantrum to express your feelings isn't productive either. Adults who have learned to accept and work with their emotions achieve a culturally acceptable medium between the extremes of too little emotional outlet and too much. Many find that it is important to let off steam as it arises instead of allowing it to accumulate into a blowup. Teachers with this kind of self-knowledge can provide a beneficial model for youngsters.

LETTING IT SHOW

You teach a lot when you share your feelings with children and allow them to see how you express your frustration, excitement, sorrow, or joy. Children learn the most when adults talk about how they feel, also letting it show in their face, body language, and tone of voice. By listening and observing, children can figure out a lot about what feelings are, what situations are likely to create which feelings, and how to express feelings (Hyson, 1994).

> Mrs. Jensen was pushed past her limit one day by the several children in her classroom with behaviorial disorders. Her friends always told her that the "reward" for being a great teacher is that you get more of the needier children. But that thought was of no comfort when she was being kicked and hit on a daily basis. Then there was the additional problem of trying to keep the other children safe from those who were out of control.

Children learn ways of expressing their feelings by watching how adults express theirs.

Much to her chagrin, Mrs. Jensen lost her patience and yelled at Tomas, making him cry. At group time, she apologized sincerely and led a class discussion about the situation. She involved the children in brainstorming about what she should have done instead. She was impressed with their responses. Karinna said, "You could have called him aside to talk." Garrett suggested, "You could have walked away."

A personal time-out is often the best answer when you are overwhelmed, and is possible where there are several adults in charge of a group of children. Unfortunately, the option of leaving the scene is seldom available for public school teachers. Even if you are the only adult with a group of children, you can still stop and take a deep breath when things begin to feel overwhelming. You do not need to respond instantly to the problem. However you do it, your model of how to calm yourself will teach your students best if you explain to them what you are doing. Children benefit in two ways when teachers briefly remove themselves, either physically or emotionally, when they become overstressed: The cooling-off period helps the teacher to deal more rationally with child behavior, and the example set by the teacher shows children a useful way of handling their own stress.

This is just one of the many possible lessons that can be taught by adult example. There are packaged curriculum programs addressing many of the important lessons about feelings, but observing an adult who is actually coping with an emotional situation is much more likely to help children learn.

APOLOGIZING

Sometimes even wonderful teachers get overwrought and lose control. This offers a teaching opportunity also, as in the following example:

> Dennis usually didn't mind the children's inevitable messes, but the director's reminder to "spruce up" for open house that night had him on edge. It seemed like everywhere he looked was a disaster area. He snapped at Kaeldra when she ripped the border edging on his bulletin board while she was trying to reach the shelf next to it. He complained to Jessie that he was spilling sand from the sand table. Then Dennis saw the easel careen forward, with violet, green, and red paint spewed all over the adjacent block area. He let out a "Hey!" so loud it silenced most of the class. Gabriella, who had tripped on the easel, cowered and looked fearful of punishment.
>
> Dennis took a few deep breaths, recovered his composure, and smiled to reassure the frightened girl. Then he told the class, "Wow, I'm really getting nervous about all the people coming to see our classroom at the open house tonight. When I saw that paint spill, I got upset. I'm sorry I yelled. I've been pretty irritable about messes all day because I want our room to look nice when your families come to visit tonight. I'll bet you want it to look nice, too. What can we do to fix this problem?" The children were eager to help and immediately got busy cleaning up the paint.

Dennis apologized for frightening the children and explained his feelings to them. Then they worked together on a solution. Because there is so much inappropriate expression of feelings in the world, and in some children's homes, it is essential that schools model better ways. For instance, how we express our anger makes the difference between a violent situation and a nonviolent one, and between a destructive use of anger and a productive one (Lantieri & Patti, 1996). Because feelings are so much a part of human behavior, the daily life of the school offers ample opportunity for such teaching. But, as Hyson (1994) says, "Early childhood educators should not be content to leave this process entirely to chance. Competent, thoughtful professionals consciously decide what emotions and emotion-related behavior to model" (p. 130).

CHILDREN'S LITERATURE

What children's books do you know that deal with the expression of feelings? Some children learn from the old favorite *Alexander and the Terrible, Horrible, No Good, Very Bad Day* (Viorst, 1972). Have you read *Spinky Sulks* (Steig, 1988) with children? Both provide examples of how *not* to have children express their feelings, but offer children the opportunity to be wiser than the book character and offer suggestions for improvement.

ACCEPTING FEELINGS

Many adults tend to deny children's feelings. They apparently think that little people have little feelings that can be easily erased. You have no doubt heard someone tell a child, "You don't hate your sister, so don't talk like that." A common response to children's unhappiness is, "Have a cookie and don't cry." Although well-intentioned, these responses don't help children learn to deal with their feelings effectively. Instead, they may learn that their feelings are wrong and end up feeling guilty. This guilt, added to repressed feelings, is likely to result in negative behavior.

USE YOUR WORDS

When Christie says, "I hate you!" she is expressing anger. The anger may or may not be justified from your perspective, but she does have that feeling and it needs to come out. Young children usually lack the language skills to express their feelings adequately (Furman, 1995). Your role as the teacher can be to help the child clarify feelings by modeling more appropriate words. In this case, your response might be "It sounds like you are angry with me."

If you can find out what made Christie angry, you can help her find the words to say specifically what she is upset about. Perhaps she wanted to be the line leader, and you chose someone else. You can accept her feelings while helping her express them more suitably. This approach involves demonstrating expressive language for her, perhaps by saying, "I can tell you are very *disappointed* that you weren't chosen." Then you can let Christie know that it is more productive to tell you that she wanted to be the line leader than to say she hates you. Teaching effective communication will be discussed further in Chapter 7.

DENYING FEELINGS

Sometimes adults try to deny children's feelings just because they so desperately want youngsters to be happy. It's not that they undervalue children's emotions, but that they worry too much about a child's sadness, loneliness, or jealousy. Therefore, they try to make those bad feelings go away as quickly as possible by submerging them in treats or diverting activities. These parents and teachers feel that they have failed a child who is experiencing an unpleasant emotion (Klein, 1975). They don't understand that important learning can result from facing those negative feelings. For instance, a child who has never faced the loneliness of being left out is less able to feel compassion for someone who is being excluded from a group.

Sometimes just having the bad feelings acknowledged can help a child get over them. Jealousy of a new sibling is a common problem that most adults don't want to accept.

> Jessica was glued to the goodbye window at preschool. She was trying to get her mother's attention for a wave, but her mother's back was to the window as she adjusted the baby's carseat. Maureen noticed the look on Jessica's face and asked if she'd like to step outside to catch her mom. Jessica spit back, "She's too busy with that baby!" and turned away, her face scrunched in anger and sorrow.
>
> Maureen appreciated Jessica's irritation since she had been the only child in her family, too, until her brother came along and burst her bubble. She was glad that she had checked out several library books about new babies, with Jessica and

another new big sister and brother in mind. She decided to read one of her favorites for story-time today, *Darcy and Gran Don't Like Babies* (Cutler, 2000).

Just the title was enough to pull in half the children, as there were several older siblings in the group. Maureen began reading in a strong voice, "Darcy didn't like the baby . . . . When someone asked her how she liked the baby, she told them. Her mother responds by telling her the baby is just like she used to be. Her dad says she will like him later on. Her neighbor rejects her statement and says, "Of course you do." Maureen makes sure Jessica can see the picture of the look on Darcy's face when the neighbor says that. Maureen adds, "It sure made her mad that nobody believed how she felt."

Then Darcy's Gran comes to visit in the story. When Darcy informs her, "I don't like the baby," Gran replies, "Me neither . . . . I don't much like their smell and I don't much like their looks, I don't like all the work they make for everyone. And besides, they get far too much attention." Now Jessica was grinning and Maureen grins back. They enjoy the rest of the story together, as Gran and Darcy come to terms with this new member of the family, and *all* of their feelings: resentment, irritation, and even some love.

Instead of trying to make children's bad feelings disappear, you can help children learn to accept and express their feelings by the example you set in accepting and expressing your own feelings. Male role models are especially important for little boys. The cultural stereotypes tend to make it harder for males to deal with emotions. The old idea that big boys don't cry hasn't disappeared from society (Edwards, 1986). Many men not only feel uncomfortable expressing sadness or fear, but they also have trouble expressing positive feelings of affection and caring. For some men, the only emotion that feels masculine is anger. Therefore, these males camouflage sensations such as grief, loneliness, and jealousy, expressing them instead through anger. Conversely, some women have difficulty expressing anger, having learned to consider anger unfeminine. The inability to express honest emotions creates obvious difficulties with interpersonal relationships.

Dennis does his part to wipe out the macho stereotypes regarding feelings in his preschool. He freely expresses affection for his young students with hugs, smiles, and verbal feedback, such as "I like being with you." He demonstrates his joy in small things: a sunny day, a delicious snack, or a child's artistic creation. He also shows feelings of sadness when the guinea pig dies. Although Dennis doesn't cover up his feelings of frustration when something goes wrong, he is careful to show negative feelings in ways he wants children to imitate. He knows the children are likely to follow his example, whether it is positive or negative.

CULTURAL DIFFERENCES

Some children get very different messages at home about how to express emotions than what they get at school. Some children come from a culture that allows aggressive expressions of anger. Others come from a culture that does not allow for any expression of emotion (Hyson, 1994). Cultures also differ in the ways children are taught to show respect for others, about whom they should trust, and polite ways of speaking (De Gaetano et al., 1998). Whether to speak loudly or softly and whether to look at the person spoken to are examples of cultural variations on politeness. The many possible differences between home and school expectations emphasize the importance of getting to know parents and coming to a mutual agreement with them on behalf of their children.

Perhaps your own cultural background makes you disagree with this text about the best ways of dealing with feelings. This book explains one viewpoint; your professional judgment will have to guide you in how to use this information in ways that work best for you and for your students.

CARING FOR OTHERS

You may have noticed that some youngsters have sharp tongues and say cruel things to other children, and others show concern for anyone having a hard time. Much of that behavior is learned through example (Eisenberg, 1992). Because adults are powerful role models for young children, your example has a great impact. When this model is coupled with reminders about people's feelings, children learn to think about the impact of their words (Edwards, 1986). In a classroom where students are being unkind to one another, the teacher needs to examine what type of role models children are experiencing.

MODELING ACCEPTANCE

"More and more early childhood teachers have come to recognize that teaching tolerance outright in the curriculum is as fundamental and as far-reaching as teaching children how to read" (Teaching Tolerance, 1997). The tolerance referred to here is the tolerance for differences and the acceptance of people who are different from you. This is a lesson clearly not learned in most of the world: wars between people of different religions, skin colors, and cultures throughout the world testify to the lack of tolerance.

How can you, as a teacher, work to counteract ethnic and racial stereotyping that creates devisiveness in the classroom and in the world? In the past, teachers have considered it enough to treat all children the same and ignore differences, with the intent to give the message that everyone is equally acceptable. However, those approaches have not been effective in the face of outside influences. It is now clear that schools must take a proactive stance in combatting intolerance. For instance, instead of hushing it up if a child repeats a racial slur, use it as a "teachable moment" for a class discussion. Instead of pretending there are no differences in skin color, offer activities that celebrate those differences. Whole boxes of crayons devoted to various skin colors can contribute to such celebrations. *Starting*

BE A ROLE MODEL

- Be kind to others
- Be honest with your feelings
- Be willing to try new things
- Practice what you preach

Small (Teaching Tolerance, 1997) is one source of activities designed to increase children's appreciation of diversity.

Sometimes you will have students who have personal characteristics that make them the target of cruelty from other children. Maybe a youngster with a bed-wetting problem comes to school smelling of urine, and another wears ragged and ill-fitting clothes. Sometimes the child is like Pat, who has such damaged self-esteem that he actually seems to invite abuse from other youngsters. These children have many needs, but one of them is the teacher's example to encourage their classmates' kindness toward them. These children are often hard to like and unappealing to be around; however, they are the ones who most need your acceptance and caring.

Starting with their families and friends, children can begin to understand and accept differences and similarities (Edwards, 1986). Later they will be able to expand this awareness to the greater world. Learning to care about others and to get along together in our diverse world are central issues in the curriculum area called *social studies.* Some teachers' guides seem to suggest that social studies only covers the food and music of other lands, so youngsters spend time learning trivial facts rather than developing attitudes and understandings that might promote the welfare of humanity (Clark, DeWolf, & Clark, 1992). If educators recognize that compassion and learning how to establish caring relationships are among the most important things anyone can learn, they will spend time in the classroom assisting the development of such social skills.

MODELING KINDNESS

Children first need to learn these ideas at the concrete level—in their own environment and through their own experience. People and problems far away are too abstract for young children's thinking. Concepts such as compassion become understandable to children when they apply the principles in their own homes, classrooms, and communities (Honig & Wittmer, 1996).

Children learn these lessons best through situations that constantly arise during the course of the day, as twenty-five people attempt to live and work harmoniously together in a classroom. Because Mrs. Jensen considers that learning to live harmoniously is an important issue, she doesn't hesitate to spend school time helping children learn to settle a group problem. She calls it her social studies curriculum and considers it time well spent. By making time for interpersonal relations skills, she shows that she considers such skills important.

She and other educators are concerned about the prevalence of bullying in school. This is a worldwide problem that affects children's ability to feel safe in school and to learn (Banks, 1997). The bullies and their victims both feel the negative effects: The bully, left unchecked, learns a pattern of abuse that carries over to future relationships, and the victim suffers from low self-esteem, anxiety, and insecurity. Too often teachers do nothing about bullying, either because they are unaware of it or because they want to discourage

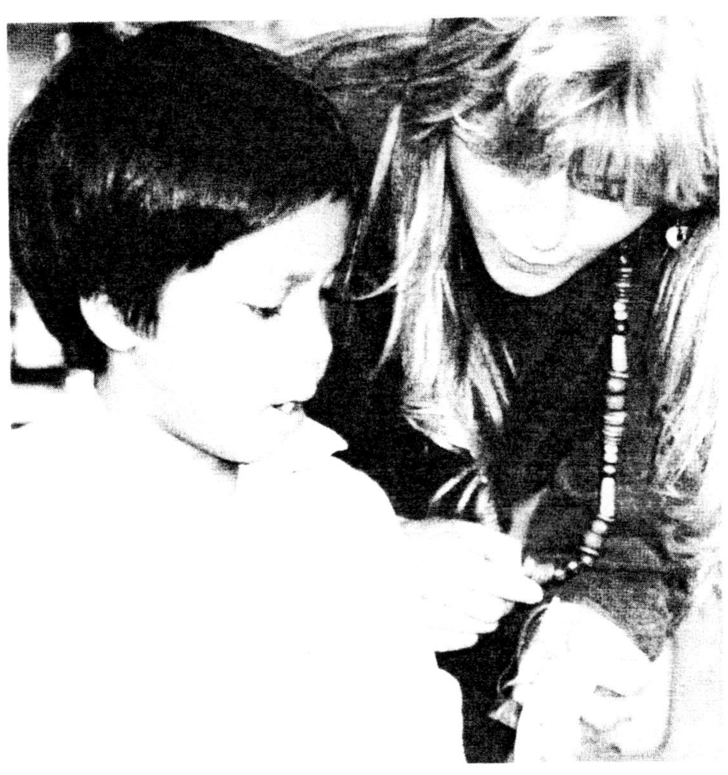

A teacher who treats children kindly and respectfully is showing youngsters how to treat each other.

tattling (Froschl & Sprung, 1999). Teachers do not ignore bullying if they realize how serious the effects are.

Mrs. Jensen lets it be known that she will not tolerate such behavior. The guidelines in her class emphasize being kind to one another, and any deviation from that is a matter of grave concern for the whole class. Any child who does not feel safe in class, on the playground, in the lunchroom, or even on the school bus is encouraged to let the teacher know. If a child has a pattern of bullying, Mrs. Jensen works with the parents and tries to get help for the child. Often, the intervention needs to focus on the family, since the cause of such problems is often based on family interactions. See Chapter 14 for further discussion of family intervention for children with serious emotional needs.

Mrs. Jensen also takes a proactive approach to bullying: She combats bullying and other unkindness when she creates a classroom climate that fosters cooperation instead of competition, when she helps children learn ways of calming themselves, and when she involves children in discussions about the kind of class they want to have. Whenever you work at meeting children's needs and at creating a caring classroom, you are combatting bullying.

Children's books may help you discuss bullying and teasing with your students: We suggest you try *Chrysanthemum* (Henkes, 1991), *Oliver Button is a Sissy* (de Paola, 1979), *The Meanest Thing to Say,* (Cosby, 1997), and *The Crow Boy* (Yashima, 1976).

Vivian Paley's stories of classrooms (1999) show us that young children are capable of caring and concern for others. Paley encourages understanding of others through the stories she shares with children: stories of helpfulness and compassion to give children the ideas and the models needed.

TAKING RISKS

Teachers can also be role models for risk taking. Why would a teacher want to encourage risk taking? Rest assured, we don't mean dangerous physical risks, but rather intellectual risks. Intellectual risks involve following up on an idea or hypothesis to see if it works. Intellectual risks may be related to science, math, art, music, or other areas. When people talk about intellectual risk in the field of science, they refer to it as generating and testing hypotheses. When they talk about the arts, they refer to intellectual risk as creativity.

WHY BOTHER?

Risk taking is an essential part of the learning process and therefore a highly desirable behavior. Unless people are willing to think about concepts and test out their ideas, they are only able to memorize what other people say is true. Such rote learning is a very limited and limiting aspect of education. People who only learn this way will never add to the knowledge of the world. Throughout history, the great scientists, mathematicians, composers, artists, and others who have made major contributions to civilization have been those who risked questioning the status quo.

Some people might argue that children who don't think for themselves are easier to manage. They might even suggest that encouraging risk taking will increase discipline problems. After all, a child who debates the fairness of adult-imposed rules and consequences can be a real pain. But you can also consider such debates a challenge with valuable teaching potential. How you feel about this idea relates back to Chapter 1 and decisions about your goals for children. Because we, the authors of this book, are committed to the goals of intellectual and moral autonomy, we definitely want to encourage children to think for themselves.

We believe you will find that teaching for autonomy, rather than conformity, makes guidance and discipline easier, not harder. As you help children learn to make their own responsible decisions, you are released from having to make and enforce all the rules. Additionally, children who are challenged intellectually to think for themselves tend to get excited about learning. As they explore their hypotheses, they become self-directed and self-motivated learners, which also makes the job of classroom management easier. The teacher is released from the job of police officer and freed for the role of educational guide and facilitator of learning.

HOW TO DO IT?

How does the teacher demonstrate risk taking? The first step is to work on fear of failure or mistakes. This fear is a serious block to trying new ideas of any type. Mrs. Jensen starts by calling attention to all the mistakes she makes herself. She freely shares her failures, such as a fall on her new mountain bike. She doesn't belittle herself for natural human failings, but rather demonstrates acceptance of them. If she misplaces a book or some needed supplies, she might say, "I got so interested in Brianna's block creation that I didn't pay attention to where I put the book for story-time today. Can you help me look for it?" Then she might use the situation to encourage children to disclose times when they, too, forgot where they put something. Her acceptance of their forgetfulness, as well as her own, provides an example for them to learn similar acceptance. It is also important for teachers to model taking risks as part of their own learning experience.

> Russian visitors were coming to Lincoln Elementary School. One of the school aides spoke some Russian, so Mrs. Jensen invited him to her classroom to teach some basic greetings. Never having heard the language before, Mrs. Jensen was right with the children at a beginner's level. First, the aide told them how to say, "My name is . . . . " "Menya zavoot," he said. Mrs. Jensen tried, "Menizoot." He repeated, "Menya zavoot." She struggled, smiling, "Menyesavoot?" The children giggled with her as she tried again. She admitted, "This is a little hard for me," and she invited the children to try with her: "Can you help?" Their keen young ears quickly picked up the nuances of sound, and within a few minutes everyone was saying, "Menya zavoot Abby. Menya zavoot Jimmie." Eventually, even Mrs. Jensen mastered it!

RELATION TO ACADEMICS

Mrs. Jensen believes that risk taking is especially related to children's progress in writing. Emergent literacy research indicates that children learn about letters and their sounds best when they work on their own hypotheses about writing and spelling (Kamii, Manning, & Manning, 1991). Therefore, Mrs. Jensen encourages children to try out their ideas through "kid writing" or invented spelling. This approach involves risk taking. Some children charge into kid writing with gusto, but others hesitate, afraid of making a letter wrong or spelling a word wrong. Some are risk takers and some are not.

The fearless ones produce pages and pages of scribbles; they also include some words they have memorized, such as their own name and *Mom, Dad,* and *I love you.* They proudly tell everyone about what they have written. Soon these youngsters are making good progress on their sound-symbol hypotheses, trying out different ideas about which letter makes which sound (Fields & Spangler, 2000). Those children who are afraid of failure may be hampered in their learning.

> Stephanie just joined Mrs. Jensen's class and obviously has not done any writing except copying. She is so terrified of making a mistake that she does

nothing for most of journal time. As Mrs. Jensen tries to encourage her that "kid writing" is just fine, Stephanie blurts out, "What if I mess up?" Mrs. Jensen tries to reassure her, but knows it will take awhile before Stephanie gets the courage to try to express herself in writing.

Ideas about perfection in one area, such as writing, can carry over to other topics and get in the way of other learning, too. Some children feel incapable of artistic creativity, always wanting someone to show them the "right" way to approach an open-ended project. Others will read the same book over and over, not just because they enjoy the book, but because they know all the words and it is safe. These children desperately need the teacher to model acceptance of imperfection and the courage to venture into the unknown. They need help becoming more comfortable with learning through their mistakes. They need such help in order to become effective learners and self-directed students.

TAKING RESPONSIBILITY

Adults tend to lecture a lot about being responsible. Picking up after yourself, taking care of materials, finishing what you start, and doing work on time are common themes. A much better way to teach children these important ideas is by modeling them yourself.

HELPING WITH CLEAN-UP

Clean-up time is a good place to start. You read about Dennis' power struggle over this issue, and you may know that cleaning up frequently causes conflict. It is often a problem at home as well as at school. Many young children are simply overwhelmed by the mess; they don't know where to start and think it is impossible to clean-up. Adults who tell kids to clean up are assuming that the children know how to do it. That is not a logical assumption. Young children need to be taught how to pick up a mess; the best way for them to learn is for you to show them what you mean by cleaning up. In other words, you work with them. Seeing you help with clean-up also gives children a clear message that the teacher thinks cleaning up is worth doing. You are an effective model. Contrast the scene below with one where the teachers merely tell youngsters to hurry up with the clean-up.

The block area was strewn with a jumble of blocks and littered with the small toy cars and trucks that had been driving on the block roads. Nancy, Dennis' assistant teacher, saw Kelsey and Danny standing in the midst of this mess looking hopeless. Nancy went over to the children and offered to help. She started picking up blocks, handing the long rectangular ones to Kelsey to put on the shelf and giving the small square ones to Danny to put away. Nancy made sure the youngsters were able to match the blocks with the outlines painted on the shelves showing what kind of block goes where. She called their attention to the different sizes and shapes as they worked together.

Soon Nancy positioned herself by the shelf and asked the youngsters to hand her all the triangle-shaped blocks. Next, the children got to choose which shape to

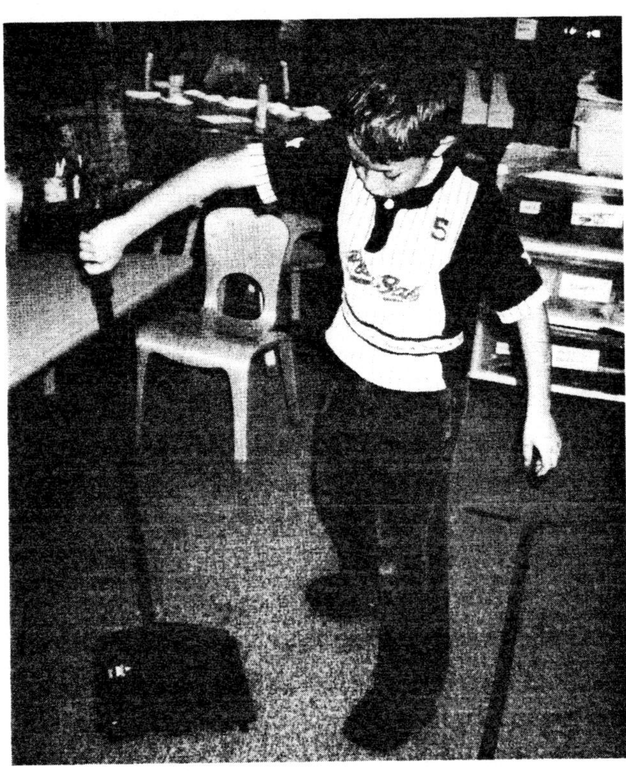

The best way for children to learn to clean up is for you to *show* them what you mean.

work on, and before long the job was complete. Kelsey and Danny felt good about their hard work, and they gained skill in organizing the clean-up of the block area. Eventually, they will be able to do it themselves with only a few verbal clues. Having Nancy work with them helped them to value the work they were doing.

Meanwhile, Dennis was working with children washing out paintbrushes. As they worked, he talked about the importance of using cold water so as not to loosen the glue holding the brush in the handle. He also encouraged his fellow brush cleaners to experiment with ways that most quickly get the paint out.

While Dennis and Nancy helped with blocks and paint clean-up, Sheri, the aide, circulated among other clean-up tasks. She stopped to help get the doll babies comfortable in their bed instead of on the floor in the playhouse. Then she complimented Shantae and Andrea on how orderly the kitchen cupboard looked before moving on to help Megan and Alex at the manipulatives table.

KEEPING YOUR PROMISES

Following through with a plan or a promise is another important area of responsibility. Like clean-up, it, too, contributes to a smoothly running classroom. Mrs. Jensen teaches this behavior effectively through modeling. She starts each day with a discussion of the day's schedule, writing it on the board while the children watch and learn about writing as well as planning. They get practice in reading as they refer back to the schedule during the day. Mrs. Jensen treats the daily plan like a contract, or promise, of what the day will bring.

If weather causes the cancellation of a nature walk that the children are looking forward to, she discusses the change and plans with them to do it another day soon. She makes sure to follow through with this plan, never deciding that the children will soon forget. She models consistent follow-through, and she talks to the children about her commitment to keeping her word. She wants to be sure they realize what she is modeling for them. As mentioned in Chapter 5, some children have no experience with consistency and follow-through in their homes. These children may need help recognizing it when they see it.

Children in Mrs. Jensen's class can count on this same follow-through on an individual level as well. If their teacher is too busy when they want to talk to her, they know she will soon get back to them.

> Mrs. Jensen was deep in discussion with Ling Ling about the story she was reading when Raymond came up and tapped his teacher on the shoulder. A tap on the shoulder is an approved signal for a child to communicate the need for teacher attention when she is in conference with another student. Mrs. Jensen smiled at Raymond and made a signal with her fingers indicating she would be with him in a short while. To make sure that she didn't forget, Mrs. Jensen wrote Raymond's name on a note to herself. Raymond went back to his seat, secure in the knowledge that his teacher would soon be with him. As soon as she was finished with Ling Ling, Mrs. Jensen went over to see what Raymond wanted. Raymond and his classmates have begun writing reminder notes to themselves in imitation of their teacher.

Sometimes Mrs. Jensen's list of requests for attention gets too long, and she knows she can't reach so many children in a timely manner. Rather than keeping them waiting, she makes appointments with them for later on. They can still count on her, even if not immediately. Of course, if children have an urgent need, they communicate it. Mrs. Jensen then helps them find whatever assistance is required. As part of encouraging their autonomy, Mrs. Jensen has shown her students how to use a variety of resources effectively rather than always relying on the teacher. Therefore, these children are quite capable of helping each other when their teacher is working with an individual child.

SHOW, DON'T JUST TELL

Instead of telling kids to do something, show them how to do the following:

- Clean up
- Keep promises
- Be safe

INDEPENDENT USE OF MATERIALS

Things go smoothly without the teacher's constant attention due, in part, to the time Mrs. Jensen has spent in helping children learn how to use materials in a responsible way. Her students have learned these lessons well because their teacher doesn't just lecture about their proper use. You guessed it: She shows them how instead.

Mrs. Jensen spends time working with children in each learning center as a way of helping them learn the independent use of materials. Independent use is much different than single use. It is not a way to limit how children use things, but rather to provide guidelines for their creative expression. Mrs. Jensen finds that her students soon take over the modeling job and begin to show one another important points. Desmond learned well that a tile is needed under the plastic clay to protect table tops. He then took the responsibility of reminding Eric when Eric forgot. Mrs. Jensen also follows the class guidelines when she uses any material. She knows that to do otherwise would undermine her efforts.

FOLLOWING THE RULES

Beth's first day of student teaching taught her a lot about the importance of adult role models. At least some children pay a lot of attention to whether adults follow the rules.

> When the teacher called everyone together for the morning meeting and everyone began to gather, Beth took a seat on the couch in the gathering area. Riley loudly informed her that, "It isn't your day for the couch." Beth asked him how he knew whose day it was, and he pointed to a list. Beth went and examined it and said, "You're right, it's not my day for the couch." Beth joined the children on the floor.
>
> After the meeting, children were dismissed to the designated learning centers. Beth was busy helping a group of children when she noticed that Riley had climbed up onto the table. She looked at him questioningly. He looked back. Beth said, "Are you supposed to be sitting on the table?" He just looked at her, and in that instant she realized that *she* was sitting on the corner of the table. She immediately acknowledged, "But I'm sitting on the table, aren't I?" Riley nodded yes. Beth replied, "Well, I'll have to get off then, won't I?" Riley waited until Beth stood up, then he jumped back down onto the floor. Later, when Beth forgot and sat down on the table again, Riley started to scramble back up again. Beth quickly got up and Riley got down.

KEEPING SAFE

"Do as I say and not as I do" won't work in teaching safety behavior, either. All the teachers at Midway Children's Center remind each other to carry scissors with points down to keep their example consistent with their words to children. They are also careful not to walk too close to a child on a swing, and they model safe street crossing when taking walks with children. When using a car or van for a field trip, teachers, as well as children, wear seat belts.

Mrs. Jensen makes sure she always pushes in her desk chair when she's not using it. Pushing in chairs is an important safety rule in her school. This rule is primarily to keep passageways clear for fire drills, but it also saves a lot of tripping over chairs on a daily basis. Mrs. Jensen helps her students internalize this safety rule by her example.

Maureen became convinced of the impact of adult models while watching preschoolers in dramatic play one day.

> Several youngsters were engrossed in a make-believe trip on the boat in the play yard. Megan ran to get some life jackets that had been donated as props. She offered them to Jimmie and Tory, who scorned them, saying, "We're the dads! We don't wear those." These children had obviously noticed during family boat outings that the children had to wear life jackets but that their fathers did not wear them.

EFFECTIVE ROLE MODELS

Role models are most effective when they are people whom children look up to: important, powerful, nurturant people (Eisenberg, 1992). Young children look up to their teachers and their parents. In fact, they tend to consider all adults powerful and infallible creatures. This belief puts a large responsibility on you as an adult who works with young children. Seize the opportunity! As children get older, they look less to adults for their models and turn more to peers they admire.

SOMEONE SIMILAR

The ability to identify with the model is important to all ages. Children are more likely to copy people who are similar to them in some way. Teachers can emphasize similarities with their students by commenting on similarities of interest and feelings. For instance, Nancy let Patricia know that her favorite color, purple, is Nancy's favorite color, too. Sheri and Danny both have pet beagles that they talk about.

Older children often look to others of the same age for models, and models of the same gender are important because of their similarities, too. Therefore, we want to be sure there are male teachers as well as female teachers for young children. Children whose first language differs from their teacher's or whose skin is a different color are less able to benefit from the model of their teacher. This tendency is one reason why it is important to recruit more teachers and aides from minority groups.

SOMEONE TO BE LIKE

You are more likely to be an effective role model if children want to be like you (Hyson, 1994). This means that youngsters need to see you as being fun and pleasant. It probably also means having a positive relationship with youngsters. They want to *be* like you because they *like* you.

Children also look up to, and identify with, sports stars and television characters. They pick up whole behavior patterns by emulating these

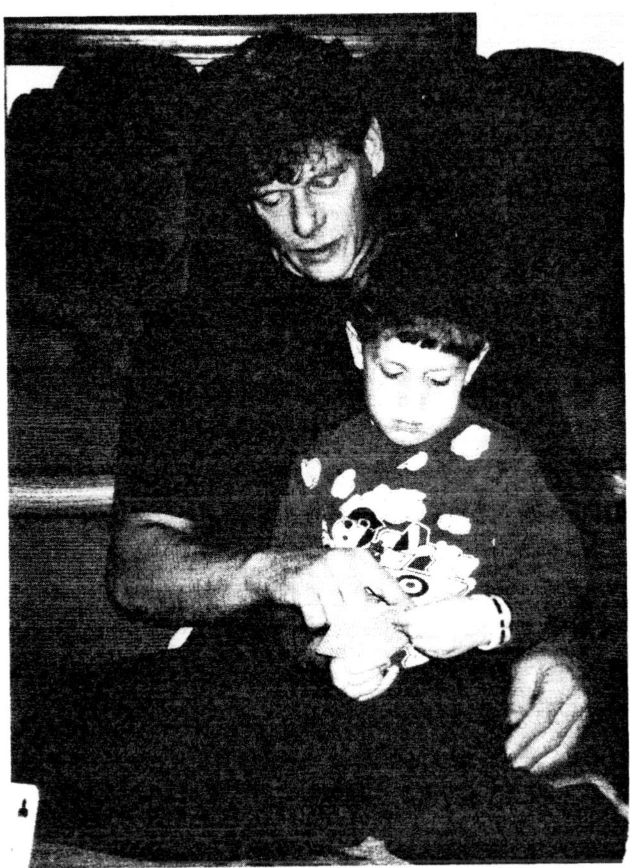

You are more likely to be an effective role model if you are someone children like and admire.

models. In television sitcoms, sarcastic put-downs are presented as humorous and entertaining, teaching impressionable young people that this is a desirable way to interact. Imitations of various superheroes demonstrate that children will even emulate the behaviors of cartoon characters and video game figures. The greatest concern regarding cartoons is the likelihood that children will copy the violent behavior they have observed.

MODELS OF VIOLENCE

There is widespread concern about the impact of huge daily doses of violence that so many children absorb. "Never before have so many young children been exposed to so many images of casual cruelty . . . . Never before has there been such an urgent need to provide our children with a living model of how differences can be resolved with honest and respectful communication" (Faber

& Mazlish, 1996). Organizations such as TRUCE (Teachers Resisting Unhealthy Children's Entertainment) actively work to eliminate violence in children's television and toys. The National Association for the Education of Young Children (NAEYC) has published a position statement cautioning about the media and violence. A strong joint statement by four national associations of health professionals links violence in television, music, video games, and movies to increasing violence among children. The American Medical Association, the American Academy of Pediatrics, the American Psychological Association, and the American Academy of Child and Adolescent Psychiatry presented this conclusion at a public health meeting on entertainment violence in July, 2000 (Holland, 2000).

If parents do not shield their children from harmful influences, schools must try to counteract the effects. Children need to know that, contrary to what they may be seeing on TV, most people really do not carry weapons; they avoid violence and talk about their disagreements instead of forcing their opinions on others. It is the responsibility of adults who work with children to help them think about and analyze the positive and negative models they are sure to encounter both in real life and on television. Youngsters will learn negative behavior patterns from models as easily as they learn positive ones. Teachers and parents must work together to ensure that the negative doesn't overwhelm the positive.

CURRICULUM PROGRAMS THAT PROVIDE EXAMPLES

The principles described in this chapter are accepted pieces of violence prevention (Lantieri & Patti, 1996) and are included in published violence prevention programs. Lesson plans to promote productive expression of feelings, caring for others, and being responsible for yourself can be found in programs such as *Tribes* (Gibbs, 1995), *Second Step* (Committee for Children, 1991), *Peacemaking Skills for Little Kids* (Schmidt & Friedman, 1992), and *Educating the Heart* (Siccone & Lopez, 2000). We prefer activities that involve children with one another, using the skill or disposition to be learned. These include exercises such as practicing giving compliments, expressing and interpreting feelings through pantomime, and partner interviews. We encourage you to critically review published programs and decide the worth of the lessons for yourself. We find that too many focus on paper and pencil or cut and paste activities rather than actual interpersonal experiences.

The principles in this chapter are also related to programs for *character education* (Lickona, 1999; Watson, 1999). Character education programs emphasize critical thinking more than do violence prevention programs.

Therefore, encouraging intellectual risk-taking fits more with character education. Violence prevention—or peace-making programs—emphasize conflict resolution more than do character education programs. The next chapter of this book focuses on effective communication for conflict resolution. We see both character education and violence prevention as necessary and interactive for creating a more humane world.

CONCLUSION

Your positive examples will result in more positive child behaviors. If you have a caring relationship with your students, your models of respect and fairness toward children will be emulated in how children treat one another. How you deal with your own feelings and those of others will affect how children handle their feelings. Your demonstrations of caring and kindness will make lasting impressions on young people. Your willingness to take risks in learning new skills and trying out new ideas will help youngsters more bravely try out their emerging skills and ideas. When you set an example of being responsible and of following good safety habits, children are more apt to pay attention than when you lecture about those issues. As an adult you have a powerful influence on young children. You are teaching by everything you do.

FOR FURTHER THOUGHT

1. Observe young children and the adults with whom they spend their days. Note the ways in which the children imitate the examples set by adults.
2. Analyze your own expression of feelings. Are you able to express fear or loneliness? Do you have a tendency to cover up other negative feelings with expressions of anger? How do you express your anger? Do you need to work on your own ability to express your feelings effectively in order to set an example for children?
3. Notice how adults respond when children get hurt or are upset. Do they deny children's negative feelings or accept them? Do they try to distract children from physical or emotional pain? What is your own common response? Do you need to work at learning new ways to respond to a child's pain?
4. Observe ways in which teachers encourage or discourage children in thinking for themselves. Do you see any relationship between a teacher's own intellectual autonomy and that teacher's encouragement of children's intellectual autonomy? How would you rate yourself for intellectual autonomy?
5. Observe the difference in classrooms where teachers merely tell children to clean up and those where teachers work with youngsters, showing them useful clean-up approaches.

RECOMMENDED READINGS

Froschl, M., & Sprung, B. (1999). On purpose: Addressing teasing and bullying in early childhood. *Young Children, 54*(3), 70–72.

Furman, R. A. (1995). Helping children cope with *stress* and deal with feelings. *Young Children, 50* (2), 33–41.

Horton, J., & Zimmer, J. (1994). *Media violence and children, a guide for parents.* (brochure). Washington, DC: National Association for the Education of Young Children.

Hyson, M. C. (1994). *The emotional development of young children: Building an emotion-centered curriculum* (ch. 8). New York: Teachers College Press.

Kuebeli, J. (1994). Young children's understanding of everyday emotions. *Young Children, 49*(3), 36–46.

Teaching Tolerance. (1997). *Starting small: Teaching tolerance in preschool and the early grades.* Montgomery, AL: The Southern Poverty Law Center.

7

EFFECTIVE DISCIPLINE THROUGH EFFECTIVE COMMUNICATION

"Get to work, young man."

"Stop acting like a baby."

"You're such a good little girl."

"No recess unless that paper is finished."

"You are being rude."

"Everything will be fine; just wait and see."

"Your picture is beautiful."

"You're okay. There's no reason to cry."

"You need to improve your attitude."

Do any of these statements sound familiar? Perhaps you heard them from your parents and teachers as you grew up. Perhaps you have said them to children yourself. You may be surprised to hear that these statements have a negative effect on behavior (Gordon, 1989). Chapter 6 discusses some of these types of responses in terms of negating children's feelings. This chapter will look at how such comments build barriers to communication in addition to teaching children that their feelings aren't okay. In his discipline classic *Parent Effectiveness Training,* Thomas Gordon (1970) calls them "roadblocks to communication."

Many parents and teachers grew up with these counterproductive ways of communicating, which have become second nature to them. These adults automatically resort to the ways of talking to children that they have heard in the past. Knowledge about effective communication can drastically alter relationships between people of all ages. Some people use the information to improve marriages, friendships, or working relationships (Gordon, 1989). Parents and teachers can apply the information to effective communication and better relationships with children. Effective communication is an essential part of effective discipline, as are good relationships.

This chapter helps you build better relationships as you communicate more positively with children. Being a role model of effective communication, plus your explicit teaching, helps children learn to use these forms of communication so that they can get along better with others. Your classroom will be a more peaceful place when you and your students talk, listen, and negotiate differences according to the guidelines shared in this chapter.

WHY CHILDREN DON'T LISTEN

Adults frequently complain that children don't listen to them, and they often have no idea why. Few adults ever consider that it might be their own fault. Think about the following situations:

1. You have just warned Kenji to be careful of that puddle, and now he's splashing right into the middle of it.
2. You have given the directions for the art activity three times, and still individual children are coming up to you and asking how to do it.
3. You hear yourself saying, "How many times have I told you not to do that?!"

These incidents may be symptoms of ineffective ways of talking to children. Of course, we can't guarantee that Kenji will stay out of the puddle no matter *what* you say, but you can improve your success rate. How you talk to kids makes a big difference in whether they listen to you. How you talk to children and other people also makes a big difference in whether they care what you have to say.

CRITICIZING AND LECTURING

It isn't too surprising that people don't listen to what is unpleasant to hear. It seems like a natural self-protective device to tune out what is unpleasant. Yet many teachers and parents express dismay when children don't listen to their persistent nagging. The adults consider frequent reminders and corrections as forms of teaching. Certainly, teaching is the intent, but the teaching approach obviously is not effective if the teaching is ignored.

No matter what their age, people rarely like to hear someone tell them how badly they have behaved. Similarly, no one wants to be called derogatory names such as *selfish* or *tattletale*. Most people also get irritated at being told how they should be acting. Well-intentioned comments analyzing possible causes of your behavior are perhaps the most infuriating of all. Remember, kids are people, too, and if you want them to listen to you, avoid talking to them in ways that turn off listening.

Think about how you would feel in the following situation: You were late for work and feeling awful about it. It was a terrible morning: Everything that could go wrong did go wrong. Your alarm didn't go off, the clothes you had washed and put into the dryer last night to wear today didn't get dry, and the bus pulled away just as you got to the bus stop.

> You finally arrived at work, frustrated, hungry, and disheveled. Your supervisor pointed out that you were late once last month, too, and said that you have been inconsiderate. She went on to tell you how disappointed she was in your thoughtlessness and suggested that you might have a problem dealing with authority and rules. She finished by lecturing you on the importance of being on time.

Would this supervisor's approach make you open to her instruction? Would you pay close attention to what she says and want to learn more from her? How would it affect your feelings about her in general? How would your attitude about work that day be affected? Most people would get very angry, tune out the supervisor, and have an even worse day as a result. Yet many teachers regularly talk to students in this way and expect improved behavior to result. Gordon (1970) calls this behavior "sending, put-down' messages." It is fortunate that kids often tune such messages out because they are so harmful to self-esteem.

GIVING ORDERS

It is fairly easy to recognize the unpleasantness of hearing about your errors. However, you may not have thought about why kids (and adults) also dislike constantly being told what to do and how to do it. These instructions communicate disrespect for the other person's ideas and abilities. When you tell people everything they need to do in a situation, you also tell them that you don't think they are capable of figuring it out for themselves. Gordon (1970) calls this communication approach "solution messages." When you communicate this kind of disrespect, you don't get much cooperation in return. You are more likely to generate resistance to your directions instead. Of greater concern are the long-term effects on the child. Such disrespect not only damages self-esteem, but it also short-circuits growth toward autonomy. When you solve problems for them, children learn not to trust their own solutions. You are creating an unhealthy dependency.

> Ariel couldn't get the glue to come out. She turned the dispenser's end, chewed on it, and squeezed as hard as she could. Finally, she just took off the lid and tried to pour glue onto her collage. When it didn't immediately come out, she shook the container. Glop! As Ariel considered the best way to approach the puddle of glue, Miss Wheeler stepped in and ordered, "Get a sponge!" Ariel frowned. She would have scooped up most of the glue with a scrap of mat board first. Then she would have gotten a sponge to finish the job. Why didn't Miss Wheeler ever let her decide how to do things, Ariel wondered.

Thomas Gordon, as well as Haim Ginott, who wrote another child-guidance classic, *Between Parent and Child* (1965), discuss how differently adults talk to children than to other adults. They point out that few teachers or parents would talk to a friend or acquaintance in the bossy, rude ways that many speak to children. It tends to sound ridiculous if you think of talking to an adult in the disrespectful terms often used toward youngsters. If Ariel had been an adult, would the teacher have spoken to her that way? More likely, Miss Wheeler would have said, "You may use my table sponge if you'd like."

INAUTHENTIC COMMUNICATION

Speaking to children with respect, as you would expect to do with adults, can be a helpful guide. But many people don't know the best ways to express themselves to people of any age. You may be one of those people who doesn't say anything when someone offends or upsets you because you don't want to be rude or unpleasant. Or, you may be bold about speaking up to defend yourself. Too often, it is hard to defend yourself without expressions of anger, which generate anger in response.

If you say nothing when someone hurts or frustrates you, your resentment builds. Your nonverbal communication will be negative, indicating your true feelings. The relationship will be damaged by the unexpressed feelings and the unresolved conflicts. This is not an honest way of relating. Children with parents and teachers who provide this model of behavior do not have productive examples to follow.

If you find yourself speaking in anger frequently, you may also be covering up your true feelings. Anger is often a secondary emotion. It results from a primary emotion such as fear, hurt, or embarrassment. Expressions of anger focus on what the other person did, without acknowledging your own feelings. Some teachers and parents feel that revealing their own fear or hurt is not compatible with their authority role. They may think that the expression of true feelings demonstrates weakness and that their job is to demonstrate power. Like holding in unpleasant feelings, expressing them as anger also damages relationships. It is dishonest and, therefore, a poor role model as well.

The idea that an adult cannot demonstrate fear, sadness, or other feelings associated with vulnerability is linked to the power-based authoritarian discipline style, with its repercussions of negative behaviors and negative self-esteem. The invincible adult role is counterproductive to long-term discipline goals in other ways as well. We have already discussed in Chapter 6 how children's ability to express their emotions in a healthy way is affected by their adult role models. Additionally, the invulnerable adult model gets in the way of authentic relationships with children because the adults cannot reveal their true selves. Authentic relationships between adults and children, like those between peers, encourage cooperation and empathy. These traits are clearly linked to more desirable behavior.

TALKING TO CHILDREN RESPECTFULLY

It is important to communicate your personal needs and limits. Doing so effectively means you state your feelings without labeling the child as bad and without ordering the child to change. In this way you balance the expression of self-respect with that of respect for others. Gordon (1970) was the first to call this simple statement of your own feelings an "*I message.*"

"I messages" are appropriate when the problem is yours: what is happening is upsetting to you personally. Children need to learn to give "I messages" when someone does something that bothers them. Sometimes adults seem to get confused and assume that all problems are the adults' problem; that view gets in the way of teaching children to express their own feelings with "I messages."

In contrast with "you messages," "I messages" do not blame or condemn another person, and they do not contain put-downs. "I messages" also don't tell someone else what to do, thus avoiding a "solution message." They focus on your needs instead of on the other person's actions. Therefore, people are more willing to listen to this type of communication; it generates little argument or defensiveness.

A complete "I message" has three components according to Gordon's book, *P.E.T. in Action* (Gordon & Sands, 1976):

1. It is specific about what the unacceptable behavior is.

2. It states your feeling.

3. It explains why it makes you feel that way.

We add another component:

4. It stops after saying those three things.

Too many people start out with a good "I message" and then ruin it by telling the child what he or she should be doing differently. Some social skills curriculum programs also make this mistake in teaching "I messages" (Sadalla, Holmberg, & Halligan, 1990). If you don't stop after stating the problem and its cause, your listener hears the instructions for improvement and tends to react negatively. The communication has turned into a solution message—another roadblock message.

It is more effective and respectful to communicate the nature of your problem and then to back off, allowing the child to make things right. The following examples show three different examples of useful "I messages."

1. While Mrs. Jensen was reading a story to the group, Abby was talking to her friend quite loudly. Mrs. Jensen looked at Abby and said, "I can't read with so much noise in the room. It gives me a sore throat to try to talk loudly enough for people to hear me." Abby had a reason for keeping her voice down and willingly complied.

2. Dennis was bending over to help Andrea with her boots when Sam came up behind, threw his arms tightly around Dennis' neck, and hung on his teacher's back. Dennis nearly fell over backward, but understood that Sam was expressing affection and meant no harm. As calmly as possible, Dennis told the affectionate child, "I'm afraid I'm going to fall over with you on my back, Sam, and I can't help Andrea with her boots this way." Sam hopped off, and Dennis gave him some attention as soon as Andrea had her boots on.

3. Mica was spilling paint on the carpet as she exuberantly worked on the class mural. Mrs. Jensen walked over to where Mica was working

and told her, "I am worried that this paint won't come out of our rug, especially after it dries." Mica got a sponge for clean-up and then put down papers to catch the drips.

RELATIONSHIPS

"I messages" assume that the person you are speaking to actually cares about how you feel. If you don't have a caring relationship with Kim, you can't expect her to be concerned when you tell her you are having a problem. Once again, we are reminded of the central role played by relationships. Piaget (1965/1932) identified mutually respectful relationships as the basis of moral development. In order to be effective with guidance and discipline, you must cultivate relationships with the children in your care.

The children in the previous examples were free to think about their teachers' concerns instead of defending themselves against accusations of wrongdoing. The children were also free to think about how they could make things right again. Did you notice that Mrs. Jensen didn't tell Mica what she needed to do about the problem, but instead respected the child to come up with a solution? This approach helped Mica feel good about herself and increased the likelihood of future desirable behavior. If Mrs. Jensen had tacked on a solution message, it would have taken away from the effectiveness of the communication. Instead, Mrs. Jensen indicated belief in the child's ability and desire to figure out a solution.

MISCONCEPTIONS

Sometimes people get confused about what an "I message" is. They think that it is any statement that starts with "I feel. . . ." Remember, an "I message" is the expression of your own perspective; it doesn't aim the blame at someone else. Be careful, or you might actually send a "you message," fooling yourself into believing that it is an "I message" (Gordon, 1970). For example, Mrs. Jensen might have told Mica, "I feel irritated when you are being such a messy painter." Her "I feel irritated" would then have only been a preface for an insult.

The real key to "I messages" has little to do with using the word *I*. Instead of saying, "I feel hurt when you kick me," it would be much more natural to say, "Ouch, that hurts!" The message is the same: It isn't calling the youngster bad for kicking; it is just expressing your feelings about being kicked.

EFFECTIVENESS

According to Curwin and Mendler (1990), "I messages" are effective for the following four reasons:

1. They say how you feel about what a child is or isn't doing.
2. They give a reason why the behavior is a problem.
3. They never criticize or blame the child.
4. They allow the child to solve the problem.

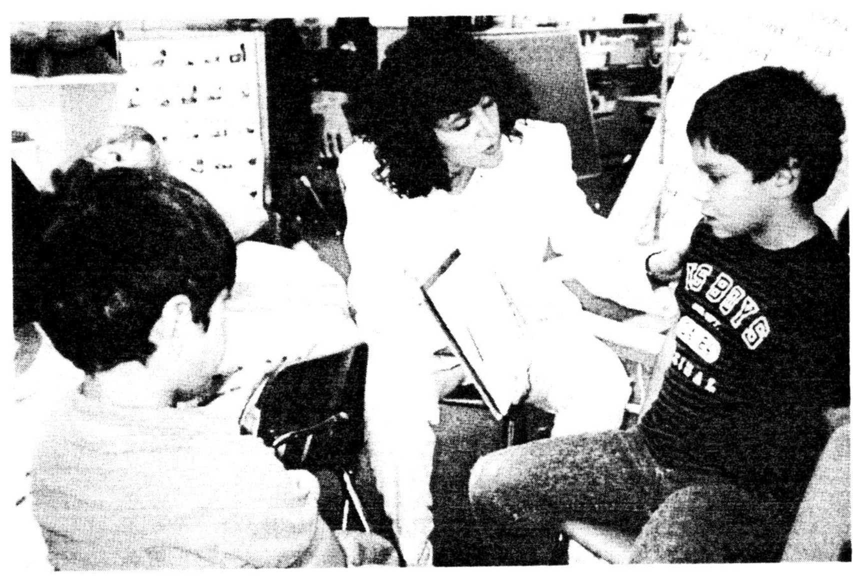

Learning to use "I messages" helps children and adults to communicate their concerns more effectively.

It takes practice to get good at "I messages," but eventually you can retrain yourself so that it comes more naturally to express your own perspective instead of judging someone else's behavior. You will find that the results are worth the effort. People of all ages will respond much more positively to what you say.

TEACHING CHILDREN TO USE "I MESSAGES"

Your model will go a long way toward encouraging your students to express themselves with "I messages," but coaching them in how to use them will help, too. Remember, the person who has the problem is the one who gives the "I message." So, when Sarah is upset because someone took something she was using, it is an appropriate time to help her use an "I message." Often, the other child involved will have a different perspective on the problem and can be helped to give his or her own "I message" in response. "I messages" are an important first step in conflict resolution. You may recall that Chapter 3 recommended "I messages" for helping children gain perspective-taking ability, too.

BEING A GOOD LISTENER

Maybe one of the reasons children don't listen to adults is that adults often don't really listen to children. Too often teachers and parents respond to children's problems by brushing them off. The reasons for this attitude, as discussed in Chapter 6, may be varied. Sometimes adults believe that children's concerns are trivial, or they worry too much about children getting

DEVELOPING POSITIVE "I MESSAGES"

Can you think of positive "I message" alternatives instead of the "you messages" used in the following examples?

1. You are taking a group of children on a walking field trip that involves crossing a few streets. Sam runs ahead of the group instead of staying with you as instructed. Frantic, you yell to Sam, "You have to stay with us! Come back here right now!"
2. A co-teacher is clearing a counter for a project and doesn't notice that five children behind her have their hands raised. You are overwhelmed by trying to meet their demands for attention alone and say to the co-teacher, "You should be more attentive to the children!"
3. A parent brings in a child late, as is her habit, which disrupts your morning gathering time. Besides, this boy really needs help with the daily separation from his mother. You wish she would bring him either earlier or later so that you could be available for him. You say to the mother, "You really need to be on time."

upset. Sometimes an adult is unable to deal with real feelings. It is also possible to be so busy that you don't realize you are not truly listening. You may even think you are paying attention to a child and still respond in ways that prove otherwise.

NOT LISTENING

Many common, well-intentioned ways of responding to what a child says amount to quick brush-offs. Trying to distract a youngster from feeling sad is one way of not really listening. Diversions may be something like the old cookie routine or the words that say, "Let's think about something nice instead." Quick reassurances that everything will be fine also communicate that you are not interested in hearing the child's concerns. Therefore, these are roadblocks to communication. Even trying to solve the child's stated problem with advice is a way of not really listening. Think about how you feel when someone does those things to you.

> Maureen has a friend, Jane, who is quick to give out advice. Maureen really hates it when she is upset about something, then confides to Jane, and gets an instant solution. The advice is always shallow and nonproductive anyway, because Jane hasn't had time to think through the problem. Naturally, Maureen has thought of all those obvious and easy solutions and already come to the conclusion that they won't work; otherwise, she wouldn't still have the problem.
>
> Because Jane doesn't know all the complexities of the situation, her thoughts are mostly irrelevant. What Maureen really wants is someone who hears and understands how upset she is. Instead, Jane's response shows that she

isn't hearing the seriousness of the problem; her offer of an easy answer clearly says to Maureen, "Your problem isn't any big deal. If I were in your place, I could solve it in a minute. You aren't handling things very well."

No wonder Gordon lists giving advice as one of the roadblocks to communication.

TALKING INSTEAD OF LISTENING

Sometimes adults are so busy telling kids what *they* think that they don't hear what a child is saying. When children bring up a problem, many teachers and parents think it is their job to tell youngsters what to do. Some talk to kids about what they "should" do from a moral standpoint, while others tend to dish out facts, trying to influence young people with logic. Still others just give orders and expect compliance. None of these approaches result in listening to the child or respecting the child's ability to figure out answers to problems. You can surely remember how you felt when you got these kinds of lectures yourself. They didn't make you feel like listening!

Passing judgment on a person confiding in you is another sure way to stop further communication. You have heard responses like "It's your own fault" or "You're not making any sense." You may have even heard worse. One of the worst things anyone can say to a young child striving hard to be grown-up is "You're being a baby." Such name-calling is just one way of shaming children and making them feel worthless. Some teachers unfortunately use ridicule and other forms of humiliation to keep youngsters from challenging authority.

Have you ever thought about praise as another way of passing judgment? In this case, you have judged that things are good, but the implication is clear that you will continue to judge and next time may come up with negative findings. This message is also counterproductive to the communication process. Gordon (1970) includes praise, along with reassuring, diverting, and probing, in his list of roadblocks to communication. These methods are attempts to help the child feel better; but like the rest of Gordon's twelve roadblocks to communication, they are nonlistening responses.

Adults can teach good listening by being good listeners. Adults can also learn a lot by listening to kids and finding out what they are thinking. In addition, you can build productive relationships with children by showing that you care enough about them to genuinely listen. When you have a good relationship with children, they try harder to cooperate with you. Good listening can reap many rewards.

PASSIVE LISTENING

One way to show you are listening is to stop talking yourself. Some people just can't seem to be quiet long enough to hear what anyone else is saying. Quiet attention to a child's words with only minimal comments, such as "Is that so?" or "How interesting," can be very effective. Even a sympathetic "hmmmm" is better than a roadblock (Faber & Mazlish, 1996). Sometimes more is required, such as asking "What do you think about that?" or "Would you like to talk about it?" These responses indicate acceptance and respect for the child's opinion. They are basically passive listening approaches.

REFLECTIVE LISTENING

Gordon (1989) suggests that active listening is even more productive than passive listening. He used the term *active listening* to describe an approach common among counselors and therapists. It is designed to ensure the accuracy of communication by reflecting back to the speaker what the listener has heard. Though the term active listening is widely used, we prefer the term *reflective listening* as being more descriptive of the process.

When you practice reflective listening, you will discover how often misunderstandings occur. Saying what it is you think the other person meant allows the speaker to confirm or correct your interpretation. The different experiences and perspectives of the people involved can give totally different meanings to the same set of words. Reflective listening involves the speaker and the listener in a mutual effort to ensure accurate communication. When you give this kind of effort to understanding a child, you show the child you care. You are also more likely to find out what's really going on.

> Barry had ignored all the reminders to get ready for P.E. and was getting belligerent when pressed to hurry. Everyone else was on the way to the gym, but Mrs. Jensen decided that Barry seemed to need her attention most at that moment. "It looks like you don't want to go to P.E. today," she said to him.
>
> "There's no use in going," he retorted. "No use?" Mrs. Jensen asked. "Yeah," he answered. "You don't get hardly any turns." Thinking about the two trampolines out this week for her twenty-five students, Mrs. Jensen figured out, "You don't get much jumping time, huh? Maybe only a couple turns?" She resisted the urge to add that it couldn't be helped. She knew she needed to listen, and it was a good thing she did.
>
> "I only get *one* turn!" Barry exploded. "You gotta put these stupid shoes on to go there, then he makes you take them off to jump, and then you have to have them back on and tied to get back in line for another turn." Mrs. Jensen noted the extra long laces on Barry's gym shoes and was beginning to think that the real problem was the shoes. She checked that out as she affirmed, "Your shoes take a long time to get on?"
>
> "I hate these stupid long laces," was the answer that confirmed her theory. Now that Barry had identified his problem, Mrs. Jensen asked if he would like some help in solving it. She showed him how to cut the laces and melt the ends so they still worked. Barry could manage these much better; putting his gym shoes on, he seemed ready to try P.E.
>
> As she walked him to the gym, Mrs. Jensen decided to ask the gym teacher if he could lighten up a bit and let the children just slip their shoes on, untied, while they waited in line for a turn. But then, maybe it would be better to have another activity for those who were waiting.

Reflective listening assists understanding and shows caring.

There are many important benefits to reflective listening. By encouraging children to talk about a problem or concern, you also encourage them to think about it. Because you are just listening and not giving solutions or advice, the children are free to figure out their own solutions. Chances are good that their solutions are similar to yours, but they are more likely to implement them because they are their own. Chances are also good that their solutions are more in tune with the children's perspective.

CAUTIONS ABOUT REFLECTIVE LISTENING

When you practice reflective listening, be sure to watch for some common pitfalls. Most people find it very hard to avoid trying to give advice. Sometimes the tendency to take over the problem is shown by inappropriate probing questions, such as "Why do you think that happened?" or "When do you feel this way?"

Reflective listening is appropriate when the problem belongs to the child; use "I messages" for your own problems. When the problem belongs to the child, the best solution is the child's own. If you decide how the problem should be solved, then you communicate a lack of respect for the child's problem-solving ability. You get in the way of children's learning when you try to figure out and solve their problems for them. The experience of personally resolving a problem teaches children how to do it and empowers them in the future. Besides, kids generally don't use adult solutions. If they do use an adult's solution, it only creates dependency.

Feeling Awkward or Phony You may initially feel awkward when trying to find the right words for reflective listening. This type of listening involves telling the speaker what you heard him or her say, but it should be your own interpretation rather than mere parroting of the same words. When you provide your interpretation, you are asking for confirmation that you did understand the speaker's intent. The process of clarifying the message encourages the speaker to continue and to delve more deeply into the subject. By clarifying the idea for the listener, the speaker tends to clarify his or her own thinking.

The reflective-listening process may sound contrived to you at first, and you may feel like a phony paraphrasing back to someone what he or she just said to you. If you are honestly trying to understand what the other person is saying, however, your sincerity will come through. Keep focused on the other person's feelings and on accurate communication; then you will not only feel more comfortable with reflective listening, but you will also be a more effective listener. Your model will help children learn to be better listeners for one another, but few preschool or even primary grade children are capable of this sophisticated type of communication.

Children's Communication Very young preschoolers not only can't do reflective listening, but they can't easily use words to tell us what is bothering them. Their vocabulary generally doesn't have precise words for feelings. In addition, they often lack a clear idea of what is bothering them. Reflective listening with very young children requires you to tune in to the children carefully and pay close attention to their nonverbal communication. With children you know, you can usually get clues from their behavior about what is bothering them. You can follow up these clues by checking out your impressions with the child: Respond to the message that the child's behavior or appearance sends to you.

The process is the same as reflecting back what you hear being said with words. Just as with oral communication, you may not receive the message accurately. When you verbalize your hypothesis about his or her feelings, the child may shake his or her head, "No." That reaction means you need to try other ideas until you get an affirmative response.

> Corrie grabbed the handlebar of Joshua's tricycle, yanking him sideways. Joshua tried to shove him away and screamed for the teacher. When Nancy arrived, 2½-year-old Corrie was saying, "Off! Off!" The teacher assumed he wanted to use a tricycle. There were other free trikes she could help him get, and she almost offered. But she thought she'd better check to see if that was really his problem. "You want to ride a trike?" she asked. He shook his head vehemently no, still clinging to Joshua's handlebar. He had planted himself firmly in front of the trike.

Nancy thought again, looking around for other clues. Then she saw the chalk dust smeared all over Corrie's hands and clothes. Nancy looked ahead on the sidewalk and saw a big colored section. "It looks like you are worried Joshua will drive over your picture," she guessed. "Yeah!" Corrie cried. Nancy then modeled some words Corrie could use to ask Joshua to please go around his drawing. They communicated, the conflict was resolved, and both boys returned to their play.

Cultural differences can present another barrier to reflective listening. For instance, some families discourage children from speaking their minds to adults (Lantieri & Patti, 1996). Some families also teach children not to look at people who are talking. So, if you are trying to have a reflective listening conversation with a child and you become frustrated that the child isn't looking at you, be sure to consider whether this is a cross-cultural misunderstanding.

HELPING CHILDREN RESOLVE CONFLICTS

Both reflective listening and "I messages" come in handy when conflicts arise. When your needs and the needs of a child conflict, sophisticated communication skills can help you to negotiate a solution. You can protect your own personal limits and still respect the needs of children. When youngsters experience conflict among themselves, you can coach them in using effective communication to resolve their differences. Your classroom can become a laboratory for learning the fine art of conflict resolution. This skill may be one of the most important subjects you can teach.

Many people think that conflict is bad and should be avoided; however, avoiding conflict usually means repressing feelings. Rarely can people live and work together in total harmony with no one's needs impinging on those of another. Conflict in the classroom and on the playground can be viewed as a learning opportunity. It is a chance for children to learn about the needs and wants of others, and it is also a chance for them to learn lifelong skills for mutual problem solving.

CONSISTENCY IN SCHOOLS

Schools have traditionally used a power model rather than a negotiation model (Gordon, 1989). Because children have so often seen threats and intimidation used as ways of resolving differences, it may take some effort to teach them a peaceful, respectful alternative. However, you will find it is worth the effort both to enhance the social skills of your students and to increase peace in your classroom.

Many of the social skills curriculum programs adopted by school districts include conflict resolution instruction based on the same principles of negotiation and consensus that Thomas Gordon described (e.g., Siccone & Lopez, 2000). The success of these programs may require that schools let go of authoritarian approaches to discipline. It is difficult to teach students a cooperative approach to resolving their problems if you model a different

SAMPLE STEPS FOR NEGOTIATING SOLUTIONS TO PROBLEMS

How are these alike and different?

Thomas Gordon's Steps

1. Identify the problem.
2. Generate solutions.
3. Evaluate solutions.
4. Make a decision.
5. Implement the plan.
6. Evaluate the plan.

William Kreidler's Steps

A. Ask: What's the problem?
B. Brainstorm solutions.
C. Choose the best.
D. Do it!

Peaceworks Steps (Schmidt & Friedman)

1. Keep both hands on the peace table while you are talking and listening. (Hands are for helping, not hurting.)
2. Tell the truth.
3. Listen without interrupting.
4. No name-calling or blaming.
5. List ideas to solve the problem.
6. Choose the best solution.

style when adult-to-child interactions are involved. If adults use a "power-on" model, instead of learning negotiation and cooperation, children learn that "might makes right."

EVERYONE WINS

Negotiating mutually acceptable solutions allows both sides to have power and respect. No one says, "You do it my way or else." No group says, "We have more votes. You lose." No one ends up angry and resentful. Therefore, general attitudes and relationships are more pleasant. Because everyone is involved in selecting the solutions, each person is more likely to follow through on them.

In addition, the solutions tend to be higher quality, reflecting the needs and ideas of all involved. The process helps children to consider the views of other people. Consideration of others and the thinking process involved in problem solving both contribute to the long-term goals of intellectual and moral autonomy. It takes a lot more work to get consensus than just to vote, but that's what makes negotiation such a great learning opportunity.

Mutual problem solving not only assists children toward long-term goals, but it also makes life more pleasant in the here and now. It relieves youngsters from the anger and the fear of punishment that accompany teacher-power approaches. It relieves the teacher from constantly having to nag, enforce, and police instead of teach. It makes school a much more enjoyable and productive place for teachers and children to be. Gordon (1970, 1989) presents the basic model for peaceful negotiation and problem solving; many other authors present variations of these steps.

IDENTIFYING THE PROBLEM

How does the problem-solving process work? You need to explain that you would like to work together with those involved to figure out a solution to the problem. First, you need a clear statement of a problem. This step is where "I messages" come in to help each side express how its needs or expectations are not being met. Reflective listening is useful for hearing the other side, and often it's necessary for discovering the actual cause of the problem. Notice how effective communication works as part of negotiations to solve the basketball conflict described next.

> "They won't let us have the ball!" complained the younger children trying to join in a basketball game during the after-school child care program. Ann, the program director, wanted all children to feel that they were a part of the group. She asked those complaining to her if they had told the bigger kids how they felt. "Yes, but they won't listen," was the answer.
>
> Ann decided it would be appropriate for her to support the communication process here. She asked the older youngsters to come over and listen to what the younger ones had to say. The little kids were pretty clear: "It's no fun for us because you never throw the ball to any little kids." "But you always lose the ball when you dribble down the court," the big kids responded.
>
> Both sides had stated their positions and it seemed to Ann that the next step should be trying to figure out a solution to the problem.

BRAINSTORMING SOLUTIONS

Once the problem is identified, everyone involved needs to help think of possible solutions. No idea is too wild, and no ideas are rejected at this point. In fact, no ideas should even be evaluated yet. Be sure to continue getting ideas until everyone has run out of possibilities. Writing down all the ideas where everyone can see them is helpful, even if the children are too young to read yet. You can refer to the list as you review, and they will recognize their ideas.

> Many ideas were proposed by the group, and Ann wrote them on a big piece of paper so all could see.
>
> "Big kids play and then little kids have a turn," suggested Kirk, a competitive and competent player.
>
> "Little kids play an easier game," offered Allison, trying to be helpful.

"Don't take the ball when we dribble," Sarah said assertively.

That seemed to spark an idea for Eric: "I know!" he said excitedly. "Let's make a rule that the little kids can either dribble the ball or they can hold it and run down the court."

"OK," chimed in Raymond. "And when they dribble, no big kids can try to get it; but if they carry it, we can try to get it away."

The brainstorming seemed over at this point and it was time for the next step in problem solving.

EVALUATING SOLUTIONS AND MAKING A CHOICE

The next step is to evaluate the suggestions. Which ones are just impossible or totally unacceptable to someone? Cross those out immediately. Now what is left? Do any of them stand out as great ideas? Continue the discussion until everyone agrees to try one or a combination of solutions. Make sure the children understand that choosing a solution means a commitment to carrying it out. Voting is not a part of the process. This is a consensus model: Everyone agrees to try a solution, and no one is forced into it by a "someone loses" or "minorities lose" method, such as a vote.

Choosing among the suggestions for the basketball conflict didn't take long. Kirk held out a bit for his idea of the big kids playing without the little kids, but the little kids nixed that one. There was lots of support for the idea of new rules that created some equality between older players and younger ones. Consensus soon emerged around that plan, and the new basketball rules were clarified.

IMPLEMENTING THE PLAN

There's more to the process than simply determining a solution. A plan isn't worth much unless you figure out how to implement it. Who will do what? When and how often? Where and how? To what standards? Who checks? When children make these kinds of decisions and plan to implement them, they tend to follow through with little teacher direction.

Eric and Raymond felt ownership of the new plan. They took leadership roles in setting up teams of fairly equal ability and getting the game going again. All the children reminded one another of the new rules as they played.

EVALUATING THE PLAN

What if the solution doesn't work? There are many reasons why it might not. Perhaps it was too difficult to implement or perhaps there were conditions you and the children neglected to consider. Evaluating the solution after you have tried it for a while is an essential final step. If you find that things aren't working, that situation isn't a signal for you to take over. It just means that the group needs to try again to generate workable solutions.

Ann watched with pleasure as the game went on for a full 45 minutes without a single problem. What a relief! Complaints and arguments had been the main event on the basketball court for days. In addition, she noticed that these new rules encouraged the younger children to practice dribbling the ball. The older children were now working in partnership with the younger ones on their team, giving them the ball and urging them to dribble it, since that protected it from being stolen. Everyone seemed to be having a good time.

Ann checked with the group the next day after school, asking them how their new "big kid—little kid" rules worked out. There seemed to be unanimous agreement that they worked great.

SAVING TIME

Does conflict resolution sound like it takes a lot of time? This is a common concern. Sometimes problem solving can be accomplished in just a few minutes; at other times, it does take quite a lot of time. However, if you have a recurring problem, that takes a lot of time, too. Teachers and parents who use this problem-solving approach report that it saves a lot of time in the long run. Instead of ineffectively dealing with the same problem over and over, time is set aside to deal effectively with the problem until it is resolved. The time spent on this problem-solving session was certainly time well spent for Ann; the problem had been disrupting play and dividing the group for quite some time.

INDEPENDENT PROBLEM SOLVERS

Obviously, conflicts don't just occur between adults and children. Children frequently find themselves engaged in a battle over a toy, a turn, or a space in the classroom or on the playground. You can save yourself time and trouble by teaching youngsters to negotiate solutions to their own problems. The model you provide in group problem solving is an important part of this teaching, but you will need to talk children through the process individually while they are learning. Kreidler's (1994) simplified ABCD version of negotiation is probably easiest for children to remember: A. Ask: What's the problem? B. Brainstorm solutions. C. Choose the best. D. Do it! Let's see how Raymond and Sam work out their problem at the sand table.

Raymond and Sam were trying to play together at the sand table again, but as always, they had very different game plans. Raymond was trying to make carefully groomed patterns in the sand. Sam was chugging around with a bulldozer, trying to get all of the sand up against the edges, exposing the bottom.

Raymond complained as the bulldozer kept undermining his space, making the patterns sluff away. Mrs. Jensen observed the conflict and got things rolling by helping them define the problem. "It looks like you two are getting in each other's way here," she commented. Then she suggested that the boys try to brainstorm a way to play together at the sand table.

Raymond frowned, wishing the teacher would just tell Sam to stop ruining his work. Then Mrs. Jensen reminded him, "You did so well at solving the stage problem. I bet you could come up with a way to fix this one!" He brightened up.

With practice, children learn to negotiate their own solutions among themselves.

> Mrs. Jensen then asked, "Do you remember how to brainstorm solutions?" Sam had liked that part; anything you thought of was okay, so you could be silly or serious. Sam was silly: "Measure every grain of sand and divide it exactly!" Raymond got into it and offered, "We could take turns at the sand table." "I know! We could build the Great Wall of China, and neither one could cross it!" Sam said excitedly, remembering a picture he had seen of the wall. Raymond thought again and came up with one last idea: "Sam could play with the funnels instead of the bulldozer."
>
> Mrs. Jensen reminded the boys that choosing the best solution meant they had to both agree on a solution to try. Measuring sounded like a challenge and both boys thought it would be too hard. Taking turns was rejected because neither wanted to be second, and Sam wasn't interested in playing with the funnels. But the "Great Wall" idea intrigued both of the boys. They asked if they could use some blocks in the sand table to make a barrier wall.
>
> Mrs. Jensen thought to herself that the idea might not work but told them to go ahead anyway. They were eager to try out their solution. It didn't perfectly hold back sand, but it was completely effective at resolving the conflict between the boys. Whenever it collapsed, they ignored their patterns and bulldozing to rebuild their barrier cooperatively, the new major focus!

If you teach children how to negotiate their own solutions, soon they will be teaching each other and won't constantly be coming to you with their arguments. Even preschool-age children are capable of problem solving. In the past, adults generally just separated children who were in conflict, or else the teacher decided who was in the right and would "win." Teaching children to arrive at a mutually satisfying solution to their disagreements is a more productive use of your time (Watson, 1999). In the process of learning to problem-solve, your young students will learn about peaceful negotiation of differences. Perhaps they will even put this skill to work as adults, possibly helping the people of the world to resolve their differences.

CONCLUSION

When we communicate with children respectfully, we can prevent many discipline problems and solve many others. When we state our own needs respectfully, children are more apt to behave considerately in the first place and are generally more willing to change their behavior if it has become inappropriate. When we listen to children respectfully, we can help them to resolve their problems, either before their behavior is adversely affected or in time to remedy the situation. When we teach problem-solving skills, children learn to use them to avoid a dispute as well as to solve one. Children's literature offers numerous books to help children think about the importance of peaceful conflict resolution and about how to accomplish it (e.g., Kreidler, 1994; Committee for Children, 1991). When sharing lessons in stories, with puppets or other group presentations, remember to help children think about how to transfer the lesson to their own experiences.

FOR FURTHER THOUGHT

1. Listen to adults talking to children. Think about those same words used with another adult. Do they sound ridiculous or reasonable? Analyze your own ways of talking to children. Do you show less respect to children than to your adult acquaintances?
2. Practice using "I messages" when someone upsets you. What are the results? Were you careful not to send a disguised "you message?" Were you able to stop yourself from also telling the other person what to do or not to do? Keep on trying. It takes time to break old habits.
3. Practice reflective listening with friends who confide in you about a problem. Be careful not to give advice or reassurance, but only to clarify your understanding of the other person's feelings. How does this attitude affect the communication? Is it difficult to do?
4. A problem to solve: Angie comes to you complaining because another child is using the swing and she wants to swing.
   a. Describe a common ineffective response.
   b. Describe a reflective-listening response.
5. A problem to solve: Matt and Jason are experimenting with magnets at preschool. Jason goes off to play elsewhere, and Matt starts crying.
   a. What might a teacher say who is skilled in reflective listening?
   b. What might a teacher say who doesn't understand about roadblocks to communication?
6. Try out the steps to negotiating conflicts as described in this chapter. Analyze the results to learn how to be more effective in the future.

RECOMMENDED READINGS

Carlsson Paige, N., & Levin, D. E. (1992). Making peace in violent times: A constructivist approach to conflict resolution. *Young Children, 48*(1), 4–12.

Faber, A., & Mazlish, E. (1996). *How to talk so kids can learn at home and in school.* New York: Fireside/Simon & Schuster.

Fine, E. S., Lacey, A., & Baer, J. (1995). *Children as peacemakers.* Portsmouth, NH: Heinemann.

Ginott, H. (1965). *Between parent and child: New solutions to old problems.* New York: Macmillan.

Gordon, T. (1970). *Parent effectiveness training.* New York: Wyden.

Gordon, T. (1974). *T.E.T.: Teacher effectiveness training.* New York: Wyden.

Gordon, T. (1989). *Teaching children self-discipline: At home and at school.* New York: Random House.

Kreidler, W. J. (1994). *Teaching conflict resolution through children's literature.* New York: Scholastic.

Schmidt, F., & Friedman, A. (1992). *Peacemaking skills for little kids.* Fresno, CA: Peace Works Inc.

Siccone, F., & Lopez, L. (2000). *Educating the heart: Lessons to build respect and responsibility.* Boston: Allyn & Bacon.

8

HELPING CHILDREN UNDERSTAND AND ACCEPT LIMITS

What do you do if prevention, modeling, listening, and problem solving don't work? What if you need to change a behavior immediately? What do you do when it's too late to prevent a problem because it is already happening? Do you then turn to punishment?

Natural and related consequences, not punishment, provide the answer for effective immediate results that are compatible with long-term positive outcomes. Punishment merely affects the immediate response and generally produces negative side effects. With related consequences, you can teach toward long-term discipline goals while still enforcing limits. The best use of consequences as a discipline tool is when the undesirable behavior is caused by a child's lack of understanding. Understanding is the goal of using consequences as a teaching tool.

Related consequences emphasize and clarify limits; they communicate through actions that certain behaviors will not be tolerated. At the same time, related consequences help children learn why that behavior is undesirable, giving them personal reasons to change. Instead of merely forcing children to do what adults know is best, related consequences help youngsters reflect on the consequences of their actions. Related consequences use children's own experiences as the basis for teaching desirable behavior. In the process, this form of discipline helps develop the personal responsibility necessary for self-discipline and moral autonomy. At the same time, this kind of discipline respects the child's right and ability to choose more appropriate action.

The concept of related consequences has been described in different terms by various authors. Publications by Piaget (1965/1932) and Dreikurs (1964) laid the foundation for the idea; subsequently, others have continued to explore why and how this discipline approach works (Albert, 1996; Gathercoal, 1998; Kamii, 1982, 1984; Reynolds, 1996).

In *The Moral Judgment of the Child* (1965/1932), Piaget points out the arbitrary nature of punishment and its lack of relation to the misbehavior as reasons for not using this approach. Piaget describes several types of alternative discipline strategies in contrast with punishment. He recommends five results of misbehavior that help children move toward moral autonomy. These results may or may not be imposed by an adult; they may simply occur as the natural outcome of the child's actions or may happen within the child's peer group in response to antisocial behavior.

1. Natural consequences: The child experiences the direct results of his or her own behavior. Piaget uses the example of a child who has a cold room as a result of breaking his or her own bedroom window.

2. Exclusion: The child who is harming others may not play with the other children until the behavior changes.

3. Deprivation: The child may not have access to materials that have been abused or misused until the behavior changes.

4. Restitution: The child pays for, or replaces, that which has been damaged or lost; the child assists a person injured through that child's fault.

5. Reciprocity: What the child has done to another is done back to the child. Piaget is very clear that this response does not mean an adult doing evil for evil, such as biting a child who has bitten another. He says that action is not only a poor model but also "absurd" (Piaget, 1965/1932, p. 208). Instead, he refers to a response such as not doing a favor for a child who has not helped with assigned chores. Thus, if the child doesn't help you, you don't help the child.

Dreikurs' concept of natural and logical consequences is basically the same as Piaget's alternatives to punishment. In his book *Children: The Challenge* (1964), Dreikurs explained consequences and elaborated on the concept in his subsequent writing (Dreikurs, Greenwald, & Pepper, 1982). Natural consequences are those that automatically result from the child's behavior with no intervention from an adult. According to Dreikurs, logical consequences are those imposed by an adult but linked to the child's actions.

In this book, we blend the viewpoints of Piaget and Dreikurs. We prefer the simplicity of a distinction between consequences that happen without adult intervention and those that require such intervention. Therefore, like Dreikurs, we make a distinction between natural consequences and imposed consequences. To emphasize the necessity of consequences being related to the behavior, we chose the term *related consequences* for imposed consequences that help a child learn. We find Piaget's several categories of consequences helpful in remembering to consider a variety of options in discipline situations. Keep in mind that some outcomes in these categories may also occur naturally or within the child's social group.

It is important to remember that related consequences are designed to help children think about why certain behaviors are unacceptable and others are desirable. This is a teaching approach in which punishment has no place. Consequences are designed to help children view themselves as capable and willing problem solvers. Punishment tends to have the opposite effect, making children consider themselves bad and teaching them to be sneaky to avoid being caught (Kamii, 1984). Punishment will be discussed further in Chapters 9 and 10.

NATURAL CONSEQUENCES

Both Piaget and Dreikurs recommend allowing children to experience the results of their actions when possible. Natural consequences are mostly a matter of getting out of the way and allowing children to learn from their experiences. Too often adults deprive children of the chance to experience the consequences of their actions because they care about the children and don't want them to have unpleasant or disappointing experiences. Unfortunately, the result is that the children don't become responsible for their own actions (Kamii, 1982). The following example is one that most teachers see frequently:

> Travis forgot his gym shoes again. It was gym day, and the P.E. teacher would not let the children participate unless they had on the proper shoes. But Travis wasn't worried; he was confident that his mom would bring his shoes for him. Sure enough, Travis' mother arrived soon, harried and disgruntled at having to fit this errand into her day's schedule. She was cross with Travis and fumed, "Why are you so irresponsible? I even reminded you this morning. You never listen."

What has Travis learned here? Instead of learning that he needs to remember his gym shoes if he wants to participate in P.E., he has learned to depend on his mother. He has become convinced that he is, indeed, irresponsible and that his mother needs to take responsibility for him. Instead of having the experience of not getting to play in the gym, Travis experiences his mother's anger. Anger teaches nothing; it only brings resentment and retaliation. It focuses the child's attention on the "mean" adult instead of on his or her own behavior. It deprives him of the opportunity to think about and learn from the outcome of his own actions.

AVOIDING OVERPROTECTION

Mrs. Jensen does try hard not to protect children from learning through their mistakes. She reminds herself not to take over their responsibilities when they forget. She doesn't nag, coax, and remind children to do the things they are supposed to remember on their own. Mrs. Jensen thinks that youngsters learning to take responsibility for themselves is more important than making sure everyone remembers to take home the book order list or even the class newsletter. She teaches effectively by helping them to figure out the cause-and-effect relationship between their actions and the results. They soon find out that they don't get to buy a book if they don't take the book order form home, get permission and money to place an order, and then return the form with the money to school. She knows that children learn through their experiences and that learning takes time.

The real world offers much more opportunity for natural consequences than school does. By its nature, school is an artificial environment that doesn't allow much opportunity for natural responses. At home, Mrs. Jensen can allow her own children to learn much more freely from their mistakes than she can at school with her students. If her own children don't put away their things at home, they naturally get lost. At school, the custodian picks things up and gets cross when they are lying around. When her own children go running outside without a coat on a cool day, she lets them find out for themselves that they need to come back for a coat. At school, she worries that parents will think she is shirking her responsibility if she lets her students go out to recess without coats. Besides, school rules don't allow youngsters to run back inside for coats in the middle of recess. Mrs. Jensen has trouble allowing natural consequences at school.

THE INEVITABLE DOES HAPPEN

Although teachers and parents are often uncomfortable with allowing natural consequences, children still manage to experience them often. They will build an unstable block tower and experience its collapse. From this natural consequence they can begin to learn about balance, physical limits, and maybe the way hard blocks feel when they land in their lap. That is, they will learn if some overprotective adult doesn't stop them by controlling their constructions. Social behavior and friendships are also molded a great deal by natural consequences (Rizzo, 1989). A child who repeatedly hurts others physically or hurts their feelings may reap the consequence of peer rejection, as in the following example:

> On the playground at Lincoln Elementary School, the ratio is 2 aides to 250 children. Here, free from the ever-watching eyes and ears of the classroom teacher, the children learn how to get along on their own. Allison had been particularly bossy to her table mates in class one morning. She told Rose to get out of the book corner and ordered Ling Ling to clean up her mess. When Allison came out for recess, they all avoided her, leaving her out of their games. She complained, "Why can't I play?" Rose answered directly, " 'Cause you always have to be the boss!" Allison was experiencing a delayed natural consequence for her earlier behavior.

The teacher can help Allison by helping her to think through this experience, not by saving her from it. Though showing sympathy for her hurt feelings is appropriate, fixing the problem Allison created will not help her learn. Some adults would insist that no child should be left out and thus would ruin Allison's lesson. A much kinder teacher response is to encourage Allison to think about how she might act differently in the future in order to be accepted on the playground.

RELATED CONSEQUENCES

Related consequences are useful when natural consequences won't work. Not only do school rules make natural consequences impossible at times, but also the natural consequences in many situations are unacceptable. Adults do have the responsibility of keeping children safe from harm.

Obviously, no one allows a child to experience the natural consequences of playing in the street. Instead, adults watch carefully and plan related consequences to help youngsters learn to stay away from traffic.

Different teachers have varying views on the safety issue as it relates to consequences. Some let children use paring knives to prepare fruit salad, supervising the use but accepting that a small cut may be the occasional result. They feel that the minimally unpleasant experience is a natural consequence that will teach care with knives. Others might be willing to use that method with their own children but don't feel comfortable doing so with other people's children. It is a matter of personal comfort level, as are the varying amounts of risk that different parents allow their children. However, there is general agreement that children cannot be allowed to take risks that could result in serious injury. Therefore, adult-imposed consequences are often the only learning experiences available. Following are examples of several different types of related consequences.

RECIPROCITY

At home, Mrs. Jensen is likely to use a reciprocity consequence by not driving Betsy to her friend's house because Betsy didn't finish helping with household chores. This differs from punishment due to the connection between Betsy not helping her mom and her mom not helping Betsy. At school, it is more often the children who impose consequences of reciprocity. For instance, Nichole may not help Mollie with her project because Mollie got mad and messed up Nichole's project last time they worked together. Mrs. Jensen helps Mollie to learn from this experience and doesn't insist on her inclusion. What if Sam hits Danny? Do you allow the consequence of reciprocity, in which Danny hits him back? Occasionally, Dennis decides that this response is the learning experience one of his preschoolers needs. Perhaps the child hasn't had enough social interaction to realize that hitting gets a negative response from peers. In that case, Dennis pretends not to notice what is happening, yet keeps an eye out to be sure no one really gets hurt.

EXCLUSION

Usually, however, Dennis doesn't allow hitting and uses related consequences, as in the following example using the consequence Piaget (1965/1932) called exclusion:

> Sam wanted to play with Danny after nap time. Unfortunately, Danny was waking up slowly and just wanted to be left alone. Frustrated, Sam got increasingly aggressive and eventually resorted to physical contact to get Danny's attention. Action escalated from nudges to pushing, and then to hitting. Danny wailed and Dennis intervened. Sensing that Danny was in no condition to verbalize his need for privacy at the moment, Dennis chose to impose the consequence of removing Sam, explaining that he could not let him hit Danny. "Hitting hurts," Dennis said as he calmly took Sam to the next room. He told

the child, "You may go back to the sun room when you are ready to use your words instead of hitting. Danny is hurt and he needs to feel safe."

Notice that Dennis did not tell Sam how long he had to stay away from Danny. Instead of using his adult power to make all the decisions here, Dennis allowed the child to be in charge of how much time he needed. He allowed Sam to reflect on his own actions and to decide when his feelings were under control. This approach helped Sam learn to take responsibility for himself and become more autonomous.

DEPRIVATION

Chapter 1 mentioned the problem of Kenji knocking over other children's block constructions. The teacher explained to Kenji that he cannot play with the blocks until he is ready to play without damaging anyone else's constructions. This is an example of the consequence involving deprivation, or not being allowed to use materials that were misused. Dreikurs (1964) introduced the idea that children must be allowed to determine when they are ready to try again to get along with their friends. Telling Kenji he may not play in the block area until he decides he can play without knocking over other children's work is very different from simply removing him. Asking him to decide when he is ready to return gives him the message that you have faith in his ability to make the necessary adjustments in his behavior.

RESTITUTION

The example from Chapter 1 in which Aaron wipes up the water he spilled is also a related consequence. Cleaning up the mess you make is a way of making restitution, a method that Piaget (1965/1932) recommends. An example of making restitution that we particularly like involves children who hurt each other through carelessness. If Desmond is throwing rocks and one accidentally hits Beau, Desmond learns much more about the dangers of rock throwing by holding a cold cloth to Beau's head than by being banished to the principal's office. Kenji and the block destruction could also be handled with restitution. If it seemed appropriate to the circumstances, the teacher might ask him to help rebuild what he knocked down. Making restitution helps youngsters see themselves as helpful people rather than bad ones. All of these examples describe ways of motivating children to build rules of conduct for themselves from within.

COMBINING WITH OTHER TEACHING

In a situation like the one with Sam, be sure you don't ignore the child's feelings that lead up to an incident, although this doesn't mean you should interrogate the children to determine who started it. That action would put the adult back in charge of the kids' behavior. Instead, think about how you can help the children deal with their feelings.

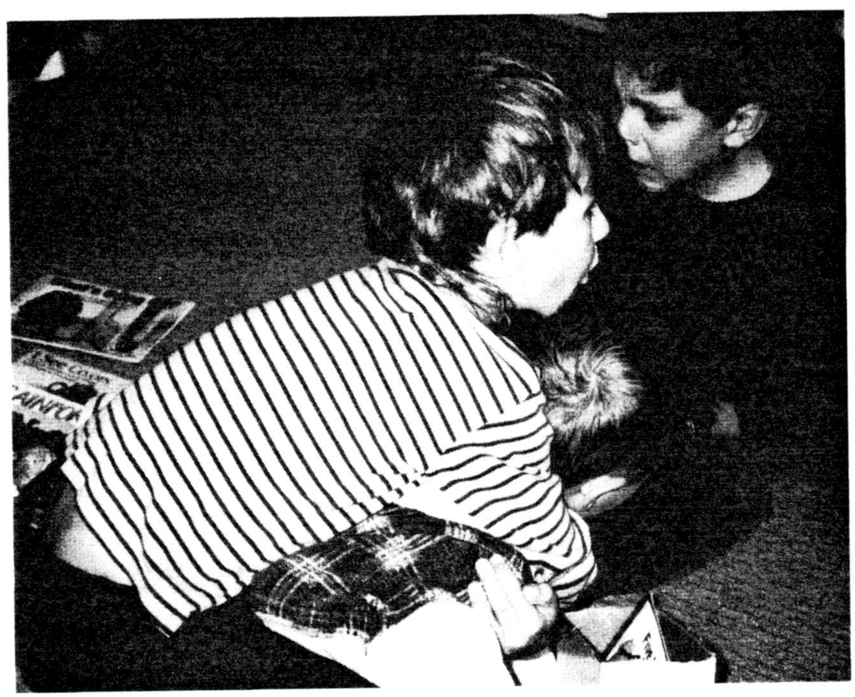

Related consequences are designed to help children understand the effects of their behavior.

Imposing consequences to stop the hitting doesn't preclude the use of other guidance techniques. For instance, after Sam and Danny have calmed down from the incident, you could work with them on the communications skills discussed in Chapter 7. Each boy could be helped to tune in to his feelings and put them into words. Hitting is often a primitive form of communication; learning higher level communication skills can help a child give up hitting.

CONSEQUENCES OR PUNISHMENT?

Many people use the term "consequences" when they really mean "punishment." "He has to face the consequences," often means a spanking or loss of privilege. In this book we are trying to make a distinction between punishment and consequences. Consequences respond to a behavior problem in a way designed to solve the problem rather than to punish the child. As they were originally described (Dreikurs, 1964), consequences were not intended to be punitive. Yet many people began using that "nicer" term when they really meant punishment, and as a result the terms became confused. Alfie Kohn's (1996) position against consequences appears to be based on such misuse of the term.

The connection between the child's behavior and the consequences must be clear to the child or else you are punishing instead of teaching through related consequences.

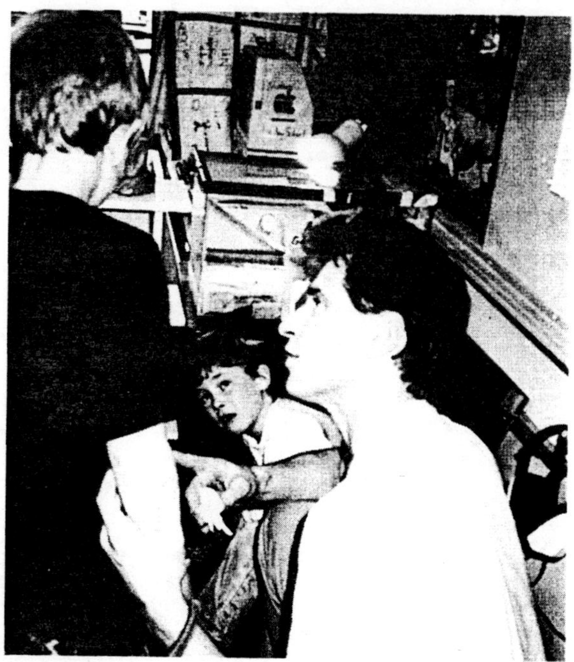

USE CONSEQUENCES WITH CAUTION

Nevertheless, related consequences can easily turn into punishment if the adult is not careful (Curwin & Mendler, 1990). Because the adult administers them, they demonstrate adult power over children. For this reason, other less-intrusive methods of discipline should be tried first. Prevention of problems is the least intrusive approach to discipline. Teaching by example, coaching, "I messages," and conflict negotiation all teach discipline without the use of adult power.

However, if none of those approaches works on the cause of the misbehavior, then another approach is needed. If a lack of understanding is the behavior cause, then consequences can help the child understand. Also, there are times when judicious, respectful, and limited use of adult power is required in order to keep children safe. That is another time to plan a related consequence. These are the two reasons to rely on consequences as discipline: to teach understanding or to enforce necessary limits while you work on the cause of a behavior problem.

The big difference between punishment and consequences is in how they make children feel about themselves. Punishment convinces a child that he or she is "bad" and damages self-esteem. Consequences aim to empower children in their efforts at self-control and to help them see themselves as good people (Gathercoal, 1998). An example of consequences empowering children is the emphasis on giving them the power to decide when they are "ready" to return to a situation from which they were removed. Restitution consequences are an example of consequences helping children see themselves as good people as well as people who can remedy their mistakes (Northeast Foundation for Children, 1998).

PLAN AHEAD

Sometimes it's hard to remember the judicious and respectful aspects of related consequences. Imposed consequences can quickly lead to a power struggle for the unwary adult. Remember Dennis' problem with the "no lunch until you clean up your mess" ultimatum in Chapter 4. Dennis had a practical rationale for that ruling: He wanted to clear the room for lunch. However, it was really Dennis, and not the situation, that was depriving Amy of her lunch. Amy's dress-up clothes weren't on the lunch table, and she couldn't see any reason why they had to be put away before she could eat. Dennis had only his power as an adult to enforce his hasty ultimatum, and that power led to the confrontation. Effective consequences strive for adult withdrawal from power rather than an application of power. Fortunately, Dennis' ego allowed him to back down, listen reflectively, and negotiate a solution with the child.

Related consequences take planning and forethought. The connection between the child's behavior and the results must be clear to the child. Dreikurs (1964) reminds parents that there is no relationship between not taking out the garbage and not getting to watch television. He suggests that there may be a relationship between a parent's refusal to fix dinner and a kitchen with smelly garbage. Therefore, being deprived of television is a form of punishment, while not fixing dinner is a consequence reasonably related to the situation.

Notice, too, that the adult must assert power over the child to enforce the no-television ruling, but refusing to fix dinner affects only the adult's own behavior. A bonus of this approach: You are much less likely to get into a power struggle if your consequence affects your own behavior instead of someone else's.

WATCH YOUR ATTITUDE

Not fixing dinner, however, can also be turned into punishment. If the adult expresses anger about the garbage, then not fixing dinner will come through as a retaliation rather than a consequence. Instead, the parent might use an "I message" and say, "I don't want to fix dinner until the garbage is out. The garbage makes the kitchen smell too bad for me to be in there cooking." It is important to be calm and matter-of-fact about imposing consequences. In fact, it is important not to *be* angry, or your anger will be all that is heard. Effective consequences involve adult intervention without anger or recrimination.

If you use the impending consequences as a threat, that treatment also turns them into punishment (Dreikurs, Greenwald, & Pepper, 1982). "Take that garbage out before I come home from work, or no dinner tonight" is not in the spirit of related consequences. There are times when you want to inform children in advance of consequences, but it needs to be done in a nonthreatening and calm manner.

Variations of the "I told you so" theme are another way to ruin the educational value of related consequences (Dreikurs, 1964). Perhaps, in addition to not fixing dinner, the parent might be tempted to say, "Maybe that will teach you a lesson." These words take the focus away from the actual problem and invite an angry power struggle. Often it is better to say nothing. Let the consequences speak for themselves.

The bottom line is respecting children. If you take away a child's dignity as you deal with his or her behavior, you damage that child. Sarcasm and humiliation have no role in teaching better behavior. Instead of trying to avenge a wrong, the helpful approach is to work on a solution to the problem. A constructive guidance approach using consequences looks for ways to make things right again. Helping a child make restitution to someone he or she has harmed is probably the most useful consequence of all.

SELECTING REASONABLE CONSEQUENCES

As a result of trying to think up reasonable consequences, Mrs. Jensen sometimes finds that there really is no good reason why some actions aren't acceptable. What was the reason for the rule against water in the sand table? She knows that children will more easily accept limits when they can see their value. She believes children deserve an explanation of reasons why certain behaviors are unacceptable. If she can't think of such an explanation, she is inclined to allow the behavior. Sometimes her decision means not conforming to school traditions, such as walking in lines.

> Walking through school hallways in regimented lines under the stern gaze of the teacher is a time-honored tradition. Yet Mrs. Jensen can't convince herself that lines are necessary or helpful.
>
> Why shouldn't youngsters be allowed to walk in quiet groups like adults? Won't they learn more about respecting others if they are in charge of their own behavior than if the teacher is standing guard? Won't many behavior problems be solved if kids aren't walking so close together and don't all have to go at the same time? Mrs. Jensen sees many children poking the child in front of them just from the sheer frustration of waiting until everyone is ready.
>
> She has been working to teach her students about walking through the halls without disturbing other classes or blocking the hallway for people coming in the opposite direction. She finds this approach a much more productive use of her energy than enforcing the lines.
>
> It is much easier for Mrs. Jensen to explain to her students the importance of not bothering others than to explain why they have to stay in a line. She feels good about the time spent helping children learn to be independent in the halls. She leads class discussions about what hall behaviors would bother other classrooms. During these discussions, Mrs. Jensen sees careful thinking; the children are definitely making progress in understanding the views of others. She sees children feeling important and proud as they practice being responsible for their own behavior in the hallway. Children who continually forget about thoughtful behavior can be helped to remember by experiencing a consequence. Mrs. Jensen simply asks forgetful children to walk with her until they think they can manage on their own.

You probably have seen a child being punished for hallway misbehavior by having to walk with the teacher and you may be wondering why we are calling this a consequence and not a punishment. Notice that the child only walks with the teacher until the child decides he or she can manage alone. Giving the child this power is important. Also remember that the adult attitude toward the child is a key factor in the difference between punishment and consequences. A helpful attitude is much different from an angry one and makes a child feel much differently about walking with the teacher. Of course, the way the child feels about the teacher in general also plays a part. Your relationship with each child is the foundation for any guidance or discipline approach.

CLEAR TEACHING GOALS

Living and working harmoniously in a group requires great mutual consideration and cooperation (DeVries & Zan, 1994). Related consequences can be very useful in helping children develop and remember these attitudes. Mrs. Jensen plans this part of her curriculum as carefully as the academic aspects. As she plans, she keeps in mind her goal of assisting the children's growth toward autonomy. She wants to give them freedom while helping them understand that freedom implies responsibility.

This responsibility includes not impinging on the freedom of others, such as the rights of other classrooms not to be disturbed. Mrs. Jensen's plans are also built around the principle of respect for each child, which she demonstrates through her belief in their ability and desire to behave responsibly. She firmly believes that all people, including children, have an equal claim to dignity and respect. She likes the way Dr. Seuss puts it in *Horton Hears a Who* (Geisel, 1954): "A person's a person, no matter how small."

Mrs. Jensen employs a variety of strategies to help her students determine the value of mutual consideration and cooperation. In addition to imposing related consequences, she also demonstrates desirable attitudes and behaviors through personal example. She makes sure that the class environment encourages harmonious social interaction, too. The best approach to guidance and discipline is usually a combination of approaches. Related consequences serve to help youngsters judge the pros and cons of a certain behavior as they experience the ramifications.

CAREFUL THOUGHT

Consequences must be selected carefully. Besides picking something related to the behavior, you need to think of a consequence that matters to kids. Telling them they have to hurry up or they'll be late may carry no clout if being late isn't important to the child. The consequence also needs to be something that you can live with and are actually willing to follow through with, unlike Joanne's threat below:

> The children kept running across the plot that had been rototilled for a garden at Midway Children's Center. They delighted in how the fluffy soil felt! The parent who had promised to build a fence to protect it kept putting off the job. Joanne tried steering the children away, telling them that the ground would get packed

COMPARING APPROACHES

You may find it helpful to compare punishment, natural consequences, and related consequences as they might be applied to a single behavior problem. Kids seem to love throwing sand, and teachers always get upset about it. They lecture endlessly about the dangers of sand in playmates' eyes. Here is how the different discipline approaches would look if Jimmie threw sand at Joshua.

Punishment

No doubt you have observed or experienced the punishment response to this behavior. There are many variations of punishment, ranging from sending Jimmie to the principal's office to having him miss recess for a week.

Natural Consequences

You probably would not see any adult deliberately use natural consequences for sand throwing, though such consequences certainly do occur accidentally. In this case, natural consequences might happen because you were unaware of Jimmie's behavior until Joshua or Jimmie got sand in his eyes. Then you could discuss what happened with them and help them relate the unpleasantness to the sand throwing.

Related Consequences

Related consequences involve adult intervention without anger or recrimination.

One type of related consequence, deprivation, is to remind Jimmie about the dangers of throwing sand and remove him from the sandbox until he thinks he can play without throwing sand. If he immediately goes back and starts throwing sand again, you need to impose a longer period away—such as the rest of the play period. Although it is preferable to encourage Jimmie to decide for himself when he is able to behave acceptably, some youngsters need guidance for such reflection.

Another type of consequence would also be appropriate if sand actually got into Joshua's eyes. Jimmie would be put in charge of helping Joshua go to the nurse's office, and then he would stay with Joshua while he got his eyes washed out. This would be a consequence of restitution. This experience should help Jimmie learn why throwing sand is dangerous.

down too hard to plant in, but they had no concept of the problem. As yet another group raced through the garden area, she gave up. Crossly, she told them, "That does it! We just won't have a garden if you step in there again!" Intimidated by her anger, the children avoided the tempting dirt for most of the afternoon.

Then Kenji blew it. Right before pickup time, he got carried away with a game of tag and tromped through the forbidden zone. A few minutes later, the parent volunteer arrived with an armful of tools to work on the fence. Kimberly piped up, "We don't need a fence anymore. We can't have a garden 'cause Kenji stepped in

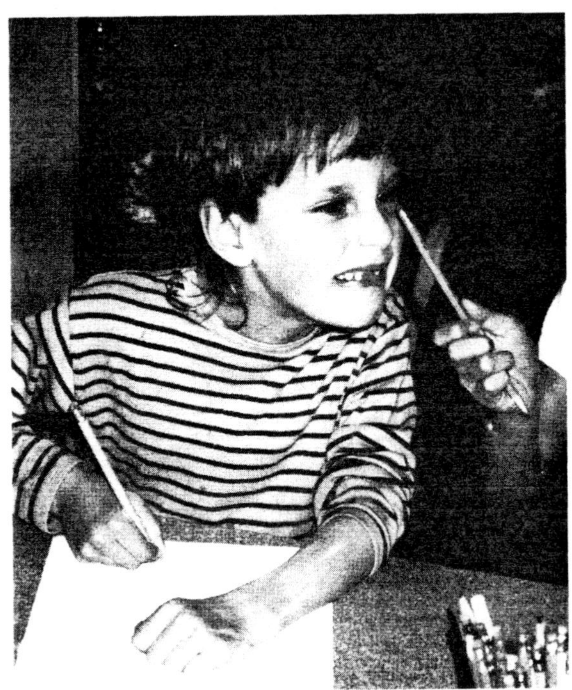
Selecting a consequence related to the action takes thought and understanding.

it!" Embarrassed, Joanne looked at the confused parent. She wondered how she could get out of this one. She really wanted to have a school garden.

CLEAR RELATIONSHIPS

Selecting a consequence related to the action takes thought and understanding. Many people misunderstand and misuse the term consequence. They impose totally unrelated outcomes on children's behavior and call them consequences. They don't realize that without the relationship between the action and the result, there is no learning involved; the result is merely punishment (Curwin & Mendler, 1988; DeVries & Zan, 1994).

Public school discipline guides often list a variety of punishments they call consequences: losing a recess for chewing gum, staying after school for talking back to a teacher, or doing push-ups for hitting someone. Totally unrelated to children's behavior, these punishments teach resentment, calculation of the risk of getting caught, and consideration of whether the benefits are worth the costs (Kamii, 1984). Gum chewing might have a reasonable consequence if there is a need to scrape gum off floors and desks. Discipline for talking back to a teacher or hitting someone should depend on the causes for those behaviors. No pat solution could address all the various sources of those behaviors. Discipline solutions are of questionable value if they are not based on the cause of the behavior as determined by information about the nature of the individual child, the particular situation, and the relationship between those involved.

APPLYING CONSEQUENCES

Mrs. Jensen frequently uses her experiences with her own children to guide her with her students. When she needs inspiration about how to apply related consequences at school, she reflects on the following successful use of them at home:

> Getting ready for school in the mornings had become an unpleasant ordeal. Mrs. Jensen not only had to get herself ready and out the door early, but she had four children who also had to get to school on time. If they missed the bus and she had to drive them, then she was late for work. It had happened once, and there were several other narrow escapes. The pressure of this situation was making her cross with the children as she hurried everyone along. It seemed that the more she tried to hurry them, the slower they moved. Her frustration was building, and her days were getting off to a bad start. Her children were leaving for school upset, too. She had to find a way out of this problem.
>
> How could she change the situation so that the children's behavior did not affect her personally? The part that was upsetting to her was the prospect of being late for work because of driving the children to their school. If only they lived close enough to walk when they missed the bus. The walk and their tardiness would be good learning experiences. But this natural consequence wasn't available because their school was ten miles away.
>
> However, the city bus route was within walking distance. Her children were experienced bus riders. Sure, it was a long, slow trip, probably involving a wait for the bus and assuring tardiness, but those were learning experiences, too. Mrs. Jensen thought the idea might work. She bought a roll of bus tokens and showed her children where they were. Then she explained that she simply couldn't be late for work and that they could take the city bus to school if they ever missed the school bus.
>
> What a relief! Mrs. Jensen could relax and be cheerful with her children in the mornings. She could make sure she left the house on time, but it was up to the youngsters to make certain they did. Sure enough, before long it happened. The four children dragged sadly back to the house after seeing the bus pull away. Their mother calmly reminded them where the bus tokens were as she left for work.
>
> The problem was the children's, not hers. She was not at all upset because she knew they would be fine. She was careful not to say, "I told you so." She merely waved as she drove off to work. That evening she could be truly sympathetic about how awful the long bus ride had been and how they felt about being tardy. However, she also sent the clear message that getting to the bus on time was their responsibility, not hers.

ALLOWING CONSEQUENCES TO HAPPEN

This learning experience worked so well at home that it has become a model for Mrs. Jensen at school. She uses the same principles and procedures when she applies reasonable consequences with her students. She withdraws from any power struggle and turns the responsibility over to the children. This plan helps her remain calm and pleasant. She knows that any anger on her part will ruin the consequences by turning them into punishment.

She used these guidelines to solve the problem of children not keeping track of their own crayons and scissors. She has classroom boxes for crayons, markers, and scissors. Any of these items found lying around after cleanup go into the boxes and become community property. Children are free to borrow them and use them, but they now belong to the class. The boxes solve several problems at once. They provide a place for the things that have been left out, a source of needed supplies, and an incentive for children to keep their own things put away. With this solution in place, Mrs. Jensen is able to turn the problem over to the children.

HELPING CHILDREN MAKE CONNECTIONS

Preschoolers may be somewhat less adept at linking cause and effect, but they are able to learn from related consequences. Dennis and Maureen know that they can use related consequences to help their students learn. Adults can assist children in thinking about cause and effect as well as about how their actions affect others. Therefore, experiences with related consequences are a valuable part of their preschool curriculum. As the following example shows, both teachers are careful not to ruin the learning experiences with sermons or scoldings.

> Colette and Leo were being too rough with Pinky the guinea pig. As the frightened creature squealed and tried to pull away, Colette grabbed its fur. Tufts of fur came out in her hand. Leo thought the tufts were neat and tugged off another bunch of fur. The teacher heard Pinky's cries and came to his rescue. As she examined his patchy coat, she decided he deserved a respite to recover. She moved his cage up out of the children's reach, explaining as she did so, "Pinky's hair has been pulled out, and I want him to have a chance to grow it back. He needs to be in a safe place for a while. After he gets better, and when you feel you can play gently with him, he can come back down."

Depriving the children of Pinky's company matches one of Piaget's recommended responses. Dennis finds that his young students respond to the inherent justice of such a consequence. They do not usually resent or rebel against a truly related outcome. Noting this fact, Dennis is challenged to think of the best possible consequences. Still, he keeps in mind that the behavior may be a symptom of another problem that needs attention.

COMBINING APPROACHES

Dennis wants to do more than merely stop the behavior; he wants to get at the cause as well. If the cause is simply that the child does not understand why an action is inappropriate, then consequences alone are sufficient. If the behavior is signaling an unmet need, as it may have when Sam hit Danny, that need must also be considered.

> When Sam was harassing and eventually hurting his friend Danny, Dennis stopped the escalating behavior by removing Sam—an exclusion consequence.

If he thought that Sam's behavior was a symptom of an unmet need for attention, Dennis could have helped Sam get that need met. If Sam had complained that Danny wasn't his friend anymore, Dennis could have listened reflectively to find out more. Maybe Sam just wanted a playmate, so Dennis could have coached him in ways to play cooperatively.

CONCLUSION

Natural and related consequences are ways of helping children construct moral rules and values by reflecting on their experience. Like teaching through example, teaching through experience is an extremely effective method. Of course, just the experiences themselves are not sufficient for learning. The child must reflect on the experiences and try to make sense out of them. It is this process of thinking about the experiences that results in learning. Children construct their own sense of right and wrong in this way. Moral rules that children construct from within are compelling to them, unlike rules that have been imposed by others. Children are best guided by their own understanding. Similarly, the values they construct for themselves are more likely to guide their actions.

Thus, consequences teach self-discipline. They not only help children take responsibility for their behavior at the time, but they also assist with the development of lifelong autonomous behavior. When you help children move toward autonomy, you work toward the ideals of a democratic society. Instead of being imposed by authority, order is maintained by each person for the benefit of all. When schools employ democratic principles and treat students according to those principles, students will rebel less and learn more.

FOR FURTHER THOUGHT

1. Observe an early childhood education program, watching for how often children experience the results of their actions and how often an adult protects them from those results. Are adults getting in the way of child learning, or are they merely protecting them as necessary?
2. Watch for situations in which making restitution would be the most educational consequence for inappropriate behavior. Are you quick to discover these situations, or is your thinking still locked in to more punitive approaches?
3. Practice planning and implementing related consequences. Do you have trouble thinking of actual relationships to the behavior? Is it hard not to use consequences as threats? Do you find times when there may be no real reason not to allow the behavior?
4. A problem to solve (use this chapter and the previous ones to help you): Chelsea knocked over Katie's block construction. Katie is yelling at Chelsea and threatening to knock down what Chelsea has built.
    a. Describe an appropriate related consequence.
    b. Describe other guidance approaches that might also be useful.
    c. Describe how this problem might have been prevented.

RECOMMENDED READINGS

Butchart, R. E., & McEwan, B. (1998). *Classroom discipline in American schools: Problems and possibilities for democratic education.* Albany, NY: State University of New York Press.

Dreikurs, R. (1964). *Children: The challenge.* New York: Hawthorne Books.

Greenberg, P. (1992b). Why not academic preschool? (Part 2): Autocracy or democracy in the classroom? *Young Children, 47*(3), 54–64.

Hendrick, J. (1992). Where does it begin? Teaching the principles of democracy in the early years. *Young Children, 47*(3), 51–53.

Kamii, C. (1982). Autonomy as the aim of education: Implications of Piaget's theory. In C. Kamii (Ed.), *Number in preschool and kindergarten* (pp. 73–87). Washington, DC: National Association for the Education of Young Children.

Piaget, J. (1965). *The moral judgment of the child.* New York: Free Press. (Originally published in 1932.)

9

CONTROLLING BEHAVIOR EXTERNALLY

In this chapter we will discuss the uses and abuses of Behaviorist theory for discipline. As explained in Chapter 1, our approach to guidance and discipline is based on Constructivist theory, a very different view. However, we recognize the validity of the basic premises of Behaviorism: Behavior that gets pleasant results is likely to be repeated. Behavior that gets unpleasant results probably won't be repeated. That is the natural response of both people and animals. This principle is used in training circus animals to perform, housebreaking a puppy, or getting laboratory rats to run a maze. Unfortunately, it is also widely used to control children's behavior. The method is called behavior modification: it sets up artificial reward systems designed to get children to behave in certain ways.

BEHAVIOR MODIFICATION

Behavior modification is based primarily on the research of Skinner (1965, 1971), who conducted experiments with laboratory animals, testing theories about using reinforcement to get rats and pigeons to perform, discontinue, or persist with specific actions. In looking for a "quick fix" to managing groups of children, schools have widely adopted and misapplied behavior modification to classrooms (e.g., Butchart & McEwan, 1998; Gordon, 1989).

PROTECTING CHILDREN AND ADULTS

The authors of this book are opposed to behavior modification as a discipline approach. We are convinced that praise, stars, stickers, tokens, and other behavior modification reinforcement systems are counterproductive to the development of self-discipline and autonomy.

Behavior modification does not teach children why certain behaviors are more desirable than others; instead, it uses rewards in attempts to coerce better behavior (e.g., Kohn, 1996). Coercion then replaces teaching as a means of changing children's behavior (Katz & McClellan, 1997). Performance based on rewards requires the presence of an authority figure who dispenses or withholds rewards; therefore, it is not consistent with the goal of autonomy. In addition, there is compelling evidence that rewards aren't even very effective in changing behavior; they may actually be counterproductive (Kohn, 1993).

We do not believe this method is a good way to elicit desired behavior and we will discuss our reasons later in the chapter. However, we think you need to understand how behavior modification works—because it does work. Even if you don't deliberately use the technique, it is an inevitable side effect of your interactions with others. It can work for you or against you. Your reactions are constantly affecting the behavior of others, just as their reactions are affecting your behavior. If the reactions are pleasant, chances are the person will repeat the action.

In Behaviorist terminology, the behavior has been reinforced. When you smile at what someone says, your action is a pleasant response. When you pay attention to what someone is doing, your interest, too, can be a rewarding response. Chapter 2 explains that the need for attention is a basic human need. It is easy to reinforce undesirable behavior accidentally if you don't know about reinforcement theory. Do the following examples seem familiar?

A. Have you seen an adult chasing after a runaway toddler? If so, you know the glee with which toddlers play this game. It is a lot of fun to have Dad or a teacher running after them and giving them so much attention. Of course, the attention encourages running away again.

B. What about adult laughter at a preschooler's rude or improper language? It may sound funny to hear such words come out of the mouth of an innocent child, but laughter as a response can unintentionally act as a reward and will ensure repetition of the inappropriate language.

C. Who tends to get the most attention from the teacher in a classroom? Is it the child who responsibly does what is asked or the one who never does? Is the teacher unconsciously rewarding the irresponsible behavior by paying attention to it?

You can more easily avoid these pitfalls if you understand how behavior modification works. It is essential to remember the link between the action and the reward. Rewards can take many different forms, depending on the person and the circumstance. Even a spanking may actually be a reward if it is the only way a child can get attention.

Close observation of children will help you discover what reactions a child finds rewarding. In the following example, Sheri and Maureen make an important discovery through observation.

> James had been making life difficult at the children's center. He was throwing tantrums regularly and often chose the block area to do it. If there was a structure standing there, he knocked it over. If the blocks were on the shelves, he pulled them all off. If they were on the floor, he scattered them and threw

them about. The staff had been trying hard to help him. They tried everything they could think of. Recently, they were implementing sanctions of reciprocity, but the method didn't seem to be working at all. James helped to clean up the mess he had made, but then he went and did it all over again. Clearly, a different approach was needed.

Sheri was watching him as he went through his block-scattering routine; she was trying to figure out what the teachers could try next. As she watched, she caught James glancing out of the corner of his eye to see if she was looking. Then Maureen came over and stopped the destructive behavior. While Maureen talked to James about the problem, she held him on her lap and rubbed his back lightly with her hand. James sat with a little smile on his face, not appearing to listen. Sheri thought the experience seemed to be a pleasant one for him. She began to think about the possibility that James was getting what he wanted through his disruptive actions. Later, she suggested that perhaps the staff had been unintentionally reinforcing James' tantrums.

The teachers made a new plan. The next time James began his inappropriate behavior, they left the area. No one paid any attention to what he was doing. Pretty soon he stopped and went over to join a group listening to a story. He seemed quite content and under control. His teachers were amazed. Always before, his tantrums had gone on and on while adults worked to calm him down. This time he had calmed himself down. It appeared that James got bored without an audience for his behavior. As the adults at the children's center continued to resist reinforcing his undesirable behavior, it disappeared.

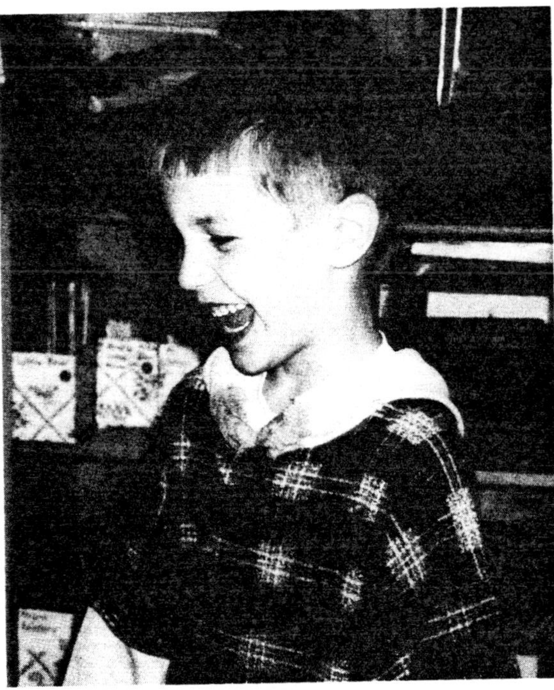

Giving children attention for misbehavior can make the problem worse.

This example demonstrates how *mislearning* occurs when an unproductive behavior is inadvertently reinforced. The child learns to use inappropriate behavior to get his needs met (Charles, 1996; Wolfgang & Wolfgang, 1995).

REINFORCEMENT THEORY

Understanding more about how behavior modification works will help you avoid having it backfire on you. Too many adults accidentally teach children to misbehave.

REWARDS

The pleasant or rewarding responses that encourage behaviors are called *reinforcers* or *rewards.* Reinforcement is generally divided into two categories: social and tangible rewards. Smiles, laughter, and attention are social reinforcers, as are a hug, a touch, or even eye contact. Words of praise are commonly used social reinforcers as well. Food is often used as a tangible reinforcer. Raisins, Cheerios, or M&Ms are handed out to children to reinforce certain actions. Seals prefer fish, and puppies like dog biscuits. Common tangible rewards used in school include stars, stickers, and smiley faces. Because older children are better able to delay gratification, behavior modification systems for them often include points or tokens, which can be accumulated and redeemed for prizes.

Social reinforcement is readily available and may occur without intent. Sometimes accidental reinforcement is fine, but at other times it isn't. Smiling at a child who has just helped a friend with her paint smock is a natural and harmless reinforcement. But the story of James' tantrums shows a situation in which accidental reinforcement causes problems, as do the examples of the runaway toddler, the rude preschooler, and the irresponsible student. It takes practice to become aware of when you are reinforcing negative behaviors. If you are attentive to the possibility, you can relax and feel free to otherwise interact naturally with children.

PUNISHMENT

Remember, there are two sides to behavior modification: the pleasant rewards and the unpleasant punishments. Chapter 10 focuses on punishment and explains its dangerous side effects. Most proponents of behavior modification emphasize the positive aspects and usually deny that punishment is used. However, any time a hoped-for reward is denied, it can feel like punishment.

> Miss Wheeler wanted to "motivate" Karin to finish her *Excel Math* worksheet on time. The girl always dawdled and just wouldn't stay focused. The teacher knew that Karin loved to use the math manipulative materials, so she said that if Karin got her sheet done by 10:30, she could join the advanced group working with the Unifix cubes. Enticed by the possibility, Karin worked diligently for ten minutes. But the deadly worksheets soon took their toll, and she started daydreaming as usual. Her wandering gaze settled on the table with the Unifix cubes. She began wondering if she could make them into a horse. Then she

remembered the time limit, glanced at the clock, and panicked: 10:27! She scrambled to finish the page, but it was hopeless. She'd blown it again! Discouraged, she thought, "I hate math!"

REINFORCEMENT SCHEDULES

Behavior modification research provides guidelines for the most effective ways of using reward and punishment: responses must be immediate, specific, and consistent (Charles, 1996). These guidelines are designed to demonstrate the relationship between the action and the result. If you want to use behavior modification, this information is essential to its effective use. Those of you who have trained puppies have used these principles.

Though Behaviorist theory considers immediate and consistent reinforcement to be essential for initially getting the desired behaviors, it does not recommend it for long-term use (Wolfgang & Wolfgang, 1995). Not only is it exhausting to constantly have to watch for a desired behavior and then immediately reward it, but it also works better to reduce the frequency of reinforcement gradually. Behavior modification research indicates that, once a response is established, unpredictable intervals between rewards have a longer lasting effect (Charles, 1996; Miller, 1996). This is called an *intermittent, variable reinforcement schedule:* You keep the behavior going the longest with the least amount of effort in this way. It also means you keep unwanted behavior going longer if you only give in to it occasionally.

Even though we don't recommend that you formally implement behavior modification, we think you should know that intermittent and variable reinforcement has the most lasting impact. This knowledge can save you from accidentally applying the principle to behavior you *don't* want. The parent who *usually* doesn't give in to her children's nagging or whining may, in fact, be teaching them to keep trying. If their behavior works sometimes, youngsters will be motivated to keep it up.

Similarly, the teacher who is trying hard not to reinforce attention-getting behavior may inadvertently be strongly encouraging it through intermittent variable reinforcement. It takes practice and self-control to follow through with a strategy of "planned ignoring" (Grossman, 1990). However, the following example shows that even young children can learn to ignore unwanted behavior. This is a use of behavior modification that we support; it aims at undoing a child's *mislearned* ways of getting attention.

Jonathan was playing photographer with a toy camera when Ross came up and tried to grab the camera from him. When Jonathan wouldn't give him the camera, Ross began to call Jonathan names, "You're a meany! Bully! Poop pants! You're a baby!"

Mrs. Jensen turned toward the noise and watched to see if her help would be needed. Would Jonathan be able to use one of the problem-solving approaches discussed and role-played at group time? Would the other children remember about not paying attention to someone disrupting their classroom?

As she watched, she was pleased to see that Jonathan ignored the name calling and simply moved to another place in the room and continued his play.

Mrs. Jensen also saw Ross look around and notice that none of the other children were paying attention to him. The teacher quickly made sure that she wasn't giving Ross her attention at that moment.

When Ross failed to get Jonathan involved in conflict and when no one else responded to his outburst, Ross went over to the rug and engaged himself with a book and a stuffed bear. Mrs. Jensen made sure to pay some attention to Ross later, asking him about the book he was looking at.

Mrs. Jensen also followed up with Jonathan. When she had an opportunity to speak to him privately, she said, "I noticed that you solved your problem with Ross by walking away when he grabbed the camera and called you names." Jonathan's proud expression showed that he knew he had managed the situation well.

IS BEHAVIOR MODIFICATION THE APPROACH FOR YOU?

Behavior modification apparently gets results, so why do so many child guidance books advise against it (e.g., Butchart & McEwan, 1998; DeVries et al., 2000; Kohn, 1996; Reynolds, 1996)? And why do so many teachers and parents refuse to use it as their discipline approach? The answers can be found in careful analysis of the system. They include the effect on autonomy as well as self-discipline and intrinsic motivation. Adults who reject reward and punishment to control children's behavior do so primarily out of concern for the child's long-term welfare.

Many adults are also personally uncomfortable with using their power to coerce someone with less power. To do so violates their value system and models a principle they reject (Greenberg, 1992a). The power involved may not be physical but rather the power of access to resources that children desire. Because this use of power is effective, the system of reward and punishment is a method of forcing children into compliance.

However, schools often focus on compliance and ignore the price paid in damaged relationships and apathetic minds (McEwan, 1998). Rather than working on the unique causes of individual children's behavior problems, many educators want to believe there is one "magic trick" to solve them all. The promises of behavior modification feed this illusion.

Some teachers use behavior modification techniques without question simply because that is what their teachers did when they were in school. Even though they may have hurtful memories of their own school discipline, and even though they may acknowledge that it wasn't useful for them, they perpetuate the system in their own teaching. The common practice of teaching as you were taught—not in teacher education classes, but as a child in school—testifies to the powerful influence of role models.

DOES IT TEACH AUTONOMY?

Moral autonomy means that a person will make decisions based on internally-constructed convictions about right and wrong (DeVries, 1999). A morally autonomous person will be respectful of others whether or not

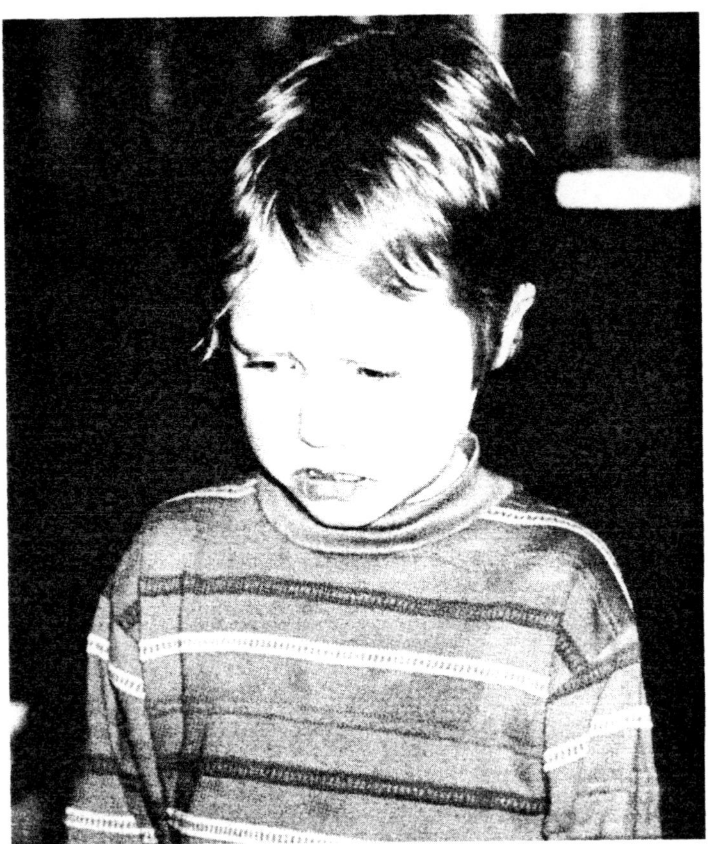

Trying to force children to behave appropriately denies them opportunity to learn self discipline.

someone in authority is watching. Both moral and intellectual autonomy require that a person be skilled in thinking about issues and coming to personal conclusions (Kamii, 1982). These skills require practice. Behavior modification eliminates the opportunity for practice with decision making or self-evaluation of behavior options (Reynolds, 1996). The person with the rewards or punishments is in charge, not the child. With behavior modification, the child's thinking centers around how to get the reward or avoid the punishment, not about what is right under the circumstances. Behavior modification creates *moral heteronomy,* which causes people to behave properly only when they think they will get caught if they don't.

> Moral qualities are not apt to be learned through techniques which are themselves of dubious moral value: manipulation, cajolery, punishment, bribery, and other "teacher tricks" (Butchart & McEwan, 1998).

By taking responsibility for the child's behavior, the adult denies the child the opportunity to learn by experience and by reflection on those experiences (Piaget, 1965). When adults are constantly in charge of children's behavior, the message to the children is that they are not capable of making good decisions for themselves. Their confidence in themselves as thinkers and decision makers is damaged (DeVries, 1999). Therefore, behavior modification creates both a lack of experience with making decisions and a lack of confidence to do so.

It is ironic that schools advocate teaching critical thinking and problem solving skills in academic subjects, but do just the opposite for social and emotional development (McEwan, 1998). This mix of incompatible approaches not only harms moral autonomy, it also counteracts the intellectual autonomy necessary for critical thinking. You cannot teach children to think for themselves about certain issues while simultaneously disempowering them in other areas (DeVries et al., 2000).

DOES IT ENCOURAGE SELF-DISCIPLINE?

With behavior modification, the teacher decides what the children should do and enforces that decision through reward or punishment. Many adults apparently think that children become self-disciplined by being bribed and coerced in this way. Actually, the opposite is true. When adults force children to behave appropriately, they deny children the opportunity to learn self-discipline. The hope of behavior modification is to make good behaviors a habit; however, the common result is to make reliance on external controls a habit (Kamii, 1982).

Making the decisions for youngsters takes away their chance to make the decisions for themselves. They have no opportunity to develop inner controls when adults are imposing external controls (Kohn, 1993). Young people who have been controlled by adults often have difficulty when they are old enough to be on their own. They don't know, or maybe don't care, what is right without the rewards. As soon as the rewards quit, the behavior quits.

HOW DOES IT AFFECT INTRINSIC MOTIVATION?

Intrinsic motivation means doing something for its own sake. The value lies in the behavior itself, and the reward is in how you feel about it: The reward is internal to you. Extrinsic motivation is the opposite; it means doing something for a reward. The value lies not in the behavior, but in what you get as a result of the behavior. The reward is external to you because it comes from someone else. Obviously, behavior modification relies on extrinsic motivation.

The relationship between self-discipline and intrinsic motivation is just part of the problem. Rewards can teach people to expect them and to perform only for them. Thus, the extrinsic motivation of rewards goes against the development of self-discipline and autonomy. Self-disciplined autonomous people don't behave appropriately only when a reward is offered. They have come to appreciate the value of learning appropriate behavior as a reward in itself. They recognize the natural benefits of positive interactions and making good choices.

Motivation Destroyed It is possible to destroy intrinsic motivation by rewarding behavior that a person was doing for personal satisfaction (Beyer, 1998; DeVries et al., 2000; Watson, 1999). Such a counterproductive result is another aspect of the problem with extrinsic motivation.

> Mandy was in third grade but loved to go to her old first-grade classroom and help. She would frequently offer to stay after school and help clean chalkboards or tidy up the shelves. Helping made her feel good, and it also made her feel grown-up. Miss Wheeler decided she should reward Mandy's helpfulness and began giving the girl a prize each time she came in to help. Somehow helping wasn't as much fun anymore, and Mandy went to Miss Wheeler's room less and less often. Neither the teacher or the girl understood the relationship between the rewards and Mandy's lessened enthusiasm.

In this case, Mandy's reaction to rewards caused her to discontinue her volunteer work. Sometimes extrinsic rewards do more critical damage. It is possible to override a child's joy in learning and change the focus to getting rewards. As Kohn (1993) says, "The more you want what has been dangled in front of you, the more you may come to dislike whatever you have to do to get it" (p. 83).

> Peige was an avid reader when she started first grade. She had been an early starter and had already read a great deal for her own pleasure. She frequently borrowed books from the classroom library to read at home, and her parents took her to the community library as well.

Competing for Stars

> Miss Wheeler was pleased with how much Peige read and wanted her other students to read more. She thought that it might help if she made a chart and put stars by each child's name for every book read. The children did like the stars and enjoyed seeing how many they could collect after their names. Competition developed among the better readers to see who could accumulate the most stars. Peige wasn't the only one who began looking for the smallest and easiest books so that she could read more books faster. She also wasn't the only one who began reading too hastily to know what the book was actually about. The focus had become winning and getting stars instead of enjoying reading.

Winners and Losers

> That was the outcome for the good readers. Youngsters who were less proficient readers were embarrassed by how few stars they had. Jimmie started pretending he had read books that Miss Wheeler knew he hadn't. Devon was more straightforward: One day he took a black marker and scribbled all over the chart. The chart had made him feel bad every time he saw it.

A Teacher Remembers

> When Miss Wheeler realized the results of her plan to encourage reading, she remembered an experience from her own school days. She remembered loving

to read in second grade and choosing to do so in much of her free time. When her teacher announced a contest to see who could read the most books before spring vacation, she decided she had to be the winner.

So, she read at recess time, she read at free time, and during all of her play time at home. It didn't take too long before she started to dislike reading. But she drove herself on because she was determined to win that contest. Her view was that if she wasn't the winner, she would be the loser. Well, she did win the contest but she lost her love of reading. She didn't begin reading for pleasure again until she was out of college.

It is a little-known fact that people who perform only for rewards perform at lower levels. This can explain much of the student apathy so observable in our schools: external controls cause students to become passive and to withdraw their interest and investment in learning. This is too often the price paid in the name of quiet, efficient, predictable classrooms (Beyer, 1998).

Rewards decrease performance Many studies have compared groups of people doing the same task, rewarding one group and not the other. Results are clear that those who were rewarded for their performance did less well than those who were not (Kohn, 1993). Rewards backfire in many ways. For instance, a program to help people stop smoking found that those who were given rewards for quitting were most likely to be smoking again in three months (Curry, Wagner, & Grothaus, 1991). Trying to get people to buckle their seat belts by giving them rewards had a similar negative impact (Geller, Rudd, Kalsher, Streff, & Lehman, 1987). Surprised? You probably are, which goes to show how much society has unquestioningly bought into a false premise.

A Guiding Principle Mrs. Jensen has a principle that guides her general use of extrinsic motivation and helps her avoid the problem Miss Wheeler had with her reading chart. She won't give rewards for anything that she hopes children will do for its own sake. Therefore, she doesn't give rewards for reading, because it can independently bring enjoyment and information. Additionally, she doesn't give rewards for being kind and caring: that behavior brings love and friendship. Instead, Mrs. Jensen helps youngsters tune in to the pleasures of reading and kindness themselves. She helps them find books they enjoy, with appropriate challenge. She also models respectful interactions so that children will learn them more readily.

There are some uses of behaviorism that Mrs. Jensen considers useful. One was for toilet training her own children. The age of the child involved and the nature of the desired behavior made rewards acceptable in that case. Another use is for "retraining" a child who has been reinforced with attention for inappropriate behaviors. Many children have learned that the best way to get attention is to do something to upset someone. This mislearning is best corrected by carefully withholding attention (ignoring) for undesirable behavior. We visualize this "undoing" the damage as like rewinding the video. Of course, you also have to be sure to meet the child's need for attention at other times.

DOES IT WORK ON THE CAUSE OF PROBLEMS?

As long as the cause of a behavior problem continues, any efforts to change the behavior can only be superficial. Like the weed whose roots live underground, the problem will pop back up again soon. Long-lasting approaches to change have to search for the cause and work on that cause. Behaviorist approaches focus on the symptoms instead of the cause (Kohn, 1996).

If a teacher has to use rewards to keep kids on task with the learning activities provided, the obvious question is, "Why?" Why aren't students interested or involved? Perhaps it is because the school work is boring (Butchart, 1998). That means putting some teacher energy into a more meaningful curriculum. Some teachers put their energy into making learning interesting and relevant. Others put their energy into bribing or threatening children to keep them on task. Which teachers do you think have students who learn the most?

Think about behavior modification and causes of behavior problems. If Kimberly behaves inappropriately because of missing social skills, does it help to put her name on the board? If unmet power needs cause Raymond to act out, does it help to send him to time-out? If a lack of understanding leads Ashley astray, does it help to deprive the class of a popcorn party?

HOW DOES IT AFFECT RELATIONSHIPS?

As we have said before, caring, mutually respectful relationships are an essential component of teaching desirable behavior (DeVries et al., 2000; Kamii, 1982; Piaget, 1965/1932). Rewards and punishment damage relationships (Blount, 1998; Kohn, 1996; Reynolds, 1996). You probably already knew that punishment damages relationships; after all, who wants to be around someone who hurts you? But, isn't getting rewards just the opposite? The answer is no.

Getting rewards means you are dependent on someone else to judge you worthy of getting something you want. This causes you to try to impress or flatter the person who gives rewards; this is not an honest relationship. Such an unauthentic relationship cannot foster the trust and genuine caring that inspire students to do their best. Even verbal judgments and rewards damage relationships (Gordon, 1970). In addition, the process of judging and rewarding is not respectful; it emphasizes the power and status differences between the person giving the reward and the person hoping to get one. Besides, if the authority figure withholds the reward, in essence the subordinates are punished by not getting it.

Relationships are damaged by the strict rule-bound discipline typical of behaviorist theory. Behavior modification programs lay out the rules and also the punishment for breaking a rule (Canter & Canter, 1992). This focus on the rules does not take into consideration the reason a rule was broken; therefore, the relationships and contexts for the behavior are ignored (Noddings, 1992). This model does not teach children sensitivity to the needs and concerns of others, since their own needs and concerns are not considered.

Mutual trust is essential to caring relationships, but the impersonal nature of a reward and punishment system damages children's trust in adults. Rather than caring and compassionate protectors, adults become feared authority

Rewards, as well as punishments, damage children's trust in adults.

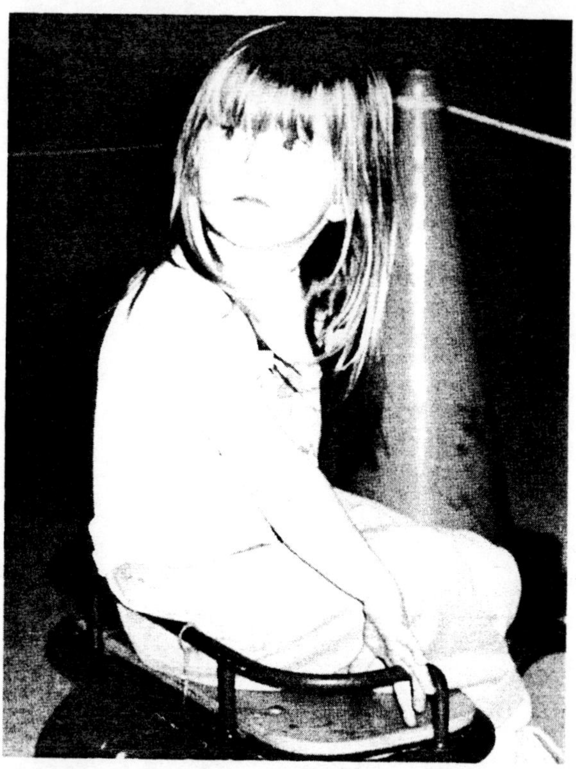

figures. The lack of trust goes both ways, as a teacher's use of such a management system implies adult mistrust of children as well. Teachers who believe that children want to be kind and cooperative will not feel the need for constantly monitoring and coercing children to do their bidding. Behavior modification is based on the belief that people will not do the right thing on their own (Beyer, 1998).

NECESSARY MOTIVATION

Having emphasized the importance of intrinsic motivation, we need to examine sources of motivation. The previous discussion implies that the only choices are intrinsic or extrinsic motivation. Yet there are many tasks and behaviors that are simply not intrinsically motivating. Does that mean we have to resort to extrinsic rewards?

Many people say, "What about the real world? Isn't it basically run by a system of rewards?" After all, who would go to work without getting paid? Isn't that extrinsic reward the reason you work? Maybe not. If you really like your job and are interested in what you do, the pay probably just makes it possible for you to follow your intrinsic motivation. It frees you from having to do something else to support yourself. If your work is boring or unpleasant, the reward of a paycheck is probably what Hymes (1990) called *necessary* motivation. You really do want and need food and shelter; therefore, you go to work. However, as stated earlier, people work less effectively if they work only for the payoff. Interestingly, paying according to the level of output ("merit pay") damages productivity the most (Jenkins, 1986).

Mrs. Jensen is aware that there are three kinds of motivation: intrinsic, extrinsic, and necessary. Many activities may not be pleasing in themselves, but they lead to goals that are. Therefore, they are done out of necessary motivation. Although teaching is intrinsically motivating to her, washing dishes falls into the "necessary" category for Mrs. Jensen. She doesn't like doing dishes, but she does appreciate a tidy kitchen. In this case, the clean kitchen provides necessary motivation. Mrs. Jensen tries to help students find such motivation for some dull tasks such as clean-up by focusing on a purpose for doing them. It is important to remember that the purpose needs to be the children's, not the teacher's.

COMMON FORMS OF BEHAVIOR MODIFICATION

Regardless of the criticism it receives, behavior modification is a tradition in the public schools. You have experienced it as a student, and you will see it as a teacher. We want you to recognize it when you see it so that you won't just go along with tradition, not realizing what you are actually doing.

REWARDS AND PUNISHMENT

You are probably most familiar with tangible rewards, such as Miss Wheeler's chart and stars. Your memories probably focus on how you felt about either getting or not getting the coveted rewards; you probably remember little about the actual purpose or content of the work. That fact is evidence of the damage done by rewards: they take attention away from what is truly valuable. Too often, schools take eager kindergartners who are excited about school and by the fourth grade transform them into bored students eager to escape school. This can partly be explained by the constant use of rewards in school: not only stickers and stars, but also popcorn parties, videos, awards, and (oh yes) grades (Kohn, 1996). Most children come to accept this system and believe that they need such help in order to do the right thing, as in the following example:

> Miss Wheeler's class coat area was a mess! The coats were all over the floor instead of on the hooks, and the boots and gym shoes were strewn everywhere. It took forever for children to find their own boots or gym shoes. Miss Wheeler decided to have a class meeting about the problem.
>
> She asked her students for ideas about what to do. The ideas ranged from punishment to reward: "Make us stay in from recess if our boots aren't where they belong," or "Give us candy if we clean it all up nice." These were the only options the children knew as their ideas were based on their experience. No one was able to think of problem-solving approaches or ways to help themselves be more responsible. Most already had experienced behavior modification discipline in kindergarten and preschool before getting to first grade.

Given the choice between reward and punishment, the children naturally chose the reward. Miss. Wheeler felt intuitively that something was wrong with giving children candy for organizing the coat area, but she didn't have a better idea, either. So, the children scurried around and tidied up, and Miss Wheeler got out her stash of reward candy. Of course, the boots, shoes, and coats were in the same mess the next day.

As we have said before, not getting a hoped-for reward is a form of punishment. Not getting candy when others do is sure to devastate a young child. It can also feel like punishment when the teacher says she likes how other kids are sitting, but she doesn't say your name when you are sitting nicely. Punishment may come in the form of not having your picture chosen for the display of good work, and it can come from being embarrassed by a public correction when you get confused about the rules. Many teachers who don't think they use punishment have students who feel punished. The nature of an authoritarian structure, with the powerful adult doling out approval or disapproval, sets up punishment situations.

Some teachers fool themselves into thinking they aren't punishing, but that children have made a choice. They say to a child who has not conformed to a rule, "I see you have chosen to give up your free time today." Or they will give a child a "choice" between two undesirable things, such as finishing the worksheet now or missing recess. These are not choices because they are not freely chosen; they are inherently dishonest ways of trying to cover up the teacher's power to punish. Despite Behaviorist assertions to the contrary (Canter & Canter, 1992), such false choices do not teach responsibility, but rather breed all the negative outcomes associated with punishment described in Chapter 10.

TIME-OUT

Time-out is a pervasive school tradition. It is often used as a behavior modification technique and considered an improvement over the old stand-in-the-corner punishment. In actuality, there is often little difference between the two (Katz & McClellan, 1991). An analysis of the various ways in which time-out can be used may help you understand the differences between Behaviorist and other approaches to discipline.

Joanne prides herself on her discipline during morning circle at Midway Children's Center. When all the children are on their designated rug scraps in their circle spots, she begins singing, "I like the way that Christie sits; she's got her legs crossed, and her hands are in her lap. I like the way that Ling Ling sits; she's got her legs crossed, and her hands are in her lap. I like the way that Ashley sits; she's got . . ." until all the children are dutifully in position. Then she begins the "educational" presentation part of her circle program. If children get out of position, she says, "I need your whole body's attention, and you can't do it that way. Please sit up crisscross-applesauce style!" Some children continue to resist the rigid posture.

Time-out is not much better than the old stand-in-the-corner punishment.

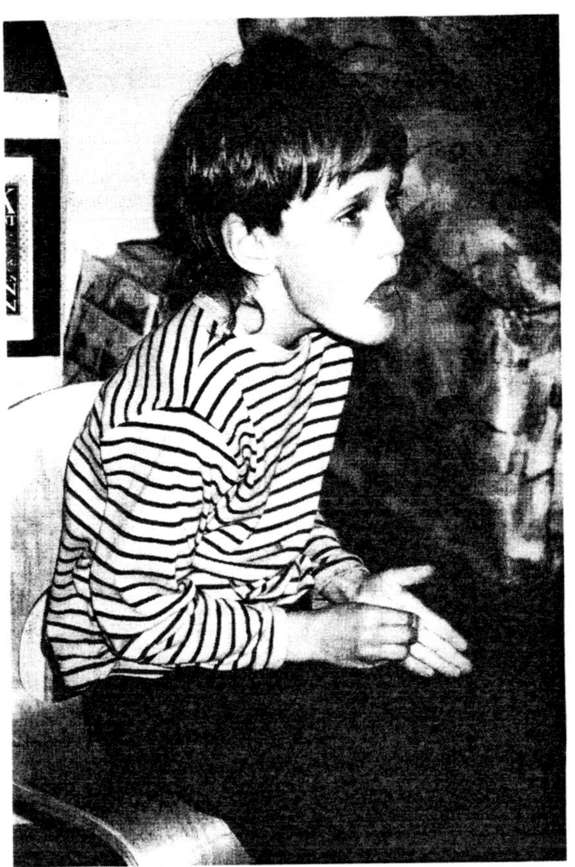

Joanne's firm rule is that the second time they get out of position, youngsters are sent to a time-out chair for the remainder of circle time. Sheri, the aide, usually has her hands full supervising the time-out chairs by the end of Joanne's "well-behaved" circle time. She wonders if this behavior modification approach is really working. The same kids are in those chairs almost every day, and the same few get the daily dose of praise. It sure doesn't seem to be teaching them anything.

Maureen uses a different approach to a similar problem, with more emphasis on self-regulation and less on external control.

Maureen's story-time before lunch has looser seating requirements. But even though children can sit where and how they please, there are still problems. Children get in each other's way or quarrel over who sits by whom. If their disagreements escalate into shoving and whining, Maureen tells them, "It's too hard for me to read while you're not getting along (an "I message"). I can see you are upset with each other (reflective listening). You need to go to the calming chairs in the other room until you can calm down enough to talk to each other about your problem. When you are ready to come back and listen to the story, you may." Maureen views time-out as a related consequence of children's failure to behave appropriately during an activity. Her term for the place, *calming chairs*, shows what she expects of their occupants. She leaves it up to the children to decide when they are capable of trying to be part of the group again—a critical feature separating consequences from punishment.

Dennis gives children a choice of not only when to return to the group, but when to leave, too. His approach gives youngsters the most control over their own behavior and helps them learn to self-monitor their feelings and needs.

Dennis knows the kids can be tired and irritable at the good-bye gathering at the end of the day. If a child is having a particularly hard time getting along with his friends during this time, Dennis sometimes asks, "Might you feel better in a place by yourself for a while? Where could you go to get some alone time?" If the child does take him up on it, Dennis is sure to add, "Come on back whenever you feel like it!" Dennis recognizes when children are too upset or tired to be in a group. He helps them learn that time alone can help them get in touch with their feelings and gain control of themselves. He thinks that the most productive time-out is one you give yourself.

Mrs. Jensen uses yet another approach to help children get their cool-down and privacy needs met. She encourages her students to decorate a designated private space in the classroom, to make it a cozy and inviting place to go when anyone feels upset. Most years, children put cushions on the floor, take stuffed animals and books there, and put pretty posters or drawings on the wall. Mrs. Jensen helps children view this spot as a safe haven where they can choose to go when they need to be alone. She also makes sure that her students get help in dealing with their feelings.

ASSERTIVE DISCIPLINE

A program called *assertive discipline* (Canter, 1976) is one example of how behavior modification has been interpreted in classrooms. Although it is a misinterpretation that violates many basic Behaviorist principles, it does come from that base. This program recommends a series of reward and punishment systems designed to gain student compliance.

Miss Wheeler had just completed a summer training course in assertive discipline. She had watched the course videos and filled out the worksheets. Now she was excited to try it out. The authors, Lee and Marlene Canter, promised a well-behaved classroom if she followed the rules. She was all prepared to write names on the board and put marbles in a jar.

On the first day of school, Miss Wheeler clearly told the children her firm rules. She began by telling them what she wanted. They were to sit in their seats until they had permission to get up. They were to follow directions the first time they were given. They were to raise their hands and wait to be called on before they spoke. The list went on.

Next, she told them what would happen when anyone disregarded the rules. For a first infraction, the student's name would be put on the board. For a second failure, the name would get a check mark by it, and the child would stay in for the first five minutes of recess. A second check mark meant the student would lose the whole recess. Anyone who received more than two check marks would have his or her parents called. (She didn't tell the children that the course had recommended that she make a point of calling the parents at work to be sure to embarrass them.)

On the bright side, Miss Wheeler said that whenever the whole class was following the rules nicely, she would drop a marble in a special marble jar. When the jar was full, they would have a popcorn party!

Kaila was worried. She said, "But I'm allergic to popcorn." Miss Wheeler decided to use the girl as an example, saying, "You didn't raise your hand before you talked, Kaila. So I will put your name on the board to help you remember to do that." Pleased with herself for having used the opportunity to illustrate the system of consequences, Miss Wheeler went on with her classroom orientation. But Kaila wasn't listening to the detailed descriptions of how to use classroom centers properly: only one book from the shelves at a time, and so on. Kaila just kept staring at her name on the board, flushed with embarrassment.

Delighted when her table was dismissed to the reading center, Kaila eagerly skipped over, taking three attractive books off the shelves and nestling into the beanbag chair to decide which one to read first. She had settled on *Frog and Toad Together,* one of her favorites from home, when she saw Miss Wheeler's feet next to where she had put down the other two books. "Who took more than one book off the library shelf?" the teacher demanded. "Kaila did it!" tattled Simon. He had learned her name off the board. Miss Wheeler looked down at the girl and reprimanded, "Kaila, because you didn't follow the instruction of one book at a time, you have chosen to have a check mark by your name. We need to follow instructions after hearing them once, and I told you the library limits this morning. You will lose part of recess now. You can use the time to think about the rules of our classroom."

Miss Wheeler caught the group's attention as she checked Kaila's name, saying, "I'm sorry, but we all need to work on remembering the rules. Maybe you can help Kaila learn so we can start getting marbles in the jar." Several children frowned at Kaila and she squirmed. She hated Miss Wheeler and her dumb rules. She hated school!

Like other forms of behavior modification, assertive discipline only deals with surface behaviors; it does not consider the child's feelings or the cause of behavior problems (Gartrell, 1987a; Hitz, 1988). Additionally, this approach doesn't consider maturation stages and the behaviors inherent in each. It uses power to gain compliance and ignores child development. Perhaps most damaging, it uses humiliation as a component of punishment, seriously damaging self-esteem. "The pain is forever!" wrote one college student, who became upset reading about assertive discipline and remembering how it felt to have her name on the board as a child. Twenty years after experiencing it, she couldn't discuss the system without crying.

Group rewards, as in popcorn parties for marbles, also do serious damage to children. Kohn (1993) calls this "one of the most transparently manipulative strategies used by people in power." He also says it "calls forth a particularly noxious sort of peer pressure" (p. 56). It isn't too difficult for children to figure out that they are being deprived because of the behavior of another child. This system doesn't harm only the child who is always in trouble and who is therefore subjected to anger from classmates. The other youngsters are being used as the punishing force and therefore are embroiled in a negative classroom community. They are learning to be judgmental and punitive rather than caring and helpful to others.

PRAISE OR ENCOURAGEMENT?

Praise is another form of behavior modification. Teachers and parents are often told to praise children for desirable behavior. It is common to hear teachers make these kinds of statements: "I like how Shelley is sitting so straight and quiet." They hope to make Shelley feel good and to make other children want to be like her. Often, it just makes the others resent Shelley as they hear the unspoken message, "Why aren't the rest of you as good as Shelley?" Even young children quickly learn to see through this type of insincere and manipulative comment. "I'm proud of you" is an even more dangerous type of praise because it is likely to make children dependent on you in order to feel okay (Kast & Conner, 1988).

Praise is a type of reward. It has the same uses and the same side effects as other forms of behavior modification (Kohn, 1996). Certainly, it has the same effects on performance, self-esteem, moral autonomy, self-discipline, and intrinsic motivation as any other reward system. This is probably hard for you to believe, as most people have bought into the idea that we are supposed to praise children. However, there is compelling evidence that praise not only is counterproductive in increasing desired behaviors (Grusec, 1991), but actually has a negative influence even on self-esteem.

How can it make people feel less good about themselves to have someone tell them they are smart or pretty or capable? Think about the importance of unconditional love for self-esteem and then think about praise: Praise doesn't say "you are important and lovable because you are you." Instead it says, "I approve of you *because* you are smart or pretty or capable." Also think about the flip side of the praise coin: If a person judges you wonderful today, that same person can make a different judgment tomorrow. Instead of making kids feel confident, praise makes them insecure and fearful of rejection (Kanouse, Gumpert, & Canavan-Gumpert, 1981).

Praise is often recommended as a tool for guidance and discipline, and most people consider it positive and helpful. Few seem to have considered that praise is an external judgment about another person (Katz & McClellan, 1997). When you praise someone, you are setting yourself up as an authority who knows what is best. This attitude implies that you are able to evaluate others' performance better than they are. The message can make children

PRAISE VERSUS ENCOURAGEMENT

Praise	Encouragement Alternatives
I'm proud of you.	I noticed that you helped Zeth with his coat. You got all the books back in their places. You did it! It looks like you're feeling good about that.
Good work!	How did you figure that out? What did you do to make it work? The end of your story made me laugh. I see you used a lot of purple paint. It looked like you enjoyed doing that.
I like how Shelly is waiting quietly	Thank you for your patience.

dependent on others to tell them whether or not they are doing well. It keeps them from judging for themselves and developing autonomy. It is also condescending because it implies a power imbalance; rarely does a lower status person praise a higher status person. Would you tell your boss you are proud of her?

GIVING ENCOURAGEMENT

So, what can you say to kids? Should you never say another nice thing? You can learn to give positive verbal feedback that is not judgmental by substituting comments that help children learn to self-evaluate and self-congratulate. Instead of telling them what *you* think about their accomplishments, you can help children identify their own feelings of pride or success. We want to convey interest, appreciation and respect, but not impose our judgment on children.

For example, instead of giving your opinion, saying something like "You did a nice job" or "I'm proud of you," you could put more energy into the process and describe what it is you saw the child do. You could say, "I saw you share the doll buggy with Devon. That made her happy." You don't need to tell the child that she is generous or kind, it is better for her to draw that conclusion for herself (Faber & Mazlish, 1996).

Giving information without evaluating is a useful alternative to praise (Brophy, 1981). This might mean commenting, "You got all the blocks put away in their right place," instead of "What a good worker you are." This example also takes the focus away from praising the person and emphasizes the behavior (Kohn, 1996). In addition, it is specific rather than general and

Praise can make children dependent on others to judge the value of their work. It inhibits self-evaluation and self-confidence.

therefore provides more information. Describing what a child did also requires you to pay more attention to the child than is required for a judgment such as "Good job!" Children recognize and appreciate the difference.

Notice the shift from external adult judgment to helping children think about and evaluate their own behavior. This type of positive feedback is often called *encouragement* rather than praise (Hitz & Driscoll, 1988). Others refer to it as *descriptive praise* (Faber & Mazlish, 1996). What you call it doesn't matter, but the effects on children do matter. Comments that focus children's attention on their own judgment of personal behavior helps children feel good about what they have done without damaging their autonomy. If it is a private statement to the child rather than a public statement to the class about one child's performance, it is less likely to be manipulative.

Teachers who model honest communication are more likely to get it from their students. *Honesty* is the key word here. Honest expressions of admiration are quite different from praise given to manipulate someone's behavior. As you work to reduce your use of praise, focus first on stopping manipulative praise, especially that which puts kids into competition with one another.

Using Effective Communication It might be helpful to think about praise and encouragement in relationship to the communication skills described in Chapter 7. Praise is another of the "roadblocks to communication" described by Gordon (1970, 1989). In contrast, encouragement can be a form of reflective listening. This type of encouragement responds to the message sent by what a child says or does. If Blake calls you over to look at his block tower, you can tell by his expression that he is pleased with himself. Reflective listening and encouragement respond to that message about his own feelings. "It looks like you feel big for making such a big tower" tunes in to the child's feelings rather than judging what he has done.

Positive "I messages" are a form of encouragement also. For instance, when a child does something helpful for you, a sincere "thank you" gives a more respectful message than praise for the behavior. On the surface, "thank you" may not sound like an "I message," and "I'm proud of you" may sound like it is. Analysis of the two statements, however, reveals just the opposite. "Thank you" actually tells your feelings and means "I appreciate what you have done." Remember not to think that any statement starting with *I* is an "I message." The statement "I'm proud of you" really is a judgment of the other person. If you decide you do want to give a value judgment, think about what you say to children in comparison to what you would say to an adult acquaintance. Then you might decide that "Congratulations," "WOW!" or "I'm impressed" is more respectful than "I'm proud of you."

CONCLUSION

Behavior modification happens whether you plan it or not. Understanding how it works can help you keep it from working against you. Recognizing that many common discipline systems are artificial forms of behavior modification can help you make more informed decisions about your own discipline plans. Thinking about the negative effects of behavior modification can help you decide whether to implement it purposefully or not. This chapter has explained why manipulative behavior modification ultimately tends to be counterproductive. It has also discussed why the manipulative aspects of rewards and praise are not compatible with a relationship of mutual respect. Such respect is crucial to the type of human relationships that nurture the development of autonomy. If autonomy and self-discipline are your long-term goals, you do not want to use behavior modification approaches to discipline.

FOR FURTHER THOUGHT

1. Think about things you do only because of the payoff or reward as opposed to those things you do purely for your own purposes. Which things do you put more effort into and get more pleasure from? What are the implications for education?
2. Observe in a classroom, watching for the focus of the teacher's attention. Is inappropriate behavior or desirable behavior more apt to get attention? What are the consequences for child behavior?
3. Closely observe your own interactions with children. Do you accidentally reinforce undesirable behavior? What can you do to focus more on the desirable?
4. Talk to children about the stars and stickers they get for school performance. Do the children focus on the learning or on the prizes? How do you think getting rewards affects a child's education and attitude about learning?

5. A problem to solve: Courtney finally wrote something in her journal today instead of just drawing in it: a major breakthrough!
   a. If you were using praise to motivate her, what might you say?
   b. If you were using encouragement to keep her going, what might you say?
   c. How are the two approaches and their goals different?
6. What's wrong with a teacher putting a marble into a jar when the class is especially cooperative, and then letting the class have a party when the jar is full?
7. How does the traditional approach to time-out differ from a related consequence?

RECOMMENDED READINGS

Butchart, R. E., & McEwan,B. (1998).*Classroom discipline in American schools: Problems and possibilities for democratic education.* Albany, NY: State University of New York Press.

Canter, L. (1988). Assertive discipline and the search for the perfect classroom. *Young Children, 43*(2), 24.

Hitz, R. (1988). Assertive discipline: A response to Lee Canter. *Young Children, 43*(2), 25–26.

Hitz, R., & Driscoll, A. (1988). Praise or encouragement? New insights into praise: Implications for early childhood teachers. *Young Children, 43*(5), 6–13.

Kohn, A. (1993). *Punished by rewards.* New York: Houghton Mifflin.

Kohn, A. (1996). *Beyond discipline: From compliance to community.* Reston, VA: Association for Supervision and Curriculum Development.

10

PUNISHMENT VERSUS DISCIPLINE

Society is gradually coming to recognize the negative effects of punishing children physically (Williams & Shaps, 1999). For example, spanking or slapping children is outlawed in most schools today (Simmons, 1991). However, many other types of punishment are still commonly used to control and direct students. Although this chapter examines various forms of punishment and their negative effects on children, this book is primarily about alternatives to punishment. Chapters 4 through 8 explained how and why other approaches work far better. In those chapters, we explained which causes indicate the approaches described there. However, we do not accept punishment as an appropriate treatment for any cause of misbehavior.

Punishment is intended to hurt or humiliate a person in response to undesirable behavior; its goal is to make a person pay for misconduct (DeVries, Hildebrandt, & Zan, 2000; Piaget, 1965/1932). Emotional pain is often more intense and lasting than bodily harm. You may have personal memories of intense embarrassment about being banished to the hallway for an offense. You might still be able to feel your childhood despair and frustration at being denied an eagerly awaited outing after an infraction of the rules. Or perhaps your worst memory of school is the shame and anger you felt from a teacher's sarcastic put-down. These are all punishments.

RESULTS OF PUNISHMENT

Most people who use punishment believe it will improve behavior. In fact, it can appear to stop the undesirable behavior because punishment may force negative behaviors "underground" (e.g., Butchart & McEwan, 1998; Straus, 1991). This quick result convinces many people that punishment is effective. However, extensive research proves that punishment is not an effective way of correcting behavior (e.g., Bredekamp & Copple, 1997; Dodge, Bates, & Pettit, 1990; Sabatino, 1991). It is clear that punishment does not improve

PUNISHMENT

Punishment does not appear to improve behavior. Even if the action being punished does stop for the moment, worse behavior is almost sure to follow. Punishment creates seriously counterproductive feelings that are demonstrated in numerous ways.

behavior. Even if the action being punished does stop for the moment, worse behavior is almost sure to follow. Punishment creates seriously counterproductive feelings that are demonstrated in numerous ways.

ANGER AND AGGRESSION

Anger is a common reaction to punishment. Children who are punished have a need to get even, to assert their own power after having been the victim of someone else's power. Because anger tends to be expressed as aggression, children often vent their anger by hitting and hurting others. The negative feelings inside these angry children inevitably surface. Having experienced punishment, they have learned from a powerful role model how to give punishment (Dodge, Bates, & Pettit, 1990; Putallaz & Heflin, 1990). Children who have been hit when they have displeased a big person are very likely to hit a smaller person who displeases them. This is very clear in the following example where Scott seems to be echoing an adult as he tries to justify hitting Ben:

> Five-year-old Scott and three-year-old Ben are working side-by-side with some magnets. Scott decides he wants the magnet that Ben has and tries to take it. Ben resists by running away from the bigger boy, clutching the precious magnet. Scott chases after Ben, catches him, and hits him to get him to relinquish the magnet. As Sheri comforts the sobbing Ben, Scott keeps saying over and over, "He didn't pay attention. He didn't pay attention."

Children who experience other forms of punishment tend to be physically aggressive, too (Vissing, Straus, Gelles, & Harrop, 1991), and they will have also learned other methods of getting even. These youngsters might call other children names, ruin their work, or take their possessions. Such unacceptable behavior is then likely to be punished, creating further misbehavior. This negative cycle is behind the behavior of many "bad kids." Unfortunately, many parents use punishment as discipline at home (Springen, 2000). The teacher then has to deal with the results at school.

> Mrs. Jensen chose her words carefully as she shared her concerns about Raymond with his parents at their conference. "When Raymond doesn't like what someone else is doing, he often hurts them." Looking concerned, his mother said, "Oh, dear. What does he do?" Referring to her observation notes, Mrs. Jensen described an incident. "When he didn't like a classmate's singing, he told her to quit it. She did for a while but started up again. Raymond hit her

Punishment can teach youngsters to use aggression to get their own way.

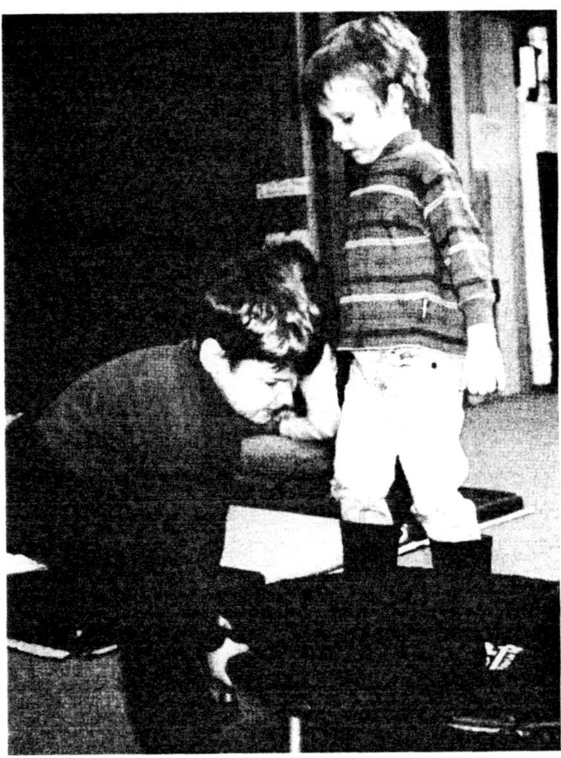

and said, 'I told you not to do that!' He usually says that right after he hurts someone." A flash of recognition came across the mother's face. She knew where he got that line! And the hitting, too! She glanced accusingly at her husband. He retorted, "That sounds like a normal kid thing."

The father questioned Mrs. Jensen, "What do you do to him when he hits?" The teacher explained how she generally handled the situations, with attention to the hurt child and modeling alternative ways for Raymond to get what he needs. Raymond's dad leaned back in his chair and said knowingly, "Yeah, well, that soft-touch stuff just doesn't work with this kid. You have to tell him not to do something and then just don't let him do it! Giving him a quick wallop works at home." The mother stared intently at the pattern on the carpet, trying to avoid both the teacher's and her husband's eyes.

Mrs. Jensen could tell she had touched on a sensitive area with this couple. Still, she was glad she had brought it up. She promised to keep them updated on Raymond's progress. In the meantime, she had some new insight about why Raymond was exhibiting such physically aggressive responses; it seemed he was following his father's model.

DAMAGED RELATIONSHIPS

Punishment also creates feelings of hostility and resentment toward the person administering it (e.g., Faber & Mazlish, 1996; Gordon, 1989; Thompson, 1998). This result is particularly serious when it damages relationships between children and their parents. Whether the negative feelings are aimed at parents, teachers, or other authority figures, those emotions get in the way of positive discipline teaching. People don't want to be around someone who hurts them or makes them feel bad. Certainly, no one is eager to listen to, or learn from, that person. Some children merely withdraw from contact, and others try to get even. Getting even takes many forms, depending on the experiences and the personality of the child. One child may be openly defiant and rude, and another may retaliate through helplessness and refusal to try anything. Still another may become a bully, using smaller children as substitute targets. All of these behaviors are self-defeating, and all are only made worse by punishment. It isn't only relationships with punishers that are damaged; children who are punished tend to have trouble with peer relationships also (e.g., Hart, Olsen, Robinson, & Mandleco, 1997; Putallaz & Heflin, 1990). Because these youngsters use aggression to get their way, other children don't want to play with them. Being rejected for hitting or shoving truly confuses the child who has been punished; their experiences of being punished teach children that hurting is an appropriate response to not getting their way. They erroneously believe that their aggressive behaviors will have positive social outcomes. All too often these youngsters end up as social outcasts, exhibiting escalating antisocial behaviors in retaliation.

DAMAGE TO SELF-ESTEEM

Punishment also damages self-esteem because children get their opinion of their worth from how others treat them (Miller, 1996). Being punished can convince youngsters that they are inferior (DeVries, 1999) and that they are bad (Vissing, Straus, Gelles, & Harrop, 1991). Feeling like a worthless or bad person is likely to become a self-fulfilling prophecy, resulting in further undesirable behavior. Many children routinely experience verbal abuse at home, internalizing the labels such as "stupid," or "damn brat" and acting accordingly. A child who is verbally or physically punished does not feel respected or valued. Any kind of punishment attacks personal dignity by putting the child at the mercy of a more powerful person. Additionally, many punishments are humiliating, as shown in the following example:

> "Beep! Beep! Beep! Beep!" sounded the intercom, as the library light kept flashing. The secretary had two people on hold on the telephone and new parents at the counter needing forms. She switched on the speaker, "Yes, this is the office." The librarian sounded distraught. "Ian bit Serge and then ran out of the room. He's somewhere in the halls, and I can't leave the group to go find him." The secretary responded, "Sorry, but I'm the only person in the office, so I can't go look for him right now." Leaning by the message board, the custodian overheard the exchange. He volunteered, "I'll go get him." Relieved, she called the library back and said, "George is going to go look for Ian. I'll let you know when we find him."
>
> The custodian strode down the hall on his mission to bring in the wayward child. Not finding him on the first floor, he went upstairs. Still failing to see the

> boy, he checked the playground. Darn it, he needed to go set up the lunchroom soon. Where was that kid? Then he thought of the bathroom. Sure enough, there were two feet standing in the back corner of a stall. "Come on out!" ordered George. The boy froze, wondering if the custodian could see him. "Come out now!" he repeated. The other boys in the bathroom giggled as George crouched to look under the door and demanded, "Move it!" Ian slowly opened the stall door, his eyes darting around like those of a trapped animal. His mind raced as his playmates, Alex and Tory, teased him about being caught.
>
> Once outside the bathroom, George scooped Ian up like a bag of potatoes. He hauled the boy past the library while the child flailed and demanded to be put down. His classmates crowded to the door to glimpse the spectacle. Humiliated, Ian's temper flared. He pounded on the back of George's leg, but the custodian just held him more tightly and headed for the office, proud to have successfully completed his mission. Dumping Ian in the detention room, George announced, "Here's your biter!" Ian felt about one foot tall as the custodian described the bathroom scene to the secretary. And Ian noted that the woman listening at the counter was his friend Kenji's mom. Ian wished he were invisible!

Unfortunately, this disrespectful treatment of children is not uncommon. The damage to a child's self-respect is immeasurable. The idea of mutual respect between adult and child is the absolute opposite of this scenario.

FEAR

Punishment controls through fear (Curwin & Mendler, 1990). This fear keeps some children from positive activities as well as negative ones. When they are punished without warning for something they didn't know was unacceptable, many children will tend to avoid any new activity. Their strategy is to use caution about anything that might possibly get them into trouble. Exploration and initiative are sacrificed to the need for safety and security. Therefore, fear of punishment can hamper academic learning. Remember Kaila in the assertive discipline example in Chapter 9? Scared of check marks on the board by her name and of classmates who blamed her for not getting marbles in the jar, Kaila rarely initiated conversation or joined activities. The following example of Zeth and the broken bracelet shows the results of a different approach:

> Zeth's face showed surprise as he held the two pieces of what had been Nelowa's bracelet, and Mrs. Jensen could see that he had not purposely broken it. Mrs. Jensen acknowledged Nelowa's concern and accepted Zeth's protests of an "accident." She encouraged each child to hear the other's side of the story.
>
> That evening, Mrs. Jensen called Zeth's parents and explained what had happened. She made it very clear that Zeth had not been "naughty," just clumsy in examining the bracelet. She discussed the concept of making restitution and asked if they thought they could help Zeth figure out a way to make it up to Nelowa for her loss.
>
> A few weeks later, Zeth arrived at school and handed a delighted Nelowa a package with a small assortment of child-size bracelets. It had taken Zeth those weeks to earn the money, buy the bracelets, and wrap them up to give to

Nelowa. Mrs. Jensen knew that Zeth's heartfelt "You're welcome!" to Nelowa's "Thank you!" could never have been the result of punishment. Zeth understood the significance of his carelessness, but he felt good about himself for making things right. He saw himself as a good boy, not a bad one.

Sadly, many adults who were themselves punished, and suffered from the results, nevertheless use punishment to control children in their care. They may realize that it harmed them, but that model has been strongly imprinted on them (McEwan, 1998).

MISSED OPPORTUNITY FOR LEARNING

Punishment actually undermines children's learning about appropriate and inappropriate behavior. Instead of youngsters thinking about the behavior that caused the problem, they end up thinking resentfully about the punishment. Punishment also focuses attention on what *not* to do rather than teaching what *to* do. Young children need information about acceptable ways of behaving, and they need help in understanding why certain actions are better than others (e.g., Hart, Olsen, Robinson, & Mandleco, 1997). In other words, they need *teaching* instead of punishment.

Caroline, the children's center director, was concerned about the row of sad faces in the back of the room during morning choice time. It was Joanne's policy to remove youngsters from play if they weren't able to get along with others. Caroline decided to discuss this policy with Joanne.

Caroline met with Joanne and shared her concern that the children who most needed practice with social skills were not getting that practice. When they were removed from play, they were no longer in the learning situation. She asked Joanne to problem-solve with her about ways to help these youngsters learn to get along instead of just expelling them from play.

As they discussed the kinds of learning experiences these problem children needed, Joanne began to think of ways to teach instead of punish. But she realized that the changes required more than one adult in the large playroom. "I'll have to ask Sheri or Maureen to work the blue room with me during choice time," she planned. That change, however, meant having fewer options available for children. The teachers would have to alternate between opening the woodworking center and the painting area. Joanne decided that the sacrifice was worth it. With two adults to intervene, teachers could help children individually resolve disputes.

Caroline was pleased with the outcome of the discussion. She and Joanne reviewed the kinds of role modeling and problem-solving assistance that would be most helpful in teaching social skills. Joanne arranged a meeting with her assistants to go over this new plan.

LACK OF CRITICAL THINKING

Punishment doesn't just limit learning about acceptable behavior: it limits learning in general. Brain research shows that events that create fear, anxiety, or humiliation have negative effects on mental growth (Butchart, 1998). A similar damage to mental capacity can even be caused by strict environments that require unreflective, automatic responses. The gruff and threatening order to "Do as you're told!" and the expectation of instant obedience are examples of this type of environment. Children raised with this type of discipline usually have low motivation to think beyond parroting memorized answers. They tend to be submissive to the ideas of others and accept what others say uncritically instead of learning to think for themselves (DeVries, 1999). Such submissiveness may sound good to some parents, unless they realize that it will mean submitting to peer pressure when the child is a teenager.

In contrast, events that encourage reflection and other thinking promote mental growth and intellectual power. An example of an event that encourages thinking is Zeth and the broken bracelet. Through his experience, he comes to realize the connection between his action and the broken bracelet, and then the connection between his work to earn money and making up for the damage. This type of discipline encourages children to think for themselves and strive to understand the world (DeVries, 1999). A brain that is exercised becomes stronger and more capable.

LACK OF INNER CONTROLS

For some kids, fear of punishment becomes the only reason to behave in socially acceptable ways. These youngsters are only likely to act appropriately when someone is there to catch them. Even then, the seriousness of the punishment is often weighed against the potential pleasure of the inappropriate action (Kamii, 1982). Often youngsters will choose to go ahead with the action and "face the music" later. Accepting the punishment can even become a sort of challenge to their courage. Not getting caught can become another type of challenge. Kohlberg's (1984) extensive studies of moral development concluded that punishment is ineffective in promoting moral development, whereas the opposite approach, a deemphasized use of adult power, assists the development of a child's internalized conscience (e.g., DeVries, 1999; Kochanska, 1991).

DECEITFULNESS

Many people whose only restraint comes from fear of punishment become incredibly sneaky (Kamii, 1982). They become skillful at lying and other forms of deceit. You have probably known people who have adopted this dishonest approach to life. They get what they want behind people's backs. Although they can act innocent, others soon catch on to them and learn to distrust them. Certainly, this behavior is not a desirable outcome of discipline.

Recent headlines tell us that juvenile crime is increasing alarmingly. The public response is to "get tough" and punish harder, while punishing the kids' parents, too. Suggestions such as publishing the names of juvenile offenders are evidence of how little most people understand about how to improve behavior. How can publicly labeling a youngster as *bad* possibly help that child behave better? When suggestions focus on prevention of juvenile delinquency instead of punishment, the plans aim at older kids who

Many truly loving and caring people are convinced that punishment is necessary. They are misinformed, basing their beliefs on tradition rather than evidence.

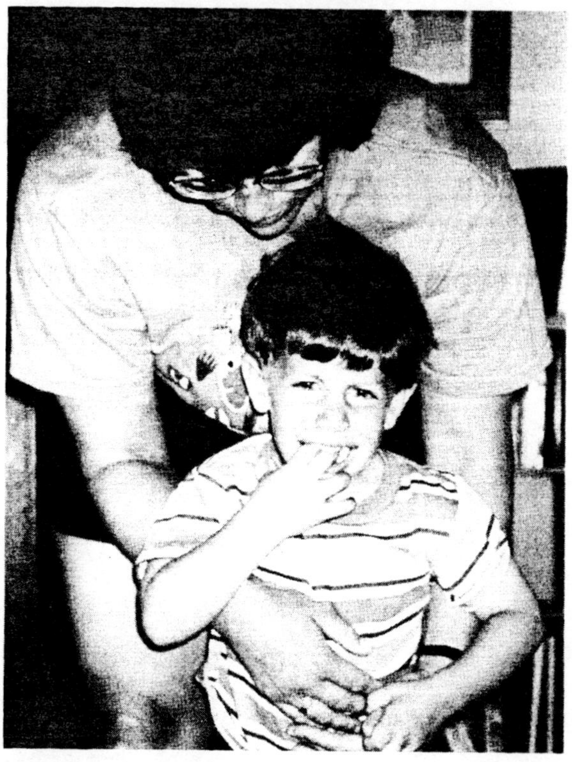

are already in trouble. Kindergarten teachers can tell you which of their five-year-old students are likely to end up in jail unless they get help; the problems begin early, and therefore need to be addressed early.

Those who would address the problems through punitive measures need to read the research showing that youngsters who are punished are most likely to turn to crime (Straus, 1991). Nearly three of every hundred American adults were in prison or on probation or parole in 1995, according to the U.S. Justice Department. Since 1980, the number of Americans under correctional supervision had almost tripled, from 1.84 million to 5.36 million, as of 1996 according to the U.S. Bureau of Justice Statistics. Punishment clearly isn't working, since building more and more prisons and incarcerating more and more people has not significantly reduced crime.

WHY PUNISHMENT IS USED

Obviously, the results of punishment are totally incompatible with the goals of self-discipline and autonomy. Punishment undermines the development of understanding and attitudes that lead to personal responsibility. Adults who rely on punishment are looking for the quick fix referred to in Chapter 1, but they may not get that result because some children are not submissive enough to give in. Children's defiance leads to escalation of punishment and even greater defiance. When punishment clearly doesn't stop the behavior, many parents and teachers still persist in using it because they don't know any other methods. However, some adults also use punishment for other reasons.

ADULT STRESS

Even adults who really don't believe in punishment and know better than to use it sometimes resort to it (Sabatino, 1991). A survey of American parents found that 70 percent believed that yelling and swearing at children causes psychological problems (Daro, Abrahams, & Robson, 1988). Yet that same study, as well as others, revealed that most parents had insulted or sworn at their children during the past year (Vissing, Straus, Gelles, & Harrop, 1991). There are times when the stresses of life push people beyond their limits, when an adult's behavior doesn't live up to his or her personal expectations. If this is a frequent occurrence, counseling is needed. If it is a rare occurrence, it is best to forgive yourself and try to redeem the situation. Mrs. Jensen had such an experience several years ago when she was driving across the state on a very hot summer day with her four children in a van with no air-conditioning. The children were uncomfortable and fussy from the heat and from being confined in the van. Andrew was screaming that he wanted out of his car seat, and Joe was teasing John by snatching his hat. There was no place to pull over and deal with the problem sensibly, so Mrs. Jensen reached back and grabbed Joe's arm, yanking him into his place with a barking order: "Sit!" She just didn't know what else to do. Besides, it actually made her feel better at the time. But later she felt bad and apologized to Joe, explaining her frustration. When everyone was calm and cooled off, the family was able to problem-solve about the situation.

Such instances are less likely in the controlled environment of Mrs. Jensen's classroom. Sometimes, however, a child does push her beyond her limits. In her professional role, Mrs. Jensen maintains her professional ethics. She would never hit a child or even grab a youngster in anger. She knows the importance of being in control of herself to effectively deal with discipline problems.

> Noah began making screeching noises again during the Spanish lesson. Señora Lupita was trying to keep the group interested in the Spanish language songs and stories she was sharing with the class, but the group was clearly becoming distracted by Noah's antics. Mrs. Jensen tried to make eye contact with him to communicate with him, but he avoided looking at her. Finally, she went and sat beside him to calm him, but his disruptions only escalated.
>
> Out of respect for Señora Lupita, Mrs. Jensen felt she had to remove Noah from the group. However, Noah was not receptive to the idea and was not cooperative when Mrs. Jensen tried to escort him away. He yelled louder and flailed around, kicking her in the process. It was an unpleasant scene, and Mrs. Jensen was very upset.
>
> She knew she shouldn't try to deal with Noah at that moment. Instead, she privately told him, "I need you to go and be quiet someplace away from me for

a while. I'm feeling too angry to talk to you about this right now. When I'm feeling calmer, we'll talk about the problem."

Any time you feel angry, you run the risk of punishing behavior rather than teaching self-discipline (Curwin & Mendler, 1988). Chapter 8 described how anger can change related consequences into punishment, just by the inevitably negative tone of voice and body language. Similarly, anger destroys the technique of holding a child to calm him or her. Restraining a child when you are infuriated is different from the reassuring embrace needed by an out-of-control youngster. It is important to know when you are not emotionally able to provide helpful guidance to youngsters and to call in someone with a fresh perspective. This action also models for children an adult's personal time-out to calm down.

MISCONCEPTIONS

Some adults say they don't believe in punishment and yet routinely rely on it. Apparently, they don't perceive their actions as punishment. Some teachers humiliate children in front of classmates and call it peer pressure. Others pride themselves on their "humor" when they cut down a child with a sarcastic response. Still others call it a "consequence" when they take away privileges totally unrelated to a behavior problem. All of these responses inflict hurt, create anger, and fail to teach. They are all punishment.

Simon was notoriously slow at cleaning up before circle time. The truth was that he didn't like going to circle time, so he dragged his feet. It distracted Joanne to have a child otherwise occupied during her circle. Today she decided to break Simon of his habit. She announced in a voice that carried across the room, "We're waiting for Simon to join our group so that we can begin our circle."

Embarrassed because all of the kids were staring at him, Simon hurried. Trying to carry both the basket of trucks and the box of animals at once, he dropped everything with a clatter. With his classmates laughing, he got even more flustered and put some trucks in the animal box. Joanne noted his error and asked, "Can anyone tell Simon which container the trucks go into?" "The orange basket!" taunted several children, enjoying what seemed to be the teacher's approval to pick on Simon. By now, Simon was nearly in tears, but Joanne couldn't see his face. She made another effort at using what she called peer pressure to bring his behavior into line. "Simon, we'll wait for three more minutes; then we'll have to start our circle. It's just not fair to keep your friends waiting." Thoroughly upset, he fumbled at putting away the rest of the toys. Finally, the teacher pronounced, "Time's up! Sorry, but you have used up too much of our time being a slowpoke." Steaming, Simon thought, "You're not sorry at all! I hate you!"

LACK OF DISCIPLINE SKILLS

Many people fear that children will go wild without fear of punishment; it is the only discipline approach these adults understand (Gordon, 1989; Reynolds, 1996). They are not informed about how other approaches to discipline set limits and communicate expectations about desirable behavior. Not understanding these other approaches, they think their choice is either

Some adults say they don't believe in punishment, yet use it, unaware that they are doing so.

punishment or a total lack of discipline, as we discussed in Chapter 1. To many people, discipline *is* punishment. That was clearly the case with the father who told Mrs. Jensen, "I just don't know what to do with him anymore. Hitting him doesn't make any difference."

Any concern about a lack of guidance and discipline is justified. Overly permissive child rearing can be as damaging as a punitive approach. Freedom without limits or responsibility is chaotic and dangerous. There are times when adults must step in to keep youngsters safe as well as to help them learn. Children must be helped to learn socially acceptable behavior and respect for the rights of others. These understandings are good for the child who learns them, as well as for those around that child. Youngsters who don't learn socially acceptable behaviors are not pleasant to be around. They damage property and are rude and inconsiderate. Naturally, no one wants to spend time with them, which leads to feelings of rejection and damages their self-esteem. Understanding the rights and needs of others is also essential to the development of self-discipline. Self-discipline doesn't result from forced behavior, but neither does it occur by itself. It is a product of careful teaching through Constructivist approaches to discipline.

SOCIAL NORMS

Many truly loving and caring people are firmly convinced that punishment will have long-term positive effects (Springen, 2000). They mean well but are

ACHIEVING EFFECTIVE DISCIPLINE WITHOUT CORPORAL PUNISHMENT

The Association for Childhood Education International (Cryan, 1987) recommends the following measures to promote effective discipline in schools without resorting to corporal punishment:

- Improve school climate with support by all school personnel
- Provide inservice training to increase staff competence and help educators see the theory-practice link
- Improve teacher training by focusing it on techniques for student motivation and effective handling of discipline problems
- Identify children's potential problems early and follow-up with counseling designed to prevent discipline problems

misinformed. Their beliefs are based on tradition rather than evidence. Education must be used as a tool to help these misinformed people learn the other, more useful approaches explained in this book. Most books on guidance and discipline are research-based and firmly reject punishment as an option. Unfortunately, a few are written by people without the background in child development or knowledge of relevant research; parents may not know the difference and can get led astray.

Some people justify punishment for broken rules based on the model of our legal system. However, our legal system is merely designed to control behavior, not to teach behavior or to sozialize citizens (Watson, 1999). "It does not make sense for educators to use the criminal-justice model as the first resort, before employing what they were professionally prepared to use—educational and mentoring approaches" (Gathercoal, 1998).

The violent traditions of society make it difficult for many people to give up punitive approaches to discipline. Movies and television promote violence as a legitimate way for the "good guys" to win. Many sporting events involve violence that is eagerly applauded, and world leaders still rely on force to settle differences. The use of force is continually glorified.

Yet society also recognizes values that should counteract the use of force to discipline children. Respect for the rights of all people is increasingly evidenced in laws and attitudes. Minority groups are speaking up and insisting on equal treatment. Perhaps the least represented group is the one with the smallest voice: the children. The U.S. Constitution guarantees equality, rights, and the protection of all. Perhaps children, too, will soon be included in this guarantee. Teachers can be effective advocates for the rights of young children. Professional organizations representing early childhood teachers, such as the National Association for the Education of Young Children (NAEYC) and the Association for Childhood Education International (ACEI), have been vocal about the subject of punishment (Simmons, 1991; Greenberg, 1992a).

CONCLUSION

We have hope that punishment will cease to be considered a reasonable means of discipline. We believe that when parents and teachers understand the dangers of punishment and learn more effective approaches to child guidance, the world will become a better place. There will be fewer angry people who need to get even with society through violence. There will be fewer people who have come to believe they are worthless. There will be less dishonesty and less energy spent to avoid getting caught. Personal inner controls and concern for others will become the norm among morally autonomous people.

FOR FURTHER THOUGHT

1. Were you punished as a child? If so, what are your memories of the way you felt and what you thought about being punished? How do your memories of physical punishment differ from those of other types of punishment? How did each method affect your self-esteem?
2. Were you raised with no discipline? Did you wish for controls and guidance? How did this experience affect your attitudes about discipline? What was the impact on your self-esteem?
3. Were you given constructive discipline as a child? How has it affected your life, your attitudes, and your self-esteem?
4. Observe aggressive young children. Do they seem to be imitating a model of adult aggression?
5. Observe socially competent young children. Do they seem to have learned from adult models for peaceful negotiation of conflict?
6. How would you explain to someone the fundamental differences between punishment and discipline? Can you relate those differences to the differences between moral autonomy and heteronomy?

RECOMMENDED READINGS

Butchart, R.E. & McEwan, B. (1998). *Classroom discipline in American schools; problems and possibilities for democratic education.* Albany, NY: State University of New York Press.

Kamii, C. (1984). Obedience is not enough. *Young Children.* 39(4), 11–14.

Williams, M.M. & Schaps, E. (Eds). (1999). *Character Education: The foundation for teacher education.* Washington, DC: The Character Education Partnership.

Part Three

MATCHING DISCIPLINE CAUSES TO DISCIPLINE APPROACHES

Part Two explained the different approaches to discipline. Although this information is essential, its organization is not in the format most useful in real life. In working with youngsters, we are first confronted with the behavior, not the discipline approach. Part Three looks at discipline from the real-world perspective: We start with the behavior and move backward to discover the cause, select the related approach, and then implement that approach.

Discipline is effective only if it addresses the cause of the problem. In Chapter 1 we explain this idea by comparing the guidance of children to gardening; getting rid of unwanted behavior is like weeding the garden—the cause of the behavior is similar to the roots of the weeds. Because it is necessary to get at the roots of a problem, parents, caregivers, and teachers are constantly challenged to determine what is causing unwanted behavior.

In the following chapters we will look at some common behaviors that disrupt school and child-care settings. We hope the examples provide useful practice in matching behaviors to probable causes. We also hope that the process of matching discipline approaches to the cause of the problem becomes more clear as you read this section. Remember, we're matching discipline approaches to the causes, not to the behaviors.

11

IMMATURITY

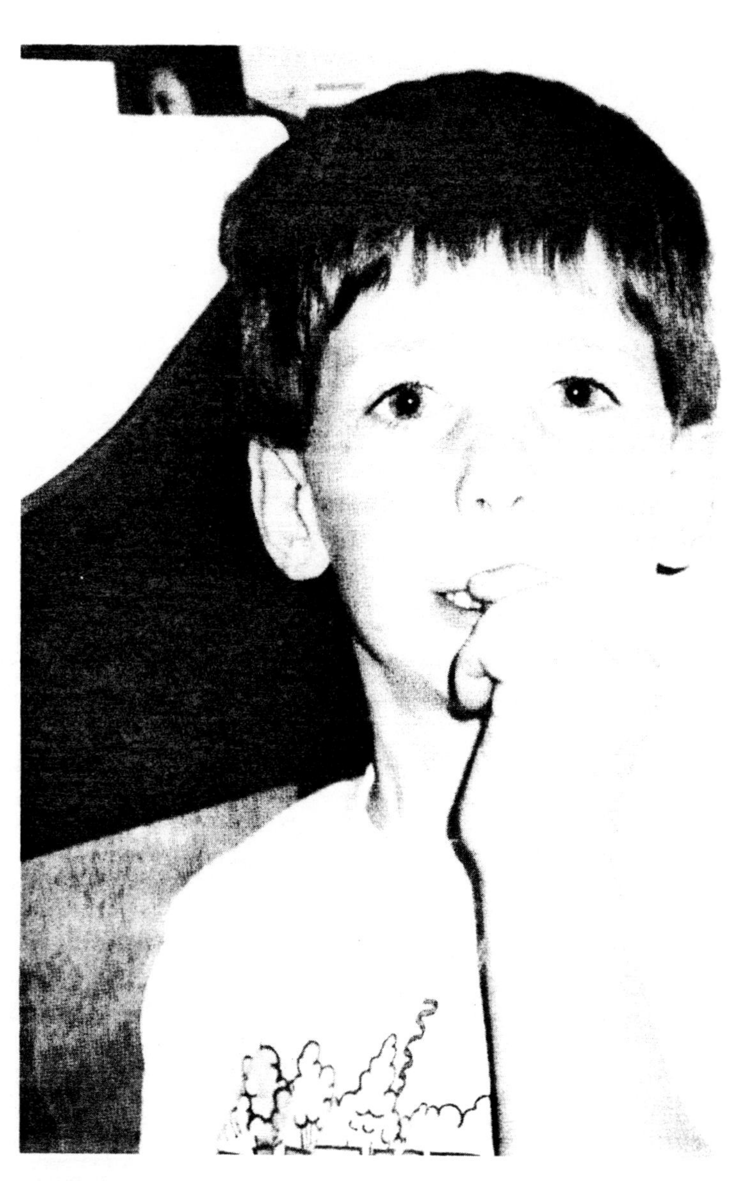

The word *immature* means not fully grown; therefore, being young means being immature. Though teenagers may use the term in a derogatory way to one another, even teenagers have a right to be immature. Just being young is often the cause of problems; the younger the child, the more this is so. Early childhood teachers face this issue daily as their students demonstrate a lack of skills needed for success in daily living. Young children are prone to spilling, falling, spitting, biting, hitting, crying, and screaming. These behavior problems can be directly traced to immature coordination, undeveloped communication ability, childish social skills, and other perfectly normal aspects of early childhood. Knowledgeable adults are able to distinguish between misbehavior and childlike behavior. This distinction is essential for helpful guidance (Curry & Johnson, 1990). Recognizing that immaturity naturally causes many problems gives you a more productive way to deal with those problems.

IMMATURE COORDINATION

Spilled juice at snack time is an everyday occurrence in preschool. It is a result of the immature coordination that is normal for young children. Providing child-sized pitchers and furniture increases children's successful independence, but it doesn't eliminate all spills. Adults with realistic expectations prepare for this inevitable outcome by having paper towels handy for cleanup. Piaget (1965/1932) calls it "making restitution" when children clean up their mistakes. We call it helping children take responsibility for themselves without making them feel bad. This approach to accidents is an example of using related consequences, as described in Chapter 8. Teachers also prevent spills from becoming a problem by locating snack tables on a washable floor surface. These preparations help teachers remain calm and allow for productive responses to mistakes. This attitude is a

SOME NORMAL BEHAVIORS OF YOUNG CHILDREN

Physical immaturity can cause:
- spilling
- bumping
- wetting
- disrupting group time

Emotional immaturity can cause:
- tantrums
- tears

Immature language ability can cause:
- hitting, kicking, biting
- tears and tantrums

Social immaturity can cause:
- hitting
- kicking
- biting
- grabbing

Cognitive immaturity can cause:
- being selfish
- telling "lies"
- taking things
- misunderstanding
- cheating

description of the approach to discipline we call *creating environments that prevent discipline problems* (see Chapter 4).

Unfortunately, not all adults realize that spilling is a natural part of learning to pour. Some act as if they think that yelling insults at a child will improve his or her pouring ability. Common adult responses to a spill are "Not again!" or "That's the third time today! Can't you be careful?" Other adults simply eliminate spills by denying children the chance to practice. Both responses are counterproductive to the child's skill development. Both approaches also damage the child's self-esteem and hinder the development of autonomy. Being yelled at makes youngsters feel ashamed and afraid to try, and having things done for them makes kids feel inept and unable to succeed. Both responses create helplessness. In contrast, related consequences help children feel capable and proud (Curwin & Mendler, 1988).

Young children frequently experience negative feedback for the clumsiness natural to their age. As a teacher, you may see a lack of sensitivity not only from other adults but also from the children's own peers. The following example demonstrates how an opportunity for making restitution can make everyone involved feel better about an accident. It is another example of a related consequence.

> Christie and Ashley were at the inventions table, busily cutting out pictures from catalogs and picking bits of ribbon, shells, and Styrofoam to glue onto larger pieces of paper. Ashley accidentally spilled some of the gooey white glue on Christie's paper. Christie started yelling in frustration and anger about her spoiled project. Ashley kept saying over and over how sorry she was, but Christie kept on screaming.
>
> Maureen quickly came to the rescue. Ashley looked frightened and fearful of punishment as the teacher came near. Maureen reassured her that accidents do happen and then turned her attention to the screaming Christie. "I know you are angry about your paper, but such loud screaming hurts everyone's ears. Let's

see what we can do to fix your paper. Ashley feels bad about spilling on it, and I'm sure she will help you clean it up. What would be a good thing to wipe up glue with?"

Ashley did indeed want to help. She suggested that Kleenex might work to wipe up the glue and ran to get some. Together, the girls carefully wiped away the excess glue, leaving Christie's paper almost as good as new. Then they were able to continue working cooperatively together.

Such accidents don't stop when children reach grade school; they are still a normal part of the children's development.

Several second graders in Mr. Davis' class were busy painting for a class project. They were working on a countertop in the uncarpeted part of the room designated for messy projects. This was fortunate since it wasn't long before the blue paint had spilled on the countertop and was dripping down the lower cabinets onto the floor. The children happily and obliviously continued to paint, while making blue shoe tracks all over the tiled floor.

Mr. Davis saw the mess and said, "I see that paint drips a lot. It's going to be a lot of work cleaning it up when you're finished; what do think will be the best way to do it?" He also asked for their ideas about how they could keep from tracking the paint from their shoes onto the carpet. He helped them find the sponges and paper towels they decided they needed, but let them take charge. He was pleased to discover that his students figured out for themselves how to wipe their shoes off, as well as how to get all the paint cleaned up. In fact, the clean-up project turned out to be even more interesting than the painting, attracting help from many who hadn't even been painting. It didn't take long before there wasn't a trace of blue paint left.

OTHER PHYSICAL LIMITATIONS

"Someone wet on the floor!" Physical immaturity sometimes means a youngster doesn't make it to the toilet on time. The accident can be a serious blow to a child's pride and must be handled with care to preserve his or her self-esteem. Mrs. Jensen remembers how her own kindergarten teacher publicly humiliated children who had accidents. They had to wash out their underpants, and then the teacher would hang them up to dry in the classroom for all to see. Mrs. Jensen is sure she can improve on that technique. She doesn't consider the incident to be a discipline issue; her only approach in the following example is to treat Meadow with compassionate respect. Mrs. Jensen knows this is not a discipline problem, but rather a maturation issue.

Meadow was working on a puzzle during choice time when she suddenly realized she had to go to the bathroom. She was very uncomfortable, but it wasn't time for the bathroom break yet. She knew she could ask permission to go any time she wanted, but it was just too embarrassing. Everyone would know where she was going. She decided to wait until the scheduled time. Oh, oh! She couldn't hold it any longer. Meadow was mortified but hopeful that no one would notice the puddle on the floor around the chair. She quickly got up and moved away from the evidence. Her skirt didn't seem too wet and maybe no one would see that her underpants were soaked. Meadow just didn't think she could stand it if anyone knew what she had done.

"Mrs. Jensen! Someone wet on the floor!" shouted Jimmie indignantly. The teacher replied calmly, "I guess it will have to be wiped up. Just don't walk there for now." Mrs. Jensen noticed Meadow's damp skirt and furtive looks. She quickly put the pieces together and realized how distressed the shy girl must be. The teacher's challenge was to get the floor cleaned, help Meadow get dry, and still preserve the child's privacy and dignity. Mrs. Jensen noticed that recess was in ten minutes, and decided to wait until then for the custodian to come and clean up. It would make much less fuss that way. Recess would also be a good time to get Meadow aside and quietly give her some dry undies as well as a plastic bag for her wet ones.

INABILITY TO SIT STILL

Children often get into trouble for moving around when they aren't supposed to. The inability to sit still for very long is another example of the physical limitations of being young (Bredekamp, 1997). Forcing young children to sit still or control their bodies for long periods of time can cause problems. Unable to satisfy this unreasonable expectation, the young child *will* move. Chapter 2 described this aspect of early childhood development, and Chapter 4 explained the importance of allowing children to move around as a way to prevent discipline problems.

Allowing children to move freely about the classroom and to find comfortable body positions lets children meet their needs to move. Teachers

Being asked to sit still for too long can cause children to be disruptive.

who are aware of children's physical development provide meaningful reasons for them to move around. These teachers are also sensitive to the group's energy level. They recognize that squirming and children's frequent requests to move—to go get a drink, to go to the bathroom, to *go!*—as symptoms of their need for movement. These teachers know that sometimes the only reasonable thing to do is to have everyone push the tables back and play an energetic game or sing an action song! The following example shows how even a normally sedentary activity like reading can accommodate the movement needs of young children.

> Mrs. Jensen asked Beth, her student teacher, to take a group to the library corner to read *The Three Little Pigs* together. Most of the children settled right in and found their place in their individual books. But Allison, Jeffrey, and Randy couldn't get settled. They pushed and jostled for seats. They juggled their books into every conceivable position, flipping pages and occasionally dropping the books. Beth was having a hard time keeping them still and focused on reading. How could she get them through the story with all of this activity and fighting? Deciding to ask for help, she excused herself from the group for a minute and described her difficulty to Mrs. Jensen.
>
> Aware of the high energy level that morning, Mrs. Jensen suggested they try acting out the story. Beth checked with the children to see if they'd like to do a play. Affirmative! She assigned the three little pigs to—you guessed it—Allison, Jeffrey, and Randy. They went to the adjacent block area to build their houses. She sent Brianna, a strong reader, along with them in the narrator/cueing role. Brianna brought the book to each construction site as the part came up in the story. Beth read the part of the wolf to help pull the play together. The piglets frantically built while the narrator read. They read their pig parts with intensity. Then they squealed in delight and scrambled to the next house as Beth huffed and puffed. No one even considered leaving the reading group for a trip down the hall.

Beth could have wasted a lot of energy trying to squelch the children's surface behaviors. Fortunately, Mrs. Jensen accurately recognized their difficulties in getting along and sitting still as symptoms of an undeniable need for movement. Her recommended discipline approach dealt directly with the cause of the problem.

Mrs. Jensen knows her students well and is in a position to know the cause of behaviors such as why Allison, Jeffrey, and Randy had a problem sitting still. But the same behavior could have had a different cause. It is possible that the "troublemakers" might have been uncooperative due to their inability to read the material. Or the problem could have been just the opposite: The material may have lacked challenge for them. Similar disruption could have been caused by one child's attention-getting tactics. Often there are multiple causes, which create an even greater challenge for helpful adult intervention.

Without information about the children involved, it is not possible to diagnose the problem accurately. Without an accurate diagnosis, discipline approaches are likely to go astray. Knowing students well enough to guess fairly accurately about the cause of problems involves establishing authentic relationships with the child and the parents (Greenberg, 1992a).

UNDEVELOPED COMMUNICATION ABILITY

Consider the activities of hitting, kicking, biting, and spitting. Although these behaviors are unacceptable, they generally only indicate a need to learn more productive approaches for expressing needs and feelings. One common cause of this type of behavior among preschoolers is their lack of communication ability. Young children are still beginners with language (Vygotsky, 1962,1934). They haven't yet had sufficient practice to find the exact words they need, and in times of stress what they do know may fall apart. A child who is angry, frustrated, or otherwise upset often has trouble expressing those feelings in words. Instead, the child hits, kicks, bites, or spits to communicate.

Productive discipline does more than simply stop the behavior; it doesn't just let kids know what *not* to do, it teaches them what *to* do. Therefore, when a lack of communication skills appears to be the cause of the behavior, adults need to help children express themselves with language. Teachers of young children can frequently be heard reminding them, "Please use your words," as in this situation with the rocking boat.

> Three children were in the rocking boat happily rocking and pretending to fish. Three-year-old Savannah went over to them and stood by the boat. The children kept on rocking. Savannah started whining and screaming at them, but used no words. The other children looked at her but did not stop what they were doing. Savannah kept on whining and screaming.
>
> Dennis came to the rescue. He bent down to Savannah and said, "You seem very upset." The child acknowledged her teacher's reflective listening with a nod and told him she wanted to play on the boat. Dennis asked her if she had used her words to tell the other children what she wanted. Savannah shook her head "No." So Dennis asked her to think of what words she could use. Savannah smiled at him and said to the children in the boat, "I want to ride."
>
> Thank heavens it worked! The children in the boat stopped and let her in, then the four of them proceeded to rock and fish. Dennis hoped that this successful experience would help Savannah remember to talk instead of scream in the future.

When a lack of language skills causes behavior problems, the proper discipline approach is to teach the missing skills. Possibly the most valuable communication skill is how to use an "I message," as described in Chapter 7. Notice how Mrs. Jensen helps Andrea find a better way of expressing herself.

> Andrea was reading by herself in a secluded spot in the room. She had had a hard day at school and needed to be alone. Suddenly Sam plopped down beside her and began reading his book aloud, laughing at how funny it was. Andrea was in no mood for such nonsense, so she kicked him. Sam yelped and indignantly complained to the teacher. "I didn't do nothing to her!" As she comforted Sam, Mrs. Jensen thought about what might have brought this on.
>
> She was aware of the conflicts Andrea had experienced during the day and knew that Andrea hadn't come out well in them. Mrs. Jensen had been pleased to see that Andrea was making good use of the soft private area of the room to comfort herself. She hadn't noticed Sam go over there, however. Maybe she could use this situation as a teaching opportunity.
>
> Mrs. Jensen went over with Sam to where Andrea was pouting, her arms crossed and a big scowl on her face. Mrs. Jensen used some reflective listening

Undeveloped communication ability can cause behavior problems.

to acknowledge what she thought Andrea's feelings were. "It looks like you wanted to be alone over here," she said. Andrea nodded, still scowling but perhaps more able to be reasonable.

So Mrs. Jensen decided to work on "I messages." She encouraged Sam to tell Andrea how he felt about being kicked. "You hurt me and made me feel bad," Sam said. Then she tried to get Andrea to use an "I message" to express her feelings: "Is there a better way for you to let Sam know what you wanted?" Andrea was able to say, "I want to be by myself." And she spontaneously added, "I'm sorry I got mad and kicked you."

Another discipline approach might have been appropriate for this behavior if there had been a different cause. You may recall that we recommended in Chapter 8 that a child who hurts another child should help the injured youngster. Do you know why that wouldn't be the best learning experience in this case? Remember, you select your discipline approach based on what you believe the child needs to learn. Mrs. Jensen saw the need for communication skills here, apparently having reason to believe that Andrea already knew that kicking hurts. Additionally, a child who desperately needs time alone is not in the best condition to offer nurturing help right then. The choice of discipline approaches was based on the teacher's perception of the child's current intellectual and emotional needs.

UNDEVELOPED EMOTION REGULATION

Hitting, kicking, biting, and spitting, as well as screaming, crying, and other out-of-control behaviors, can also be caused by an inability to regulate emotions. As explained in Chapters 2 and 6, learning to express emotions productively is not automatic, and some children require more assistance than others. Children first need help in separating minor frustrations from major traumas. Have you noticed that young children tend to scream as if their lives were threatened even when the problem is something they forget in five minutes? Once they get big problems sorted out from little problems, they can more easily work on useful ways to respond to the numerous little problems they will encounter every day. Remember, we aren't trying to get them *not* to express how they feel, but rather to express their feelings in a reasonable way. Notice how Mrs. Jensen works on this process with James:

> James was involved in a math game when Mrs. Jensen gave the five-minute warning for clean-up and lunch time. James immediately flung his cards and playing board into the air and wailed, "I didn't get to finish my game!" Then he got up and ran out of the classroom. Mrs. Jensen found him standing in the hall beside the door with his fists clenched, eyes shut, and face red. She could see that he was working on getting control of himself, but that trying to reason with him right then wouldn't work. She kept an eye on the students in the room, seeing that they were cleaning up. A couple of them were even cleaning up James' mess. Soon the others were on their way down the hall to lunch. "Have a good lunch," Mrs. Jensen said as they left.
>
> Then she had time to help James. He no longer had clenched fists, his eyes were open, and his face wasn't quite as red. He did have a few tears, though. "You really wanted to play that game, didn't you?" Mrs. Jensen said sympathetically. "Yeeeeeeeeeees, I never got to play that one afore. I want to play it!" replied James angrily.
>
> Mrs. Jensen asked James to come back to the room and look at the classroom calendar with her. She showed him that they would have math game time every day this week and the next and the next. James began to relax, and acknowledged that he could play the game tomorrow. "Can I go to lunch now?" he asked, obviously feeling much better.
>
> As she walked down the hall with him, Mrs. Jensen asked James if throwing the game had made him feel better. "Yes, but I'm not supposed to do that, am I?" he answered. "What do you think?" smiled Mrs. Jensen. "No." Then Mrs. Jensen asked him why he thought he wasn't supposed to. "I don't want to hurt the game," he replied. It wasn't a perfect answer, she thought, but James had come a long way in these first three weeks of school. Last week he was spitting when he was upset.
>
> She thought that in addition to help with emotion regulation, maybe he needed more time to make transitions. Perhaps the pressure of a tight school schedule was making it harder for him to control his feelings. The next day Mrs. Jensen approached James a little before the five-minute warning and asked him to be in charge of flicking the lights as the warning signal. This put James in charge and gave him a feeling of power over the situation that had been upsetting him.

Notice that Mrs. Jensen used a combination of guidance approaches, based on her assessment of the cause of James' outburst. She used reflective listening to acknowledge his feelings, she allowed him to express his feelings in words, and she helped him put the problem into perspective. All these responses helped him with his emotion regulation. In addition, she used her observations of his behavior to determine that transitions were hard for him and that he might be helped by feeling more control over his day.

UNDEVELOPED SOCIAL SKILLS

Learning the complexities of human interaction takes at least a lifetime. No wonder small humans with very little experience often have problems. To make matters worse, society groups these inexperienced beings into crowds where they have to compete for limited space and resources. Some children don't face this test until kindergarten age, but many are thrust into preschool or group care at much younger ages. They are expected to "get along" by "sharing" the attractive toys and being "nice" about letting others infringe on their play territory. When children are unable to rise to these challenges, adults generally consider it a discipline problem. Those who understand discipline as teaching respond in one way, but those who view discipline as controlling behavior respond in another (DeVries & Kohlberg, 1987).

> "Teacher, Leo won't let me have any little people!" complained Colette. The two children were playing at the same table with a set of miniature people and an airport setup. Leo was hoarding all of the small figures in his play space.

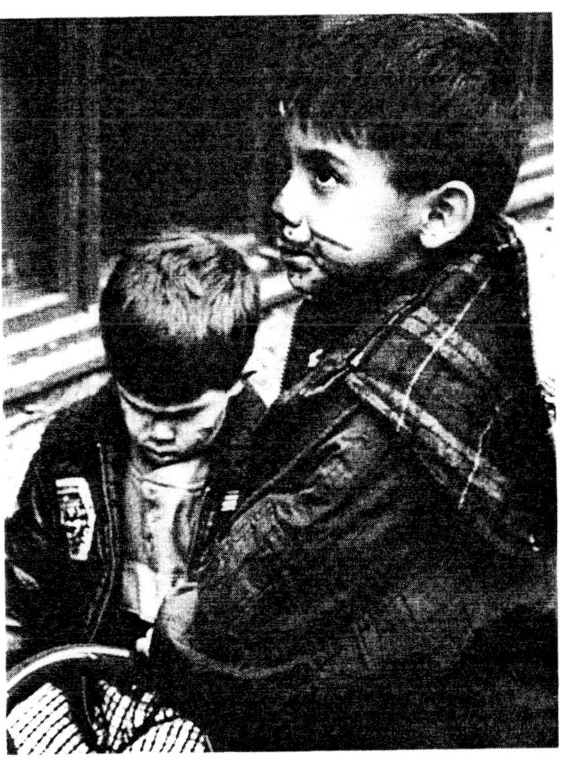

Undeveloped social skills are normal for young children, which creates frequent conflict as well as teachable moments.

Joanne immediately came to the rescue. "Leo, you must share the people with Colette. All the toys at the center belong to everyone." Leo still wouldn't part with his pile of figures, so Joanne got firmer. "Leo, if you can't share, you must go to the time-out chair and think about being kind." Leo knew he was beaten. Either he had to give up some of the people, or he would lose out all together. Sullenly, he sorted out some of the least attractive figures and shoved them at Colette.

Sheri, the aide, watched this incident with interest. Because her hours at the center were from mid-morning to mid-afternoon, she noted the contrasting teaching styles of the morning and afternoon head teachers. Sheri had to admit that Joanne's style got the incident over with quickly, but children definitely got along better in the afternoon under Dennis' management system. After lunch, Sheri closely observed as Dennis handled a similar situation.

Kelsey and Joshua dragged the zoo box out to the sun room. Kelsey busied herself by putting the cages together, while Joshua sorted out all the animals. There were two sets mixed up, and one was notably newer. By the time Kelsey had the zoo ready for occupancy, Joshua had decided that he didn't want to play with her after all. He was building his own cages with the Lincoln Logs. He had all the shiny new animals hoarded away in a basket next to him. Noticing that she only had the scuffed-up critters with broken legs, Kelsey protested, "You can't have all the good animals!" Joshua retorted, "I got 'em first!" The disappointed girl said tearfully, "But I was building the cages for them." "Well, I've got my own cages," he told her. Kelsey repeated her position, her voice rising, "But you can't have all of those good ones!" She grabbed at the basket, but Joshua snatched it out of reach and pushed her away.

Overhearing their disagreement, Dennis helped them think about their problem through reflective listening. "You both want the same animals?" he began. Kelsey clarified, "He's got *all* of the good ones! All that's left are these old broken ones." Dennis continued, "You don't want to play with the older animals?" "Yeah, they don't even stand up," she complained. Kelsey demonstrated by attempting unsuccessfully several times to get the three-legged zebra to stay up.

Addressing both children, he encouraged them to brainstorm solutions. "Well, what can you do with the old animals?" "Throw them away!" said the disgusted girl. Then she remembered that if they threw them away, she wouldn't have any. She restated her claim, "But I want half of the new ones!" Dennis invited Joshua's input: "What do you think we could do with these animals?" "Fix 'em?" the boy suggested, wondering if it were possible. "How would you fix the animals?" the teacher inquired. Joshua said knowingly, "You fix animals at the ventrananium!" His old dog had been hit by a car, and he knew all about animal doctors. "You're right. Veterinarians do help fix broken animal bodies," Dennis replied.

Eager to show off what he knew about vets, Joshua volunteered to transform his zoo into a hospital. Not sure she was satisfied with Joshua's solution, Kelsey asked, "But can I have some of the new animals?" "Okay, but I want all of yours with the broken legs," insisted the boy. He had an idea about making legs out of paper straws from the collage box. They would look kind of like the bandage his dog had worn. Kelsey agreed, and they exchanged critters. Dennis doubted that the straw appendages would work, but that problem wasn't as important as the fact that the children had come up with a solution they could both accept. Someday the preschool would probably have to throw away the old animals and get more new ones.

Sheri could see that Joshua was feeling more cooperative at the end of this exchange than Leo had after being forced to share the airport people. Yet Dennis had had to spend several minutes working with the youngsters on the problem. Sheri found a chance to ask Dennis, "Why didn't you just tell Joshua to give some of the new animals to Kelsey instead of spending so much time with that problem?"

Dennis was glad to discuss his approach with Sheri; she seemed to have a good rapport with the children, and he hoped she would stay in this job for a while. He explained that children don't learn to solve problems if a teacher solves problems for them. He also shared his view that forced sharing creates selfishness rather than generosity. He communicated his goals of teaching youngsters how to get along and helping them learn to consider the feelings of others. He told Sheri that he considered this knowledge one of the most essential outcomes of early childhood education; therefore, he was happy to spend his time working on it.

He commented further on the time element, mentioning that he seemed to spend less and less time on arguments between youngsters as the year progressed. Sheri was inclined to agree; Dennis spent more time on individual problems, but Joanne had many more continuing problems to deal with.

Sometimes the problem seems to be about sharing toys or materials, but actually has another source. As we explained in Chapter 3, many young children don't know how to initiate play with another child (Ramsey, 1991). It is common for these youngsters to grab a possession away from someone they really want as a playmate. Sometimes they will punch or shove to get attention from someone they want as a friend. This behavior is a primitive way of saying, "I like you." Adults who don't understand young children will simply try to stop the behavior. Adults who realize the cause of the problem will help children learn more productive ways of making friends. It is difficult to stop unacceptable behavior unless you help children find another behavior to take its place. In the following example, Eric learns something about using one of the play entry approaches described in Chapter 3.

Eric, a very quiet 4-year-old, was watching three girls who were engrossed in playing "puppy dog." One girl was the dog and the other two were leading her around, each one with a leash on the same puppy. Eric went up to them and tried to take hold of one of the leashes. "No, go away!" the girls told him.

Dennis saw Eric's ineffective attempt at joining the puppy dog play and went to see if he could help. "You want to play with them, don't you?" he asked Eric. When Eric affirmed that he did, Dennis suggested a play entry strategy: "They have two leashes but only one dog; maybe they will let you be a dog too if you ask them."

Eric went over to the girls but hesitated to speak to them, so Dennis supported the shy little boy by saying, "Eric wants to ask you if he can be a dog too, since you have two leashes." Then Eric was able to add, "I be dog?" The

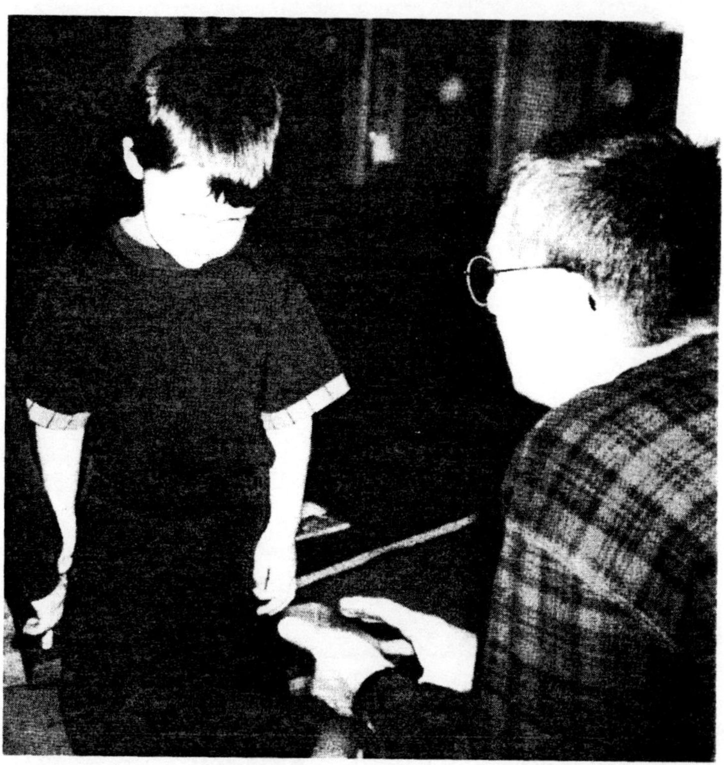

It is difficult to change unacceptable behaviors unless you help children learn more productive ones.

> girls answered, "OK," and unhooked one leash from the girl being a puppy and hooked it into Eric's belt loop. Dennis was happy to see that the children played cooperatively until it was time for snack. This was a big breakthrough for Eric.

Children don't automatically figure out how to successfully enter play as they get older; many primary grade children still use inappropriate methods for gaining a playmate. It is not unusual for first graders to shove or grab something from a person they want to play with. These children still need lots of help figuring out how to accomplish their social goals.

EGOCENTRISM

Young children want their own way, and they want it now. Adults would actually like the same thing, but they have learned not to insist on it. Adults have learned that other people's wishes don't necessarily match their own. They have also learned that give-and-take is part of getting along with others. Young children need help in learning these things. In the meantime, their behavior often appears selfish and inconsiderate (DeVries & Zan, 1994) and is difficult to deal with. They wander off during group time and start a distracting activity, they take what they want regardless of who is using it, and they generally disregard others. That's because they are so concerned with their own wishes, they cannot think about anyone else's.

Many adults believe that such behavior should be punished, but those who understand child development know otherwise. Punishing selfish behavior doesn't make children more thoughtful; it only makes them more careful about being caught and resentful about sharing (Kamii, 1982). Youngsters will become more considerate and less selfish only when they are able to understand that other people have important needs and feelings, too. This understanding takes time to develop and requires experience in order to be learned. Constructive discipline gives children both time and experience.

> Max was thrilled to see the new toy car that he could really ride in; he could hardly wait to get in it. As he drove around and around in it, he wore a huge grin on his face. But after about 15 minutes, other children began asking when they could have a turn. Danny finally decided to take things into his own hands; he climbed onto the back of the car and tried to force his way in.
>
> Nancy, the assistant preschool teacher, saw serious trouble brewing and hurried to head off any injuries. "One at a time," she cautioned as she gently removed Danny from the car. She assured Danny and the others who wanted a turn that she understood their desire to drive the car. At the same time, she tried to defend Max's feelings. "How would you feel if someone got on the car when you were driving it?" she asked. However, it is hard for young children to understand another person's feelings. All Max and Danny knew was that they wanted a turn. All Max knew was that he didn't want to stop.
>
> To assure others that they would get a turn, Nancy helped them make a sign-up sheet for showing whose turn was next. The preschoolers had used this system for other situations and understood the significance of writing their names on the chart. But Katya still complained, "Max is taking too long a turn!" Nancy agreed that something needed to be done with so many children wanting to use the attractive new toy.
>
> She asked the youngsters what they thought would be the right amount of time. Should it be the length of a song on a CD, or should they use an egg timer, or did they have another idea? Nancy knew that clocks were meaningless to these children and she didn't want to be the time-keeper: the "ogre" who makes people give up their turns. With Nancy's help, the children began learning ways of resolving such conflicts. By the end of the school year, they independently made sign-up sheets and turned on the CD player as a timer.

What if Nancy had taken a different approach? What if she had just solved the immediate problem either by forcing Max to give up the car to Danny or by removing Danny to time-out for his behavior? Or what if she had just tried to distract Danny with another activity instead? Many people would consider those to be good solutions, yet they would not help the children learn anything useful. Notice the errors made by the adult in this next situation.

> Several preschoolers were lined up waiting to foot paint. Kyle finally just couldn't wait any longer. He plunged past the others waiting in line and started shoving his way into the paint pan. The other children hollered at him indignantly. Teacher Joanne reacted quickly and firmly. She pulled Kyle away

Inability to understand that others also want a turn causes problems in sharing.

> and told him that he would have to go to the back of the line. Kyle began wailing loudly. Needing to get back to supervising the messy activity, Joanne asked her assistant, Maureen, to quiet Kyle. While Maureen was desperately trying to think of what to do, her eye fell on the gerbil cage next to Kyle. "I think you are scaring Pinky," Maureen told the crying boy. Kyle's attention was successfully diverted to the gerbil, and the problem was over for the moment.

Is this what we want to teach children about dealing with their own feelings? What about the feelings of the other children when Kyle crowded them? Neither teacher tried to help him understand the viewpoint of those who were waiting in line. Kyle needs help learning to deal with his own feelings and those of others. They are important realities that prepare a child to function effectively in society, whereas feigned concern about the gerbil's feelings is only a manipulative tactic.

A more productive approach to handling Kyle's problem involves only a subtle shift in the teacher's response. The teacher could have used the guidelines (provided in Chapter 8) for implementing a related consequence. Instead of just pulling Kyle away, Joanne could have told him to leave *until* he decided to get back into line and wait his turn. This method gives him some power over his own situation and focuses his attention more clearly on the problem. Instead of just thinking about how mean the teacher is, he is free to think about how he can change his behavior to get a turn (Curwin & Mendler, 1988). A related consequence addresses the immediate problem but needs to be supplemented with other approaches. Kyle also obviously needs help understanding the feelings of other children. Therefore, it would be useful for him to listen to how they feel about his crowding. Kyle also would benefit from the security of knowing that he would get a turn eventually. The sign-up sheet and the egg timer used with the trampoline line would address the children's needs in this situation. A combination of causes calls for a combination of approaches.

By the time they get into the primary grades, children usually have gained a little awareness of the needs of others. However, they still need help thinking about what others want when it conflicts with what they want. At this stage, they can make better progress with exchanging viewpoints through "I messages." Primary grade children can be helped to use "I messages" effectively as a starting place for negotiating resolution to conflicts, as these second-grade boys did.

> Max, Anders, and Jeremy were playing a game they had made up that involved kicking a ball within the confines of a large box. Guy was watching them kick the ball back and forth, asking if he could play but being refused. Guy saw Mr. Davis on the playground and told him, "They won't let me play." The other boys defended themselves by saying, "You play too rough and you always kick the ball out." Guy retorted that he didn't kick the ball out any more than Max did. Max then replied, "You wouldn't let us play with you and your friends last recess so you can't play with us now." Jeremy and Anders nodded in agreement.
>
> Mr. Davis asked Guy how he felt about not being allowed to play. Guy said he felt bad. Then Mr. Davis asked the other boys how they felt when Guy didn't let them play. They said they, too, felt bad; Max especially seemed to feel that a payback was necessary. Mr. Davis acknowledged everyone's feelings, saying "It's not fun to feel bad." He could see by Guy's face that he suddenly realized how his earlier rejection made his friends feel.
>
> Mr. Davis decided to work on some problem solving by asking Jeremy, "Can you think of anything the four of you could do to solve this problem?" Mr. Davis addressed Jeremy because Jeremy's body language indicated he was less upset over the previous recess interaction and therefore could probably reason better. Jeremy stepped back, took a deep breath, and said, "Well, we could make a deal. If we let you play, you have to let us play." Guy agreed to that, and Anders and Jeremy were willing to include Guy. Max was holding out, saying, "Not until next recess; this recess we want to play alone." But then Anders whispered to Max, "This is the last recess of the day." "Oh yeah," acknowledged Max.
>
> Guy saw his chance and piped up, "Come on, Max. Two against two!" Anders said, "I'll be your partner, it will be us against them." Max relented and all four boys went back into the box and played ball. At one point Jeremy fell down and Guy ran over and pulled him up. He seemed to want to make up for hurting his friends' feelings earlier.

OTHER IMMATURE PERCEPTIONS

Lying, stealing, and even cheating can be caused by children's lack of understanding. Before you decide you have a budding criminal on your hands, work on helping the child understand.

LYING

Young children often get fact and fantasy mixed up (Piaget, 1965/1932). Many adults get very angry when they believe a child is "lying." However, as explained in Chapter 3, the problem may be more a result of being young than one of immorality. Nevertheless, not telling the truth is unacceptable behavior in society. Children still need to learn how to sort out truth from untruth. They also need to learn why the truth is preferable. Effective communication strategies can help us teach both.

> Sam constantly bragged about his amazing exploits, patterned after those of cartoon superheroes. Dennis didn't want to call Sam a liar, but he did want the child to learn. Therefore, he responded with an active listening comment that read between the lines: "It sounds like you wish you were big and strong and could do all those things." This response got Sam onto a reality track for the rest of the conversation.
>
> When Sam told these stories to his preschool friends, they weren't so kind. They argued, "You did not!" Sam's reaction was to argue back and defend his incredible statements. Dennis decided Sam needed more specific feedback. He took the child aside and kindly but frankly told him, "Your friends can't believe you when you tell them things they know can't be true." Dennis continued with more information. "If you tell people things that aren't true, they might not believe you when you tell them the truth." Sam needed time to digest this idea, but Dennis was there to assist his growth over time. Dennis' goal was to help Sam sort out the difference between *real* and *pretend* without losing his joy in pretending.

STEALING

Almost everyone has an experience with "stealing" as they grow up. Taking what doesn't belong to you is a serious crime in society. Many adults believe

Adults can help children learn how to sort out the difference between truth and fantasy.

they must harshly punish children for stealing to save them from a life of crime. Parents and teachers with more knowledge of young children realize the need for helping them learn about ownership (Curwin & Mendler, 1990). Punishment may stop kids from taking something if they think they may get caught, but it won't help them understand why it is unacceptable to take what isn't theirs. Related consequences will help children learn this concept and also increase the likelihood that they will respect others' ownership, even when no one is around to enforce it. A consequence for stealing involves making restitution by replacing what was taken. In the following example, Tory is helped to understand why taking the scissors is a problem, but he is allowed to return them without confrontation.

> Amy complained that there weren't any of the new scissors left. Dennis was surprised. Only two people were cutting, and there should have been three pairs of new scissors. He checked the cubbies and noticed a bunch of cut-paper creations in Tory's. Thinking Tory might have inadvertently scooped up the scissors with his work and stuffed them into his cubby, Dennis picked through the pile. As he moved Tory's backpack aside, Dennis felt a scissors shape pressed against the cloth. A pair of scissors had been stuffed deep into the pack. There was a chance the pair was Tory's own from home, but it wasn't likely. Perhaps he just wanted a good pair of scissors at home.
>
> Rather than putting the boy on the defensive or making him feel guilty by accusing him of stealing, Dennis called a brief class meeting. He announced that one pair of scissors couldn't be found; now there weren't enough for the school. Dennis expressed confidence that they might show up. He concluded, "If anyone finds them, please put them in the lost-and-found basket in the back hallway." Tory looked self-conscious and trapped when Dennis began the meeting. But the final comment brought some relief to his face. No one could see the lost-and-found basket from the classroom. It was back by the cubbies! He could sneak those scissors into it, and no one would see.
>
> An hour later, Dennis glanced in the lost-and-found basket. There were the scissors. He brought them back into the classroom and put them on their tray. Seeing Tory eye them, Dennis offered, "Would you like to use them?" As the child eagerly reached for them, Dennis inquired, "Do you have a good pair of scissors at home?" "Nope," Tory frowned. Dennis replied, "I'll tell your parents where you can buy this kind. Okay?"

CHEATING

How often do you hear complaints from your students that another child is cheating? Sometimes the accused isn't following the rules, sometimes the complainer doesn't understand the rules, and sometimes both are confused.

> Three boys are playing the Transportation game. The procedure is to roll a die, move your game piece the appropriate number of spaces, land on a picture of a vehicle, and draw a card from the pile. If you land on a vehicle that goes on land and also draw a card that reads "by land," you get to keep the card. Having the most cards means winning.

> Suddenly Blake calls out, "Teacher, teacher, Jeffrey's cheating!" Mrs. Jensen comes to see and notices that Jeffrey has five "by water" cards. He earnestly defends himself saying, "I'm not cheating." Mrs. Jensen asks Jeffrey what he thinks the game rules were. "I have the boat (game piece), so I get to keep all the 'By water' cards," he explains. Blake is outraged at that explanation and insists, "You don't get to keep the card unless it matches the place where you land." The other child in the game agrees with Blake.
>
> Mrs. Jensen helps the three boys look at the written rules for the game, which confirm Blake's view. She asks the boys if they want to play by the written rules or make up different ones, like Jeffrey's. Jeffrey is outvoted and he also realizes that he had misinterpreted the game. He is disappointed but agrees to play by the written rules.

Mrs. Jensen focuses on clarifying children's perceptions, not on placing blame. She knows that blaming a child for not understanding does no good.

CONCLUSION

This chapter provides only a few examples of the problem situations children encounter simply because they are young. Sometimes the problem requires only your respectful acceptance of the nature of young children, such as when you are dealing with wet pants or spilled juice. If youngsters can be part of fixing the problem, it helps them feel good about themselves. Sometimes the problem requires you to change your expectations to match the abilities of young children, such as adjusting your plans when youngsters can't sit still any longer. At other times you can help children's growth by teaching them a strategy for making friends, or a skill, such as modeling self-expression through "I messages." Adults can significantly aid children's social maturation by helping them try to understand another child's viewpoint, which is part of learning to negotiate solutions for interpersonal conflicts. Effective guidance for young children also involves knowing when behavior that looks like lying or stealing is really only a reflection of a child's point of view.

When you are searching for the cause of a discipline problem, be sure to consider lack of maturity as a possibility. Remember, your role as the teacher is to allow youngsters the time they need to grow as well as to provide the experiences they need to learn. It may help you to cope with frustration if you can also remember that it isn't their fault when they are inept.

FOR FURTHER THOUGHT

1. A problem to solve: Jason grabs the ball that Tanya and Eric are playing with and runs away laughing. The other two children are hurt and indignant.
   a. Describe the probable cause of the problem.
   b. Describe the guidance approach that addresses that cause.

2. A problem to solve: It is group time at preschool and several children have wandered away to play elsewhere. Most of the children are enjoying the songs and stories in the group, but tend to get distracted by some of the other activities.
   a. Describe the probable cause of the problem.
   b. Describe a guidance approach that helps with that cause.

3. Analyze actual behavior problems and guidance approaches in a setting where you know the children. Cases in which you are the adult providing the guidance will probably prove most instructive.
   a. Describe the situation.
   b. Based on your knowledge of the children involved, state the probable cause.
   c. Describe the adult intervention that addresses that cause.
   d. Describe the children's response to intervention.
   e. If the approach was not helpful, was it unsuccessful because it did not address the actual cause or because one intervention was not enough?
   f. If a different cause is suggested, plan a different strategy for next time.

RECOMMENDED READINGS

Bronson, M. B. (2000). Research in Review: Recognizing and supporting the development of self-regulation in young children. *Young Children, 55*(2),32–37.

Charney, R. S. (1997). *Habits of goodness: Case studies in the social curriculum.* Greenfield, MA: Northeast Foundation for Children.

Katz, L. G., & McClellan, D.E. (1997). *Fostering children's social competence: The teacher's role.* Washington, DC: NAEYC.

Oken Wright, P. (1992). From tug of war to "Let's make a deal": The teacher's role. *Young Children, 48*(1), 15–20.

Ramsey, P. G. (1991). *Making friends in school: Promoting peer relationships in early childhood.* New York: Teachers College Press.

12

UNMET NEEDS

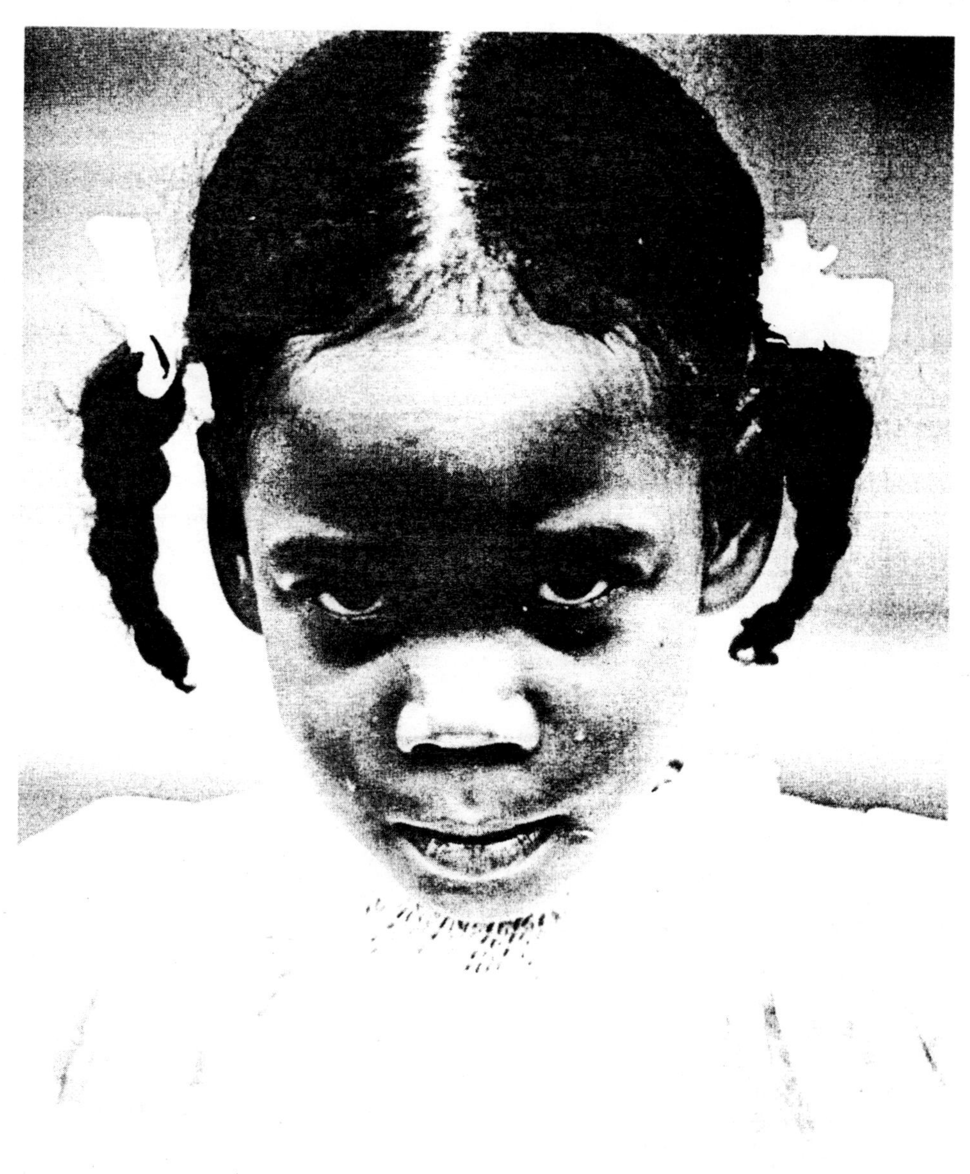

Like a baby's cry, a young child's actions can signal a variety of unmet needs. Although they now have some words, young children may not be articulate enough to communicate their problems. Often they may not even be consciously *aware* of what they need. What's more, even if they do know what they need and can verbalize it, they may not have any idea of what to do about it. Thus, the adult's role is threefold: to help identify the need(s), to help the child learn to communicate them, and to facilitate problem solving so that the needs can be met. This chapter discusses some typical emotional and physical needs that cause problems if left unmet.

This book has used a gardening analogy to explain the importance of dealing with the cause of behavior problems: Discipline that does not focus on the cause of the problem is like weeding your garden without getting the roots of the weeds. The gardening analogy also seems to help explain the importance of meeting children's needs to improve their behavior. Consider the gardener's response to carefully planted seeds that are not growing as expected. Even a novice gardener knows the basic needs of plants—light and water. Checking these needs would be a first step: If the patio table umbrella is shading the plants, move the table. If the roof overhang is keeping rain off, bring the hose over. If you can't figure out the cause of the problem, then you get an expert opinion. But you never "punish" the plants for not growing: you continue to nurture them by meeting their needs to the best of your ability.

Sometimes plants grow, but not the way you wanted. What if you had a trellis for your sweet peas but they were growing along the ground instead? Would you be upset with the sweet peas or would you gently guide the tender shoots onto the trellis? Guiding the growth of children is a lot more complex and demanding than growing plants, but the attitude of the careful gardener can guide the teacher of young children.

PRIVACY NEEDS

Adults, as well as children, often have difficulty properly identifying their own need for privacy. General grumpiness is frequently a sign of a need to be alone. In the following example, the cause of the child's antisocial behavior should have been recognized sooner. The youngster was finally helped to figure out how to get his need met, however. As we explained in Chapter 4, it is important that the school environment offers opportunities for privacy.

> Curt yelled, "Don't talk! I'm trying to concentrate!" as he sat at a table with three other children who were sounding out words for their daily journal writing. The other children were carefully saying each word aloud in an effort to hear the individual sounds and figure out which letters were in the word. Curt was busy with an intricate drawing in his journal and appeared to be feeling very cross. He repeated his demands for quiet several times and finally crawled under the table to work.
>
> Unfortunately, when Julie got up to show her work to the teacher, she bumped Curt's leg in the process, saying, "Sorry." The bump must have made his pencil move where he didn't want it to. Curt began sobbing and yelling, "She made me mess up! I hate girls! I hate that one girl!"
>
> The tantrum was in full swing when Mrs. Jensen came over and told him, "You can lay under the table and cry for one more minute if you need to, Curt, but then you need to get up and figure out how to solve your problem. I'll help you as soon as you are ready." Then she quietly reassured the other children at the table that Curt was upset but he would get over it. She also acknowledged Julie's bumping Curt as an accident.
>
> It was less than a minute before Curt stopped crying and came out from under the table. As Mrs. Jensen led him away for a private conversation, he again yelled, "I hate girls!" His teacher used reflective listening about his feelings, sympathetically saying such things as: "You were having a really hard time concentrating with other children around." And "You are very upset about making that scribble on your drawing." Mrs. Jensen put Curt in charge of solving his problems. She asked him what he could do if he needed to be alone to work and she asked him what he could do about the scribble.
>
> Having his feelings accepted, Curt was able to think about solutions. He decided that he wanted to work alone at a desk, so Mrs. Jensen helped him find an acceptable one. He also admitted that he could erase the scribble since it was done in pencil. He calmed down and went back to work.
>
> Mrs. Jensen recognized that Curt needed some time alone. He seemed more stressed than usual today, though he seemed generally high-strung. She berated herself for not intervening sooner and helping him find a spot alone before things escalated to the point they did. She also noted that Curt needed help with emotion regulation, since this wasn't the first time he had fallen apart over a fairly small problem. Of course, the unmet need for time alone made it harder for him to control his emotions. As is so often the case, there are interwoven causes for Curt's behavior problem.

POWER NEEDS

Sometimes the more you try to get a child to do something, the more resistance you meet. She *won't* put her boots on, he *won't* eat, and nap time is a constant fight. Such behavior is often a symptom of a child's healthy desire to have some control over his or her own life (Curry & Johnson, 1990). Arising conflicts can easily turn into fruitless power struggles. If the adult in charge insists, "You have to eat your lunch," the child insists, "I'm *not* hungry!" A limitation like "No, you can't go outside without your boots. There are puddles under the swings" evokes the response, "I *hate* those red boots!" To the statement, "Your mother still wants you to take a nap," the child replies, "I'm *not* tired!"

The problem may not be about hunger or boot color at all, and the child may actually be tired enough to sleep like a log. These responses may be expressions of the need for personal power. Recognizing this need, the attending adult can, within reason, give the child as many opportunities for choice as possible (Katz & Chard, 1993). She must eat, but which food does she want to eat first, her apple or her sandwich? How does she want to eat her apple, like a worm nibbling through or around and around like a circling caterpillar? He must rest, but which nap story would he like, *Rumpelstiltskin* or *Strega Nona?* Does he want a back rub or to be rocked? She must wear her boots to play in the swings with the puddles under them, but if she wants to play in the fort or the playhouse, she can race out to them in her shiny shoes.

Unmet needs for choice and other personal power can cause behavior problems.

These are *real choices,* both desirable to the child and acceptable to the adult. They give children a chance to satisfy their need for control in a world governed by many rules they don't yet understand. And by allowing them some control at levels appropriate to their age, you will find that children are much more able to allow you to control decisions that must be made by adults. As they experience the desired power, they also develop valuable problem-solving skills. The following situation is an example of a child being allowed some power, choice, and opportunity for problem solving.

> The youngsters at the children's center were going outside to play, and they were excited to get out after being cooped up indoors by bad weather. The joyful hustle and bustle of coats and boots was interrupted by Angelina's wail. She threw her boots across the floor and her coat on top of them. Then she sat crying and hitting her heels on the floor. Sheri, the aide in charge of helping everyone get ready, asked another staff person to help with the other youngsters and went over to Angelina to see what the problem was. It turned out that the little girl had new shoes, and she wanted to wear them instead of taking them off and putting her boots on.
>
> Sheri explained carefully to Angelina that her new pink shoes would get ruined if she wore them out in the mud. Angelina continued to cry and say that she wanted to wear her new shoes outside. Sheri tried reasoning with the child while upholding the rule about not going outside without boots, but Angelina kept crying loudly. Suddenly Sheri remembered what she had learned from the head teacher, Dennis, about giving children choices. Sheri changed her tactics and asked Angelina what she thought she might do to protect her shoes if she kept them on.
>
> Angelina's sobs ebbed as she began to talk about some ideas and possible solutions. Sheri stayed with her as the others trooped outdoors with another adult in charge. Finally Angelina decided to wear some big boots from the emergency supply box, which were large enough to fit over her beautiful new shoes. She was pleased with this solution and happily marched outdoors in the giant boots. Later, Angelina asked Sheri for help. She had decided to change into her own boots, explaining that it was hard to run in the other pair. Sheri noticed that Angelina's concern about wearing her new shoes seemed to evaporate once she had an opportunity to make a decision for herself.

OWNERSHIP NEEDS

"Amy won't share!" This cry is familiar to all who spend their days with preschoolers. In Chapter 11, we explored both undeveloped social skills and egocentricity, both of which contribute to sharing problems. However, it is also important to consider whether or not it is necessary for a child to share at this time. Adults as well as children have a need for ownership of possessions and territory. Notice that office workers want their own designated spaces, and the contents of each person's desk are personal and private. Adults are not required to share the personal items they bring from home to make work more comfortable. Yet we routinely demand more generosity from young children. The need for ownership must be balanced with social expectations for sharing (Curry & Johnson, 1990).

> Dennis addressed the problem of personal possessions at preschool by designating a large box as the "precious place." Youngsters who brought things from home that they didn't want others to touch could put their belongings there and be assured that they would be undisturbed. It was a child's decision when and if to bring something out for the group to enjoy.
>
> Mrs. Jensen found that putting a child's name on a personal possession helped children share. She figured out that having the item labeled as their own fulfilled the need for ownership and freed youngsters to be more generous. First graders enjoyed labeling, which became part of their emerging literacy activities. They began using the approach for staking temporary claim to class materials as well. Thus, when Eric was working on a jigsaw puzzle and had to leave it to go out for recess, he placed a sign on it that said, "Do not tuch. Eric." The children in the class respect such written notices, which solves many potential conflicts.

Both these teachers defend children's temporary or permanent ownership rights. Rather than making children selfish, this defense of their rights actually helps them to be more generous (Hendrick, 1988). When children have their ownership rights respected, they learn how to respect those of others. When they are not busy defending their rights to an item, they are more likely to give it up voluntarily.

ATTENTION NEEDS

Often, behavior labeled as disruptive can actually be a plea for attention—a cry for help! It may take some reflection to realize that a child's irritating behavior is a cry for attention. You may know kids who get attention by showing off, and you have probably seen others who seem to deliberately seek a reprimand for misbehavior. Even negative attention, after all, is attention.

> Courtney's daily "owies" are almost microscopic in size, but she insists that they need a band-aid or a cold pack or a kiss. Mrs. Jensen wants to help her find better ways of feeling important and cared for. Courtney is a strong writer, so Mrs. Jensen helps her get attention and approval through sharing her writing with others. Gradually the "owies" diminish.
>
> Mrs. Jensen thinks Ashley's tattling probably comes from a need for attention, too. She tries hard to give each child some undivided attention. It's so hard that she wishes she could clone herself.

The desire for attention is a legitimate need, yet it is often difficult to meet that need adequately in large group settings. Ratios of ten or more students to one teacher can make it difficult for even the most conscientious child-care worker to give enough personal attention to each individual. Public school classes of twenty or twenty-five children create an impossible challenge. There *is* a limit to how many children you can fit into your lap at once! Levels of need vary among children, depending on their personality types

Some inappropriate behaviors are caused by a need for attention.

and their stages of development. Levels also vary from day to day, and they are often related to the children's rest and stress levels. In addition, sometimes home life can fail to provide adequate attention.

A teacher's awareness of current home factors can provide valuable information, even about children from the best situations. A parent's absence or increased work hours, newborn siblings, or even visiting houseguests can create a need for extra attention. In the following case, teachers combine information from home with observations at school to solve the mystery of Alex's behavior.

> Alex was humming loudly and squirming around in his seat. Alicia, sitting next to him, complained that she couldn't hear the reading teacher. The teacher asked Alex if he heard Alicia. Alex was quiet for awhile, but soon began to hum loudly again and wriggle in his seat. The reading teacher became impatient and sent him back to his regular classroom with instructions to tell his teacher why he returned.
>
> After school, Mrs. Jensen talked to the reading teacher and asked about Alex. She said that as soon as she heard the door open, she knew it would be Alex walking through it. She had been having the same problem with him all day. Some checking revealed that Alex's mother was out of town for a meeting again. Mrs. Jensen remembered then that Alex always has this sort of problem when his mom is gone; she should have realized the cause sooner. It definitely would have been helpful to have been informed about the mother's travel.

Mrs. Jensen made a special effort to give Alex individual attention when he came to school the next morning. She asked when his mother was coming home, and said, "I'll bet you really miss her when she's gone, don't you?" When he went to his reading class, the reading teacher invited him to sit beside her and also talked with him about how long before his mom came home. With this support and extra attention from his teachers, Alex was able to cope with his unmet need for his mother's attention. The humming and squirming stopped.

In some cases, disruptive behavior for attention is not a temporary problem. Some youngsters have a well-learned pattern of trying to get attention and status by disrupting class. No doubt you remember these class clowns from your school days. Their behavior is a sad symptom of low self-esteem and a cry for help (Grossman, 1990). These children need to unlearn their counterproductive strategies; however, as long as their disruptive behavior gets attention, they will continue it. Helping a youngster unlearn a behavior is sometimes called the *extinction* of that behavior. In order to extinguish an unacceptable behavior, you must *never* reinforce it. We consider behavior modification acceptable when it means ignoring inappropriate behavior. This action helps correct mislearning by extinguishing previously reinforced unacceptable behavior (Curwin & Mendler, 1990). Chapter 9 describes behavior modification and explains that occasional reinforcement may actually entrench the behavior more firmly than consistent rewards do. But in the following example, a teacher manages to not reinforce negative behavior:

A group of children was listening to a tape recording of a book about birds and following along in their own copies of the book. The children were enjoying the tape and the book; the vibrant and detailed illustrations helped hold their interest. Then Jeffrey quit listening and began to open and close his book loudly. The other children complained that he was making too much noise and they couldn't hear. Mrs. Jensen went over to Jeffrey and quietly asked him to please stop disturbing the other children. As soon as she walked away, he began the same behavior and got the same complaints from the other youngsters. Refusing to give attention to the behavior this time, Mrs. Jensen said nothing to Jeffrey but instead calmly walked over and turned up the volume on the tape recorder a little so that the others could still hear. Jeffrey's eyes showed his surprise. Because he was no longer getting any attention from his classmates or teacher, he began to follow the text again. Afterward, he had many comments about the birds in the book.

It takes time and patience, but eventually behavior learned through reinforcement will stop once the reward of attention stops. Mrs. Jensen was able to respond effectively to the cause of Jeffrey's behavior because she had made a special effort to understand him and his problems. She knew that Jeffrey not only needed to have his inappropriate behavior ignored, but also needed to have his desire for attention met in another way. Mrs. Jensen did want to give Jeffrey the attention he craved, but not in response to inappropriate behavior. She had been working with his parents on the problem and was making an effort to notice him when he was working well in school. Rather than make an issue over this minor incident, she appreciated that his inappropriate behavior was happening less and less frequently. They had already survived Jeffrey's initial surge of worse behavior, which Mrs. Jensen had known would be the first result of ignoring his inappropriate behavior. They were through the worst and on the road to recovery.

Although ignoring inappropriate bids for attention may be the best approach for some children's growth, there are many other children who may be inadvertently ignored. It is easy to overlook some very quiet children. The too-quiet ones should cause more serious concern than the too-loud ones because they may have given up. They may have quit trying to get their needs met. They often appear blank or unhappy, uninvolved in activities, and generally unsuccessful. Sometimes these children assume victim roles, but more often they seem to fade into the background. You may find yourself wishing that they would actively disagree with something, get upset, or show *some* strong emotion—even if it's disruptive! The source of this kind of problem generally lies outside the school. Chapter 13 discusses ways of getting help for children with more serious unmet needs.

NEEDS FOR SUCCESS AND CHALLENGE

Youngsters who don't complete school assignments often get into trouble. Children who don't participate in planned activities in preschool worry both teachers and parents. There are reasons for their behaviors. Forcing a child to comply or punishing noncompliance does not address the reasons. The traditional loss of recess for not completing work is a classic example of counterproductive discipline. What should you do instead? The answer depends on the cause of the behavior.

You will get clues to the cause by observing the child's specific behaviors and by noting the circumstances surrounding the problem. Does the child look upset or anxious when confronted with the task? Or does the child appear distracted? Is the child interested in something else instead? If so, what is he or she interested in? What kinds of tasks go uncompleted? Does the child only avoid writing, for example, or does he or she avoid all work? Depending on the answers to these kinds of questions, you may decide that the child lacks the ability to succeed at the task, or you might decide that he or she is not sufficiently challenged by it. You may discover that the child does his or her math just fine but can't read the material to complete the science work. Each of these different findings suggests different responses. The goal is to address the problem in such a way that you help the child find success and satisfaction in his or her work. Treating each child as an individual is an important key in meeting this goal.

If Jimmie won't read because the book is too hard, one useful response is to help him find a book at his level. Another response would be to help him improve his reading skill by inviting a volunteer to read to him daily. Perhaps

Helping children to be successful with school work avoids a common cause of misbehavior.

OBSERVATION GUIDE FOR SCHOOLWORK PROBLEMS

- Does the child look upset or anxious when confronted with the task? Or does she merely appear distracted?
- Is she interested in something else instead? If so, what is she interested in?
- What kinds of tasks go uncompleted? Does she only avoid writing, for example, or does she avoid all work?

reading in partnership with a friend who is a little more skillful would be more fun as well as more productive.

If Joel is acting up at math time because he is bored, find a more appropriate challenge for him. Help him find material at his level that is related to topics of personal interest. Yes, math can be relevant, too. Many teachers now help their students find math in the real world and use it to solve real problems.

If Ashley never uses the large-muscle equipment at preschool because she is afraid, help her find activities that will increase her confidence in her physical abilities. Perhaps helping her make friends with Kelsey, who is more physically active, would encourage her. Ashley spends a lot of time in the playhouse area; you could suggest large-muscle activities that fit in with her pretend play.

The need for success, coupled with the need for appropriate challenge, continues as the young child matures. Finding the right balance for each child is essential to avoiding the problem behaviors caused by either boredom or frustration. Instead of assuming that children are misbehaving when they don't match our expectations, it is more helpful to examine the appropriateness of our expectations first.

NEED FOR SECURITY

We usually equate security with safety. Part 2 of this text discussed safety in terms of both physical and emotional security. Clear, consistent limits in both the physical and emotional realms are essential to a safe and secure environment. Although adults generally focus on their obligation to keep children physically safe, children's behavior deteriorates if they lack emotional security (Katz & McClellan, 1997).

Although children can be extremely kind to one another, we also see instances of cruelty. Children sometimes suffer greatly from the thoughtlessness of other youngsters at school. Because their emotional security is being seriously threatened, these children are unlikely to thrive and grow in that setting. Young children are just beginning to develop their sense of how to treat other people. Although we need to give children as much opportunity as possible to learn through experience, we must not allow them to learn at the expense of their peers.

"Tony made a mean face at me and I don't like him," said Rosa as she walked away from Tony. Tony started to cry. This was the second time that week that Tony had been reduced to tears from something Rosa said. Rosa was his next door neighbor, and they had played together all their lives. Now she was rejecting him.

Tony is a good-natured, slow-moving child who is large and very portly. He has eczema, which puts off some children. He has experienced frequent rejections due to his skin condition and due to his lack of athletic ability. He always seems surprised and very hurt by these rebuffs. Apparently Rosa was the one he thought he could count on.

Mrs. Jensen tried to mediate. She put a comforting hand on Tony's shoulder and took him over to Rosa. However, Rosa stated again that she didn't like him and he wasn't her friend. Mrs. Jensen asked Rosa to look at Tony's tears and see how badly she made him feel. She also asked Tony if he had meant to make a mean face. He assured the teacher and Rosa that he had not meant to.

However, Rosa was not receptive, so Mrs. Jensen gave up on that approach. Instead she told Tony, where Rosa could hear her, that she was glad he hadn't made a mean face. Mrs. Jensen added that she thought maybe Rosa had made a mistake, and that everyone makes mistakes. She then tried to meet Tony's need for security by telling him that she was glad he was in the class and by inviting him to come and sit by her for the next activity. Rosa went to the water table and played by herself for awhile. Mrs. Jensen thought that was a good choice for helping Rosa get rid of her obvious grumpiness; it gave her time to herself and also the benefit of the calming influence of water play.

The next day, Mrs. Jensen started the day with some puppet role playing. One puppet asked to play with the other but was told, "You're not my friend, I don't like you." The first puppet hung its head as it sadly turned away. The children were enthralled. Rosa's little mouth was hanging open and her eyes were like saucers.

Mrs. Jensen re-enacted the scene, but this time when the first puppet asked to play, the other one said "Come on, I'd like to play with you." This time the first puppet's head was high and it snuggled up next to the other. "What does the puppet's face look like now?" asked Mrs. Jensen, holding up the puppet that asked to play. Rosa was the first one to loudly proclaim, "Happy!" Encouraged, Mrs. Jensen reminded her class that they could make their classmate's faces and feelings happy or sad by the words they said to them.

However, by late morning—about the same time as the day before—Rosa again became anti-social; she pulled her chair away from Tony, announcing "I don't like you, you're not my friend." Once again, Tony started to cry. Again, Mrs. Jensen intervened, saying to Rosa, "How is Tony feeling right now? Look at his face." This time Rosa stopped pulling her chair away; with a look of amazement, she turned and looked at Tony blubbering away. Within a heartbeat she reversed direction, pulling her chair up close to him. She touched Tony and said, "I'm close now."

Mrs. Jensen almost cried to see this response. She knew that Rosa didn't have the words to explain what was going on, but she had made a moral choice that awed Mrs. Jensen. Of course, this was just a first step in the right direction. Mrs. Jensen knew she needed to help Rosa find private space when she felt grumpy. She also knew that Tony needed special support for peer acceptance.

For children to feel secure in a group, they need to know that others will not be allowed to harass, humiliate, or threaten them. When adults observe such behavior, they need to interact to help the perpetrator recognize how the other child's feelings are being affected. It is time for the adult to accept an authority role and set limits.

Substitute teachers often get treated badly, too. They have a difficult time because youngsters must test this new person's limits. If the usual adult in charge is wishy-washy about limits, children will constantly test that person, too. Testing behavior may appear "naughty," but it is actually an effort to learn what is acceptable in a given situation (Curry & Johnson, 1990). This knowledge provides youngsters with the security of clear expectations. Just as they need safety limits set, children need to have clearly communicated and firmly held behavioral expectations. Although they naturally push against their limits, their tests help them find out where the boundaries are and if those boundaries are flexible.

Teachers who strive for mutual respect with children will involve youngsters in determining appropriate limits and help children understand the reasons for limits. It is wise to have much freedom for individual decisions and choice, but that freedom must have clearly defined limits that protect everyone. Mrs. Jensen, for example, is firm about kindness and safety for all people and animals in her classroom. She also insists on responsible treatment of equipment and materials. Her expectations can be condensed into three easy to remember guidelines: Be kind. Be safe. Be careful.

When behavior limits are unclear, children will act out as a way to learn their boundaries.

CLASSROOM GUIDELINES

Children need limits as well as freedom. These guidelines are easy for young children to learn: Be kind. Be safe. Be careful.

A child having a tantrum may also be a child who needs the security of limits. Children need the emotional security of knowing that someone will help them keep themselves under control. When they experience anger, they can actually terrify themselves with their rage and rapidly escalating emotions. Because they are still learning how to regulate their emotions, they can be overwhelmed by the strength of their feelings and be unable to escape them. Your intervention can actually be a relief, reassuring them not only that you won't let them hurt others, but you also won't let them hurt themselves. Calmly holding a child close and offering comfort will help some youngsters calm down. Others need to be left alone so as not to reinforce the tantrum through attention. However, children must be protected from doing damage to themselves, to others, or to their environment. As they fight to get control of their own actions, children are comforted by the reminder that there are limits outside of themselves.

NEEDS FOR LOVE AND ACCEPTANCE

This basic need is explained in Chapter 2. When these needs are not met, people have difficulty with all other facets of life. Young children need love and acceptance from the significant adults in their lives, and they also need acceptance and friendship from other children.

PEER ACCEPTANCE

This book has emphasized the importance of helping children understand that other people have feelings and thoughts different from theirs. But sometimes you encounter a child who doesn't seem to care how others feel and your best efforts at teaching perspective taking have no effect.

> By the end of the first week of school, Mrs. Jensen could see that Jason was going to be a challenge. He had been creating problems all week: grabbing things from classmates, pushing and shoving to get in front of others, and showing no remorse for hurting them. Mrs. Jensen had helped Allison explain to Jason that it hurt when he shoved her, but Jason wasn't interested.
>
> Mrs. Jensen soon realized that Jason's problem wasn't that he *didn't understand* the impact of his action, but that he didn't *care* whether the other kids were upset. This was a bigger challenge than a child's lack of knowledge. Her job as a teacher was to figure out why Jason didn't care and then to work on that cause.

Mrs. Jensen found out that such children typically have a history of peer rejection (DeVries & Zan, 1994). They don't have friends and don't expect to have any. This puts them in a position of having nothing to lose by offending other children. If Jason doesn't think Randy will play with him anyway, he naturally cares more about whether he gets the most clay than whether Randy is mad at him for grabbing it all. Therefore, the cause of disinterest in other children's viewpoints is an unmet need for acceptance from peers. Of course, this is a self-perpetuating problem: the less Jason considers other children's feelings, the less likely they are to accept him in their activities.

> Mrs. Jensen decides that what Jason needs most is a friend. She wonders if she can get Alan to take Jason under his wing. Alan is a popular boy with good social skills who would provide a useful role model for Jason. Mrs. Jensen privately explains to Alan that Jason needs help learning how to get along and asks if Alan would be willing to play with Jason and teach him how. Alan lives up to her expectations of his compassionate nature and agrees.
>
> Being sought out as a reading buddy and a playground teammate by a highly desirable companion is a major change for Jason. Alan's sponsorship gains Jason's temporary acceptance by others, but Alan reminds him that he has to share the ball if he wants to keep on playing. Now Jason does have something to lose by ignoring how others feel. As a result, Mrs. Jensen has a chance to help Jason learn perspective taking. Jason's whole life just took a turn for the better.

TEACHER ACCEPTANCE

Asking teachers to love all the children in their care may be unrealistic; however, at least one definition of love sounds possible: "a strong enthusiasm for another." It *is* reasonable to expect a teacher to have an enthusiastic approach toward children. This enthusiasm can be demonstrated by efforts to create an environment and a program that continually attempt to meet the needs of all the children enrolled. Your efforts are a way of showing love, whether you actually *like* a child or not. What is important is that you accept all children as they are. By respecting each child's unique position and potential, the teacher's role is to care for, guide, and encourage all the children as they grow. Some children are just hard to like. Much as you try not to have favorites, you must admit that some kids (and adults, too) are just a lot more pleasant to be around than others.

> Sandy was once again yelling at the other children, and Miss Wheeler again wished that Sandy hadn't been placed in her room. What a nuisance she was. She was always getting into fights with the others, and constantly talked out of turn but would never answer a question when called on. As if those difficulties weren't enough, Sandy lost everything. She never had a pencil, never knew where her reading book was, and always lost her lunch box. Miss Wheeler had tried everything. It seemed that Sandy was constantly taking time-out for interrupting or fighting. And Miss Wheeler had finally begun taking everything away from Sandy that she might lose. Sandy's only reaction was to pout and look like she was going to cry, but Miss Wheeler thought it was an act because there were never any tears. Now look at the child! She was crawling under the table instead of sitting on her chair. What next?

Miss Wheeler clearly doesn't like Sandy, and neither do the child's classmates. Her behavior gets constant rejection from others. As a result of this rejection, Sandy has learned that she is a bad girl. The more she believes this lesson, the more she acts accordingly. As strange as it may sound, her reaction is normal and human. People who feel unlovable tend to act unlovable, which makes them feel worse and act worse (Rabiner & Cole, 1989). What a vicious cycle! The only hope for Sandy is to break the cycle by introducing experiences that teach her good things about herself. It won't be easy to change her self-image. At first, she will be so uncomfortable with positive feedback that she will act even worse (Miller, 1996). This behavior is the normal reaction of a person with low self-esteem: It is unsettling to be treated in any way incompatible with one's own self-image. Therefore, Sandy's first response to good feedback will be to act worse in order to show others who she really is. It takes dedication and perseverance to help a child unlearn a negative self-image. Planting a positive image in its place is essential to a child's success in life.

The following example shows how adults can start the process by gaining a more positive perspective on a child.

> At one staff meeting of Midway Children's Center, everyone was complaining about Leo, who was exhibiting particularly undesirable behavior. To relieve the negative focus, Caroline, the director, suggested an exercise. She asked everyone to think of just one thing they really liked about Leo. Some were embarrassed to find themselves struggling at first to come up with a positive point. Gradually, though, they each brought to light one part of the child they could genuinely say they liked. Musical himself, Dennis said he liked Leo's singing. Even though Leo was usually disruptive during music time, at least he was on key! Nancy liked his eyes. Sure, they were constantly darting around,

checking to see if anyone was observing his mischief, but Nancy had to admit they were bright, beautiful brown eyes, just like her mother's. Maureen respected his self-assurance. He may have been bossy, but at least he was capable, an attribute Maureen valued. As the list grew, the teachers felt themselves coming to a new appreciation of the boy they had been complaining about earlier. It didn't erase their irritation with his behavior, but it did put that behavior into a little more positive perspective. They were then in a better frame of mind to brainstorm about ways to help him.

The children who are hardest to like are the ones that need your acceptance the most (Katz & McClellan, 1997). Their unmet needs for love may be acute, causing behavior that is extremely demanding. If you feel unable to meet their needs, they can become an irritation and a drain. Or they can become a challenge! It depends on your attitude.

It can be exciting to work with difficult children; although they may take the most out of you, they are also potentially the most rewarding. You will be delighted when a child who usually hits in anger progresses for the first time to venting that anger verbally. At that important moment, you can see the results of your coaching. A habitually disruptive child who makes it through a whole day, or even a whole hour, without having a negative effect on the group can give you hope for humanity! It also allows you to congratulate yourself on helping that child channel his or her energies more productively.

CONCLUSION

When children have behavior problems caused by unmet needs, effective teachers can help them get those needs met in acceptable and productive ways. Accurately determining when a child has an unmet emotional need and responding to that need can eliminate many unproductive discipline efforts. Additionally, you can make a difference in a child's whole future by intervening in the early years and not allowing the problem to escalate.

As you work at helping children get their needs met, you will come to appreciate the obvious "problem children." They are literally crying out for help; you can't ignore them. But they are also generally the survivors. The too-quiet child may have the serious problem. Consider this child as you read Chapter 14.

FOR FURTHER THOUGHT

1. A problem to solve: Several children in your child-care center refuse to help at clean-up time before lunch.
   a. What is one possible cause? Describe the guidance approach that addresses it.
   b. What is another possible cause? Describe the guidance approach that addresses it.

2. A problem to solve: Jenny keeps forgetting to put her papers into her cubby. At the end of the day a mad scramble ensues, often accompanied by tears, while everyone searches for Jenny's papers.

    a. What is one possible cause? Describe the guidance approach that addresses it.
    b. What is another possible cause? Describe the guidance approach that addresses it.

3. Analyze actual behavior problems and guidance approaches in a setting where you know the children. Cases in which you are the adult providing the guidance will probably be the most instructive.

    a. Describe the situation.
    b. Based on your knowledge of the children involved, state the probable cause.
    c. Describe the adult intervention that addresses that cause.
    d. Describe the children's response to intervention.
    e. If the approach was not helpful, was it unsuccessful because it did not address the actual cause or because one intervention was not enough?
    f. If a different cause is suggested, plan a different strategy for next time.

RECOMMENDED READINGS

Bean, A. L. (1999). *The bully-free classroom.* Minneapolis: Free Spirit Publishing.

Berger, K. S. (1998). *The developing person through the lifespan.* New York: Worth.

Developmental Studies Center. (1998). *Ways we want our class to be: Class meetings that build commitment to kindness and learning.* Oakland, CA: author.

Harris, T. T., & Fuqua, J.D. (2000). What goes around comes around: Building a community of learners through circle times. *Young Children, 55* (1), 44–47.

13

CHILDREN EXPERIENCING DISABILITIES

by Dr. Eileen Hughes

Teachers in child-care centers, preschools, and primary grades are working with diverse populations that require a broader and deeper understanding of teaching and learning principles than in past years. Educators in early childhood and early childhood special education are engaging in dialogue and research resulting in principles for effective teaching and learning for all children. The most current version of the guidelines for developmentally appropriate practices (Bredekamp & Copple, 1997) includes recommendations for working with culturally and developmentally diverse children. As early childhood educators and early childhood special educators collaborate in the same educational settings, the need for closer examination of learning environments that are driven by sound educational principles has emerged. The following observation is an example of the "growing pains" the two fields experience as educators learn how to best provide a supportive environment that fosters meaningful relationships among all its members. The following observation took place in a community child-care center that has a history of including children with disabilities.

> Four-year-old Eric is swinging in the blue swing that was designed so he can sit independently. Eric has cerebral palsy that affects his ability to speak and walk. A girl with disabilities from another class is pushing him, and Joan, an instructional assistant, is standing next to him. Two other women surrounding Eric are professionals from the special education program who are visiting the center to gather information about Eric's development. The woman with the clipboard and pencil is leaning in front of the swing as she talks to Eric. She says, "Isn't that nice she is pushing you?" Her tone reflected talk to a younger child. "Oh, Tonya gave you a big push (She emphasizes the word *big*). And you like that." Eric smiles and laughs. She continues, playing what almost resembles a peek-a-boo game by moving her face away then moving back when the swing comes forward. Eric laughs hard as she continues. At one point the woman asks Eric if she can swing,

> and he shakes his head, "No." A blonde girl sucking her thumb is standing back observing the playground. An adult asks her, "Can you use that swing?" She looks puzzled and says, "No, cause I am a big girl (She emphasizes the word *big*). "Who is the swing for?" "Eric," the girl responds in a matter-of-fact tone.

The adults surrounding Eric send messages to the other children through their actions and words. The children on the playground may have perceived Eric as a younger child for several reasons. Eric was surrounded by several adults and was being talked to as though he was a much younger child. The number of adults standing around Eric also sets him apart from the other children and is not common practice for the other children. Jerome Bruner (1987) discusses how the social context and language that children are exposed to contributes to the ways they will construct knowledge of their social world.

> It is by such subtle means, as well as by more direct linguistic forms such as metaphors and symbols, narratives and images, that the child picks up the vast array of messages about social categories, expectations of behavior, etc. that she needs to cope with the social and conceptual world. (Bruner, 1987, p. 24)

In the earlier observation, Eric was "included" in his preschool setting; however, educators were not reflecting on the ways the other children might be influenced and how this would affect their relationships with Eric. The time has come to look beyond teaching isolated social skills. It is also time to look beyond simply placing children with disabilities in typical classrooms as the end goal of inclusion. We must examine how approaches of teaching and learning reflect our image of children: all children and each child.

As young children with disabilities are being included in settings with their peers, we must create environments to support children's construction of understandings about differences and commonalities. We must work for understandings that build healthy and meaningful friendships, relationships, and associations.

Historically, different philosophical perspectives and practices have characterized the two fields of early childhood and early childhood special education. Early childhood special education has had a strong grounding in behavioral perspectives that, at times, promoted deficit-driven models, focusing primarily on what the child can't do. This focus resulted in teaching isolated skills instead of encouraging meaningful learning experiences in a relevant context. The field of early childhood special education has recognized the limits of a strict interpretation of applied behavioral analysis (Wolery & Wilbers, 1994). Early childhood education has had strong roots in a more maturational or developmental view and continues to draw upon other disciplines and perspectives. Professionals in both fields are faced with the shifts in current research on teaching and learning. Thus, current practices are being influenced by a more comprehensive and deeper understanding of the ways in which young children learn.

In any field, theoretical perspectives may translate to principles that are interpreted into teaching practices. In our daily lives as teachers, we work with children making thousands of decisions. Often we teach without the necessary time required for reflection or understanding of how our actions are congruent to theory, principles, or beliefs. Misunderstandings of theoretical perspectives can lead to the misuse of teaching practices. For example, one of the most misunderstood practices in the field of early childhood, or early childhood special education, is the use of "reinforcers." The use of reinforcers (verbal, activity/event, or tangible) can become a way of motivating children to do what we think is best. We see that children will "behave" if we give them a sticker or make recess contingent on finishing all their assignments. However, the child's actions are short-lived and the child is relying on an external motivator instead of learning to behave himself. Sometimes teachers in situations that demand immediate attention fall prey to the use of quick-fix thinking and strategies. At times, these strategies become applied to all children with little regard to what the individual child actually learns.

Sometimes teachers are placed in a position to "catch" a child so that a "consequence" for that behavior can be delivered. Operating under these conditions, a teacher could allow the child's actions to camouflage the potential and strengths of that child. For example, a Head Start teacher explained how the staff she worked with was very discouraged with a child who had difficulty playing with other children. The child used language that was not appropriate for the classroom and had difficulty staying with most activities. The staff was quick to time-out the child and jump in to correct the child's actions. The Head Start teacher decided to videotape the child when he was engaged and interested in activities or experiences to learn more about his interests. She found that on the playground he was very curious about the environment and took joy in explaining to her about the bark on the tree or the ice that was forming on the ground. When she shared her discoveries with the staff, the staff was surprised at the child's knowledge and the amount of time he was able to focus his attention. The Head Start teacher and her staff were learning to "reframe" the way they viewed the child's actions (Olson, Burgess, & Streissguth, 1992).

The use of praise is another overused strategy often observed with children with disabilities. Because the field of special education has promoted the use of reinforcers, teachers have become quick to comment on the actions of children. Sometimes, the teacher will say things such as, "I like the way you _______ " or "Good Job." These comments tend to be frequent and are often almost automatic. Certainly, our intentions are to recognize the positive actions of the child; however, the teacher may also be creating a dependency on teacher approval. Thus, the child's actions are short-lived and probably for the wrong reasons.

As classrooms become more heterogeneous, teachers find themselves needing effective classroom management systems for a wide array of disabilities. The authors recognize that there may be situations that require curricular modifications or individualized teaching strategies for some children. There are times when special educators and early childhood educators must collaborate to determine ways to individualize or make

As classrooms become more heterogeneous, teachers find themselves needing effective classroom management systems for a wide variety of disabilities.

curriculum modifications for a particular child. When educators work in teams, they can collaborate to make appropriate decisions related to objectives, teaching strategies, and curricular modifications. These decisions must be based in an environment and curriculum that support moral and intellectual autonomy, respect for others, positive self-concept, and problem-solving for all young children. The following examples show ways for thinking about a Constructivist approach to guidance for children with disabilities.

THE SOCIAL ENVIRONMENT

Previous chapters explained why effective classroom management is dependent in part on the way children feel about themselves and each other. A classroom that supports the self-esteem of all its members will foster healthy relationships among children. When children observe you modeling respect and caring actions, they are more likely to have socially desirable behavior. Supporting children to become socially competent and to develop perspective taking is essential for effective classroom management. Social skills, as well as understanding the viewpoints of others, are necessary for children to solve conflict, understand the meaning of fairness, and build a community of learners.

As teachers, we must recognize the importance of the classroom as a place where young children learn about the roles, responsibilities, norms, expectations, and patterns of interacting. Corsaro (1985) suggests that young children come to understand themselves as members in a group through their peer culture. In the cultural context of their classrooms, young children acquire prosocial behaviors and come to understand the intricacies of relationships and ways of acting with others. Children co-construct their understanding about the values of the community and their classroom environment. Through interactions with each other, young children exchange their ideas and understandings to co-construct knowledge and assign meaning to experiences. In addition, adults in the environment provide ways of ascribing meaning to experiences, or behaviors that give information about group norms. Thus, educational settings that support children of varying abilities must mirror the beliefs, perceptions, and "inclusive" values of its members.

Mallory and New (1994) advocate that the Social Constructivist theory offers a framework for understanding inclusionary education and that the Reggio Emilia approach from Italy exemplifies programs that demonstrate practices that are consistent with this theory. One of the many meaningful underlying principles of this approach is that all children are viewed as being capable, having "special rights" and contributions to a community of learners (Edwards, Gandini, & Forman, 1998). Differences in children are recognized, valued, and used to develop knowledge about a child. In fact, the teachers in Reggio Emilia talk about the "image" of the child as being capable and having potential. This image of the child is projected on all children and is central to how educators interact with children, design environments, and build curriculum. When children with disabilities share the same educational setting with their nondisabled peers, there can be an opportunity for teachers and children to assign meaning to the experiences that create understanding related to "disability." We, as teachers, can construct with children the meaning of disability through our daily interactions that involve acceptance, understanding, and recognition of potential and capability.

Nondisabled children may be uncomfortable with unusual behaviors exhibited by children with disabilities. A child with a disability may not be able to communicate using speech and instead may use non-verbal actions. A child may have the power of speech, yet exhibit behaviors that are ambiguous and difficult to interpret. When a child's actions are misunderstood, or behaviors are disruptive to the classroom, a teacher must consider the actions she will take that will help the other children come to understand how to interact with the child with disabilities. Punitive actions or other actions that give negative messages about a child undermine the culture of the classroom. They are not consistent with a caring community that supports self-esteem; instead, they lead to an increase in conflict situations.

Helping nondisabled children to understand or assign meaning to atypical behavior teaches them perspective-taking and lessons about differences among people. Children in preschool settings often compare themselves to each other as it relates to their age or size. Using these dimensions to compare themselves to each other is what children at this developmental age know how to do. As young children step out of diapers and assert their independence with peers, they come to understand how they are alike and different. When children who have disabilities display behaviors that appear disruptive to others, it can be confusing to the ways children typically learn about differences among themselves. The way a teacher rejects or accepts differences, behaviors, or characteristics of children provides a model for the other children. At the same time that you are supporting the nondisabled children, you can also build the self-esteem and self-image of the child with disabilities. Thus, the social context for young children should provide dimensions that will support: (a) perspective-taking, (b) the strengths of each child, and (c) relationships among children.

PERSPECTIVE-TAKING

Perspective-taking helps children to: (1) learn about multiple viewpoints and different ways of thinking, (2) problem-solve, and (3) accept other children who have different characteristics. Teaching children about "seeing" another view can help nondisabled children to understand children who exhibit unfamiliar or confusing behaviors. Children with disabilities may display behaviors that appear odd, confusing, or even frightening to other young children.

> Becky, a six-year-old child with significant disabilities, attends a community preschool and is the only child with a disability in her class. A five-year-old boy in her class observes Becky as she lays screaming on the floor. The boy comments to his friend, "She is a baby. She is six and I am five. You know what? She wears diapers and she stinks." The boy's comments reflect a question about why Becky, who is taller and older than himself, still wears diapers. Becky's teacher responds to the young boy, "You wore diapers, I wore diapers, and Becky needs diapers now."

Becky's teacher views her role as a guide for the children to provide an explanation for Becky's behavior. She wants the children to understand about Becky, and at the same time support a positive image of Becky as a member of the group. Becky's teacher knows preschool children compare themselves using physical characteristics to understand similarities and differences. She believes that Becky's behaviors are confusing to the other children as they compare her to themselves. Further explanation in a private conversation between the teacher and the boy might alleviate the child's concern. By responding to the nondisabled children's concerns, teachers can help them to understand the behaviors of their peers with disabilities. This can lead to a supportive classroom environment and reduce conflict with children with disabilities.

In another classroom, three-year-old Thomas teaches us how to interpret the behaviors of a child with disabilities. His response reflects an acceptance of difference and shows perspective-taking.

> Four-year-old Eric is in the same preschool class as Thomas. Eric has cerebral palsy that influences his mobility and the ways he moves his arms. It is not uncommon that when Eric sits next to his peers he inadvertantly moves his arm and hits them. Several of the boys in the class are bothered by his action and call for the teacher. For example, on one occasion a boy next to Eric yelled out, "Hey, he's hitting me and I can't draw." Eric's intentions are sometimes unclear. His arm movement might have been involuntary, but over time it may have become intentional as he gained attention from others when he touched or "hit" them.
>
> Thomas, who often plays alongside Eric, is observed as he plays with a small plastic playhouse. Eric is on the floor opposite the house and Thomas. Eric moves his arm and as he moves, he knocks the house over onto Thomas. Thomas looks surprised and replies, "Darn house." Thomas does not interpret Eric's actions as an intentional act to disrupt his play, nor does he call for the teacher.

A lesson to learn from Thomas is to observe how nondisabled children can give meaning to behaviors in ways that build acceptance for the differences among children. Teachers can consider ways to extend Thomas' observations and use them to help other children who view situations less positively.

Perspective-taking is taught through the ways teachers invite ideas from individuals in a group. The goal is to help children realize there are other perspectives than their own, that other children also have things to say and want turns. In the following dialogue, Jason, who is diagnosed with ADHD, is trying to dominate the group discussion. Jason is still learning to take turns and sometimes has difficulty knowing how to express his ideas in a group setting. The teacher strives to include him in the group without removing or "punishing" him.

The following transcription is taken from a circle time activity with Jennifer, a preschool teacher. The children are in an ongoing discussion about dinosaurs. The dialogue reflects only a portion of the circle time discussion that started when Jason volunteered to share his "weekend." The children are encouraged during Monday's circle time to share stories about their weekend, and on this Monday Jason is telling about a dinosaur movie he watched at home.

Jason:	Quiet everybody! (yelling) It was my weekend!
Teacher:	Let's listen to Aaron.
Aaron:	The dinosaurs umm, eat umm, dirt umm . . . they make it
Jason:	No they don't eat dirt!
Teacher:	Jason, Aaron thinks that some dinosaurs might have eaten dirt.
Jason:	They don't eat dirt!
Teacher:	You might think that they don't.
Jason:	I know it's not dirt . . . I know it's not dirt.
Teacher:	But this is what Aaron thinks; you might think something different.

Aaron: They eat dirt and they eat whales except they're not s'posed to.

Teacher: And what do they eat that they're not supposed to?

Aaron: Whales that they're not s'posed to, the killer ones, killer whales.

Jason: Aaron did all my weekend, nobody gets a question.

Teacher: Geoffrey has something to say. Let's listen to Geoffrey.

Jason: Nobody gets a question. (loudly over everyone) Nobody. Nobody gets a question! Mine.

Christopher: I have my hand up.

Jason: No you don't. I'm not gonna . . . put your hand down I'm not gonna let you have a question. . . . You can't have a question. (yelling) Nobody gets a question. Put your hand down!! Put your hand down!

Teacher: I'm sorry, Geoffrey. I couldn't hear.

Jason: Put your hand down Christopher and do it now! (being forceful) Christopher if you s'pose to do that, I'm gonna tell.

Teacher: Jason, I'm having a hard time hearing Geoffrey.

Jason: Nobody gets a question.

Teacher: I'm having a hard time hearing Geoffrey.

Jason: Nobody does.

Teacher: We're having an open discussion.

Jason: If you are gonna say that, I'm just gonna say the loudest words that I—.

Teacher: Will you listen to me for a minute? We started talking about dinosaurs. All of us are sharing our ideas. We're discussing about dinosaurs. Some people think differently and that's okay. So we're all discussing. Geoffrey is going to finish what he's saying and then we're going to let Austin and Christopher talk. Okay, if you would like another chance to talk just put your hand up and that will let me know.

Jason: This is my weekend!

Teacher: I know, you told us about the movie that you watched, I was real excited to hear all of the fun stuff that you learned about dinosaurs. That was real interesting. I'm really glad that you shared.

Jennifer teaches the other children to express their ideas while at the same time teaching Jason rules and limits for remaining in circle with his friends. First, Jennifer restates to the children their ideas, noting the children's different ideas about what dinosaurs eat. Second, Jennifer is patient with Jason, allowing him to express himself. Third, she helps Jason to remember the class rules by repeating that he must raise his hand and he must listen to the ideas of the other children. Jennifer is not used to working with children like Jason. However, Jennifer is working in collaboration with a special education support team to support Jason in his community child-care settings. Jennifer and the special education team are learning new ways of supporting all children as they reflect on their observations in the social context.

Earlier in the chapter the Reggio Emilia approach was mentioned and cited as providing teachers in America with examples of ways to support children with disabilities that values and recognizes their abilities (Smith, 1998). One of the many ways teachers in this child-care system teach perspective-taking is to literally design a physical environment that allows children to "reflect" on their images and to see materials, or themselves, from many different views. This concept has been applied to the teaching of self-image and children with disabilities. Mirrors are often situated in the classroom, allowing children to "play" with their images and to come to know themselves in relationship to others. Recently, the author observed an infant with cerebral palsy as she moved from side to side in front of a mirror. She moved to catch the light from the window and played with the mirror, touching at the reflection of her face. She smiled, looked away, and repeated these actions. This could have been a wonderful opportunity to encourage other children in the group to join in the play. This example is mentioned here to encourage you to think about the concept of perspective-taking that can be "provoked" even in the design of the environment. Thus, as you develop your approach to guiding young children in your classroom, you will need to consider the ways to support all children learn about the differences among themselves.

RECOGNITION AND SEEING STRENGTHS

Creating an environment with capable children who view each other with respect and who value the attributes of each member means teachers must make visible the strengths and gifts of each child. In the following kindergarten classroom, Miss Forrest prevents a potential classroom disruption when she observes Mark, a child with developmental delays, who squirms and bothers the other boys sitting next to him. Until this year, Mark has always had a teaching assistant assigned to his classroom. This year, in Miss Forrest's class, Mark is spending time away from the teaching assistant. Mark has difficulty in groups and seeks the attention of his peers by getting close in their face or hitting them. Often children react to his actions by entering into interactions that disrupt the class activities. Note the way Miss Forrest anticipates Mark's actions, recognizes his interests, and in the midst of the classroom discussion shifts her lesson to prevent the mounting conflict from the back of the room.

> The children in Miss Forrest's class are engaged in a group discussion about a wood carving experience from yesterday. A small group of boys in the back of the room begin to talk to each other and start to hit each other, causing others in the group to turn around. Miss Forrest is making a list of the children's ideas, writing down their comments on a poster board at the front of the room. She then

Highlighting the abilities and strengths of all children helps them engage in healthy interactions with each other.

> observes Mark getting restless and sees the other boys start to enter into interactions with Mark. At this point, Miss Forrest calls Mark up to the front of the class and asks him if he will draw something he remembers from yesterday. She rewords her direction to help him comprehend. She hands him the pen to draw on the paper and asks him to write some letters. Miss Forrest interprets Mark's actions to the class. She says that he is drawing an idea he remembers and that he is using his words to write about his idea. Mark turns to his classmates, grinning as though pleased with himself, and gestures as he uses his limited speech.

In this example, Miss Forrest redirects Mark's attention to avoid creating more problems for the group. She knows that Mark has difficulty in large groups as he does not comprehend at the level of the other children, and his way to seek attention is to bother others. Further, Miss Forrest knows that Mark takes an interest in drawing (making undistinguishable marks). She then interprets Mark's "letters" for the children. Miss Forrest gives Mark attention and prevents a further escalation of actions that might disrupt Mark and the other children. In addition, she makes Mark's abilities visible to the other children.

In the Reggio Emilia approach, (Edwards, Gandini, & Forman, 1998), teachers acknowledge that a "handicap" is just one of many differences among people. In the instance above, Miss Forrest was co-constructing with the children the ways that Mark was different. At the same time, she was building a sense of self for Mark that would support his relationships and positive associations with the other children. This guidance strategy is a very different approach than what many typically observe when a teacher would "time-out" Mark for "inappropriate" behaviors.

By recognizing children's strengths and bringing them to the attention of the group, you create a climate for children to observe and interpret the variety of ways to understand "difference." When children learn that the differences among themselves are positive and can be strengths for the group, children will be better able to create healthy relationships with each other. Note the way the teacher in the following classroom observes ways to highlight the strengths of the children in her room.

> Jacob is diagnosed with ADHD and attends a local community child-care setting. His teacher is aware that Jacob has difficulty with other children. It is not an uncommon occurrence that children will move away from Jacob when he tries to control a play situation. The teacher is also aware of the different ways Jacob sees an event, observation, or situation that the other children sometimes miss. For example, at Christmas time four children are constructing a Santa Claus to hang in their playhouse. The children are on the floor, drawing the various parts of the Santa on butcher paper. One child decides to draw the head, another girl decides she will draw the body, and someone else decides to draw the legs. The children work next to each other on their separate parts. Jacob, who is engaged in a playdough activity across the room, runs over to the children and says, "Hey you guys, that is never going to work." The children stop momentarily, then continue to work on their parts. The teacher, overhearing Jacob and observing the children, intervenes and comments, "Jacob has an idea." One of the children looks up and says, "What, Jacob?" Jacob proceeds to explain that the parts won't go together. The teacher asks Jacob for his idea. Jacob tells the children that some parts are too small for the head and it will look "funny." The children ask Jacob what they should do. Jacob says they should start over and make Santa bigger. The children exchange ideas with Jacob and come up with the idea to trace the teacher.

There are many ways the children could solve their problem. The teacher, knowing that Jacob has difficulty working with others, decides to use this opportunity for a learning situation. She focuses the group's attention to Jacob's idea and supports Jacob in his own way to gain entry into the group activity. Because the children have observed Jacob to be someone that gets into trouble with the other children, the teacher facilitates an interaction with Jacob. She also guides the other children to construct a more positive image of their peer who can offer creative and imaginative ideas.

In another preschool, two-and-a-half-year-old Meona is supported Becky as an "expert" in making puzzles by her teacher to view. Becky is the only child in her class with developmental and language delays, and she frequently demonstrates behaviors that draw attention to her. These behaviors at times cause some children in her class discomfort. Similar to Jacob's teacher, Becky's teacher supports the children in her class to "see" the strengths of others.

> Becky is observed by Meona every morning when she arrives to preschool and pulls out the puzzles. One morning Meona pulls out a puzzle and sits across from Becky. The teacher stands nearby and observes the two girls. Meona, watching Becky, looks to her teacher and says, "Maybe Becky will help me." The teacher responds, "Maybe. You could ask her." Meona turns to Becky and says, "Will you help me?" Becky looks briefly at Meona and continues doing her puzzle. Meona watches Becky and chants to herself, "Maybe she will, maybe she will."

Becky's teacher uses this interaction between the two girls to support Meona's initial observation of Becky as someone who is capable and can offer help. Becky's teacher knows Becky does not comprehend the words of others and has limited speech abilities. However, she supports Meona's idea that Becky can help with the puzzle. She allows Meona to think about Becky as someone who has abilities in puzzle making. The teacher could also extend this situation to support Becky in her own ways to show Meona how to put the puzzle together. This observation also illustrates how children are able to view children with significant disabilities as having something valuable to contribute.

In another preschool, five-year-old Allison observes her friend Christine, who has cerebral palsy and cannot walk or talk, as someone who is capable of communicating. While Allison is only five years old, like Meona she gives meaning to Christine's behaviors that suggest she views Christine as someone who is capable. Both Meona and Christine are able to "see" the strengths despite their friend's obvious physical disabilities or other developmental delays.

Allison, overhearing Christine vocalize "Aaaaaaaaah," says, "She said Aaaaah; that means Allison." On another occasion Allison, who is sitting across from Christine, notices Christine look up at the top of the toy shelf. Allison says, "She is looking up. She wants the toy house."

Allison assigned meaning to Christine's behaviors that suggests she: (1) recognizes and acknowledges her subtle behaviors and (2) interprets Christine's vocalizations in ways that suggest Allison views Christine as someone capable of communicating and expressing her desires.

When you highlight the strengths of children with disabilities you can also build their self-esteem. At the same time you can support opportunities for their further interactions with peers.

ENCOURAGING FRIENDSHIP

As explained in Chapter 4, friendship among young children is critical to their intellectual and emotional development. When children feel good about themselves, the dynamics of the classroom are likely to be more friendly. When children feel confident and liked by their peers, the classroom will likely have less conflict among children.

Young children with disabilities are at risk for difficulties when socializing with their peers (Guralnick & Groom, 1988). Children with developmental delays can have difficulty initiating and maintaining interactions with other children. The attitudes and perceptions of nondisabled children can also influence their relationships with children with disabilities. In Constructivist

Children with disabilities need even more planned opportunities to interact with others. Group work helps children with diverse abilities find a place among peers.

classrooms, teachers encourage children to work collaboratively to encourage the incidental, or spontaneous, opportunities for social interaction. Children with disabilities will need even more opportunities to interact with others. At times you will need to modify your values, objectives, or activity routines to consider the social needs of the child with disabilities. In the following example, Miss Wheeler puts her own values first instead of the social needs of the children.

> Eric is painting alongside Martha and Vanessa. Martha blows paint from her paintbrush. Vanessa laughs and does the same with her paintbrush. The two girls continue giggling as they play a game. Eric watches the two girls and holds up his brush to his mouth to do the same. Because he has difficulty moving his arm, the brush hits his cheek and he ends up with paint on his face. Miss Wheeler sees the paint and, being very careful to keep Eric clean, wipes his face. The children watch as the teacher wipes Eric, then they return to their game. Eric tries again to enter into the game of the other children and again gets paint on his face. Miss Wheeler remarks to Eric, "I guess you are done." She wipes his face and hands and removes him from the table.

Miss Wheeler has good intentions. However, the way she interacts with Eric ends the potential for Eric's interactions with other children. Miss Wheeler did not recognize the potential for social interaction for Eric and the two girls at the time. If we value the importance of social and emotional development, we must create environments for all children that support interactions.

In Miss Forrest's combined kindergarten/first-grade class, children are observed to work and play in very natural ways. In fact, the climate in the classroom supports the five children with disabilities in their associations with the other children. Miss Forrest, from the first day of the school year, encourages children to go to each other when they need help doing their school work. She identifies the strengths of each child to the group and the members in her class seek resources from each other as a natural part of their daily activity.

Children with disabilities, like all children, need to feel good about themselves. Sometimes teachers tend to focus too much on the child's "needs." Teachers may unintentionally give messages that work against building the self-esteem or enhancing the image of the child with the disability. In the example given, Miss Wheeler could have allowed Eric to join in the play with Vanessa and Martha. Due to her misguided intervention, the girls saw Eric as messy and in need of being cleaned up instead of as someone to play with. Instead, teachers can help children to see different perspectives, to recognize strengths, and to support the children's need for interactions. It is in these ways that teachers can work toward effective classrooms that encourage healthy relationships and consequent harmony among children.

THE PHYSICAL ENVIRONMENT

The physical arrangement of the learning environment provides children with a foundation for understanding the expected classroom behaviors and norms of the classroom community. When children with disabilities are included in environments that are developmentally appropriate, you may need to individualize aspects of the environment. Attention to the social and physical dimensions of the environment can prevent the escalation of behaviors that might cause havoc to a class by the end of a school day. Some children with ADD, ADHD, or FAS, or other developmental delays have difficulty focusing their attention against a background of various sounds and visual information. Regardless of the type of disability, children who have difficulty focusing their attention may vary in their abilities to select or ignore information in the environment. For example, children may appear to be inattentive to verbal directions if they are attending to a noise in the classroom. Research suggests that reducing stimulation may help children focus their attention; however, a sterile environment void of materials may not be the answer (Jones, 1991). Children with ADHD may have difficulty inhibiting impulses from inside their bodies, not just from their environment. Overall, children with attention problems will benefit from the same high quality environments for all children that invite active participation and engage children in meaningful activities (Landau & McAninch, 1993). In developmentally appropriate environments, the teacher will arrange the environment to allow children quiet time or privacy, mobility, and so on. However, there may be times a particular child may need you to tailor or adapt the physical structure of the environment to meet his or her individual needs. The following suggestions are guidelines to consider when adapting the physical environment if a child has difficulty with attention or another type of developmental delay.

CONSIDERATIONS FOR SEAT ARRANGEMENT

Some children have difficulty sitting in large or small group activities. There are some days when a child starts the day calling for attention in a group and by the end of the day the child has hit, yelled, and created lots of discomfort in the classroom. Young children call for help or seek attention for many different reasons, and it's not always easy to know the cause for the disruptive behavior. Children diagnosed with ADHD may experience a symptom called overactivity; teachers often describe these children as fidgeting or always getting up and down (Landau & McAninch, 1993). The arrangement of the classroom environment can influence the child's interactions with the environment and resulting behaviors (Landau & McAninch, 1993; Weaver, 1994). For example, when children who have difficulty remaining in their seats are placed in classrooms with rows of desks that inhibit mobility or choices in activities, teachers will likely have problems. Offering choices in learning areas and offering different areas for seating creates an environment more conducive to the learning of all children, especially those who have trouble remaining in their seats. In addition, offering choices for types of seating is also encouraged. For example, comfortable furniture, such as beanbag chairs or soft pillows, offer an alternative to the reading area and invite sitting for longer periods of time.

When a child has difficulty paying attention to the important information in the environment, you can seat the child in front of you or in the center of the group. By seating the child in a visible location, the child can see you better in order to receive directions, both verbally and visually. It is also important to make sure the child is not seated close to environmental sound sources, such as fans, radiators, and so on. Children who are distractible may attend to these background noises and miss the verbal directions from the teacher.

In some instances, a child may need support to calm himself or herself in order to sit with the group. Sometimes teachers can plan relaxation exercises or warm-up exercises prior to "work." These exercises allow the child a chance to learn to focus by moving his or her body in space and to gain greater control over the body. There may be different types of strategies for calming or relaxing children depending on the individual child's characteristics. The following example is one way a preschool teacher helped relax a child with ADHD:

> Maureen found that when she holds four-year-old Matthew on her lap for morning circle, he is able to listen to the other children for longer periods. Rather than punishing Matthew for his difficulties during circle time, Maureen finds that gentle touching and comforting on her lap provides a way to relax this child. Maureen helps him to listen to the other children in this way. Over time, Maureen moves Matthew off her lap and places him next to her where she can put her arm around him when necessary.

Not all children will respond the same as Matthew. However, we can learn to observe when children need support. Sometimes a teacher might be quick to isolate or otherwise punish a child who cannot sit with others. In the previous example, Maureen is building a caring relationship with Matthew while providing the support and attention that allows him to remain a member of the group. Asking the questions, "Why is the child wanting to leave his place in the group?" and "What types of support soothe or calm the child?" are the beginnings to problem solving and identifying adaptations to the environment. Some teachers may question if Matthew is receiving preferential treatment by being allowed to sit on the teacher's lap. Teachers may believe that if Matthew is allowed to sit on their laps, then the other children will want the same treatment. Interestingly, Maureen is faced with the situation one morning when a child questions, "How come he always gets to sit there?" Maureen searches for a good response. However, before she can answer a young girl in circle answers matter-of-factly, "Cause it helps him." Nothing more is said and the children continue with their circle time activity. The teacher concludes that the children are learning about caring, individual differences, and fairness through this situation.

In Miss Forrest's classroom, Mark, who was introduced earlier in the chapter, will sometimes be seated in the front row for group discussions so that the teacher can move to be close to him if necessary. She is conscious to not always have Mark right next to her, but she knows that until he can remain with the other children without adult attention, she will need to observe his actions closely.

A child with ADHD may have difficulty returning to the same assigned place in the room for seating. In some instances, seating the child next to other children who will provide reminders for expected classroom behaviors can be a support. Offering choices for seating that are acceptable can also be an alternative. For example, you might tell the child, "You may sit next to Joe or here next to Mary." You allow the child some choice, but provide appropriate options for his or her choice.

Sometimes thinking about the physical environment makes teachers forget about the social environment when they make decisions about classroom management. In the following classroom, the children are not socializing with Becky because of where she sits.

> Becky has difficulty sitting in the small chairs in her classroom. Because she falls out of the chairs, she is given a desk and a larger chair against the wall. Over time, the children in the class, as well as Becky, learn that the desk against the wall is "Becky's table." No other child or adult could use the chair, and this becomes a special place meant only for Becky.

Because the table accommodates only Becky, the opportunities for social interactions are limited, and Becky's isolated physical place becomes her social place in the classroom community. Another alternative is to consider adding more chairs with a wide base of support to prevent tipping. Becky would then have opportunities for interactions with the other children.

In a similar situation, four-year-old Eric cannot walk and is often placed at the table or on the floor by his teacher. In preschool children learn quickly that if you want to talk to your friends, you must find a place next to them at circle or at snack so you can whisper or talk as you wait for the teacher or for the next activity. When adults choose where a child sits, the child may miss the opportunity for interactions that occur when sitting next to friends. For Eric, who cannot move on his own to find a seat, the teacher might ask him where he would like to sit and he could point or vocalize. By offering Eric a choice, the teacher also gives him the opportunity to pick a friend to socialize with, just like the other children. You need to consider the social dynamics of the group and the individual child as well as issues of classroom management.

ORGANIZATION, ACTIVITY AREAS, AND MATERIAL SELECTION

Early childhood classrooms generally offer an array of materials and activities to invite the participation of children with different interests, abilities, and ages. Children who have a difficult time focusing their attention on activities may need more reminders, visual coding systems, or supports to organize themselves in the early childhood environment. For example, an environment that is carefully organized and provides clear messages for the storage of materials will support the child who needs extra environmental cues. A child who is distractible needs to have a place that is clearly identifiable for organizing his or her personal belongings. Materials that are labeled and organized for easy classification help all children, especially those who have difficulty making associations. Visual cues, such as color coding, sometimes help children learn to organize and store their materials.

Some children may need support through the use of physical boundaries that designate their work area. Consider the following situation that illustrates how teachers provide boundaries for Victor.

> Victor has difficulty keeping his tools for drawing or painting on his own paper, and the other children are bothered by Victor's invasion of their space. The teacher defines Victor's work area by giving him a tray to work on at the table. Victor's teacher places carpet squares on the floor to define his area when he plays on the floor with materials that have many parts. Many teachers provide small decorative baskets or containers that help children to put materials away and keep a sense of order in the room. In addition to needing physical boundaries, some children may need to have a limited number of materials or types of choices available at one time. For example, when Victor has half a box of crayons to use instead of the entire box of crayons, he can organize his work place.

In early childhood classrooms, it is not uncommon that activity areas will change to reflect the types of projects or curriculum that attract children's interests. There may be some children, such as those with FAS, who will need more preparation or a longer period of time to adjust to changes in the environment. If the changes are unexpected, the children may have an even harder time adjusting. You can prepare the child for anticipated changes ahead of time or the child could help to make the changes in the class. The child might be included by helping you to move or sort materials in preparation for making changes in the classroom. When children have difficulty with changes in their routines or physical environment, an observant teacher can work to prevent problem behaviors.

There are times you need to seek the support of other team members to identify alternative teaching strategies for a particular child. For example, some children are calmed if they are in certain positions on the floor where they are given physical support and can move parts of their bodies. This way of preparing children helps them to focus their attention to an activity. Some children can concentrate better with gentle rocking to soothe their bodies. Other children do

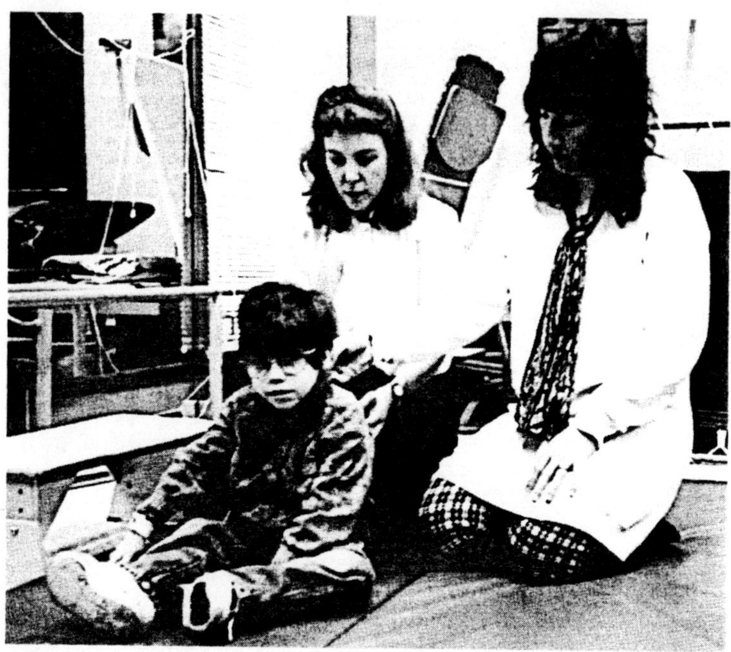

Early childhood teachers and special education staff can work together to identify alternative teaching strategies for children with special needs.

not like to be touched and become bothered when sitting close to another child. Other children need physical boundaries to help them concentrate.

Special education staff can support teachers when making adaptations for children who challenge the typical environment. In the following classroom example, the teacher and special education teacher work together to modify the environment for Elias.

> Elias has difficulty organizing himself and has a hard time putting on his clothes to go outside. In the process of trying he often ends up in fights with the other boys. The teacher collaborates with the special education staff in identifying that Elias has a hard time with the sequence of putting on his clothes. Understanding this helps the teacher to understand why he engages in fighting. The teacher and special education staff figure out ways to use the environment to support Elias. The teacher finds that if she placed his cubbie against the wall and provides a limited place for putting on his coat, Elias takes less time to put on his clothing. He can then be ready to go outside with the other children. The special educators provide a small bench for him to put on his boots. The additional boundaries allow Elias to remain in the area. The modifications in the environment provide boundaries that help Elias to focus on preparing to go outside.

Another aspect of the Reggio Emilia approach that has meaning to the education of young children with disabilities is the belief that children have "100 languages" (Edwards, Gandini, & Forman, 1998). Our Italian educators have much to teach us about the different ways children have to express themselves. In the Reggio Emilia child-care system, you will find many different wonderful raw materials for children to use to express their ideas, theories, or expressions. This concept, as applied to children with developmental delays, is meaningful especially when some children have limited use of verbal language for expression. If children can express themselves through the use of various media (sculpture, music, wire, paper, raw materials), it is more likely that children will have an outlet for expression that might reduce behaviors of frustration.

Identifying dimensions in the physical environment that influence the onset of a child's inappropriate behavior is extremely helpful. Such identification makes it more likely that special education staff can understand the cause of the problem and the needs of the child in the environment. Special education staff can then provide meaningful support to the early childhood teacher and the child in the early childhood classroom environment.

ORGANIZATIONAL STRATEGIES

As noted in Chapter 5, a teacher can prevent problem situations by providing familiar routines and planning carefully for transitions, waiting periods, and group times. The same principles that you use to make decisions related to these organizational strategies will especially apply to children with disabilities. However, as with other aspects of the curriculum, you may need to adapt or modify the principles when a child with disabilities has difficulty with the typical classroom routines or transitions. You will need to be sensitive to children who do not respond well to changes in the classroom routines or who cannot transition easily.

ROUTINES

Several aspects of the classroom routines can be individualized for the child who has difficulty with the usual approaches. First, a teacher can prepare children for the routines by having a visual calendar or photographs for the routines posted. Children who have difficulty remembering the sequence of routines (for example, children with FAS) can be prepared at the beginning of the day and during the day. Second, a child's time during the routine can be altered, perhaps allowing an activity to continue longer. Third, you can help children who have difficulty making changes to prepare for any changes in the routine. Children are reassured if they can prepare in advance for the change of routines and be part of the planning for change.

TRANSITIONS

It is not uncommon for children with ADHD or FAS to react negatively to the normal transitions that occur in an early childhood classroom. It is reported that children can spend up to 15 percent of the school day in some type of transition between activities or routines (Jones, 1991). Preparing plenty of time for transitions can help the child who has outbursts when asked to shift activities. The child may need individual directions, as well as the directions given in the group. In addition, the preparation for transition times can be introduced with visual drawings or photographs. A calendar of photographs of the day's activities can be posted for the child to revisit each day and at different times during the day. You can also explain to the child in advance of the transition what will happen next and present positive aspects to the change of activity. It can also be helpful for you to explain the beginning and end of the activity in preparation for the change.

RULES AND LIMITS

One of the goals of early childhood educators is to help young children learn to view themselves as capable and as competent decision-makers. Guiding children to make decisions about their actions can support this goal. This is congruent with the research of Piaget and his colleagues related to the development of moral autonomy, which is the underlying principle of this book. This principle applies to children with disabilities as much as to other children. Therefore, the basic guidelines for effective guidance are the same for children with special needs as for others: Building mutually respectful relationships based on caring is essential to moral autonomy for all children. Planning that prevents behavior problems is probably even more important for children with disabilities than for others. Such planning helps keep problems from escalating and turning into power struggles.

It is important to understand that some children will need more support, guidance, or personal attention because of the nature of their individual learning patterns. Children with difficulty paying attention or following rules do not necessarily have "deviant" behavior. Teachers need to understand why children are making mistakes, ignoring rules, and calling for help or attention. When you know why children are acting out, you can make more appropriate decisions for when and how to individualize. We make informed decisions about why and when to bend the rules when we understand the characteristics of children who have disorders such as FAS or ADHD.

It is reported that when children have ADHD, teachers tend to repeat directions over and over (Landau & McAninch, 1993). To avoid such repetition, teachers can anticipate these situations and work with children who usually challenge the rules and limits. Some children with FAS will have difficulty expressing themselves and understanding language, or will have an inability to predict consequences for their behavior. Support from the special education staff or a school psychologist can assist the classroom teacher to determine when to modify teaching strategies. In some instances, it will be necessary to work with family members for seeking resources that involve counseling or intervention beyond the classroom. Team members can exchange viewpoints and develop strategies for individual students.

CLASSROOM INSTRUCTIONS

Children who are impulsive are likely to miss details while listening to group directions and will then make mistakes. Some children with ADHD may have difficulty organizing themselves or their workplace. There are several ways you can prevent or reduce these problems. You can help prepare children to listen, focus on important parts of class instructions, and plan how to approach their work. The following suggestions might assist you when working with children who have trouble listening and understanding directions.

Direct, brief, and concrete class directions will help. Combining auditory and visual information may also be helpful. For example, classroom schedules, rules, or instructions might be posted for visual reference, using pictures for younger children. Planning and offering time for children to ask questions will also help. Another strategy is to prepare students for an activity by helping them get organized. For example, you might ask children, "What do you need?" "What do you do now?" These types of questions help children set up their workplace (Weaver, 1994). Some children might need more one-on-one contact.

Children who are impulsive may have frequent outbursts when asked to listen in a group or to remain at one activity. You can prevent outbursts by including the child in the class demonstration or giving that child a job. The teacher thereby engages the child and, at the same time, encourages self-esteem. Another suggestion is to allow these youngsters more breaks than the other children receive.

Even more than most of us, children with ADHD do not like to feel forced to comply. Power struggles and rebellious actions are not uncommon when teachers do not understand the characteristics of these children. Although these children need structure and predictable routines, they also need to feel as though they have choices. For example, the children may be allowed to choose when and where to take breaks outside or in the reading area.

RELATED CONSEQUENCES

Chapter 8 explained the use of related consequences for children to give them experiences helping them understand why certain behaviors are unacceptable and others are desirable. Children who are impulsive or who have FAS typically have difficulty predicting consequences and often show poor judgment. Children who have difficulty understanding consequences will not understand why their behavior is acceptable or unacceptable. If children are asked to explain their actions, they often say what they think the teacher wants to hear. The use of related consequences can provide valuable learning experiences about cause and effect, which is especially necessary for youngsters who have difficulty with this concept. These children will need many repeated experiences in order to make the connections between their actions and the meaning of those actions.

COMMUNICATION AND RESOLVING CONFLICT

Children who have difficulty following the classroom norms or rules need good models of communication that help them to clarify their problems and to express themselves. Some children will have difficulty understanding and communicating effectively. Sometimes these children may appear to understand classroom directions, but their actions will be just the opposite of the direction. The child may not actually understand what was being asked and is not intentionally being disrespectful or disobedient.

The principles for helping children problem-solve and create their own solutions are the same for all children; however, some children may need additional attention.

As noted in Chapter 7, children need models of communication that do not contain "put-downs." The suggested "I message" statements (Gordon, 1989) are particularly useful when considering ways to express your concerns. "I messages" are less likely to make children feel accused of wrongdoing or to make them defend their actions.

Class Meetings Strategies for negotiating solutions, such as the ones suggested in Chapter 7, are useful ways for children to create classroom norms or rules. Children learn to take ownership of their problems and at the same time learn to negotiate their own solutions to resolve their differences. These strategies help children with disabilities who reject adult authority and who need help in learning about related consequences. For example, a child may have an outburst by throwing blocks. A teacher might bring the problem to the other children without mentioning names. For example, "Today I noticed that blocks were left in the block area and some children were throwing the blocks. What could happen if we throw blocks? What could happen if we leave blocks laying around the room?" The children can generate solutions and follow the steps as outlined in Chapter 7. The teacher might follow-up by reviewing these class "rules" privately with the child who had the outburst. In addition, the teacher might prepare the child the next day by going over ideas generated by the class. The principles for helping children to problem-solve and create their own solutions remains the same for all children; however, some children may need additional attention.

TEACHER COLLABORATION

As teachers in special education and early childhood special education come together to work with children in early childhood settings, situations can occur that require teachers to study their actions and exchange points of view. In the following vignette, team members exchange viewpoints to decide how best to work with a child with developmental delays.

> Malcom is playing at the table with the other children, who are given water, flour, and salt to mix and make goop. The children have this opportunity throughout the year and, over time, have become familiar with how much of the ingredients they need to make the consistency of goop that works best for them. Malcom sometimes has difficulty playing alongside other children, and sometimes tries to tell the other children what to do. He sometimes holds onto the cup so that the other children won't get a turn. On this day he is putting in more cups of water than the other children want. He is also splashing the water, and the other children are getting upset.
>
> The classroom teacher and special education teacher observe this situation. They use the observation for discussing their philosophies and to plan how best to work with Malcom in the early childhood classroom. Both the classroom teacher and the special education teacher feel they need to work with this situation, as it is becoming a problem for Malcom and the other children. The classroom teacher listens to the special education teacher express her ideas about ways to deal with Malcom's behaviors. "I think Malcom needs to know his limits and that it is appropriate to take turns and to use only the amount of water necessary for the goop." The special education teacher suggests the following: "We should put up a sign on the wall that provides a clear visual cue that only one cup of water is needed for the goop. If he uses more than that, then he is put in time-out and he cannot play in the area any more."
>
> After listening to the special education teacher the early childhood teacher responds, "I don't agree that Malcom should be timed-out. I don't believe in time-out for this class and that would be something different we do only for Malcom. Another thing is that I purposely don't put up a recipe at this time of the year because the children are learning how to transform the materials into the right consistency for goop. By putting up the recipe, I am giving them the answer."
>
> The two teachers are willing to listen to each other's point of view to decide how to best support Malcom. The teachers explain their positions while remaining open to the idea that their position might change after understanding

the other person's viewpoint. In this case, the special education teacher listens to the classroom teacher's rationale and philosophy and poses the question, "How can we let Malcom know his behavior is not acceptable?" The early childhood teacher agrees that Malcom is being told too many times to cease his activity. At the same time, she does not want to punish him. She understands Malcom has more difficulty monitoring his actions than the other children in the room.

The teachers then brainstorm a variety of ideas for helping Malcom realize he cannot continue to disrupt the play of others, or control the play area. The teachers agree that a reasonable related consequence might be to exclude him from the activity, but that he needs to be part of the decision. The teachers decide that Malcom also needs to be prepared for the related consequences on a daily basis or when there are activities such as these that are potentially "messy." The teachers explain to Malcom that he can choose to play where he wants and clarify the expected ways to use the area. They then warn, "If you have difficulty sharing the toys or if you splash water, you will need to make other play choices until you decide that you can share and not make a mess."

This example offers teachers ways to think about their work with special education staff when individualizing and adjusting the classroom rules to assist a child who has difficulty knowing his limits.

Videotapes offer another valuable way for teachers to understand another point of view and to reflect on teaching practices. When teachers have videotapes for observation and documentation, they can review the tape several times. They can observe the actions of the children, the actions of the teacher, and the actions of the child with disabilities. Using the video as a means to revisit the teaching and learning experiences can be a tool for dialogue among the teachers. Videos also offer a way to really study children rather than merely observing them (Forman & Fyfe, 1998; Hughes, 1999).

CONCLUSION

The principles related to guidance presented in other chapters also apply when children display inappropriate behaviors due to various disabilities. Understanding the causes for those behaviors and how they can be influenced by the curriculum and environment will help teachers to make decisions for ways to individualize. Viewing children with disabilities as contributing strengths to the classroom environment is central to the decisions about the modifications. Helping nondisabled children to recognize these strengths will support healthy environments and foster strong self-esteem in all children.

FOR FURTHER THOUGHT

1. As a teacher in a child-care center or in a public school, you will have children with different types of disabilities in your class from year to year. Consider how you will prepare your class when you have a disabled child that might scream or exhibit odd behaviors to communicate his or her frustration. How will you reduce the fear or confusion that the other children may feel? How will you model ways for the children to understand the confusing behaviors? How

might you provide explanations that respect the disabled child and consider the child's image with his or her peers?

2. A good practice in early childhood education is to include using the strengths of all children in your class. How will you design your curriculum and environment to support the strengths of all children? Consider how you will recognize the strengths of children with disabilities. How can you observe for these strengths and bring them to the attention of the other children?

3. As an early childhood educator you may find yourself working with special education teachers. You will need to share your ways of planning curriculum and be able to explain how you make it meaningful. Consider how you might work with special educators to understand the design of your curriculum. How will you make decisions for when and how to individualize your curriculum? How will you work with special educators who may not have the same background in early childhood as you do?

4. Videotaping our classrooms can offer a powerful tool for reflecting on our teaching practices and the learning environment. Consider how you might videotape experiences throughout the day to sample ways your classroom supports the guidance approach as discussed throughout this book. Look specifically at ways that your interactions with children, your curriculum, and the design of your environment are positive for building self-esteem and work to help children make their own decisions. What supports are in place for the children with disabilities? Use the videotape as a means to have a dialogue among your team members. Focus on a particular question or issue.

5. Some children with disabilities will have difficulty following directions, classroom routines, or transitions. As an early childhood educator, you are interested in ways to prevent classroom problems. In what ways can you organize your classroom to individualize for a certain child and maintain the same rules for the other children? How will you prepare your classroom to prevent or reduce the disruption that might arise from an individual child?

RECOMMENDED READINGS

Edwards, C., Gandini, L., & Forman, G. (1998). *The hundred languages of children: The Reggio Emilia approach-advanced reflections*. Connecticut: Ablex Publishing Corporation.

Erwin, E., Alimaras, E., & Price, N. (1999). A qualitative study of social dynamics in inclusive preschool. *Journal of Research in Childhood Education, (14)*, 1.

Jones, B. (1991). *A Sourcebook on attention deficit disorder: A management guide for early childhood professionals and parents*. San Antonio, TX: Psychological Corporation.

Mallory, B., & New, R. (1994). Social Constructivist theory and principles of inclusion: Challenges for early childhood special education. *Journal of Special Education, 28*(3), pp. 322–337.

New, R., & Mallory, B. (1996). The paradox of diversity in early care and education. In E. J. Erwin (Ed.), *Putting children first* (pp. 143–167). Baltimore: Paul H. Brookes.

Weaver, C. (1994). *Success at last! Helping students with attention deficit (hyperactivity) disorders achieve their potential*. Portsmouth, NH: Heinemann.

14

SPECIAL EMOTIONAL NEEDS

By: Lory Britain, Ph.D. and Sierra Freeman, M.Ed.

Mariah and Alex have been working intently in the block corner for 20 minutes, carefully placing blocks in a trail around the edge of the rug in the block area. As they begin the next step of their plan to vertically place one pillar block on each rectangle block, Jason enters the block area. He selects a toy car and drives in along the block trail, knocking some of the pillars down. After Mariah and Alex begin to protest, Jason kicks the block trail, scattering blocks around the block area and into other parts of the classroom. The teacher comes over to the area to facilitate the children's problem solving and to support Jason in expressing his needs and emotions.

All teachers of young children have observed similar emotional outbursts and disruptions in children's play at one time or another. The task for a Constructivist teacher is to understand the meaning of the experience from the child's perspective and find clues as to how to best respond.

Perhaps a child acting like Jason simply didn't get enough sleep last night, or perhaps the teacher needs to look at how his or her classroom is arranged to encourage children to play together well. Even a single event, such as the birth of a new child, could certainly provoke such emotional outbursts. However, for Jason, the circumstances go much deeper.

For Jason, repeated exposure to family violence in his early years impacted several areas of his development. Jason's difficulty entering into play and his low tolerance for frustration is but one example of the many ways children from stressful home environments might behave in the classroom. While one child with a similar history might frequently react by withdrawing from classroom participation, another child experiencing a short term disruptive home environment could behave similarly to Jason.

This highlights the challenges teachers have in supporting children with both chronic and temporary emotional and behavioral problems. These children come from many different environments and have had experiences that have not supported their development in healthy ways and/or have traumatized or stressed them in significant ways. Helping all children to have successful classroom experiences requires considering how their experiences outside the classroom influence their behavior in the classroom. Understanding the relationship between children's development and emotional well-being and their life outside the classroom is a first step.

This chapter provides background information on specific circumstances that put children at risk for emotional and behavioral problems. Strategies to provide constructive guidance for these children are presented with consideration to related issues in Chapters 12 (Unmet Needs) and 13 (Children Experiencing Disabilities). As teachers consider circumstances outside the classroom environment and their effects on children's classroom behavior, they will also need to ask themselves the question, "What is my role here?" This chapter concludes with guidelines that help you answer this question.

RISK FACTORS

Even though the range of situations and environments that put young children at risk each involve varied circumstances, there are commonalities when viewed from the child's perspective. Consider, for example, a home environment void of developmental stimulation where the television is blaring continuously. Children's books are absent, and toys, if there are any, are broken and piled around the room with other objects and garbage. Add to this picture adults who are either physically or emotionally unavailable to converse with the child or offer verbal encouragement and appropriate affection. Whether this chaotic and neglectful home environment is a result of parental drug abuse, adult mental health issues, or a traumatized parent preoccupied with coping with domestic violence, the child most likely experiences his or her world similarly. It is difficult for these youngsters to view the world as a safe and predictable place that cherishes and encourages them.

Singular traumatic events or short term situations, such as the death of a significant family member, divorce, moving, or even the birth of a sibling, without adequate emotional support for the child can disrupt the child's already existing view of the world and call for special considerations in the classroom environment.

THE EFFECT OF EXPERIENCE ON THE DEVELOPING BRAIN

More and more is being discovered and understood about the influence of the environment on children's brain development, both before birth and during the beginning years of life. The Constructivist belief that children construct knowledge from their interactions with their physical and social world now take on an even deeper meaning. Just as loving and nurturing environments help children develop empathy and trust, the opposite can also be true.

According to current brain research, abuse and neglect have far reaching effects. "Prenatal development and the first two years are the time when the genetic, organic, and neurochemical foundations for impulse control are being created. It is also the time when the capacities for rational thinking and sensitivity to other people are being rooted—or not—in the child's personality" (Karr-Morse & Wiley, 1997, p. 45). Children's cognitive abilities can be profoundly affected, as can their capacity for the regulation of emotions and interpersonal responsiveness.

BEHAVIORS

There are a variety of risk factors and unmet needs that can affect a child's development and behavior. Though the severity and kinds of situations that each child is faced with may vary greatly, they can provoke similar behaviors in different children. Some of the most common behaviors found are having tantrums, aggressiveness, distractibility or inability to focus, shutting down emotionally, acting clingy, crying, taking on an adult role, or having unsafe boundaries. For example, a child who has not formed healthy adult attachments might tend to seem emotionally distant, as might a child who is experiencing or witnessing abuse in the home. Likewise, children found in similar circumstances or experiencing similar traumatic events may respond completely different from one another. For example, one child who has been exposed to domestic violence in the home might respond by withdrawing while another becomes unusually aggressive.

Some children who are experiencing short term abrupt disruptions, such as parental separation, might be extremely clingy and have separation anxiety, while others might react by showing signs of aggression and hostility.

As educators, you will not always find yourself in a position to know enough about each child's home life and developmental history to determine which factors to attribute to a child's specific behavior. However, as a teacher, you can carefully observe the child in the classroom environment as a means of making changes that support the child's learning and development. There will be times when teacher-child interactions, modifications to the physical environments, and changes to the curriculum are not sufficient to meet the needs of a child. In this case, the use of other professionals for support and services may be necessary.

OBSERVATIONS

You can probably think of countless times that you have stopped to watch a child while he or she works at a given task, or paused to observe a group of children during play. These observations provide useful information about what the child knows, feels, or can do, and also can serve as a guide for planning meaningful and relevant curriculum. "The value of anecdotal notes is in both the immediate picture they give you of the children's activities and the cumulative information you will acquire" (Chaille & Britain, 1997, p. 61). Life in the classroom can be very busy, and stepping away from the children for even a few minutes can, at times, seem impossible. However, observations can be both formal and informal, or scheduled and unscheduled.

One of the most valuable observation strategies to use when trying to figure out how to support children with behavioral difficulties is to look for

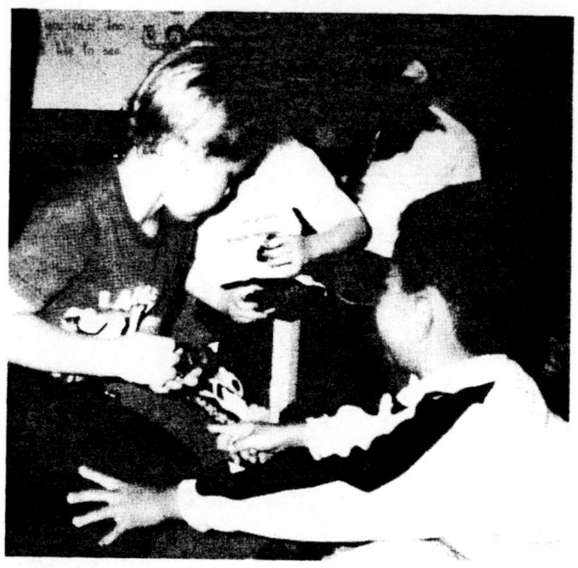

Watch for patterns of behavior and events as you observe to understand a child's difficulty in the classroom.

patterns of behavior and events. How does the child begin the day? What precipitates or comes before the event or outburst? How does the child respond to the frustration and how do adults and other children respond to the child's behavior? And finally, what is going on simultaneously in the room, such as loud noise or transitions?

There are many methods for observation that you can use in the classroom, and as a teacher you will need to develop the strategy that works best for your classroom environment. Ideally, it is best to use a variety of strategies. Some educators find that having a time to sit back and observe without engaging the children is useful for gaining insight into the functioning of the class as a whole, as well as into individual children's needs and abilities. Taking time to do this can be difficult in a busy classroom environment and may take some planning and coordination with other teachers. Another useful method is to keep a note pad and pencil with you to jot down quick notes that can be used for reference later when writing more detailed observations or having a discussion with other professionals. Chaille and Britain recommend making an observation "necklace" by clipping a sticky note pad to a pencil and wearing it on a cord during class time (1997, p. 59). This allows teachers to have their hands free in the classroom but to still have their observation pad with them when they see a situation that they want to explore further. When neither method is feasible, making a quick mental note during class time and then sitting down later and writing an observation can be useful as a means of keeping records or documentation. Videotaping classroom time can also provide a wealth of information about the classroom dynamics and about individual children's behaviors when reviewed at a later time. Observations are useful documentation if you should decide that you need to consult with a specialist or make a report or referral at a later date.

Objective written and verbal communication between educational settings can help the child as well as provide teachers with a greater sense of understanding and subsequent effectiveness. When challenging children move suddenly, teachers can be left with an uncomfortable sense of unfinished business and of not knowing what will happen. On the other end, teachers who first have a child exhibit signs of emotional disturbances often don't have any background information to help them fully support the child.

A THERAPEUTIC APPROACH: STRATEGIES AND TECHNIQUES

The constructive guidance and discipline approach presented in this book is useful for all children, especially those who present challenging behaviors. However, additional considerations, such as examining a child's needs both inside and outside of the classroom, are often needed with children having behavior problems stemming from emotional issues. Extra support and strategies for these children are sometimes called *therapeutic approaches*. This term means strategies and techniques that provide healing, compensatory, and/or supplemental experiences for children under stress. These therapeutic approaches can strengthen the children's ability to cope with stress and to develop appropriately. To understand the concept of "therapeutic approach" as being healing and/or preventative, consider the following concrete analogy: Hand lotion is often used therapeutically to heal our hands when they are chaffed from either dry weather conditions or the use of strong cleaning detergents. Lotion is also used preventatively so that the weather conditions do not dry out the skin. In the same way, the approaches presented in the following section help heal children whose environments has not promoted their well-being, and it helps prevent children from developing long-term emotional issues when their current circumstances are stressful.

A therapeutic approach must be built upon a strong foundation of developmentally appropriate practices central to quality early childhood programs (Ferber, 1996). Children's emotions, ideas, and explorations are always central in a predictable yet flexible early childhood classroom. However, the nature of the issues that children bring into a classroom, often creates the need for particular attentiveness to their emotional development and their ability to develop trusting relationships.

Many researchers have looked at the characteristics and skills that help children face stressful situations and other environments that might put them at-risk for emotional difficulties. These skills and characteristics are generally accepted as indicating resiliency in children (Garbarino et al., 1992). These range from the ability to recognize and express emotions and being flexible, to having problem solving skills and a strong sense of competence and self-esteem. Sociability, autonomy, the ability to comfort oneself by seeking comfort from others, adaptability and frustration tolerance, and competence are also part of this picture. As we describe these therapeutic strategies, you will begin to see the links between these strategies, meeting children's needs, and supporting resiliency skills and characteristics. It is important to remember that supporting resiliency in children goes hand-in-hand with a mindful eye on the vulnerability of young children. Equally important when selecting strategies to best support children with emotional and behavioral issues in the classroom is to reflect on "What is the meaning of the behavior for the child?" and "How can I best support the child in getting his or her needs met?" The following strategies will be useful for such times when a healing and/or preventative approach is called for.

PRINCIPLE ONE: THE CULTURE OF THE CLASSROOM MUST SUPPORT THE APPLICATION OF THERAPEUTIC STRATEGIES

Each classroom has a culture of its own, similar in some ways to the way that we think of other countries and particular ethnic groups having a distinct culture. This classroom culture reflects the relationship between children, as well as what routines are established in the classroom by the teacher in response to the needs of the children. Examples include how the room is laid out, what activities are presented, the language the adults use in response to children, the daily schedule, and so on. You can see that this includes everything that has been presented in the book thus far. This way of looking at classroom practices is based upon the belief that children construct meaning from interactions with their social and physical world. This is why it is so important for a teacher to carefully observe and reflect on all his or her classroom practices for consistency in values and goals for the children.

You will need to consider if all components of your classroom are consistent with a therapeutic environment that supports respect, the encouragement of problem solving, predictability and safety, and flexibility and nurturing. Does your classroom encourage what was described earlier as *resiliency characteristics?* For example, creating an environment that encourages children to feel a sense of competence means more than words of encouragement. It also means that this goal will be supported by having a range of easily accessible materials that facilitate children's exploration. This also would include thinking about how many materials to have accessible or how to organize them in ways that are not too stimulating for sensitive children.

Another component of the classroom culture that is important to all programs, and in particular programs inclusive of children with special needs, is the creation of a sense of classroom community. Collaboration and cooperation, rather than competition, can be encouraged and supported by several elements in the classroom, such as an emphasis on the collective good that includes individual views and empathy, the valuing of new ideas and variations, the choice of materials, a focus on problem-solving and child-centered decision making, and respect and encouragement for all children (Britain, 1992).

PRINCIPLE TWO: THE PHYSICAL ENVIRONMENT SHOULD BE ARRANGED TO BE RESPONSIVE TO THE ISSUES AND DEVELOPMENTAL LEVELS OF EACH CHILD

Children with special emotional needs may need additional considerations in the physical environment. Consider the various home environments that can put

Children with special emotional needs may need extra consideration as you plan the class environment.

children at risk and consider special circumstances that can be emotionally challenging to young children. As described in the beginning of this chapter, many home environments that do not support the children's developing sense of well-being may be unpredictable, traumatizing, void of stimulating materials, harsh, or unresponsive. In a different way, circumstances such as death, divorce, and moving might present the child with feelings of loss, fear, and insecurity. Consequently, many different circumstances can contribute to children's needs not being met outside of the classroom environment. Children's home environments, and subsequent behaviors as described earlier, can provide guidelines for thinking about the physical room arrangement.

Chapter 4 discusses the importance of considering traffic patterns, allowing for movement, and providing for privacy. Clear traffic patterns and visual cues can take on an even greater significance for children whose home environments are chaotic, cluttered, or constantly changing. These not only can be reassuring to children, but can give them guidelines on how to move from area to area and make choices based on visual possibilities.

Mona's home has clothes, litter, and broken toys strewn all around. Naturally, she has little experience with looking around a room, seeing clear choices about what to do or how to play. When Mona first entered preschool, her teacher had the room arranged so that high shelves between learning areas visually blocked the view between all other areas of the room. Mona, consequently, remained all day in the first area that she saw. When the teacher analyzed the environment and realized the lack of clear traffic patterns, she rearranged the room so that each area was distinct and separate, but children could see the other areas and how to get to them. When the teacher made these changes, she also considered the importance of keeping each area without undue distraction from the other areas, as discussed in the previous chapter. Gradually, Mona took her cues from the environment and began to make other choices and venture into other learning areas. The teacher also made sure that materials were displayed within each area in a clear and organized way to make choices within the areas apparent to Mona.

Similarly, children from unpredictable and/or chaotic home environments will probably have a need for both privacy and calmness. Private corners in the classroom can also provide a place for nurturing interactions between a child and teacher, something so critical for children in stressful circumstances. This arrangement can also give teachers the time to privately read books with a child that address emotionally relevant issues, such as divorce, family violence, and body issues. Children who are reacting to others with aggression and who cannot be redirected with problem solving can retreat to the private space with or without a teacher to learn to self-monitor their reactions to frustration.

Creating a soothing environment for children can help meet children's needs for relaxation and calmness. Children who have been traumatized by loss, abuse, or exposure to violence might react by being hyper-vigilant, clingy, and/or easily distracted and agitated. Subdued colors, lighting, and uncluttered walls with carefully selected pictures can be both child-centered and relaxing to these children. In these circumstances, more is definitely not better! Carefully consider the impact of visual and auditory stimulation on children's behaviors.

In one toddler classroom, the teachers decided that playing classical music would be therapeutic and calming. Surprisingly, some of the children's activity levels escalated to the point that other children felt agitated. Analyzing the situation with another teacher, they discovered that the music, as soothing as it seemed, caused the teachers to talk loudly to one another, and this contributed to a hectic feeling environment. The music was subsequently turned off, and the children became calmer. Sometimes, reducing noise levels requires more drastic solutions. When one therapeutic program moved into a new classroom with high ceilings, the staff discovered that the voices echoed in the room, causing people to talk loudly, which in turn agitated children to the point that they would cover their ears. Eventually, sound-absorbing tiles were put in near the ceiling, the noise level of the room dropped, and the children and teachers became more relaxed.

In the same way that a soothing environment with allowance for quiet space can help children that are agitated or easily distracted, a quiet protected space can help children who are withdrawn, an important behavior not to ignore. A critical strategy for developing a quiet space for withdrawn children is to have the space be protected, yet allow children to view other activities and to eventually make choices to engage with others. For example, the teachers suspected that Seth's life possibly included ongoing traffic of strangers in and out of his home throughout the evening. Seth was always reluctant to enter the classroom and would stand by the door looking vigilant. He would also startle easily. The teachers rearranged the room allowing entry into the main part of the room from a private reading area, equipped with a rocking chair and books, that offered a clear view into the main part. Seth gradually developed the habit of entering the first area, reading a book while simultaneously looking around the room, and then transitioning into the main room and becoming involved with the other children. Similarly, a loft that overlooks the room, yet is cozy with soft surfaces and quiet toys and books, can provide a child with a simultaneous sense of security and power. Both security and power are often needed by children whose needs for either are not met at home.

Because children with emotional issues are often particularly challenged in their social interactions with other children, the teacher should analyze their physical environment to provide for social interaction and a variety of group sizes. For example, some areas might accommodate the larger groups of children working on a block structure, while other areas might be spaced to better accommodate two or three children. The size, shape, and positioning of tables, whether they are up against or perpendicular to a wall, all influence how children interact socially. Take the time to step back and observe what social interactions and groupings naturally occur in various areas of your room or around certain types of furniture arrangements. Consider the needs of individual children in this dimension and how the physical environment might be adjusted to help meet their needs.

PRINCIPLE THREE: THE CLASSROOM ROUTINES SHOULD BE PREDICTABLE WITH AN ALLOWANCE FOR INDIVIDUAL FLEXIBILITY AND RESPONSIVENESS

In the same way that a carefully considered physical environment, including attention to room arrangement and the presentation of materials, can help meet children's needs, classroom routines can provide children with a sense of predictability, security, and safety that might be missing in their lives outside of the classroom. The challenge for teachers is to maintain predictability while still being flexible and responsive to their individual needs. Sometimes this might seem like incompatible goals; however, several strategies can make this possible.

Establish your routine with consideration for the physical and emotional needs of the particular children in your classroom. Be sensitive to the individual pace of children. For example, are they arriving hungry? Do they consequently need to have a meal available as the first thing after arriving? Do the issues in their families' lives make the time they might arrive unpredictable? If so, establish a routine so that children can ease into the classroom activities without feeling like they are disrupting the established flow. Do some children need extra long periods of self-directed play since they are slow to enter play or because their lives at home are not relaxing? You should take their needs for physical activity into consideration. It is possible these children endure crowded living conditions at home with no outside play area.

A discussion about the class schedule can give children a sense of knowing what to expect. It can also provide opportunities for children to make choices and consequently feel a sense of power. Empowering children and giving them choices has been a theme throughout this book. For children with emotional issues who so often lack power over many aspects of their lives outside the classroom, providing opportunities for them to make decisions is critical. For children who also need predictability, make sure that the choices you are offering them are realistic. Offer clear options, such as extending choice time, although not so long as to make lunch rushed and chaotic.

As described in the previous chapter, some children with developmental disabilities need supplemental cues for transition times. This might include longer warning times or visual cues, such as picture cards about what to expect next. For children whose tolerance for frustration is low due to either environmental or developmental challenges, this strategy can be an effective tool.

Another way of honoring children's needs for both predictability and flexibility is to acknowledge that all the children do not always have to participate in the same routine. For example, the following scenario describes how one teacher met a child's need for quiet and still helped her transition into circle time participation.

> Every time Sasha came to circle time, she would become agitated and start to shove the children around her, eventually ending up rolling around and kicking in the center of the group. This extreme behavior not only perplexed and concerned the teacher, but was both upsetting and distracting to other children who eagerly came to participate in the circle time activities. The teacher decided to step back and observe Sasha when she was relaxed and engaged in play activities in other times of the day. What the teacher noticed was that Sasha was very focused on puzzles, working intently even with other children around her. The teacher's goal was to honor what seemed like Sasha's need for individual time and to help her transition into group time. She set up a special tray for Sasha with a puzzle on it and allowed her to sit just outside the circle if she could work quietly. Each day, the teacher would repeat the expectation of quiet during circle time and invite Sasha to join the circle when she was ready to participate. Some days Sasha would leave her puzzle work and participate in circle time for a short while and then, upon getting agitated, return to her individual work with gentle reminders. The teacher would remind Sasha that it was her choice, but still made the expectations clear. After several months of this strategy, Sasha eventually became more relaxed and fully participated in circle time activities with the other children.

PRINCIPLE FOUR: POSITIVE, NURTURING RELATIONSHIPS SHOULD BE ENCOURAGED AND SUPPORTED WITH A FOCUS ON PROBLEM-SOLVING

Positive, nurturing relationships are essential for helping children face issues in their lives that challenge them emotionally. Thinking about children's

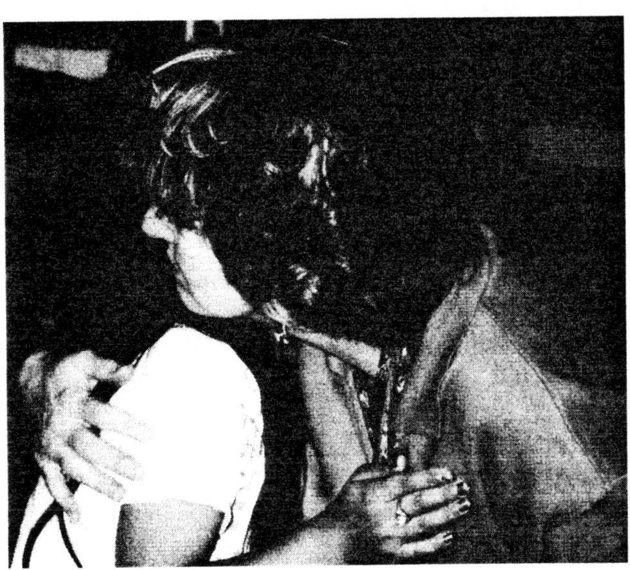

The stability and support provided by a nurturing caregiver can help children cope with emotional issues outside the classroom.

unmet needs outside of the classroom environment can provide clues to what children's relationship and friendship needs are within the classroom. Although a relationship with a beloved teacher is not a substitute for a nurturing relationship with a parent or primary caregiver, it can be a positive force for emotionally challenged children. Additionally, positive social interactions with other children promotes development in all areas, including the cognitive domain. Helping children to develop good social problem solving, conflict resolution, and play skills will benefit children whose environment has not supported these skills.

Each day, as children enter the classroom, teachers should ensure that all children feel beloved and cherished in that environment. This can be harder to accomplish with children whose behaviors sometimes create difficulties in the classroom. For these children, special provisions need to made to insure that they have the opportunity to connect with primary adults in the classroom in a close and nurturing way. Several strategies are key to achieving this goal.

First, children need to feel unconditional acceptance for who they are and what they feel separate from the behavior that they exhibit. For example, a teacher's remarks to a child who has just hit another child should focus on the hitting and the need to keep all children safe rather than that the child was "wrong" or "too wild." Validating and accepting all the children's feelings as neither right nor wrong is also part of this separation of behavior from who the child is. Often, children who are acting aggressively are the ones that need the most reassurance from you.

Second, special provisions will need to be made so significant adults in the classroom have individual time with the children who need it. The staff-child ratio must be low enough to enable adults to respond to children's needs in a timely manner. In many classrooms, this is not an easy task! Student interns, community volunteers, and parent volunteers provide ways to enhance your ratio of adults to children. Analyze your classroom arrangement so that you have a private place for individual time, yet you can still have a clear view of the rest of the activities. Establish communication strategies with other adults in your room so that when you are spending individual time with a child, they can be extra vigilant of the other classroom dynamics.

And third, part of allowing a child to feel unconditional acceptance lies in how teachers respond to children's ideas and explorations. Thinking back on some of the home situations that put children at risk, it is easy to envision an environment where adults are not emotionally able to respond to children's ideas and suggestions, much less greet them with enthusiasm. If you truly think about experiences in the classroom from the child's perspective, you can have an understanding of how important it is to greet children's ideas with enthusiasm and openness.

> One day a teacher turned around and saw Nathan standing barefoot in the sand table, saying, "Look teacher, my toes can wiggle in the gushy sand!" Because the teacher realized that it was not safe for a child to stand in the sand table, she knew Nathan would need to get down. However, instead of telling him that it was not safe and to get down, the teacher said, "It must feel good to have your toes wiggle. I'm worried about you being so high on the table, though. What could we put the sand in on the floor so you could feel the gushy sand in a safe way?" Together they got a plastic tub, placed it on the floor, and filled it with sand. The teacher even took her shoes off to feel the sand, too. Instead of feeling shamed, Nathan felt that his idea was wonderful and felt safe with his special teacher time.

Most early childhood teachers are aware of the importance of children having positive interactions with their peers. The discussion and guidelines presented in Chapter 3, "Intellectual and Social Development Affect Discipline," are particularly meaningful for children who are experiencing special emotional needs. Sometimes, however, these children can challenge even the most experienced teacher to facilitate children in positive social interactions.

Several factors might be relevant as you consider strategies beyond what usually helps children develop problem solving and conflict resolution skills, and assists successful social interactions. Does the child have an unmet need due to an inadequate home environment or a disruptive event in his or her life that must be met before social interactions can be successful? Can you meet that need in the classroom by, for example, providing a nutritious meal for the child in the morning or creating special individual time for you and the child? Perhaps the child needs quiet, alone time because his or her environment outside the classroom does not provide for this, such as in the case of a homeless shelter. Do any developmental delays, coupled with emotional difficulties, create even more challenges for the child? Sometimes children with emotional challenges are also delayed, for example, in their language development and symbolic play level. These children will need more sustained, attentive coaching for peer entry attempts and the development of pretend play. Teachers sometimes need to remain in play time with the child longer than might otherwise be necessary as the child gradually gets involved in play. A perceptive teacher, in these cases, will stay involved in the play and gradually back off and observe as the child becomes engaged in a significant way with other children.

Consider the home environment of the child. What have their experiences been that would provide inappropriate role models for social interaction, such as aggression, harsh controlling words, and the use of physical force? It's important to be reflective and consider experiences from the child's perspective, but to still proceed with caution in your analysis. In these cases, you might need to make referrals and seek other professional support.

As with all strategies intended to provide therapeutic support for children experiencing difficulties, helping children achieve and maintain positive social interactions does not exist in isolation. How your room is arranged, what materials you select for the curriculum, and how the culture of the classroom fosters children feeling cherished and respected all contribute to the likelihood of their growth and success in this area.

PRINCIPLE FIVE: SUPPORT AND VALIDATE CHILDREN'S FEELINGS AND HELP THEM IDENTIFY AND RESPOND TO THE FEELINGS OF OTHERS IN APPROPRIATE WAYS

At the core of all the strategies suggested that are integral to a therapeutic approach is the support of children's emotional development. This concept is basic to most early childhood programs, but a heightened awareness of how everything that happens in your class can support this goal is warranted (Hyson, 1994). A child's world outside the classroom can be frightening and seem out of control, leaving the child without a means to cope with these feelings. Although, in many cases, you have little impact on the children's environment outside the classroom, you can provide an environment to help them with their feelings and to develop important coping skills.

Supporting children emotionally can be broken down into more concrete components. The first step is helping children develop the ability to recognize and express feelings in themselves. Curriculum, literature, music, and circle time activities are all useful in this regard, but some of the most powerful supports involve in-the-moment responses by teachers.

> Tommy enters the classroom with an angry scowl on his face, shoving his way past children as he goes to hang up his coat. The teacher is aware that Tommy's parents are going through a divorce. She is also sensitive to the fact that anger is not the only feeling Tommy is experiencing right now. Sadness and fear have also come into play. The teacher knows that she must simultaneously keep the other children safe, set limits for Tommy, and support all his feelings. What she decides to do first is support his feelings by saying, "I can see you're angry and I know you might be feeling sad and scared now about your Dad." Immediately, Tommy's face changes from an angry scowl to a sad look. Using eye contact to see if the other teacher can take over the classroom, the teacher asks Tommy if

he would like to go in the library corner with her and read a special book about divorce she found for him. As they go off together, Tommy is able to learn more about his own feelings and feel validated and supported.

Recognizing feelings in others, and thereby developing perspective-taking and empathy, is the other side of emotional development. This can be developed through activities such as creating a story about a beloved pet who died, group meetings, and carefully selected literature, and by "in-the-moment" opportunities which help children learn to identify how their actions affect others around them. For example, sometimes younger children need to look for visual cues, such as facial expressions, to identify how other children feel. Phrases like, "Can you tell me how Melissa might be feeling by looking at her face?" supports this process.

Chapter 6, on teaching desirable behavior through example, discussed the importance of accepting feelings and being a role model for children learning to identify feelings in others. As discussed in Chapter 4 and the previous chapter, teachers can and should act as role models of the self-expression of feelings. Often, children experiencing disruption in their home lives or environments that put them at risk for emotional difficulties have confusing, conflicting feelings. Children might experience an intense loss through death, moving, or even removal to foster care. Under these conditions, adults may not be sharing their feelings with them in an age-appropriate way. Children might be told too much or too little. Having a teacher model an appropriate demonstration of adult feelings and helping children identify their own feelings can contribute to a child's sense of well-being and ability to cope.

Sometimes, a teacher might feel torn between supporting children's feelings in the moment and taking into consideration the response of other children within close proximity.

In one program during snack time, Jenine described, in an agitated way, a violent scene about hitting and people getting "bumped off." The teachers listened, thinking that she was describing something that happened at her house last night. Meanwhile, the other children were becoming quiet with frightened expressions on their faces. As it turned out, Jenine was describing a video game (still inappropriate for children to witness). In retrospect, the teachers wished they had said to Jenine in the beginning, "That sounds like it was scary and important to share. Let's go sit in the block area and we can talk."

Having consistent phrases used by all teachers and adults in the classroom helps support children's feelings, gives clear messages about their acceptance, and provides a sense of safety.

Another important component of supporting children's emotional development is helping children develop the ability to comfort themselves, including seeking comfort from others. Children whose environments are chaotic or seem unpredictable and inconsistent might not view adults as sources of comfort. Similarly, they might not have any experience identifying their needs and knowing when they need to retreat to a quiet corner of the room for relaxation. A perceptive teacher can help children find strategies

EXAMPLES OF PHRASES TO HELP SUPPORT CHILD'S FEELINGS

Tell me how you feel
Can you tell ____ how you felt when _____
I can see by your face that you might be _____
It seems to me that you are angry and I need to help keep you safe.
I feel _____
Look at _____'s face, can you guess how she might be feeling.
Let's look at this chart and see if you can pick a face that shows how you are feeling
How did it make you feel when _____
It's okay to feel _____, but I can't let you throw blocks at other children
Use your words to tell _____ how you feel

both to know when they need to quiet themselves and what to do, such as read a book or hold a stuffed animal or other comfort object, as well as ask an adult for comfort. These strategies help children cope before they find themselves out of control or withdrawn in an unhealthy way.

PRINCIPLE SIX: ACTIVITIES AND MATERIALS APPROPRIATE TO THE NEEDS AND ISSUES OF THE CHILDREN CAN HELP PROVIDE HEALING AND SUPPORTIVE EXPERIENCES

As confirmed throughout this book and highlighted in the previous chapter, therapeutic goals and constructive guidance and discipline must be grounded in a developmentally appropriate curriculum that is child-centered, flexible, emergent, and based on giving children choices and opportunities for problem solving. For a child with special emotional needs, the following curricular considerations are particularly meaningful.

The previous chapter discusses the importance of meaningful curriculum with topics driven by the children's interests and issues. For example, a classroom that had a child in it whose dog died might paint a mural of all the things the dog liked to do (Goldman, 2000). When working with children with emotional and behavioral needs, these sorts of activities can help children to make sense of their environment and to develop appropriately. As an example, in one classroom that had several children whose families were either homeless or transient and had to use pay phones when making a call, the class designed and decorated a phone booth out of a cardboard box. The project involved a discussion around phone use and emergency calls, measuring the door, problem solving about stability, decorating, and then using the phone booth in symbolic play.

The above project is also an example that highlights the importance of selecting and/or creating relevant symbolic play materials. Look to the children's lives for inspiration about what might be appropriate. Family figures, cars, camping props, police stations, phone booths, babies, and baby items are but a few examples of props that might allow children to symbolically represent issues that are pertinent to their lives. Common traditional school curriculum at the beginning of the school year often involves activities that revolve around "self", "my body," and "my family." These concepts are meaningful throughout the entire year for children whose sense of self has been stifled by environmental conditions.

There is also the issue of children who do not seem to be able to participate in pretend and other types of play (Koplow, 1996). For example, there are children who have taken on an adult role in their home environment and children whose language and symbolic representational ability has been thwarted by relationship and attachment issues. Helping these children feel safe and secure in their environment, selecting relevant play props, and engaging in play with them can help them gradually participate fully.

In addition to play props that allow children to transform and represent their world symbolically, materials that can be physically transformed by children in shape, form, or substance (Chaille & Britain, 1997) provide a context for children to experiment and feel both powerful and soothed. Particularly empowering and soothing to children are the transformational materials, such as sand, water, play dough, cornmeal, mud, and dirt, which changes through mixing, combining, poking, and shaping. For many children with emotional issues, these tactile experiences are needed for their developmental progression. Also, for children who need extra guidance around social interactions, these materials lend themselves easily to collaboration as well as individual work.

Painting, drawing, writing (including "pretend" writing), dance, singing, and movement are all examples of ways children can express and represent their feelings and issues to themselves and others. This representational ability is related to children's ability to communicate with others. Unfortunately, children whose early experiences did not support the development of a positive, caring relationship with a trusted adult and appropriate communication will need attentive support with these representational experiences. Accessible materials, open-ended creative activities, and gentle encouragement with some adult participation are part of setting the stage to encourage children to express themselves through these mediums.

Children's literature is a significant part of using representational materials therapeutically. The use of literature to support children's experiences and emotions is called bibliotherapy. Experienced teachers are well aware of both the magic and power of using a carefully selected book to both help prepare children for an upcoming event or to validate and reflect the emotional impact of past or ongoing experiences. Books can suggest healthy strategies for children to use in challenging situations.

The power of books to help support children through troubled times lies in the teacher being familiar with existing books and to have them readily available to be read to, or with, the child at the appropriate time. Children can't wait to have their feelings validated or solutions to troubling situations given until a trip to the library is possible. Being able to pull just the right book about death, for example, off the shelf when a child comes in upset

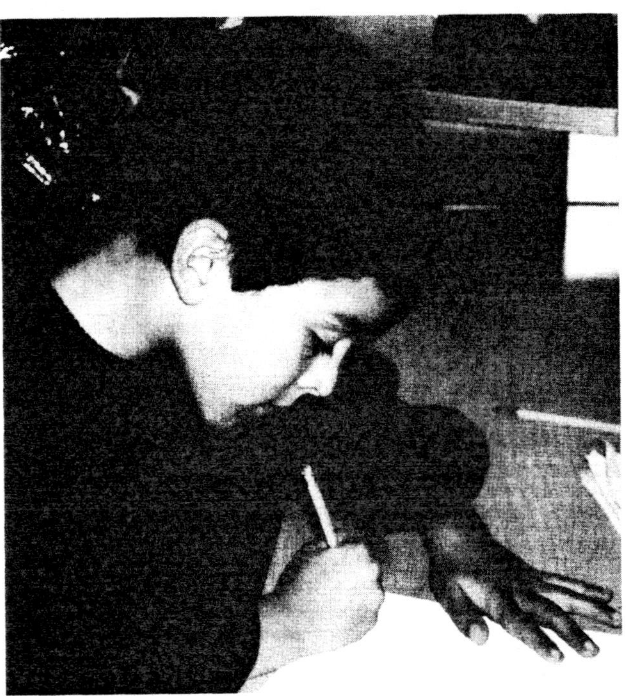

Writing, drawing, painting, singing, and movement allow children to express and represent their feelings.

after attending his grandma's funeral can be a powerful and healing experience. The book *Unsmiling faces: How preschools can heal* (Koplow, 1996) has an excellent bibliography listing children's books on sensitive topics. Parenting Press, in Seattle, Washington, specializes in books that help children and parents through difficult times. Children's librarians in pubic libraries usually have lists on such topics as well.

One of the key decisions you will need to make when deciding when or how to read books on difficult and/or emotional topics has to do with the choice to read the book to the class or to an individual child, as well as to have the book available on the children's bookshelf. A book about domestic violence, for example, might be too frightening and confusing to read to a group of children who have never been exposed to it and might be best read to individual children or small groups of affected children so that you can monitor and support their responses. On the other hand, a book about personal touch, such as *It's My Body* (Freeman, 1982), would be valuable to read in a group with an interactive and supportive format. However, as with all sensitive issues, the teacher must be prepared to respond to a child disclosing sensitive information in a group context.

Using children's literature therapeutically involves the same principles as reading all books to children, such as creating an interactive format where children share their ideas and feelings, and all ideas and feelings are validated.

Another important consideration when planning a curriculum to support children is that many children coming from high risk environments might not have the opportunity to develop an ability to problem-solve with materials and to explore cause-and-effect relationships. Constructivist activities involving physical knowledge such as ramps, inclines, balls, pulleys, and pendulums not only focus children on relationships, but also provide a sense of power and choice over materials and their actions on the materials. Asking children to predict, "What would happen if?" when using these materials increases their awareness. These types of activities (Chaille and Britain, 1997) often will focus children, who otherwise act distracted and/or aggressive, on problem solving for sustained periods of time.

The storage and dispersal of materials in the classroom sometimes needs to be done in different ways for different children. For example, children whose needs for ownership and privacy may not be met in their home environment may benefit from having personally marked containers or backpacks with their school belongings in them. Homeless children who suddenly find themselves in unfamiliar places with little or no personal belongings or comfort objects will especially benefit from this strategy. Related to this issue are particular habits around the hoarding of food and/or materials that could indicate unfulfilled needs. Responding with a reassurance, such as "You may have more when you are done" and then providing the child with more food, can help the child feel satisfied and cared for.

PRINCIPLE SEVEN: TEACHERS NEED TO BE AWARE OF ISSUES PARTICULARLY RELEVANT TO THE LIVES OF CHILDREN WITH EMOTIONAL NEEDS

Part of your challenge in working with children with special emotional needs is to educate yourself about the multiple issues relevant to understanding the behaviors of these children. The following section about children's boundaries is an example of only one such issue and how it impacts teaching strategies.

Children who have been sexually abused, traumatized, and/or deprived of healthy relationships with trusting adults may exhibit issues around what is known as "boundaries." Sometimes this can be confusing for teachers whose natural instinct is probably to be physically affectionate and responsive with young children. These children might readily be affectionate with adult strangers in the classroom or not pick up on cues when other children do not want to be touched. On the other extreme, children may not want adults or other children near their bodies at all. In one therapeutic early childhood and family support program, the Relief Nursery, Inc. in Eugene, Oregon, a key goal is that children will maintain and develop a sense of self-protection of their bodies and personal space. As a teacher, your role is to be educated about indicators of sexual abuse and other warning signs of serious emotional problems that warrant referral. Your role is also to support children in developing and recognizing appropriate boundaries. Modeling, helping children listen to each other's limit setting, reading books about appropriate and inappropriate touch, and role playing are effective means to help children both recognize other children's boundaries and to be empowered to set clear limits for themselves.

As you begin to educate yourself further about the dynamics of risk factors for young children and about children's special emotional needs, considering the implications for classroom practices will lead you to think further about your role as a classroom teacher.

EXPANDING THE TEACHER ROLE

A teacher who understands children's development from an ecological model (Brofenbrenner, 1979), meaning children's interactions and experiences in the family, neighborhood, and community play a role in their development and well-being, has new issues to consider, such as, "What is my role here and what part do I play outside of the immediate classroom environment?" Reflecting on these kinds of questions can help you respond appropriately to the needs of children while caring for your own emotional needs as a teacher. Consider, for example, Angelica, a child who is homeless and arrives at school during cold weather with only a thin sweater on. From what you can gather from Angelica's comments at school, you have reason to believe that her mother has recently left a domestic violence situation and is considering returning to her partner. How do you support Angelica? What do you do, if anything, that might extend outside of the classroom? And, most importantly, how do you take care of yourself so that you do not continually wake up at night troubled by Angelica and her mother's situation? Another situation that might challenge you to consider your role as a teacher is, for example, when a child's father breaks down during a parent-teacher conference and confides in you about the troubling details of his divorce situation. Again, what is your role here in supporting this child's development and how deep into this discussion with his father do you go? Sometimes these questions are referred to as "professional role" or "professional boundary" issues.

The NAEYC Professional Code of Conduct (1998) provides helpful guidelines to help early childhood teachers be clear about their role. For example, in the above case, it might be useful to remember that, "In cases where family members are in conflict, we shall work openly, sharing our observations of the child, to help all parties involved make informed decisions. We shall refrain from becoming an advocate for one party."

REFERRALS AND TEAMING WITH SPECIALISTS

As a teacher, you will no doubt encounter children whose emotional and behavioral issues require the support and expertise of specialists outside of the classroom. It will be important to understand when to seek support and to make referrals, as well as to know what resources are available in the community where you are teaching. It is vital to always understand your school or agency's policies and procedures about making referrals to other agencies.

Teaming with specialists from other agencies can be a means of providing both direct support for a child and consultation services for you, as a teacher.

Sometimes children's emotional needs require help beyond what a teacher is able to provide.

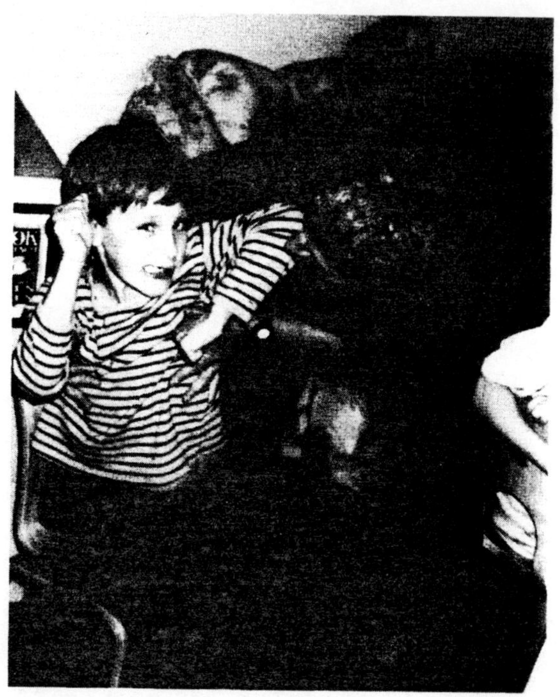

Appropriate referrals for a child with special behavioral needs might be, for example, for a special education evaluation or for mental health services. Your written or taped observations of a child in the classroom environment can be especially useful when making a referral or sharing concerns with other professionals.

Having an awareness of community social service, health, and basic needs resources will not only aide you in making the appropriate referrals but can also greatly enhance your relationship with the parents of children in your class, if you are in a role to share your knowledge with them. Because parents in stress often have difficulty taking the first step to locate resources to help themselves, it is important to be aware that a handout with community resources, phone numbers, and contact person can be more effective than just mentioning the names of agencies.

REPORTING

The NAEYC Professional Code of Conduct (1998) states that when we "Have reasonable cause to suspect child abuse or neglect we shall report it to the appropriate community agency and follow up to ensure that appropriate action has been taken." As an educator it is your legal responsibility to do so. This role is often called being a "mandatory reporter" and it is vital to clearly understand the reporting procedures of your state and your community. It is also important that you understand the reporting procedures for your own school or agency. It is helpful to have a clear grasp of these procedures before a situation in which you must make a report arises. Making reports can be both stressful and uncomfortable. It is valuable and often essential to debrief the situation with another professional for support and guidance.

PROFESSIONAL DEVELOPMENT

As is made evident by the complexity of the issues surrounding children with special emotional needs, there is no limit to how much more information a teacher can have to help to understand children better. Professional development not only helps you support children more fully, but it also can provide you with a sense of competence and knowledge about appropriate professional boundaries that will help sustain a sense of self care in your role as teacher.

SUPERVISION, PROFESSIONAL SUPPORT, AND SELF CARE

One of the most important steps in answering questions, such as ones presented in this chapter, and maintaining a clear professional role is debriefing troubling situations with a supervisor, principal, co-worker, or a team of other professionals. Just as a Constructivist teacher provides support for children to problem-solve, professional support can provide a safe environment to explore issues around children with emotional challenges and strategies for working with them. Regular reflective supervision not only helps you analyze and debrief about relevant child issues, but also provides guidance in maintaining clear professional boundaries.

Garbarino et al. (1992) talks about the importance of providing support for teachers around the emotional intensity of dealing with traumatized children and with children experiencing emotional difficulties. In recent years, more has been learned about the potential for professional caregivers, such as teachers, therapists, social workers, and health care providers, to experience what is commonly known as "burnout" while helping others deal with troubling situations. Debriefing with supervisors and co-workers, paying attention to your stress levels and your own mental and physical health, and developing good self-care habits around relaxation and recreation are essential.

CONCLUSION

Sometimes, after learning about all the various conditions and events that can make children vulnerable, it is easy to feel overwhelmed and wonder how a teacher can possibly help children in these situations. While there are clear limits to the role of the classroom teacher, you should remember that a child's relationship with a beloved teacher can do much to ameliorate or "soften" some of the disturbing events or environments outside of the classroom. And an early childhood teacher who carefully observes and maximizes the strategies to support the child in the classroom can exert a positive influence on the child's overall development and sense of well-being.

FOR FURTHER THOUGHT

1. When families are in short-term or chronic states of crisis, they often have difficulty taking the first step toward accessing resources. Investigate what kinds of resources are available in your community to help families meet basic needs, such as food, shelter, and clothing, as well as medical attention and counseling. What other needs might families have? Collect brochures and/or phone numbers and contacts from the agencies to be able to help parents take that first step in meeting family needs.
2. Suggestions were given in this chapter for resources of children's books that can be used to help children deal with difficult and challenging issues. Explore those resources and others to compile your own list of children's books. Organize the list by age group (i.e., preschool and elementary school age) and by topics that you feel are meaningful.
3. When children come to the classroom with special emotional needs resulting from issues in their lives outside of the classroom, teachers can be pulled in directions beyond their typical daily classroom role. What are some situations that would be especially challenging for you and how might you proceed? What would you need to take into consideration when establishing clear boundaries about your role as a teacher?
4. This chapter covered many different issues and discussed overlapping emotional and behavioral responses to various stressful situations. How might the issue of family culture influence children's responses to stress and what would you need to take into consideration as you respond to children's needs? What are some other situations that you might find yourself confronted with in your classroom involving cultural sensitivity that would be challenging for you as you support children emotionally?
5. Refer to Chapter 13, Children Experiencing Disabilities. What is the potential for special emotional needs when children experiencing some of the disabilities described are living in an environment that does not support their well-being?

RECOMMENDED READINGS

Carlsson-Paige, N., & Levin, D. E. (1998). *Before push comes to shove: Building conflict resolution skills with children.* St. Paul: Redleaf Press.

Chaille, C., & Britain, L. (1997). *The young child as scientist: A Constructivist approach to early childhood science education.* New York: Longman Press.

Essa, E., & Murray, C. (1999, Summer). Sexual Play: When should you be concerned? *Childhood Education,* pp. 231–233.

Garbarino, J., Dubrow, N., Kostelny, K., & Pardo, C. (1992). *Children in danger: Coping with the consequences of community violence.* San Francisco: Jossey-Bass Publishers.

Hyson, M. (1994). *The emotional development of young children: Building an emotion-centered curriculum.* New York: Teachers College Press.

Karr-Morse, R., & Wiley, M. (1997). *Ghosts from the nursery: Tracing the roots of violence.* New York: The Atlantic Monthly Press.

Koplow, L. (Ed.) (1996). *Unsmiling faces: How preschools can heal.* New York: Teachers College Press.

Slaby, R., Roedell, W., Arezzo, D., & Hendrix, K. (1995). *Early violence prevention: Tools for teachers of young children.* Washington DC: NAEYC.

15

ANALYZING DISCIPLINE PROBLEMS

You have read about many approaches to discipline and many causes of discipline problems in this book. In case the information is whirling around in your head and you're not sure what to do with it, this final chapter presents guidelines for how to put it all together in a usable fashion. However, it is not a recipe for no-fail discipline, but rather assistance in the difficult task of analyzing discipline problems and matching them with appropriate discipline approaches. Each child and each situation is unique, requiring your professional judgment about discipline.

KEEPING GOALS IN MIND

The first step in exercising your judgment is to examine your goals for discipline. Chapter 1 discusses the importance of keeping long-term goals firmly in mind as you plan discipline strategies. This book has emphasized the long-term goals of enhancing self-esteem, self-discipline, and moral autonomy. It is crucial that no discipline approach damage a child's growth in these areas. This book attempts to explain how inappropriate forms of discipline counteract progress toward these long-term goals. Rewards, punishment, and other manipulative approaches to discipline have become mainstream practices; teachers must understand that these practices work against their long term goals.

Short-term goals are also important, although meeting them must not conflict with long-term goals. There are certain behaviors that are so disruptive or dangerous that they must be stopped immediately, leaving the teaching aspect of discipline for the next step. If children's actions put them into danger, it is essential to act quickly and decisively. Talking directly to the children involved is much more productive than yelling directions across a room. An emergency situation may require a warning shout, which will be useful if the teacher's voice is usually calm and controlled. However, teachers who routinely raise their voices in an effort to control a group will find that a raised voice quickly loses effectiveness.

FINDING THE CAUSE OF THE PROBLEM

If the situation is not an emergency, or after an emergency situation is over, you are free to think about the most appropriate discipline approach for long-term goals. This step requires a search for the cause or causes of the discipline problem. Many times you will find several, interactive causes of a problem. This means you need to address several causes in order to provide effective help. Discipline that deals only with the symptoms rather than the causes of behavior problems is doomed to failure; the problem behavior will continue to surface until the reason for that behavior is addressed. Too often teachers respond to the behavior instead of the causes (Butchart, l998). This problem is well demonstrated in schools with posted sets of rules and the pre-planned punishments for breaking each rule.

The causes of a problem are not always obvious, and it may take serious study and even some trial and error to get at the root of the matter. The chart in Figure 15–1 may help you in the process of analyzing a discipline problem pattern for an individual child. The organization of this chart follows the organization of the book in moving from the least intrusive to the more intrusive approaches to solving behavior problems. First we consider the possibility that the adult needs to change and then gradually consider more and more serious needs of the child.

AGE-TYPICAL BEHAVIOR

As you start to search for the cause of a behavior problem, first ask yourself whether the offending behavior may simply be typical of that child's stage of maturation. Some adults don't realize, for instance, that a two-year-old is not being naughty when she wets her pants. These adults might punish the child or try bribing her in efforts to change this behavior, unaware that a two-year-old who isn't potty-trained is exhibiting maturationally normal behavior. The child can't change the behavior until she is older. Chapters 2 and 3, as well as Chapter 11, offer other reminders of age-appropriate child behaviors that may frustrate adults. Your soul-searching may reveal that the "problem" is actually adult intolerance or a misunderstanding of childlike behavior (Curry & Johnson, 1990). In that case, the cause of the problem is the adult's attitude; therefore, that attitude, not the child's behavior, needs to be changed.

INAPPROPRIATE ADULT EXPECTATIONS

The next step in finding the cause of a behavior problem involves examining whether or not inappropriate adult expectations may have created the problem. We do have sufficient information about child development and learning to eliminate inappropriate teacher expectations, including poor educational practices, as causes of behavior problems. Chapters 4 and 5 describe many common ways in which well-meaning teachers and

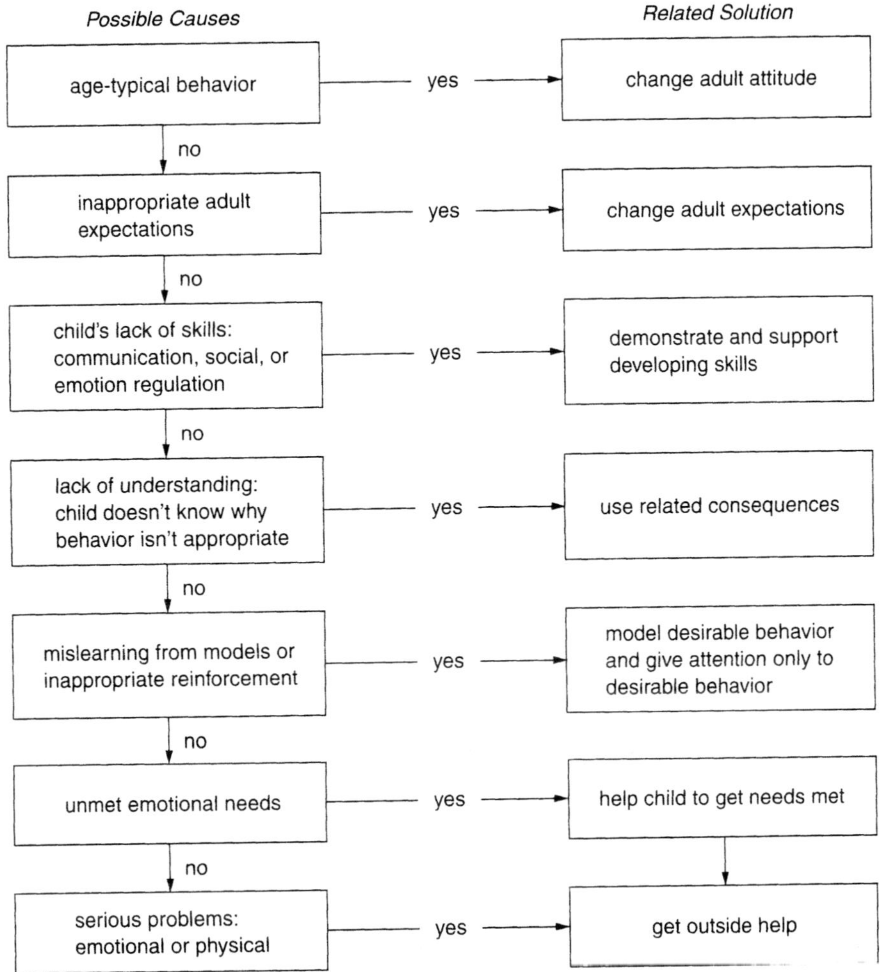

Figure 15–1
Matching problem causes to solutions.

caregivers accidentally cause discipline problems. Adults create problems when they require young children to sit still and be quiet for more than a few minutes, to wait with nothing to do, or to engage in learning activities designed for older youngsters. The National Association for the Education of Young Children offers guidelines for appropriate programs (Bredekamp, 1997) and curriculum (Bredekamp & Rosegrant, 1992) that teachers can consult to make sure discipline problems are not being caused by an inappropriate environment. If you suspect that the environment is causing children to react negatively, the solution is to change the situation rather than try to change the children. This preventive discipline approach saves both teachers and children a lot of trouble. The adult response in the following example demonstrates the value of this approach.

> After eating lunch each day, the children in the child-care program are expected to clear off their table setting and sit back down to wait for a teacher to call them to brush their teeth. Sometimes there is no wait time, but sometimes it can be a couple of minutes, depending on how many children have finished eating. Sheri knows this is not an ideal situation, but it seems to be the only way to handle the tooth brushing with twenty children and only two sinks.
>
> The children don't seem to have a problem with this, with the exception of James. James sits down for about ten seconds and then has to get up and move around the room, usually causing a disturbance in the process, or he wanders into the unsupervised kitchen.
>
> Sheri has repeatedly reminded James about sitting and waiting his turn. He seems to know what is expected of him but doesn't seem to be able to do it. Sheri decides that this situation just isn't appropriate for James and makes a plan to accommodate his needs. The chairs need to be stacked to sweep the floor after lunch. This has usually been done by the staff after the kids leave school, but Sheri asks James if he would like to help out and be the chair stacker after lunch. James jumps at the chance to do this real and important work—and to get to move around and use his muscles instead of trying to sit still. Now James is the proud official chair stacker instead of the kid in trouble every day. What a difference this makes to his self-esteem!

MISSING SKILLS

Once you have satisfied yourself that you are accepting children at their maturational level and providing an age-appropriate environment and curriculum, you can go on to look for other causes of discipline problems. Young children have a lot to learn about how to get along, how to deal with their emotions, and how to communicate effectively. If you suspect that lack of skill in any of these areas is causing the problem, a discipline approach that works on needed skills is the solution. Most of us work at developing these skill throughout our lives, so it is to be expected that young children will need help with them.

Chapters 3, 6, 7, and 11 present ways of helping children learn social skills and effective communication techniques. Adults can demonstrate and assist in desirable modes of self-expression and interacting with others (DeVries, Hildebrandt, & Zan, 2000). Probably the most important lesson you can teach has to do with perspective taking, the understanding other people's viewpoints. This requires a combination of communication and social skills because people need to be able to express their feelings clearly in order to facilitate an exchange of viewpoints. Teachers can help children find words so that they can share their views and feelings with their peers, thus decreasing egocentricity. Helping children learn how to play with others

Teachers can help children find words so they can share their views and feelings with peers, thus becoming less egocentric.

and make friends goes along with teaching them perspective taking. Other useful approaches include the use of "I messages" and problem-solving techniques to teach children effective conflict resolution (Gordon, 1989).

Emotion regulation, discussed in Chapters 2 and 6, is related to enhanced communication and perspective taking skills. When children are able to find the words to express their sorrows and frustrations, they have a way of getting support and an acceptable way of letting off steam. When they begin to understand that there may be another side to a situation, they are often comforted. For instance, being able to understand that the child who wronged them did so by accident often has a calming effect. Similarly, beginning to learn that things don't always go their way because others also want their own way can help children cope with a disappointment. In addition, most children need specific assistance with learning how to comfort themselves and how to delay gratification. Teaching children social skills, effective communication, and emotion regulation are important discipline strategies that promote lifelong harmonious social interaction.

LACK OF UNDERSTANDING

Perhaps the child has the needed skills but has chosen not to use them. Sometimes children behave in unacceptable ways because they don't understand why they shouldn't. Perhaps the cause of the problem is a lack of knowledge about how to behave or about the results of certain actions.

Young children need assistance in learning about cause-and-effect relationships. They need to learn that their behaviors have certain results, or consequences (Dill, 1998).

Chapter 8 explains how natural and related consequences help youngsters to understand *why* certain behaviors are undesirable or desirable. Adults often have trouble allowing children to learn from experience because of the desire to protect them. Although you do need to keep children away from harm, you don't want to protect them so much that they lose the opportunity to learn. Finding out that you get cold if you don't dress for the weather or that you get hungry if you don't eat are valuable educational lessons. They are examples of natural consequences (Dreikurs, 1964). Related consequences are adult-imposed, but they link the behavior to a result that demonstrates why the behavior needs to be changed. Too often, adults expect children to learn from lectures and forget that experience is the best teacher (Butchart, 1998). Natural and related consequences are effective forms of guidance that help children gain knowledge, which in turn guides youngsters in self-regulating their behavior.

MISLEARNING

Sometimes children have learned the wrong things. Chapters 9 and 12 describe how youngsters often get attention for undesirable behavior and how this attention encourages the behavior to continue. These children have learned to get their emotional needs met in counterproductive ways. In this case, the needed discipline approach involves reteaching. Children need to unlearn old ways of getting attention and learn new ones (Curwin & Mendler, 1990). Judicious use of behavior modification techniques guides teachers in ignoring undesirable behaviors and reinforcing desirable ones.

Another type of mislearning is a result of undesirable role models. Chapter 6 discusses the problems of media violence and how it impacts the behavior of children and youth. The need to counteract this influence cannot be overstated (Faber & Mazlish, 1996). Sometimes the undesirable role models are older children, family members, or sports heroes. Unfortunately, educators frequently model power tactics that model a "might makes right" approach (Butchart, 1998).

Whatever the source, positive role models who build trusting relationships with children are desperately needed as the antidote. Teachers must be moral, caring, and socially skilled so they can demonstrate important skills and understandings in word and deed (Watson, 1999). The most effective models "transparently" model desirable behavior by talking to themselves out loud, demonstrating the thought processes behind their actions (Dill, 1998).

UNMET EMOTIONAL NEEDS

If you are sure that a child knows better and is capable of behaving better, but is still acting out, you need to look deeper for the cause. Sometimes undesirable behavior is motivated by children striving to feel okay in spite of experiences that have left them with emotional deficits (Curry & Johnson, 1990). Strong survival instincts motivate these youngsters to try to get their needs met, and they frequently act out in extremely disruptive ways that show misguided efforts toward "wholeness." But other youngsters with emotional deficits give up and retreat into their shells. The latter may be easier to deal with but are ultimately an even greater cause for your concern and attention.

Chapter 12 discusses how unmet needs in such areas as trust, pride, love, and power can contribute to discipline problems. If unmet needs are the cause of the problem, a truly effective discipline approach must involve attempts to help children get those needs met. These attempts may be made in conjunction with other approaches that will make the symptoms more manageable, such as related consequences. It is important to keep the cause of the problem in mind, however, and continue to work on helping the child get his or her needs met.

SERIOUS PROBLEMS

Teachers frequently find that a child in their care has a problem that they cannot adequately address by themselves. Chapters 13 and 14 discuss sources of help for children with severe problems. In some cases, the child's entire family must be helped in order to benefit the child. There is a limit to what can be expected of teachers and caregivers, and they must insist on outside expertise for these situations.

Sometimes teachers find themselves at odds with parental preferences and are torn between what they believe is right for the child and the commitment to honoring families. These are times for consulting the NAEYC Code of Ethics included in the appendix (Feeney & Kipnis, 1999).

MATCHING DISCIPLINE TO THE CAUSE

As you try to use the various guidance and discipline approaches described in this book, remember that each is useful only to the extent that it deals with the cause of the problem. Each discipline approach is aimed at a different type of cause. Using all available evidence to discover the cause is the first step. The solution is usually fairly evident from there—if you keep in mind that the solution needs to aim at the cause. Too often, people forget that the solution is to treat the cause; they slip back into the old ways of responding to the behavior instead of the cause.

AN EXAMPLE

Perhaps it would be helpful to analyze an actual problem behavior using the chart in Figure 15–1. See how Mrs. Jensen worked as a "detective" to discover the cause of Kayla's problem:

> Kayla arrived late this morning and is very quiet during morning circle. When the class begins to work together on writing, Kayla sits alone. Since Kayla usually participates in writing groups, Mrs. Jensen is confused by the girl's behavior.

Given this evidence, do you think that Kayla's behavior is age-typical or the expectations are inappropriate? Since the others are participating and Kayla usually does, neither of those possibilities seem to be the cause of the problem.

> Mrs. Jensen encourages Kayla to find someone to work with, but Kayla insists that the other children don't like her. The teacher decides to let her alone for the time being. A little bit later, she notices Kayla sitting under the table looking sad.

Mrs. Jensen thinks hard, trying to figure out what is going on. Kayla usually enjoys working with her friends and seems to be well accepted by the other children. Therefore, the teacher doesn't think that the problem is caused by missing communication or social skills. Mrs. Jensen continues to explore other possibilities. She wonders if Kayla is testing the limits to see if there is any good reason to work on her writing.

> Mrs. Jensen reminds Kayla that the class is working on play scripts for Friday Fun Day, when they will act out their plays for one another. Mrs. Jensen expresses concern that Kayla won't get to be in a play. Kayla makes no response.

The teacher decides she is giving Kayla far too much attention for her negative behavior. Mrs. Jensen wonders whether her urging and attention has actually been encouraging Kayla's pouting. She decides to shift her attention to the children who are writing.

> After a little while, Kayla brings Mrs. Jensen a picture of a broken heart with a girl crying on it. Next to this picture, she has written her name. She looks so sad that Mrs. Jensen is concerned.

She thinks this is starting to look like unmet emotional needs. She decides she must find out what is happening in Kayla's life.

> She gives Kayla a hug and asks her about her picture. Kayla only says, "That's me feeling sad."

At lunch time, Mrs. Jensen makes some phone calls and discovers that there had been some domestic violence at Kayla's house the night before. The police had been there and Kayla was aware of the trouble. Mrs. Jensen revises her theory about the cause of the problem from unmet emotional needs to serious emotional needs. She knows that it will be especially important for her to provide a sense of love and security for Kayla at school.

This example explores all the possibilities on the chart, but you will find that most problem analysis stops far short of serious problems. Yes, it may seem like most of your discipline problems have that cause because a child with serious problems can take up so much of your time. But in actuality, you have dozens of minor incidents daily that are caused by lack of perspective-taking skills, lack of ability to enter play, or lack of communication skill. We hope you do not have many problems caused by inappropriate expectations. However, if you do, you know what to do about it.

EVALUATING GUIDANCE PROGRAMS

Much of the current curriculum material for guidance and discipline is in relation to violence prevention, due to the recent tragic rate of school violence. Many violence prevention guides focus on "managing behavior," which tends to be a focus on symptoms rather than on the causes of inappropriate behavior. The most consistent rule enforcement will not help the child who mistreats others due to unmet attention needs. The most detailed lessons in social skills will not help the child who lashes out due to low self-esteem. Genuine change will come only when the child's needs are met and self-esteem is secure. Superficial change due to a focus on symptoms may submerge the actual problems and allow them to grow more serious. These problems will eventually emerge again and be manifested through more serious negative behavior.

Teachers and caregivers working with young children have a unique window of opportunity to make a difference. Children's attitudes about themselves and their world are still malleable during the early childhood years (through age 8). By the time students are adolescents, it is often too late for them to change their views and their behavior.

SAFETY FIRST

Discipline approaches aimed at teaching missing skills and understandings are different from your job of keeping children safe. In an emergency you must first stop unsafe behaviors or assist an injured child. It is not a "teachable moment" when children are in danger, injured, or upset. However, this does not mean that the needed teaching should be ignored. After the crisis has passed and the children involved are comforted and calmed, you can work on the skills or understandings that can keep the problem from happening again.

WHOSE PROBLEM IS IT?

Another way to analyze a discipline problem is to ask yourself, "Whose problem is it?" Gordon (1989) suggests the usefulness of separating those problems that belong to the child from those that belong to you, the adult. When you know whose problem it is, you have a start on how to solve it (see Figure 15–2). To find out who owns a problem, look at who is bothered by the behavior.

YOUR PROBLEM

If the child is perfectly content with the situation and you are the unhappy one, the odds are that you own the problem. If you are bothered by children's messiness, exuberance, or lack of logic, you definitely own the problem. These characteristics are part of being young and aren't likely to change until children are no longer so young. This type of problem leaves you with only one reasonable solution: Change yourself. Perhaps you can increase your understanding of youngsters to the point of increasing your acceptance of them. For some teachers, the solution is to find work with older children.

ADULT'S PROBLEM	CHILD'S PROBLEM
DISCIPLINE APPROACHES	DISCIPLINE APPROACHES
Express "I message" Change expectations Change environment Change curriculum Remove yourself	Reflective listening Related consequences Coaching in skills Help with unmet needs

MUTUAL PROBLEM

Problem-solving negotiations

Figure 15–2
Whose problem is it?

Other common examples of discipline problems that belong to the teacher include children taking blocks out of the block area, leaving the group at circle time, or talking out of turn. The children exhibiting these behaviors certainly are not bothered by it, and rarely are other children offended by these situations. If the problem is the teacher's, then the teacher is the only one motivated to find a solution.

SOLUTIONS TO YOUR PROBLEM

When you own the problem, you have several options. One is to change your expectations so that you no longer perceive the behavior as unacceptable. For example, you may decide to allow blocks to be used in other centers as long as they are eventually returned to the block storage area. You may also decide to allow children a choice about attending circle time, as long as they don't disturb those who are participating. You might even decide to allow more informal talking and not require raised hands.

Your options also include changing the situation to prevent the problem from recurring. You may decide to locate the block center next to the pretend-play area because the blocks so frequently get taken for use in playhouse scenarios. You may decide to shorten circle time and make it more lively so that the children's attention won't wander. You might decide to encourage more small group rather than large group activities, thereby reducing the need for formal turns in discussion. All of these solutions involve creating a more developmentally appropriate learning environment for young children, as discussed in Chapters 4 and 5.

If you cannot overlook the behavior or change it by modifying the situation, then you still have other options. If the child is capable of changing the behavior, you might find an "I message" effective (Gordon, 1989). Matter-of-factly telling a youngster, "I can't read this book when you climb on my back," provides information about the situation and your wishes. It does not suggest that the child is being "bad," nor does it reinforce the behavior with undue attention. If you have established caring relationships with the children around you and have respected their feelings, they are likely to respect your feelings expressed as "I messages." Saying "I don't like to be hit" may be the way for you to deal with another problem. This approach also demonstrates to children how they can deal with some of their own interpersonal problems.

If that method doesn't work, you still have options. If you have tried the other approaches without success, you may decide that the behavior has a cause that needs attention. As Lillian Katz suggests, if you have tried the same discipline approach more than two or three times with the same child and it hasn't worked, you can assume it isn't going to be effective for that child (Katz & McClellan, 1991). Perhaps you need to investigate the possibility that the cause of the problem includes mislearned approaches for getting attention, as described in Chapters 9 and 12. In that case, the option of walking away from the offending child not only can meet your needs, but also can address the cause. When you withhold attention from inappropriate bids for it, you help the child unlearn the misguided behavior. There are some behaviors, however, that are too disruptive or dangerous to ignore. These instances may be good times for related consequences that teach why certain actions cause problems. These strategies try to make the problem also belong to the child by getting the child involved in a solution.

THE CHILD'S PROBLEM

Many times the problem does belong to the child in the first place, but the adult takes it on. We describe this situation in Chapter 8 when we introduce the mother who repeatedly brings the child's forgotten library book to school. Remember, children won't see a need to change behavior that is not causing a problem for them. Therefore, it is crucial that we acknowledge when the problem belongs to the child. Natural and related consequences get the adults out of the way and let the child experience the problem. These approaches quickly teach youngsters what behavior needs changing. Through natural and related consequences, children experience the problem, understand its cause, and are motivated to solve it.

When a child's problem is of a social/emotional nature, reflective listening (described in Chapter 7) is useful. When you listen carefully and reflect back a child's words, you are not taking over the problem and offering solutions (Gordon, 1989). Rather, you are being a supportive sounding board to help the child arrive at his or her solution. This approach helps children learn to own their problems and demonstrates an effective communication technique for them. Reflective listening respects children's ability to solve their problems, which not only enhances their self-esteem but also provides practice in autonomous decision making.

Before you respond to a discipline problem , first ask yourself, "Whose problem is it?"

MUTUAL PROBLEMS

Sometimes a situation arises that makes lots of people unhappy. But even if it only makes two people unhappy, the problem does not belong to just one person. Perhaps a group of youngsters can't start their math game because they can't agree about who should have the first turn. Now mutual problem-solving skills are required: It is important to find a solution that is acceptable to everyone involved. Chapter 7 describes how to brainstorm solutions and look for one that pleases all participants. This process may be a formal and time-consuming operation with a large group, or it may be a quick negotiation between two youngsters or between an adult and a child. Using this process solves many discipline problems, and teaching it to children provides them with a lifetime tool (Kriedler, 1991).

TAKING TIME FOR DISCIPLINE

Some teachers and parents want solutions too fast. They don't want to take the time to work through problem solving. They provide their adult solutions instead of listening reflectively, and they even force desirable behavior through fear or coerce it through rewards. These adults are short-circuiting the learning process that defines constructive discipline (Watson, 1999). Instead of helping children become autonomous and self-disciplined, this quick-fix attitude makes them dependent, rebellious, and sneaky (Kamii, 1984).

TIME FOR CHILDREN TO LEARN

Teaching desirable behavior is a process of helping children learn a complex set of concepts and skills. Adults need to understand that children's exploration of behavior and social interaction is as natural for them as their exploration and manipulation of a new toy or another interesting object. Children need to try out certain behaviors to see how they work in relation to themselves and others. Given a predictable environment, along with sufficient practice, guidance, and time, youngsters will discover through their explorations that there is a logical pattern or consequence of actions. Children need to experience repeated connections between their behaviors and the results of them. As they reflect on these experiences, they construct their knowledge of productive behaviors, which eventually allows them to self-direct their actions as morally autonomous people. Such an important process does not happen quickly. Understanding gradually evolves as the child internalizes experiences and information over time. But the results are important enough to be worth waiting for.

TIME FOR COOL-DOWNS

It is hard to quit rushing. Sometimes teachers hurry to implement effective teaching techniques in a discipline situation. Perhaps two children are fighting. You know that they need to use their words to express their feelings and then negotiate a solution through problem solving. It is tempting to immediately start in on this important teaching as you separate the antagonists, but they are red-faced, short-breathed, and still swinging. Will they hear your voice of reason right now? A wise teacher allows a cool-down time before trying to teach more acceptable social skills.

TIME FOR ADULTS TO PLAN

Adults usually don't give themselves time to plan effective discipline. Behavior modification, with its emphasis on immediate feedback, has contributed to the common view that discipline must be instantaneous. Therefore, adults see a child doing something unacceptable, and they feel pressured to respond immediately. However, thoughtful, reasoned responses on any subject take time. None of us does our best thinking without reflection time. Many teachers and parents confess to using discipline approaches they don't like simply because they couldn't come up with a better one *at the time*. It rarely occurs to them to allow sufficient time for effective planning in the area of discipline.

If you discovered a child had a language development problem, you would study the situation and consult others as you carefully planned proper intervention strategies. However, when the subject to be learned has to do with proper behavior, adults tend to act without thinking. Next time you are confronted with a discipline problem that you don't have an immediate answer for, try telling the child or children involved that you need time to think about it. Such a response demonstrates the seriousness of the situation and also models the use of thoughtful reflection in problem solving. Of

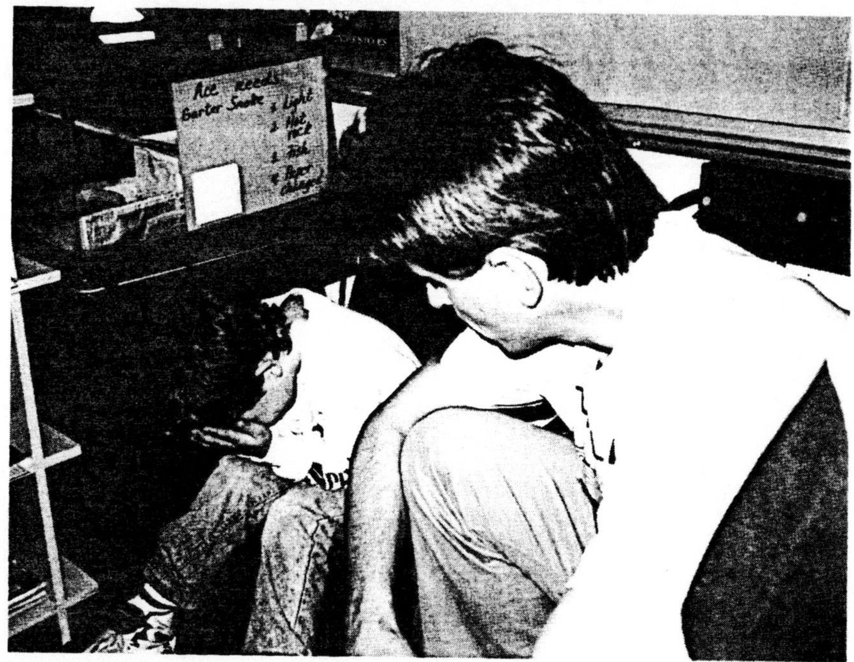

Quality solutions to problems can't be rushed.

course, for ongoing and predictable discipline problems, it's possible to plan ahead and have a guidance plan ready to implement.

We effectively learn through the role models in our lives. Unfortunately, most of us have learned some highly inappropriate discipline methods from our own childhood. When we react quickly instead of thoughtfully, our actions are often influenced by old models. The automatic response generally corresponds with the one our own teachers used. If we want to implement better ideas about effective discipline, then we must make a constant effort to override our automatic responses with rational ones. Be careful and take your time.

THE ROLE OF RESPECT

Few of us experienced discipline with respect in our childhoods. American mainstream society says it values children, but demonstrates little respect for them. Many of us experienced punishment and behavior modification: coercive tactics that damage both character development and intellectual development (DeVries, 1999). Adults in our lives may have also criticized us when they wanted to improve our behavior. The idea that criticism helps people to improve is widespread. Yet, in fact, it discourages us, and it does not improve behavior. When children's efforts result in feedback about their shortcomings, they are discouraged.

Discouragement leads to quitting, not to trying harder. Alternatively, encouragement (described as an alternative to praise in Chapter 9) leads to trying harder.

Respect accepts the child as a child, not as an imperfect adult. Respecting children means that we provide situations in which they can thrive while still acting their age. It also means that we give them as much choice as possible. When we respect youngsters, we don't force or manipulate them to bend to our will. However, that attitude doesn't mean they are allowed to run wild and be undisciplined. Respect for children guides us in helping them learn effective behaviors and understand the reasons for them. When we respect children, we help them to respect themselves. The resultant self-esteem combines with self-discipline skills to create morally autonomous people—something our society needs more of.

CONCLUSION

The teacher with the knowledge and the caring to implement this sophisticated approach to discipline deserves society's highest respect. Few observers realize how much effort and thought goes into a smoothly functioning program for young children. Teachers make hundreds of important initial decisions about the environment and the program, and they must make hundreds more each day as they implement their plans and keep youngsters constructively involved. We hope that this book is helpful to your own professional growth toward implementing the best possible approaches to discipline for young children. We hope that it helps you to envision and create educational relationships in keeping with democracy and human dignity.

FOR FURTHER THOUGHT

1. Think about your goals for guidance and discipline. Do you feel clear about what you hope to accomplish?
2. Analyze an actual ongoing discipline challenge using the chart in Figure 15–1 and the accompanying explanation as a guide. Does this analysis help you to consider your own possible role as a cause of discipline problems? Have you discovered a cause you had not previously considered? Have you discovered a need for outside help? Does this analysis approach help you to match guidance approaches to the causes of discipline problems?
3. Analyze another discipline situation using the chart in Figure 15–2. Have you been unsuccessfully trying to get children to take responsibility for your problem? Have you been inadvertently taking responsibility for theirs? Does this analysis help you to match your responses to the situation more effectively?
4. Practice taking your time with responses to undesirable behavior. Give yourself cool-down time and planning time. What are the children's reactions? Do they seem to learn from your example? Are your interventions more effective?

RECOMMENDED READINGS

Butchart, R. E., & McEwan, B. (1998). *Classroom discipline in American schools: Problems and possibilities for democratic education.* Albany, NY: State University of New York Press.

Dill, V. S. (1998). *A peaceable school: Cultivating a culture of nonviolence.* Bloomington, Indiana: Phi Delta Kappa.

Williams, M. M., & Shaps, E. (Eds). (1999). *Character education: The foundation for teacher education.* Washington, DC: The Character Education Partnership.

Appendix A

MEDIA VIOLENCE AND CHILDREN: A CALL TO ACTION!

Media Violence and Children: A Call to Action!

2000 - 2001

Media is a powerful force in childrens lives. Many children now spend more time in front of a screen than in school. Even when children are not in front of the screen, what they do and learn is highly influenced by the toys & related products marketed with TV shows and other media. The problem is made even worse because much of what children see on the screen is violent. It undermines lessons we teach at home and school about how people treat each other and encourages the use of violence to solve problems. Recent school shootings highlight the dangers of glamorizing the use of violence as a way to solve problems.

Media violence has become a public health issue that affects us all. Let us work together to reduce the problems created by media violence for our children and society.

Teachers and parents, please join the TRUCE Campaign Against Media Violence.
Our Action Guide with help you to:

- Promote children's informed and responsible use of media.
- Counteract the negative effects of media violence on children.
- Take action to reduce media violence in children's lives and in society.

Facts About Children, Media, and Violence

Research shows:

- Children average 35 hours per week of screen time-including TV, video games and videos.
- Heavy TV viewers are less imaginative, more aggressive, and have poorer concentration.
- Viewing media violence can make children more aggressive, fearful, disrespectful and insensitive to the effects of violence.
- The average child sees 8,000 murders and 100,000 other violence acts by the end of elementary school.
- Children's TV has 5 times as many acts of violent per hour as adults TV (26 vs. 5).
- A recent Harvard University study showed that G-rated movies average 9.5 minutes of violence.
- Most violent children's media is linked to toys and other products. The best selling new media-linked toy lines in 1999 were Star Wars and professional wrestling.
- A 1998 Gallup poll found 76% of parents believe the media has a negative influence on their children.

For more information write: TRUCE PO Box 441261, West Somerville, MA 02144
PLEASE COPY AND DISTRIBUTE

Teachers Resisting Unhealthy Children's Entertainment

ACTION GUIDE

- **Help children develop thoughtful and responsible media viewing habits.**
    - Decide together how much "screen time" is okay each day or week. (With young children, we recommend starting with the least amount that can work with your schedule and your child's.)
    - Discuss and work out which shows are okay and which are not.
    - Make a chart (with simple picture illustrations for non-readers) of shows which your children want to watch and which you can agree are good choices. Check the chart regularly to help you discuss how things are going.
- **Talk with other parents about how they deal with TV.**
    - Share your concerns and approach to TV and other media. Use this TRUCE guide.
    - Discuss how you will deal with TV and other media when your children are at each other's houses.
    - Ask your child's school to help promote such discussions.
- **Limit the effects media violence has on your child by trying to limit the number of highly realistic toys and other products that are linked to TV programs.**
    - Encourage creative and imaginative play rather than play that mainly imitates what children see on TV.
    - Provide toys that children can use in many ways over a long period of time, such as blocks, playdough, dress-ups, and props for dramatic play (e.g., old telephones).
- Choose toys carefully. (Use the following guide and the TRUCE Toy Action Guide to help you with your toy choices.)

Toy Selection Guide

Look for toys that:

- Can be used in a variety of ways.
- Promote creativity and problem solving by letting children decide what to do.
- Can be enjoyed at different ages and stages and grow with the child.
- Will continue to be fun and engaging over time.
- Can be used with other toys for changing and more complex play.
- Promote respectful, non-stereotyped, non-violent interactions among children.
- Will add a new dimension to play beyond a child's current toys.

Some examples:

• table blocks • ocean, farm, and rainforest animals or insects • construction sets (Legos, Lincoln Logs, etc.) • people and animal props • tool sets • flashlights • dolls with accurate features • clay • basic art supplies • blocks • cars, trucks, boats, planes and trains • dress-up clothes and house-wares • bean bags • balls • jump ropes • playing cards • puzzles • tape stories • medical kits • musical instruments •

For more information write: TRUCE PO Box 441261, West Somerville, MA 02144

Teachers Resisting Unhealthy Children's Entertainment

ACTION GUIDE

◆ Talk with children about what they see on the screen.

Questions to Help Parents and Children Talk Together About TV and Other Media *

One effective way to influence the messages that children learn from the media is talking to them about what they see. Aim for a give-and-take discussion rather than a lecture where you give the answers. Through an open discussion you can find out children's ideas, fears, misconceptions and provide other ideas.

- You can each talk about your reactions (both positive and negative) to what you saw.
  - *What did you think about that show / game?*
  - *Did you like it when _____________ happened? Why do you think it happened?*
  - *I didn't like it when _____________. I wish they didn't have to hurt each other. What do you think?*
- You can help sort out fantasy from reality.
  - *What was pretend and what was real? How could you tell?*
  - *Help clarify confusion by saying things such as, "In real life things don't work that way."*
  - *I wonder how they made _____ happen on that show.*
  - *How can we tell the difference between these ads and the show wonder why they made the ad like that?*
- You can help compare what they saw to their own experience.
  - *Could anything like _________ happen to you? When? How could it be the same / different?*
  - *What would you do if you were in that situation?*
- You can talk directly about the violence and other mean-spirited behavior that children see on the screen.
  - *What do you think about how ______ solved their problem? If you had a problem like that what could you do / say?*
  - *Can you think of a way to solve that problem where no one gets hurt?*
- You can ask questions that focus on stereotyped images and behaviors.
  - *I wonder why it's always men with big muscles who go to fight? Did you notice that? What do you think about it?*
  - *It seems like the women always need to get rescued by the men. Have you noticed that? I wonder why?*
  - *I wonder why the "bad guys" have foreign accents? always wear dark colors? have darker skin?*

* adapted from *Remote-Control Childhood* by Diane Levin

For more information write: TRUCE PO Box 441261, West Somerville, MA 02144

PLEASE COPY AND DISTRIBUTE

Appendix B

CURRICULUM GUIDELINES FROM THE NATIONAL ASSOCIATION FOR THE EDUCATION OF YOUNG CHILDREN

1. **The curriculum has an articulated description of its theoretical base that is consistent with prevailing professional opinion and research on how children learn.**

   Curriculum should be grounded in the most current knowledge of child development and learning. The prevailing world view reflects a developmental, interactive, Constructivist approach to learning that is not limited to the almost exclusively Behaviorist approach that has permeated curriculum and assessment in this country for the past several decades.

2. **Curriculum content is designed to achieve long-range goals for children in all domains—social, emotional, cognitive, and physical—and to prepare children to function as fully contributing members of a democratic society.**

   Curriculum should address the development and learning of the whole child. This means that curriculum in primary grade schools must attend to social, emotional, and physical goals as well as cognitive goals. Likewise, programs for 3- and 4-year-olds need to address cognition as well as social, emotional, and physical development. In addition, curriculum content and processes should reflect democratic ideals of community involvement, liberty, freedom of choice, equality, fairness, and justice.

3. **Curriculum addresses the development of knowledge and understanding, processes and skills, dispositions and attitudes.**

   The acquisition of knowledge and the mastery of skills is accomplished so as to ensure that children will be disposed to apply the knowledge or skill and so that children associate positive feelings with the learning (Katz & Chard, 1989). For example, if reading instruction is limited to a drill and practice on phonics and word-attack skills, children may choose not to read because they find no pleasure or satisfaction in reading or do not understand what they decode. On the other hand, if children are motivated to get meaning from reading, they are more likely to respond to instruction in the use of phonetic cues.

4. **Curriculum addresses a broad range of content that is relevant, engaging, and meaningful to children.**

   The human mind is a pattern detector; the child naturally attempts to make meaning out of every experience. As a result, what is meaningful is always more easily learned, understood, and remembered. Effective curriculum develops knowledge and skills in a meaningful context, not in isolation. For example, children learn numerals and number concepts by counting real objects, not by filling in workbook pages. Children learn letters and their sounds from using them in their name, signs, or stories that are meaningful to them rather than by tracing them on a page or reciting the alphabet repeatedly. The younger the child, the more important it is to provide curriculum content that is close to the child's experience and therefore more likely to be meaningful.

5. **Curriculum goals are realistic and attainable for most children in the designated age range for which they were designed.**

   Curriculum planning should adjust for normative differences in children's development and learning. Children should not be expected to comprehend abstract/symbolic concepts or master skills or content that can be acquired much more easily later on. To some extent, this guideline addresses the issue of efficiency in teaching and learning. For instance, first, second, and third grade teachers all report that children cannot comprehend place value; teachers spend hours trying to teach this abstract concept, and children either become frustrated or resort to memorizing meaningless tricks. This is an example of an unrealistic objective that could be attained much more easily later on.

   Curriculum decisions about when children are expected to acquire knowledge and skills are based on age-group, individual, and cultural expectations. Curriculum expectations of young children are flexible and dynamic rather than deterministic and lock-step since there is no universal sequence of skills development. The curriculum allows for children to work at different levels on different activities and does not require all of the children to do the same thing at the same time. Decisions about when knowledge and skills are introduced and/or expected to be accomplished are based on knowledge of the prior experiences of individual children in a group, knowledge of prerequisite intellectual structures, and knowledge about typical patterns of development and learning.

6. **Curriculum content reflects and is generated by the needs and interests of individual children within the group. Curriculum incorporates a wide variety of learning experiences, materials and equipment, and instructional strategies to accommodate a broad range of children's individual differences in prior experience, maturation rates, styles of learning, needs, and interests.**

   Curriculum planning should anticipate the interests that are typical of children of different ages and should also emerge from the interests that children demonstrate. Interest can also be generated by exposing children to events, materials, and people that children would not experience otherwise. Educators must choose which of the children's interests to support and which to ignore. In addition, educators have a responsibility to nurture certain interests, particularly those that are tied to cultural values, such as the value of children's autonomy and creative experience.

7. **Curriculum respects and supports individual, cultural, and linguistic diversity. Curriculum supports and encourages positive relationships with children's families.**

   The curriculum embraces the reality of multiculturalism in American society by providing a balance between learning the common core of dominant cultural knowledge (for example, the English language, democratic values) and knowledge of minority cultures. Curriculum accommodates children who have limited English proficiency. All of the cultures and primary languages of the children are respectfully reflected in the curriculum.

8. **Curriculum builds upon what children already know and are able to do (activating prior knowledge) to consolidate their learning and to foster their acquisition of new concepts and skills.**

   For example, there is no body of knowledge possessed by all children of the same age, just as there is no universal sequence of learning. Because children bring meaning to learning experiences based on their past experiences and individual development, different children acquire different learnings from the same experience. As a result, curriculum for young children should not be based on a rigid scope and sequence but should help children connect new learning to what they already know and are able to do.

9. **Curriculum provides conceptual frameworks for children so that their mental constructions based on prior knowledge and experience become more complex over time.**

   Conceptual organizers such as themes, units, or projects give children something meaningful and substantive to engage their minds. It is difficult for children to make sense of abstract concepts such as colors, mathematical symbols, or letter sounds when they are presented at random or devoid of any meaningful context.

10. **Curriculum allows for focus on a particular topic or content while allowing for integration across traditional subject-matter divisions by planning around themes and/or learning experiences that provide opportunities for rich conceptual development.**

    Children's learning is not compartmentalized or divided into artificial subject-matter distinctions. The purpose of integrating curriculum is to reflect the natural way children learn and also to help children make connections between what they learn at home and in the program, between what they learn in school and in the real world, and between different disciplines or subject-matter areas (British Columbia Ministry of Education, 1990). The curriculum provides for long blocks of time to bring naturally related subjects together and does not require minimal time allotments for instruction in discrete subject matter. For example, children read and write about a science experiment they have done, or measure and estimate the number of blocks they will need to build a store.

11. **Curriculum content has intellectual integrity; content meets the recognized standards of the relevant subject-matter disciplines.**

    Regardless of the age of the child, educators have a responsibility to respect the knowledge base of the appropriate disciplines when formulating curriculum. In an attempt to simplify content, curriculum developers sometimes present inaccurate, misleading, or potentially confusing information. If the specific content is related to a particular discipline, then it should be as accurate as possible (although children's constructions of knowledge will not mirror adult conceptions). For example, science curriculum should be factual and not promote magical thinking in children; likewise, children should be exposed to literature, poetry, and the works of art and music of recognized quality.

12. **Curriculum content is worth knowing; curriculum respects children's intelligence and does not waste their time.**

    Content should be included in curriculum for specific age groups because it is important for children to learn to function capably in their world. Content goals should include what children can learn efficiently and effectively at this time. Children and teachers should not have to waste time trying to address content that is meaningless or could be learned much more easily when the child is older.

13. **Curriculum engages children actively, not passively, in the learning process. Children have opportunities to make meaningful choices.**

    The curriculum provides for children's direct experience before moving to more abstract levels of understanding. The curriculum or learning experience builds on children's prior learning and previous knowledge; thus, sensory experience is not prerequisite in every situation but is vital when introducing new concepts or information. Encouraging and permitting children to make real choices fosters interest and engagement. For instance, children should have opportunities to express their own ideas in writing and to read books of their choosing as well as those that the entire group will address.

14. **Curriculum values children's constructive errors and does not prematurely limit exploration and experimentation for the sake of ensuring "right" answers.**

    Overemphasis on standardized test scores and the acquisition of basic skills has made teachers and parents uncomfortable with the natural process of the child's construction of knowledge. The fact is that teachers can learn a great deal about children' thinking and reasoning and level of cognitive development by attending to their "wrong" answers.

15. **Curriculum emphasizes the development of children's thinking, reasoning, decision making, and problem-solving abilities.**

    Curriculum emphasizes both content and process, what children need to know and be able to do. Curriculum content gives meaning to process, rather than focusing on isolated facts. Skills are taught in the context of activities that are meaningful to the child, rather than teaching skills in isolation (Lloyd-Jones & Lunsford, 1988).

16. **Curriculum emphasizes the value of social interaction to learning in all domains and provides opportunities to learn from peers.**

    Social interaction with peers and adults is essential for children to develop real understanding. Social interaction also provides opportunities for children to learn cooperation and other kinds of positive social behavior. Multiage grouping is one strategy to promote social interaction among individual children and their more capable peers, an effective way of enhancing language competence, and generally assisting children's progress to the next level of development and understanding.

17. **Curriculum is supportive of children's physiological needs for activity, sensory stimulation, fresh air, rest, hygiene, and nourishment/elimination.**

    Curriculum should respect and meet children's physical needs while also promoting children's independent functioning and ability to meet their own needs. Children should not be required to sit still for long periods without a break. Under no circumstances should children who need regular opportunities to move their bodies be kept indoors to complete tasks or be deprived of food as punishment.

18. **Curriculum protects children's psychological safety; that is, children feel happy, relaxed, and comfortable rather than disengaged, frightened, worried, or stressed.**
    Decisions about curriculum should respect children's psychological safety. For instance, the content itself should not generate fear or confusion, nor should the premature expectation of mastery of skills generate stress.

19. **Curriculum strengthens children's sense of competence and enjoyment of learning by providing experiences for children to succeed from their point of view.**
    Sometimes teachers seem to use the following as their primary criterion for selecting curriculum: "But the children just love it!" Enjoying the curriculum is an important but insufficient criterion for curriculum selection. Worthwhile curriculum does not have to entertain children; instead, children's enjoyment can derive from positive feelings about self and meaningful learning as they realize their own progress and growing competence.

20. **Curriculum is flexible so that teachers can adapt to individual children or groups.**
    The curriculum suggests alternatives as well as assumes that teachers will use their own professional judgment.

Appendix C

CODE OF ETHICAL CONDUCT AND STATEMENT OF COMMITMENT

GUIDELINES FOR RESPONSIBLE BEHAVIOR IN EARLY CHILDHOOD EDUCATION

NAEYC recognizes that many daily decisions required of those who work with young children are of a moral and ethical nature. The NAEYC Code of Ethical Conduct offers guidelines for responsible behavior and sets forth a common basis for resolving the principal ethical dilemmas encountered in early childhood care and education. The primary focus is on daily practice with children and their families in programs for children from birth through 8 years of age, such as infant/toddler programs, preschools, child-care centers, family child-care homes, kindergartens, and primary classrooms. Many of the provisions also apply to specialists who do not work directly with children, including program administrators, parent and vocational educators, college professors, and child care licensing specialists.

CORE VALUES

Standards of ethical behavior in early childhood care and education are based on commitment to core values that are deeply rooted in the history of our field. We have committed ourselves to

- appreciating childhood as a unique and valuable stage of the human life cycle
- basing our work with children on knowledge of child development
- appreciating and supporting the close ties between the child and family
- recognizing that children are best understood and supported in the context of family, culture, community, and society
- respecting the dignity, worth, and uniqueness of each individual (child, family member, and colleague)
- helping children and adults achieve their full potential in the context of relationships that are based on trust, respect, and positive regard

CONCEPTUAL FRAMEWORK

The Code sets forth a conception of our professional responsibilities in four sections, each addressing an arena of professional relationships: (1) children, (2) families, (3) colleagues, and (4) community and society. Each section includes an introduction to the primary responsibilities of the early childhood practitioner in that arena, a set of ideals pointing in the direction of exemplary professional practice, and a set of principles defining practices that are required, prohibited, and permitted.

The ideals reflect the aspirations of practitioners. **The principles** are intended to guide conduct and assist practitioners in resolving ethical dilemmas encountered in the field. There is not necessarily a corresponding principle for each ideal. Both ideals and principles are intended to direct practitioners to those questions which, when responsibly answered, will provide the basis for conscientious decisionmaking. While the Code provides specific direction and suggestions for addressing some ethical dilemmas, many others will require the practitioner to combine the guidance of the Code with sound professional judgment.

The ideals and principles in this Code present a shared conception of professional responsibility that affirms our commitment to the core values of our field. The Code publicly acknowledges the responsibilities that we in the field have assumed and in so doing supports ethical behavior in our work. Practitioners who face ethical dilemmas are urged to seek guidance in the applicable parts of this Code and in the spirit that informs the whole.

ETHICAL DILEMMAS ALWAYS EXIST

Often, "the right answer"—the best ethical course of action to take—is not obvious. There may be no readily apparent, positive way to handle a situation. One important value may contradict another. When we are caught "on the horns of a dilemma," it is our professional responsibility to consult with all relevant parties in seeking the most ethical course of action to take.

SECTION I: ETHICAL RESPONSIBILITIES TO CHILDREN

Childhood is a unique and valuable stage in the life cycle. Our paramount responsibility is to provide safe, healthy, nurturing, and responsive settings for children. We are committed to supporting children's development, respecting individual differences, helping children learn to live and work cooperatively, and promoting health, self-awareness, competence, self-worth, and resiliency.

IDEALS

I-1.1—To be familiar with the knowledge base of early childhood care and education and to keep current through continuing education and in-service training.

I-1.2—To base program practices upon current knowledge in the field of child development and related disciplines and upon particular knowledge of each child.

I-1.3—To recognize and respect the uniqueness and the potential of each child.

I-1.4—To appreciate the special vulnerability of children.

I-1.5—To create and maintain safe and healthy settings that foster children's social, emotional, intellectual, and physical development and that respect their dignity and their contributions.

I-1.6—To support the right of each child to play and learn in inclusive early childhood programs to the fullest extent consistent with the best interests of all involved. As with adults who are disabled in the larger community, children with disabilities are ideally served in the same settings in which they would participate if they did not have a disability.

I-1.7—To ensure that children with disabilities have access to appropriate and convenient support services and to advocate for the resources necessary to provide the most appropriate settings for all children.

PRINCIPLES

P-1.1—Above all, we shall not harm children. We shall not participate in practices that are disrespectful, degrading, dangerous, exploitative, intimidating, emotionally damaging, or physically harmful to children. *This principle has precedence over all others in this Code.*

P-1.2—We shall not participate in practices that discriminate against children by denying benefits, giving special advantages, or excluding them from programs or activities on the basis of their race, ethnicity, religion, sex, national origin, language, ability, or the status, behavior, or beliefs of their parents. (This principle does not apply to programs that have a lawful mandate to provide services to a particular population of children.)

P-1.3—We shall involve all of those with relevant knowledge (including staff and parents) in decisions concerning a child.

P-1.4—For every child we shall implement adaptations in teaching strategies, learning environment, and curricula, consult with the family, and seek recommendations from appropriate specialists to maximize the potential of the child to benefit from the program. If, after these efforts have been made to work with a child and family, the child does not appear to be benefiting from a program, or the child is seriously jeopardizing the ability of other children to benefit from the program, we shall communicate with the family and appropriate specialists to determine the child's current needs, identify the setting and services most suited to meeting these needs, and assist the family in placing the child in an appropriate setting.

P-1.5—We shall be familiar with the symptoms of child abuse, including physical, sexual, verbal, and emotional abuse, and neglect. We shall know and follow state laws and community procedures that protect children against abuse and neglect.

P-1.6—When we have reasonable cause to suspect child abuse or neglect, we shall report it to the appropriate community agency and follow-up to ensure that appropriate action has been taken. When appropriate, parents or guardians will be informed that the referral has been made.

P-1.7—When another person tells us of a suspicion that a child is being abused or neglected, we shall assist that person in taking appropriate action to protect the child.

P-1.8—When a child-protective agency fails to provide adequate protection for abused or neglected children, we acknowledge a collective ethical responsibility to work toward improvement of these services.

P-1.9—When we become aware of a practice or situation that endangers the health or safety of children, but has not been previously known to do so, we have an ethical responsibility to inform those who can remedy the situation and who can protect children from similar danger.

SECTION II: ETHICAL RESPONSIBILITIES TO FAMILIES

Families are of primary importance in children's development. (The term *family* may include others, besides parents, who are responsibly involved with the child.) Because the family and the early childhood practitioner have a common interest in the child's welfare, we acknowledge a primary responsibility to bring about collaboration between the home and school in ways that enhance the child's development.

IDEALS

I-2.1—To develop relationships of mutual trust with families we serve.

I-2.2—To acknowledge and build upon strengths and competencies as we support families in their task of nurturing children.

I-2.3—To respect the dignity of each family and its culture, language, customs, and beliefs.

I-2.4—To respect families' childrearing values and their right to make decisions for their children.

I-2.5—To interpret each child's progress to parents within the framework of a developmental perspective and to help families understand

and appreciate the value of developmentally appropriate early childhood practices.

I-2.6—To help family members improve their understanding of their children and to enhance their skills as parents.

I-2.7—To participate in building support networks for families by providing them with opportunities to interact with program staff, other families, community resources, and professional services.

PRINCIPLES

P-2.1—We shall not deny family members access to their child's classroom or program setting.

P-2.2—We shall inform families of program philosophy, policies, and personnel qualifications, and explain why we teach as we do—which should be in accordance with our ethical responsibilities to children (see Section I).

P-2.3—We shall inform families of, and when appropriate, involve them in, policy decisions.

P-2.4—We shall involve families in significant decisions affecting their child.

P-2.5—We shall inform the family of accidents involving their child, of risks such as exposures to contagious disease that may result in infection, and of occurrences that might result in emotional stress.

P-2.6—To improve the quality of early childhood care and education, we shall cooperate with qualified child development researchers. Families shall be fully informed of any proposed research projects involving their children and shall have the opportunity to give or withhold consent without penalty. We shall not permit or participate in research that could in any way hinder the education, development, or well-being of children.

P-2.7—We shall not engage in or support exploitation of families. We shall not use our relationship with a family for private advantage or personal gain, or enter into relationships with family members that might impair our effectiveness in working with children.

P-2.8—We shall develop written policies for the protection of confidentiality and the disclosure of children's records. These policy documents shall be made available to all program personnel and families. Disclosure of children's records beyond family members, program personnel, and consultants having an obligation of confidentiality shall require familial consent (except in cases of abuse or neglect).

P-2.9—We shall maintain confidentiality and shall respect the family's right to privacy, refraining from disclosure of confidential information and intrusion into family life. However, when we have reason to believe that a child's welfare is at risk, it is permissible to share confidential information with agencies and individuals who may be able to intervene in the child's interest.

P-2.10—In cases where family members are in conflict, we shall work openly, sharing our observations of the child, to help all parties involved make informed decisions. We shall refrain from becoming an advocate for one party.

P-2.11—We shall be familiar with and appropriately use community resources and professional services that support families. After a referral has been made, we shall follow-up to ensure that services have been appropriately provided.

SECTION III: ETHICAL RESPONSIBILITIES TO COLLEAGUES

In a caring, cooperative workplace, human dignity is respected, professional satisfaction is promoted, and positive relationships are modeled. Based upon our core values, our primary responsibility in this arena is to establish and maintain settings and relationships that support productive work and meet professional needs. The same ideals that apply to children are inherent in our responsibilities to adults.

A—RESPONSIBILITIES TO CO-WORKERS

IDEALS

I-3A.1—To establish and maintain relationships of respect, trust, and cooperation with co-workers.

I-3A.2—To share resources and information with co-workers.

I-3A.3—To support co-workers in meeting their professional needs and in their professional development.

I-3A.4—To accord co-workers due recognition of professional achievement.

PRINCIPLES

P-3A.1—When we have a concern about the professional behavior of a co-worker, we shall first let that person know of our concern, in a way that shows respect for personal dignity and for the diversity to be found among staff members, and then attempt to resolve the matter collegially.

P-3A.2—We shall exercise care in expressing views regarding the personal attributes or professional conduct of co-workers. Statements should be based on firsthand knowledge and relevant to the interests of children and programs.

B—RESPONSIBILITIES TO EMPLOYERS

IDEALS

I-3B.1—To assist the program in providing the highest quality of service.

I-3B.2—To do nothing that diminishes the reputation of the program in which we work unless it is violating laws and regulations designed to protect children or the provisions of this Code.

PRINCIPLES

P-3B.1—When we do not agree with program policies, we shall first attempt to effect change through constructive action within the organization.

P-3B.2—We shall speak or act on behalf of an organization only when authorized. We shall take care to acknowledge when we are speaking for the organization and when we are expressing a personal judgment.

P-3B.3—We shall not violate laws or regulations designed to protect children and shall take appropriate action consistent with this Code when aware of such violations.

C—RESPONSIBILITIES TO EMPLOYEES

IDEALS

I-3C.1—To promote policies and working conditions that foster mutual respect, competence, well-being, and positive self-esteem in staff members.

I-3C.2—To create a climate of trust and candor that will enable staff to speak and act in the best interests of children, families, and the field of early childhood care and education.

I-3C.3—To strive to secure equitable compensation (salary and benefits) for those who work with, or on behalf of, young children.

PRINCIPLES

P-3C.1—In decisions concerning children and programs, we shall appropriately utilize the education, training, experience, and expertise of staff members.

P-3C.2—We shall provide staff members with safe and supportive working conditions that permit them to carry out their responsibilities, timely and nonthreatening evaluation procedures, written grievance procedures, constructive feedback, and opportunities for continuing professional development and advancement.

P-3C.3—We shall develop and maintain comprehensive written personnel policies that define program standards and, when applicable, that specify the extent to which employees are accountable for their conduct outside the workplace. These policies shall be given to new staff members and shall be available for review by all staff members.

P-3C.4—Employees who do not meet program standards shall be informed of areas of concern and, when possible, assisted in improving their performance.

P-3C.5—Employees who are dismissed shall be informed of the reason for their termination. When a dismissal is for cause, justification must be based on evidence of inadequate or inappropriate behavior that is accurately documented, current, and available for the employee to review.

P-3C.6—In making evaluations and recommendations, judgments shall be based on fact and relevant to the interests of children and programs.

P-3C.7—Hiring and promotion shall be based solely on a person's record of accomplishment and ability to carry out the responsibilities of the position.

P-3C.8—In hiring, promotion, and provision of training, we shall not participate in any form of discrimination based on race, ethnicity, religion, gender, national origin, culture, disability, age, or sexual preference. We shall be familiar with and observe laws and regulations that pertain to employment discrimination.

SECTION IV: ETHICAL RESPONSIBILITIES TO COMMUNITY AND SOCIETY

Early childhood programs operate within a context of an immediate community made up of families and other institutions concerned with children's welfare. Our responsibilities to the community are to provide programs that meet its needs, to cooperate with agencies and professions that share responsibility for children, and to develop needed programs that are not currently available. Because the larger society has a measure of responsibility for the welfare and protection of children, and because of our specialized expertise in child development, we acknowledge an obligation to serve as a voice for children everywhere.

IDEALS

I-4.1—To provide the community with high-quality (age and individually appropriate, and culturally and socially sensitive) education/care programs and services.

I-4.2—To promote cooperation among agencies and interdisciplinary collaboration among professions concerned with the welfare of young children, their families, and their teachers.

I-4.3—To work, through education, research, and advocacy, toward an environmentally safe world in which all children receive adequate health care, food, and shelter, are nurtured, and live free from violence.

I-4.4—To work, through education, research, and advocacy, toward a society in which all young children have access to high-quality education/care programs.

I-4.5—To promote knowledge and understanding of young children and their needs. To work toward greater social acknowledgment of children's rights and greater social acceptance of responsibility for their well-being.

I-4.6—To support policies and laws that promote the well-being of children and families, and to oppose those that impair their well-being. To participate in developing policies and laws that are needed, and to cooperate with other individuals and groups in these efforts.

I-4.7—To further the professional development of the field of early childhood care and education and to strengthen its commitment to realizing its core values as reflected in this Code.

PRINCIPLES

P-4.1—We shall communicate openly and truthfully about the nature and extent of services that we provide.

P-4.2—We shall not accept or continue to work in positions for which we are personally unsuited or professionally unqualified. We shall not offer services that we do not have the competence, qualifications, or resources to provide.

P-4.3—We shall be objective and accurate in reporting the knowledge upon which we base our program practices.

P-4.4—We shall cooperate with other professionals who work with children and their families.

P-4.5—We shall not hire or recommend for employment any person whose competence, qualifications, or character makes him or her unsuited for the position.

P-4.6—We shall report the unethical or incompetent behavior of a colleague to a supervisor when informal resolution is not effective.

P-4.7—We shall be familiar with laws and regulations that serve to protect the children in our programs.

P-4.8—We shall not participate in practices which are in violation of laws and regulations that protect the children in our programs.

P-4.9—When we have evidence that an early childhood program is violating laws or regulations protecting children, we shall report it to persons responsible for the program. If compliance is not accomplished within a reasonable time, we will report the violation to appropriate authorities who can be expected to remedy the situation.

P-4.10—When we have evidence that an agency or a professional charged with providing services to children, families, or teachers is failing to meet its obligations, we acknowledge a collective ethical responsibility to report the problem to appropriate authorities or to the public.

P-4.11—When a program violates or requires its employees to violate this Code, it is permissible, after fair assessment of the evidence, to disclose the identity of that program.

STATEMENT OF COMMITMENT

As an individual who works with young children, I commit myself to furthering the values of early childhood education as they are reflected in the NAEYC Code of Ethical Conduct.

To the best of my ability I will

- Ensure that programs for young children are based on current knowledge of child development and early childhood education.
- Respect and support families in their task of nurturing children.
- Respect colleagues in early childhood education and support them in maintaining the NAEYC Code of Ethical Conduct.
- Serve as an advocate for children, their families, and their teachers in community and society.
- Maintain high standards of professional conduct.
- Recognize how personal values, opinions, and biases can affect professional judgment.
- Be open to new ideas and be willing to learn from the suggestions of others.
- Continue to learn, grow, and contribute as a professional.
- Honor the ideals and principles of the NAEYC Code of Ethical Conduct.

This Code of Ethical Conduct and Statement of Commitment was prepared under the auspices of the Ethics Commission of the National Association for the Education of Young Children. Stephanie Feeney and Kenneth Kipnis did extensive research and prepared a "Draft Code of Ethics and Statement of Commitment." Following a five-year process involving the NAEYC membership, the Code of Ethical Conduct and Statement of Commitment was approved by NAEYC's Governing Board in July 1989.

Responsibility for reviewing the Code and preparing recommendations for revisions is assigned to NAEYC's Panel on Professional Ethics in Early Childhood Education. The first set of revisions was adopted in 1992 and the second set was approved by NAEYC's Governing Board in November 1997. The Code is reviewed for possible revision every five years.

The Statement of Commitment expresses those basic personal commitments that individuals must make in order to align themselves with the profession's responsibilities as set forth in the NAEYC *Code of Ethical Conduct. It is a recognition that the ultimate strength of the Code rests in the adherence of individual educators.*

Stephanie Feeney, Ph.D., is professor and early childhood education specialist at the University of Hawaii at Manoa. She is a former member of NAEYC's Governing Board. **Kenneth Kipnis,** Ph.D., professor of philosophy at the University of Hawaii at Manoa, has written on legal philosophy and ethical issues in law, medicine, engineering, and other professions.

This copy of the Code is a reprint of NAEYC's brochure *Code of Ethical Conduct and Statement of Commitment (Washington, DC: National Association for the Education of Young Children, 1998).*

Appendix D

YOUNG PEOPLE WITH DISABILITIES
A Booklist

This booklist presents titles of books for children and adults about young people with disabilities. It is the intention of this booklist to open a door to understanding and knowledge.

Juneau Public Libraries
City and Borough of Juneau
1993

BOOKS FOR KIDS

Berkus, Clara Widess. ***Charlie's chuckle.***
This is a delightful picture book with an out-of-the-ordinary young hero, an adventurous seven-year-old boy who happens to have Down syndrome. This thought-provoking tale will encourage youngsters with special needs to recognize their talents, while teaching children of all ages and abilities that everyone has an important contribution to make.

Booth, Barbara D. ***Mandy.***
Hearing-impaired Mandy risks going out into the stormy night to look for her beloved grandmother's lost pin.

Burnett, Frances Hodgson. ***The secret garden.***
Mary Lennox, a bad-tempered little girl, goes to live with her uncle and her crippled cousin, Colin, on their large estate. There she learns of a secret garden shut up for ten years since the death of her uncle's wife. With the help of a small robin, Mary and Colin learn the healing power of nature and the magic of love.

Carrick, Carol. ***Stay away from Simon!***
Lucy and her younger brother examine their feelings about a mentally disabled boy they both fear when he follows them home one snowy day.

Caseley, J. ***Harry and Willy and Carrothead.***
Three boys overcome prejudicial ideas about appearances and become friends.

Clifton, Lucille. ***My friend Jacob.***
A young boy talks about Jacob, who, though older and mentally slower, helps him and becomes his very best friend.

DePaola, Tomie. ***Now one foot, now the other.***
When his grandfather suffers a stroke, Bobby teaches him to walk, just as his grandfather had once taught him.

Gilson, Jamie. ***Do bananas chew gum?***
Sam has "this learning disability thing." In a new town and a new school, he hopes to overcome the old "dumbhead Sam" image. With help from those who think something can be done, Sam is on his way.

Haldone, Suzanne. ***Helping hands: How monkeys assist people who are disabled.***
A photo-essay focusing on a teenager with quadriplegia and his capuchin monkey that is trained to provide help and companionship.

Krementz, Jill. ***How it feels to live with a physical disability.***
This book introduces readers to 12 young people, ages 6 to 16, who have been challenged by physical disabilities. The author devotes a chapter to each story, writing in first person from the child's point of view.

Kuklin, Susan. ***Thinking big; the story of a young dwarf.***
Text and photos depict the life of an eight-year-old dwarf who lives in an average-sized family and attends a regular school.

Lasker, Joe. ***Nick joins in.***
When Nick enters a regular classroom for the first time, he and his new classmates must learn about each other's abilities.

Lasker, Joe. ***He's my brother.***
An older brother talks realistically, yet empathetically, about Jamie, whose physical and mental development are uneven.

Lee, Jeanne. ***Silent Lotus.***
Although she cannot speak or hear, Lotus trains as a Khmer court dancer and becomes eloquent in dancing out legends.

MacLachlan, Patricia. ***Through Grandpa's eyes.***
A young boy learns a different way of viewing the world from his blind grandfather. He even learns to see the smile in his grandmother's voice.

Marron, Carol A. ***No trouble for Grandpa.***
David, a child with a disability, has trouble accepting the fact that his baby sister is going to share his visit with his grandfather.

Martin, Bill. ***Knots on a climbing rope.***
A grandfather and his blind grandson, Boy-Strength-of-Blue-Horses, reminisce about the young boy's birth, his first horse, and an exciting horse race.

Peterson, Jean. ***I have a sister—my sister is deaf.***
A young girl describes how her deaf sister experiences everyday happenings.

Pirner, Connie White. ***Even little kids get diabetes.***
A young girl who has had diabetes since she was two years old describes her adjustments to the disease.

Rabe, Bernice. ***Where's Chimpy?***
This book shows Misty, a little girl with Down syndrome, and her father reviewing her day's activities in their search for her stuffed monkey.

Rabe, Bernice. ***The balancing girl.***
A first grader thinks up her greatest balancing act ever to benefit the school carnival.

Rankin, Laura. ***The handmade alphabet.***
The language of signing celebrates its beauty and rich imagery in this wonderfully illustrated book.

Russo, Marisabina. ***Alex is my friend.***
Even though Alex has difficulty getting about because of his disabilities, his friend does not mind because they still have good times together.

Smith, E. ***A service dog goes to school.***
Follows the selection, raising, training, and placement of a service dog named Licorice. Includes a list of service dog schools and organizations.

BOOKS FOR ADULTS

Anderson, Winifred. ***Negotiating the special education maze.***
A step-by-step guide to the special education system beginning with the first evaluation. Included are how the system works, what services are available, and what rights are protected under federal law.

Batshaw, Mark L., M.D. ***Your child has a disability; a complete sourcebook of daily and medical care.***
This sourcebook includes information on getting a diagnosis, genetic counseling, causes, and descriptions of individual disabilities and approaches to treatment. Dr. Batshaw is Physician-in-chief at Children's Seashore House.

Buck, Pearl. ***The child who never grew.***
While social and educational programs have vastly improved since Ms. Buck's day, the emotions of the author, whose daughter has mental retardation, is timeless.

Children with . . . : A parent's guide.
Woodbine House has published a series of books for parents and educators of children with disabilities. Many of these books address single disabilities and are entitled "Children with. . . ." They are well written, informative, and current.

Krementz, Jill. ***How it feels to fight for your life.***
Fourteen children tell how they battle pain, uncertainty, and the changes brought about in their lives by serious illnesses.

Little, Jean. ***The stars come out within.***
Continues the life story of the Canadian writer who grew up visually impaired and later completely lost her sight.

MacCracken, Mary. ***Turnabout children: overcoming dyslexia.***
Ms. MacCracken writes of her years as a teacher of children with learning disabilities. A warm and loving story.

Moore, Cory. ***A reader's guide for parents of children with mental, physical, or emotional disabilities.***
This guide includes more than 1,000 books and other literature on disabilities. Areas covered include: advocacy, "where-to-write," technical aids, journals, newsletters, and bibliographies.

Schwartz, Sue. ***The language of toys.***
This book teaches parents how to improve their child's communication skills at home with fun, easy-to-follow exercises.

Simons, Jeanne and Oishi, Sabine. ***The hidden child: The Linwood method for reaching the autistic child.***
Ms. Simons and her co-author have chronicled her successful treatment program in this informative book.

Thompson, Mary. ***My brother, Matthew.***
This is a realistic, compassionate tale about how family life typically focuses on the needs of a child with a disability, and the effects that may have on the other children in the family. Siblings often need help understanding and adjusting.

Trainer, Marilyn. ***Differences in common: straight talk on mental retardation, Down syndrome and life.***
An engaging collection of more than fifty essays, this book spans the life of the author's son, Ben, born with Down syndrome more than 20 years ago. Ms. Trainer discusses such issues as public attitudes, family adjustment, job training, parenting, mainstreaming, and education.

The Americans With Disabilities Act was signed into law on July 26, 1990. Enactment of the ADA reflects the belief that each individual is entitled to equal opportunity. The surest path to our nation's vitality and strength is through the contributions of all its citizens.

References

Adler, A. (1917). *Study of organ inferiority and its psychological compensation.* New York: Nervous Disease Publications.

Adler, A. (1927). *The practice and theory of individual psychology.* New York: Harcourt Brace Jovanovich.

Albert, L. (1996). *Cooperative discipline.* Circle Pines, MN: American Guidance Service.

Azmitia, M., & Montgomery, R. (1993). Friendship, transactive dialogues, and the development of scientific reasoning. *Social Development, 2,* 202–221.

Banks, R. (April 1997). Bullying in schools. *ERIC Digest,* EDO- PS - 97-17.

Baumerind, D. (1967). Child care practices anteceding three patterns of preschool behavior. *Genetic Psychology Monographs, 75,* 43–88.

Beal, C. R. (1994). *Boys and girls: The development of gender roles.* New York: McGraw-Hill.

Beane, A. L. (1999). *The bully free classroom.* Minneapolis: Free Spirit Publishing.

Bebeau, M. J., Rest, J. R., & Narvaez, D. (1999). Beyond the promise: A perspective on research in moral education. *Educational Researcher, 28*(4), 18–25.

Berger, K. S. (1998). *The developing person through the lifespan.* New York: Worth.

Berk, L. (1996). *Infants and children: Prenatal through middle childhood.* Boston: Allyn & Bacon.

Berk, L. E. (1994). Vygotsky's theory: The importance of make-believe play. *Young Children, 50*(1), 30–39.

Beyer, L. E. (1998). Uncontrolled students eventually become unmanageable. In R. E. Butchart & B. McEwan, *Classroom discipline in American schools: Problems and possibilities for democratic education* (pp. 51–84). Albany, NY: State University of New York Press.

Bhavnagri, N. P., & Samuels, B. G. (1996). Making and keeping friends: A thematic unit to promote understanding of peer relationships in young children. *Childhood Education, 72*(4), 219–223.

Billman, J. (1992). The Native American curriculum: Attempting alternatives to teepees and headbands. *Young Children, 47*(6), 22–25.

Bloch, M. N., Tabachnick, B. R., & Espinosa-Dulanto, M. (1994). Teacher perspectives on the strengths and achievements of young children: Relationships to ethnicity, language, gender and class. In B. L. Mallory & R. S. New (Eds.), *Diversity and developmentally appropriate practices: Challenges for early childhood education.* New York: Teachers College Press.

Blount, J. (1998). The visceral pleasures of a well-worn rut. In R. E. Butchart & B. McEwan, *Classroom discipline in American schools: Problems and possibilities for democratic education* (pp. 85–108). Albany, NY: State University of New York Press.

Bodrova, E., & Leong, D. J. (1998). Development of dramatic play in young children and its effects on self-regulation: the Vygotskian approach. *Journal of Early Childhood Teacher Education, 19*(2), 115–124.

Boutte, G. S., & McCormick, C. B. (1992). Authentic multicultural activities: Avoiding pseudomulticulturalism. *Childhood Education, 68*(3), 140–144.

Bowman, B. T., & Stott, F. M. (1994). Understanding development in a cultural context: The challenge for teachers. In B. L. Mallory & R. S. New (Eds.), *Diversity and developmentally appropriate practices: Challenges for early childhood education.* New York: Teachers College Press.

Bredekamp, S. (Ed.). (1997). *Developmentally appropriate practice in early childhood programs serving children from birth through age 8* (expanded ed.). Washington, DC: National Association for the Education of Young Children.

Bredekamp, S., & Copple, C. (Eds.). (1997). *Developmentally appropriate practice in early childhood programs.* Washington, DC: National Association for the Education of Young Children.

Bredekamp, S., & Rosegrant, T. (Eds.). (1992). *Reaching potentials: Appropriate curriculum and assessment for young children.* Washington, DC: National Association for the Education of Young Children.

Bredekamp, S., & Rosegrant, T. (Eds.). (1995). *Transforming early childhood curriculum and assessment* (Vol. 2). Washington, DC: National Association for the Education of Young Children.

Britain, L. (1992). *Having wonderful ideas together: Children's spontaneous collaboration in a self-directed play context.* Unpublished doctoral dissertation, University of Oregon, Eugene.

British Columbia Ministry of Education. (1990) Primary program resource document. Victoria, British Columbia: Author.

Brofenbrenner, U. (1979). *The ecology of human development.* Cambridge: Harvard University Press.

Bronson, M. B. (2000). Recognizing and supporting the development of self-regulation in young children. *Young Children, 55*(2), 32–37.

Brophy, J. E. (1981). Teacher praise: A functional analysis. *Review of Educational Research, 51*(1), 5–32.

Bruner, J. (1987). The transactional self. In J. Bruner & H. Haste (Eds.), *Making sense: The child's construction of the world.* New York: Methuen.

Burk, D. J. (1996). Understanding friendship and social interaction. *Childhood Education, 72*(5), 282–285.

Buss, A. H., & Plomin, R. (1984). *Temperament: Early developing personality traits.* Hillsdale, NJ: Lawrence Erlbaum.

Butchart, R. E. (1998). Introduction. In R. E. Butchart, & B. McEwan, *Classroom discipline in American schools: Problems and possibilities for democratic education* (pp. 1–16). Albany, NY: State University of New York Press.

Butchart, R. E., & McEwan, B. (1998). *Classroom discipline in American schools: Problems and possibilities for democratic education.* Albany, NY: State University of New York Press.

Canter, L. (1976). *Assertive discipline: A take charge approach for today's educators.* Los Angeles: Lee Canter and Associates.

Canter, L., & Canter, M. (1992). *Assertive discipline: Positive behavior management for today's classroom.* Santa Monica, CA: Lee Canter & Associates.

Caspi, A. (1998). Personality development across the life course, In Damon and Eisenberg (Eds.), *Handbook of child psychology* (pp. 311–388). New York: John Wiley & Sons, Inc.

Chaille, C., & Britain, L. (1997). *The young child as scientist: A Constructivist approach to early childhood science education.* New York: Longman Press.

Chaille, C., & Silvern, S. B. (1996). Understanding through play. *Childhood Education, 72*(5), 274–277.

Charles, C. M. (1996). *Building classroom discipline.* White Plains, NY: Longman.

Clark, L., DeWolf, S., & Clark, C. (1992). Teaching teachers to avoid having culturally assaultive classrooms. *Young Children, 47*(5), 4–9.

Clayton, M. K. (Spring 1997). Teacher tips: Helpful ideas for the responsive classroom teacher. *The Responsive Classroom,* 4–5.

Coie, J. D., & Dodge, K. A. (1998). Aggression and antisocial behavior. In Damon and Eisenberg (Eds.), *Handbook of child psychology* (pp. 779–862). New York: John Wiley & Sons, Inc.

Coloroso, B. (1994). *Giving your child the gift of inner discipline.* New York: William Morrow.

Committee for Children. (1991). *Second step: A violence-prevention curriculum.* Seattle: Committee for Children.

Corsaro, W. (1985). *Friendship and peer culture in the early years.* New York: Ablex.

Corso, M. (1993). Is developmentally appropriate physical education the answer to children's school readiness? *Colorado Journal of Health, Physical Education, Recreation and Dance, 19*(2), 6–7.

Cryan, J. R. (1987). *The banning of corporal punishment: In child care, school and other educative settings in the United States.* A position paper of the Association for Childhood Education

International. Wheaton, MD: Association for Childhood Education International.

Cunningham, P., Hall, D., & Defee, M. (1998). Nonability-grouped, multilevel instruction: Eight years later. *The Reading Teacher, 51*(8), 652–664.

Curran, J. M. (1999). Constraints of pretend play: Explicit and Implicit Rules. *Journal of Research in Childhood Education, 14*(1), 47–55.

Curry, N. E., & Johnson, C. N. (1990). *Beyond self-esteem: Developing a genuine sense of human value.* Washington, DC: National Association for the Education of Young Children.

Curry, S. J., Wagner, E. H., & Grothaus, L. C. (1991). Evaluation of intrinsic and extrinsic motivation interventions with a self-help smoking cessation program. *Journal of Consulting and Clinical Psychology, 59,* 318–324.

Curwin, R. L., & Mendler, A. N. (1988). *Discipline with dignity.* Alexandria, VA: Association for Supervision and Curriculum Development.

Curwin, R. L., & Mendler, A. N. (1990). *Am I in trouble? Using discipline to teach young children responsibility.* Santa Cruz, CA: Network Publications.

Damon, W. (1983). *Social and personality development: Infancy through adolescence.* New York: Norton.

Daro, D., Abrahams, N., & Robson, K. (May, 1988). *Reducing child abuse 20% by 1990: 1983–86 baseline data.* Chicago: National Center on Child Abuse Prevention Research.

Davidson, J. (1980). Wasted time: The ignored dilemma. *Young Children, 35*(1), 13–21.

De Gaetano, Y., Williams, L. R., & Volk, D. (1998). *Kaleidoscope: A multicultural approach for the primary school classroom.* Upper Saddle River, NJ: Merrill/Prentice Hall.

Derman-Sparks, L. (1999). Markers of multicultural/antibias education. *Young Children, 54*(5), 43.

Developmental Studies Center. (1998). *Ways we want our class to be: Class meetings that build commitment to kindness and learning.* Oakland, CA: author.

DeVries, R. (1999). Implications of Piaget's Constructivist theory for character education. In M. M. Williams & E. Shaps (Eds.). *Character Education: The foundation for teacher education* (pp. 33–39). Washington, DC: The Character Education Partnership.

DeVries, R., Hildebrandt, C., & Zan, B. (2000). Constructivist early education for moral development. *Early Education & Development, 11*(1), 10–35.

DeVries, R., & Kohlberg, L. (1987). *Constructivist early education: Overview and comparison with other programs.* Washington, DC: National Association for the Education of Young Children.

DeVries, R., & Zan, B. (1994). *Moral classrooms, moral children.* New York: Teachers College Press.

DeVries, R., & Zan, B. (1995). Creating a Constructivist classroom atmosphere. *Young Children, 50*(6), 4–13.

DeVries, R., & Zan, B. (1996). Assessing interpersonal understanding in the classroom context. *Childhood Education, 72*(5), 265–268.

Dill, V. S. (1998). *A peaceable school: Cultivating a culture of nonviolence.* Bloomington, Indiana: Phi Delta Kappa.

Dixon-Krauss, L. (1996). *Vygotsky in the classroom: Mediated literacy instruction and assessment.* White Plains, NY: Longman.

Dobson, J. (1970). *Dare to discipline.* Wheaton, IL: Tyndale House.

Dodge, K. A., Bates J. E., & Pettit, G. S. (1990). Mechanisms in the cycle of violence. *Science, 250,* 1678–1683.

Dreikurs, R. (1964). *Children: The challenge.* New York: Hawthorne Books.

Dreikurs, R., Greenwald, B., & Pepper, F. (1982). *Maintaining sanity in the classroom: Classroom management techniques.* New York: Harper & Row.

Drug Strategies. (1998). *Safe schools, safe students: A guide to violence-prevention strategies.* Washington, DC: Drug Strategies.

Duckworth, E., and Cleary, J. (1990). A story for Larry. *New Directions for Child Development, 47,* 71–76.

Educational Productions, Inc. (2000). Supporting transitions: Easing the troublespots. *Preventing Discipline Problems* (video series). Beaverton, OR: author.

Edwards, C., Gandini, L., & Forman, G. (1998). *The hundred languages of children: The Reggio Emilia approach-advanced reflections.* Connecticut: Ablex Publishing Corporation.

Edwards, C. P. (1986). *Promoting social and moral development in young children: Creative approaches for the classroom.* New York: Teachers College Press.

Eisenberg, N. (1992). *The caring child.* Cambridge MA: Harvard University Press.

Eisenberg, N., & Fabes, R. A. (1998). Prosocial development. In Damon and Eisenberg (Eds.). *Handbook of child psychology* (pp. 701–778). New York: John Wiley & Sons, Inc.

Eisenberg, N., & McNally, S. (1993). Socialization and mothers' and adolescents' empathy-related characteristics. *Journal of Research on Adolescence, 3,* 171–191.

Elswood, R. (1999). Really including diversity in early childhood classrooms. *Young Children, 54*(4), 62–66.

Erikson, E. (1963). *Childhood and society* (2nd ed.). New York: Norton.

Essa, E., & Murray, C. (1999, Summer). Sexual Play: When should you be concerned? *Childhood Education,* pp. 231–233.

Faber, A., & Mazlish, E. (1996). *How to talk so kids can learn at home and in school.* New York: Fireside/Simon & Schuster.

Feeney, S., Christensen, D., & Moravcik, E. (1996). *Who am I in the lives of children?* Upper Saddle River, NJ: Merrill/Prentice Hall.

Feeney, S., & Kipnis, K. (1999). *Ethics and the early childhood educator: Using the N.A.E.Y.C. code.* Washington DC.

Feiring, C., & Lewis, M. (1991). The development of social networks from early to middle childhood: Gender differences and the relation to school competence. *Sex Roles, 25,* 237–253.

Ferber, J. (1996). Therapeutic teacher, therapeutic classroom. In L. Koplow (Ed.). *Unsmiling faces: Preschools that heal.* New York: Teachers College Press.

Fields, M. V., & Spangler, K. L. (2000). *Let's begin reading right: Developmentally appropriate beginning literacy.* Upper Saddle River, NJ: Prentice Hall.

Forman, G., & Fyfe, B. (1998). Negotiated Learning Through Design, Documentation, and Discourse. In C. Edwards, L. Gandini, & G. Forman (Eds.). *The hundred languages of children: The Reggio Emilia approach-advanced reflections* (2nd ed.). Connecticut: Ablex Publishing Corporation.

Freeman, L. (1983). *It's my body.* Seattle: Parenting Press.

Froschl, M., & Sprung, B. (1999). On purpose: Addressing teasing and bullying in early childhood. *Young Children, 54*(3), 70–72.

Furman, R. A. (1995). Helping children cope with *stress* and deal with feelings. *Young Children, 50*(2), 33–41.

Garbarino, J., Dubrow, N., Kostelny, K., & Pardo, C. (1992). *Children in danger: Coping with the consequences of community violence.* San Francisco: Jossey-Bass Publishers.

Gareau, M., & Kennedy, C. (1991). Structure time and space to promote pursuit of learning in the primary grades. *Young Children, 46*(4), 46–51.

Gartrell, D. (1987a). Assertive discipline: Unhealthy for children and other living things. *Young Children, 42*(2), 10–11.

Gathercoal, F. (1998). Judicious discipline. In R. E. Butchart, & B., McEwan, *Classroom discipline in American schools: problems and possibilities for democratic education* (pp. 197–216). Albany, NY: State University of New York Press.

Geller, E. S., Rudd, J. R., Kalsher, M. J., Streff, F. M., & Lehman, G. R. (1987). Employer-based programs to motivate safety belt use: A review of short-term and long-term effects. *Journal of Safety Research, 18,* 1–17.

Genishi, C. (Ed.). (1992). *Ways of assessing children and curriculum.* New York: Teachers College Press.

Genishi, C., Dyson, A. H., & Fassler, R. (1994). Language and diversity in early childhood: Whose voices are appropriate? In B. L. Mallory & R. S. New (Eds.), *Diversity and developmentally appropriate practices: Challenges for early childhood education.* New York: Teachers College Press.

Gibbs, J. (1995). *Tribes: A new way of learning and being together.* Sausalito, CA: Centersource Systems, LLC.

Gilligan, C., & Wiggens, G. (1987). The origins of morality in early childhood relationships. In J. Kagan & S. Lamb (Eds.), *The emergence of morality in young children.* Chicago, IL: University of Chicago Press.

Ginott, H. (1965). *Between parent and child: New solutions to old problems.* New York: Macmillan.

Glasser, W. (1992). *The quality school: Managing students without coercion.* New York: Harper Perennial.

Goldman, L. (2000). We can help children grieve: A child-oriented model for memorializing. *Young Children, 51*(6), 69–83.

Gonzalez-Mena, J. (1993). *The child in the family and the community.* USR, NJ: M/PH.

Gordon, A., & Browne, K. W. (1996). *Guiding young children in a diverse society.* Boston: Allyn & Bacon.

Gordon, T. (1970). *Parent effectiveness training.* New York: Wyden.

Gordon, T. (1989). *Teaching children self-discipline: At home and at school.* New York: Random House.

Gordon, T., & Sands, J. S. (1976). *P.E.T. in action.* New York: Bantam.

Greenberg, P. (1987). Ideas that work with young children: Child choice—another way to individualize—another form of preventive discipline. *Young Children, 43*(1), 48–54.

Greenberg, P. (1992a). Ideas that work with young children. How to institute some simple democratic practices pertaining to respect, rights, responsibilities, and roots in any classroom (without losing your leadership position). *Young Children, 47*(5), 10–17.

Greenberg, P. (1992b). Why not academic preschool? (Part 2). Autocracy or democracy in the classroom? *Young Children, 47*(3), 54–64.

Grossman, H. (1990). *Trouble-free teaching: Solutions to behavior problems in the classroom.* Mountain View, CA: Mayfield.

Gruber, H. E., & Voneche, J. J. (Eds.). (1977). *The essential Piaget: An interpretive reference guide.* New York: Basic Books.

Grusec, J. E. (1991). Socializing concern for others in the home. *Developmental Psychology, 27,* 338–342.

Gunnar, M. R., Mangelsdorf, S., Larson, M., & Hertsgaard, L. (1989). Attachment, temperament, and adrenocortical activity in infancy: A study of psychoendocrine regulation. *Developmental Psychology, 25,* 355–363.

Guralnick, M. J., & Groom, J. M. (1988). Peer interactions in mainstreamed and specialized classrooms: A comparative analysis. *Exceptional Children, 54,* 415–428.

Hall, N. S. (1999). *Creative resources for the anti-bias classroom.* Albany, NY: Delmar Publishers.

Hannaford, C. (1995). *Smart moves: Why learning is not all in your head.* Arlington, VA: Great Ocean Publishing.

Harris, T. T., & Fuqua, J. D. (2000). What goes around comes around: Building a community of learners through circle times. *Young Children, 55*(1), 44–47.

Hart, C. H., Burts, D. C., Durland, M. A., Charlesworth, R., DeWolf, M., & Fleege, P. O. (spring/summer 1998). Stress behaviors and activity type participation of preschoolers in more and less developmentally appropriate classrooms: SES and sex differences. *Journal of Research in Childhood Education, 12*(2), pp. 176–196.

Hart, C. H., Olsen, S. F., Robinson, C. C., & Mandleco, B. L. (l997). The development of social and communicative competence in childhood: Review and a model of personal, familial, and extrafamilial processes. *Communication Yearbook, 20,* 305–373.

Harter, S. (1998). The development of self-representation. In Damon and Eisenberg (Eds.). *Handbook of child psychology* (pp. 553–618). New York: John Wiley & Sons, Inc.

Hartup, W. W., & Moore, S. G. (1990). Early peer relations: Developmental significance and prognostic implications. *Early Childhood Research Quarterly, 5*(1), 1–18.

Hendrick, J. (2001). *The whole child: Developmental curriculum for the young child* (7th ed.). Upper Saddle River, NJ: Merrill/Prentice Hall.

Hitz, R. (1988). Assertive discipline: A response to Lee Canter. *Young Children, 43*(2), 25–26.

Hitz, R., & Driscoll, A. (1988). Praise or encouragement? New insights into praise: Implications for early childhood teachers. *Young Children, 43*(5), 6–13.

Holland, J. J. (July 26, 2000). Games, Media linked to violence. (news article). Washington DC: Associated Press.

Honig, A. S., & Wittmer, D. S. (1996). Helping children become more prosocial: Ideas for classrooms, families, schools, and communities. *Young Children, 51*(2), 62–70.

Horton, J., & Zimmer, J. (1994). *Media violence and children, a guide for parents.* (brochure). Washington DC: National Association for the Education of Young Children.

Howes, C. (1988). Same- and cross-sex friends: Implications for interaction and social skills. *Early Childhood Research Quarterly, 3,* 21–37.

Hughes, E. (1999). If you have sun and you have rain you get a rainbow: Creating meaningful curriculum. *Journal of Early Childhood Teacher Education,* (20), 2.

Hunt, R. (1999). Making positive multicultural early childhood education happen. *Young Children, 54*(5), 39–42.

Hymes, J. (1990). *Teaching the child under six* (3rd ed.). West Greenwich, RI: Consortium Publishing.

Hyson, M. C. (1994). *The emotional development of young children: Building an emotion-centered curriculum.* New York: Teachers College Press.

Jambunathan, S., Burts, D. C., & Pierce, S H. (1999). Developmentally appropriate practices as predictors of self-competence among preschoolers. *Journal of Research in Childhood Education, 13*(2), 167–174.

Jenkins, G. D., Jr. (1986). Financial incentives. In E. A. Locke (Ed.), *Generalizing from laboratory to field settings.* Lexington, MA: Lexington Books.

Johnson, C., Ironsmith, M., Snow, C. W., & Poteat, G. M. (2000). Peer acceptance and social adjustment in preschool and kindergarten. *Early Childhood Education Journal,* 27(4), 207–212.

Jones, B. (1991). *A sourcebook on attention deficit disorder: A management guide for early childhood professionals and parents.* San Antonio, TX: Psychological Corporation.

Jones, E. (1977). *Dimensions of teaching learning environments: Handbook for teachers.* Pasadena, CA: Pacific Oaks.

Jones, E., & Nimmo, J. (1994). *Emergent curriculum.* Washington, DC: National Association for the Education of Young Children.

Jones, I., & Gullo, D. F. (1999). Differential social and academic effects of developmentally appropriate practice and beliefs. *Journal of Research in Childhood Education, 14*(1), 26–35.

Kagan, J., Reznick, J. S., Clarke, C., Snidman, N., & Garcia-Coll, D. (1984). Behavioral inhibition to the unfamiliar. *Child Development, 55,* 2212–2225.

Kaiser, B. & Rasminsky, J. S. (1999). *Meeting the challenge: Effective strategies for challenging behaviors in early childhood environments.* Ottawa: Canadian Child Care Federation.

Kamii, C. (1982). Autonomy as the aim of education: Implications of Piaget's theory. In C. Kamii (Ed.), *Number in preschool and kindergarten* (pp. 73–87). Washington, DC: National Association for the Education of Young Children.

Kamii, C. (1984). Obedience is not enough. *Young Children, 39*(4), 11–14.

Kamii, C. (Ed.). (1990). *Achievement testing in the early years.* Washington, DC: National Association for the Education of Young Children.

Kamii, C. (2000). *Young children reinvent arithmetic: Implications of Piaget's theory.* New York: Teachers College Press.

Kamii, C., & Ewing, J. K. (1996). Basing teaching on Piaget's constructivism. *Childhood Education, 72*(5), 260–264.

Kamii, C., Manning, M., & Manning, G. (Eds.). (1991). *Early literacy: A Constructivist foundation for whole language.* Washington, DC: National Education Association of the United States.

Kanouse, D. E., Gumpert, P., & Canavan-Gumpert, D. (1981). The semantics of praise. In J. H. Harvey, W. Ickes, & R. F. Kidd (Eds.), *New directions in attribution research* (Vol. 3). Hillsdale NJ: Lawrence Erlbaum Associates.

Karr-Morse, R., & Wiley, M. (1997). *Ghosts from the Nursery: Tracing the roots of violence.* New York: The Atlantic Monthly Press.

Kast, A., & Conner, K. (1988). Sex and age differences in response to informational and controlling feedback. *Personality and Social Psychology Bulletin, 14,* 514–523.

Katz, L. G., & Chard, S. C. (1993). *Engaging children's minds: The project approach.* Norwood, NJ: Ablex.

Katz, L. G., & McClellan, D. E. (1991). *The teacher's role in the social development of young children.* Urbana, IL: ERIC Clearinghouse Document, ED313168.

Katz, L. G., & McClellan, D. E. (1997). *Fostering children's social competence: The teacher's role.* Washington, DC: National Association for the Education of Young Children.

Kemple, K. M., David, G. M., & Hysmith, C. (1997). Teachers' interventions in preschool and kindergarten children's peer interactions. *Journal of Research in Childhood Education, 12*(1), 34–47.

Klein, C. (1975). *The myth of the happy child.* New York: Harper & Row.

Kochanska, G. (1991). Socialization and temperament in the development of guilt and conscience. *Child Development, 62,* 1379–1392.

Kohlberg, L. (1984). *Essays in moral development. Volume 2: The psychology of moral development.* New York: Harper & Row.

Kohn, A. (1993). *Punished by rewards.* New York: Houghton Mifflin.

Kohn, A. (1996). *Beyond discipline: From compliance to community.* Reston, VA: Association for Supervision and Curriculum Development.

Koplow, L. (Ed.). (1996). *Unsmiling faces: How preschools can heal.* New York: Teachers College Press.

Kostelnik, M. J. (1992). Myths associated with developmentally appropriate programs. *Young Children, 47*(4), 17–23.

Kreidler, W. J. (1994). *Teaching conflict resolution through children's literature.* New York: Scholastic.

Kriedler, W. J. (Spring, 1991). Dispute resolution in education: Creating "peaceable classrooms" in elementary schools. *Forum: National Institute for Dispute Resolution,* 5–8.

Kritchevsky, S., Prescott, E., & Walling, L. (1969). *Planning environments for young children: Physical space.* Washington, DC: National Association for the Education of Young Children.

Kupersmidt, J. B., Coie, J. D., & Dodge, K. A. (1990). The role of poor peer relationships in the development of disorder. In S. R. Asher & J. D. Coie (Eds.), *Peer rejection in childhood.* New York: Cambridge University Press.

Landau, S., & McAninch, C. (1993). Young children with attention deficits. *Young Children, 48*(4), 49–58.

Lantieri, L., & Patti, J. (1996). *Waging peace in our schools.* Boston: Beacon Press.

Leppo, M. L., Davis, D., & Crim, B. (Spring 2000). The basics of exercising mind and body. *Childhood Education, 76*(3), 142–147.

Levinthal, D. (2000, July 23). 3 percent of American adults are under corrections supervision. *The Dallas Morning News.*

Lickona, T. (1999). Character education: Seven crucial issues. In M. M. Williams & E. Shaps (Eds.), *Character Education: The foundation for teacher education* (pp. 40–45). Washington, DC: The Character Education Partnership.

Lillard, A., & Curenton, S. (1999). Do young children understand what others feel, want, and know? *Young Children, 554*(5), 52–57.

Lloyd-Jones R. & Lunsford, A. A. (Eds.). (1998). The English Coalition Conference: Democracy through language. Urbane, IL: National Council of Teachers of English.

Lubeck, S. (1985). *Sandbox society: Early education in black and white America—A comparative ethnography.* Philadelphia: Falmer Press.

Lubeck, S. (1994). The politics of developmentally appropriate practice: Exploring issues of culture, class, and curriculum. In B. L. Mallory & R. S. New (Eds.), *Diversity and developmentally appropriate practices: Challenges for early childhood education.* New York: Teachers College Press.

Maccoby, E. E. (1986). Social groupings in childhood: Their relationship to prosocial and antisocial behavior in boys and girls. In D. Olewus, J. Block, & M. Radke-Yarrow (Eds.), *Development of antisocial and prosocial behavior* (pp. 263–284). New York: Academic Press.

Mallory, B., & New, R. (1994). Social constructivist theory and principles of inclusion: Challenges for early childhood special education. *Journal of Special Education, 28*(3), 322–337.

Mallory, B. L., & New. R. S. (Eds.). (1994). *Diversity and developmentally appropriate practices: Challenges for early childhood education.* New York: Teachers College Press.

McCracken, J. B. (1993). *Valuing diversity in the primary years.* Washington, DC: National Association for the Education of Young Children.

McEwan, B. (1998). Contradiction, paradox, and irony. In R. E. Butchart & B. McEwan, *Classroom discipline in American schools: Problems and possibilities for democratic education* (pp. 135–156). Albany, NY: State University of New York Press.

McNeilly-Choque, M. K., Hart, C. H., Robinson, C. C., Nelson, L. J., & Olsen, S. F. (1996). Overt and relational aggression on the playground: Correspondence among different informants. *Journal of Research in Childhood Education, 11*(1), 47–67.

Miller, D. F. (1996). *Positive child guidance* (2nd ed.). Albany, NY: Delmar.

Miller, J. B. (1993). Learning from early relationship experience. In S. Duck (Ed.), *Learning about relationships.* Newbury Park, CA: Sage.

Murphy, D. (1986). Educational disadvantagement: Associated factors, current interventions, and implications. *Journal of Negro Education, 55,* 495–507.

NAEYC. (2000). Police leaders call for investment in quality programs to fight crime. *Young Children, 55*(2). 68–72.

Nash, C. (1979). *A principal's or administrator's guide to kindergarten.* Toronto: Ontario Institute for Studies in Education.

National Council of Teachers of Mathematics. (1995). *Assessment standards for school mathematics.* Reston, VA: author.

National Research Council. (1994). *National science education standards.* Washington, DC: National Academy Press.

Noddings, N. (1992). *The challenge to care in schools: An alternative approach to education.* New York: Teachers College Press.

Noddings, N. (January 1995). A morally defensible mission for schools in the 21st century. *Phi Delta Kappan,* 365–368.

Northeast Foundation for Children. (Summer, 1998). Punishment vs. logical consequences: What's the difference? *Responsive Classroom,* 1–2.

Olson, H., Burgess, D., & Streissguth, A. (1992). Fetal alcohol syndrome (FAS) and fetal alcohol effects (FAE): A lifespan view with implications for early intervention. *Zero to Three, 13*(1), 24–29.

Paley, V. G. (1999). *The kindness of children.* Cambridge, MA: Harvard University Press.

Phillipsen, L. C., Bridges, S. K., McLemore, T. G., & Saponaro, L. A. (1999). Perceptions of social behavior and peer acceptance in kindergarten. *Journal of Research in Childhood Education, 14*(1), 68–77.

Piaget, J. (1960). *The child's conception of the world.* Totowa, NJ: Littlefield, Adams. (Original work published in 1929.)

Piaget, J. (1964). *Judgment and reasoning in the child.* Totowa, NJ: Littlefield, Adams. (Originally published in 1928.)

Piaget, J. (1965). *The moral judgment of the child.* New York: Free Press. (Originally published in 1932.)

Pica, R. (1997). Beyond physical development: Why young children need to move. *Young Children, 52* (6), 4–11.

Powell, D. R. (1994). Parents, pluralism, and the NAEYC statement on developmentally appropriate practice. In B. L. Mallory & R. S. New (Eds.), *Diversity and developmentally appropriate practices: Challenges for early childhood education.* New York: Teachers College Press.

Powlishta, K. K. (1995). Gender segregation among children: Understanding the "Cootie phenomenon." *Young Children, 50*(4), 61–69.

Powlishta, K. K., & Maccoby, E. E. (1990). Resource utilization in mixed-sex dyads: The influence of adult presence and task type. *Sex Roles, 23,* 223–240.

Pritchard, M. S. (1996). *Reasonable children: Moral education and moral learning.* Lawrence, Kansas: University Press of Kansas.

Putallaz, M., & Heflin, A. H. (1990). Parent-child interaction. In S. R. Asher & J. D. Cole (Eds.), *Peer rejection in childhood* (pp. 189–216). New York: Cambridge University Press.

Rabiner, D., & Cole, J. (1989). Effect of expectancy inductions on rejected children's acceptance by unfamiliar peers. *Developmental Psychology, 25*(3), 450–457.

Ramsey, P. G. (1991). *Making friends in school: Promoting peer relationships in early childhood.* New York: Teachers College Press.

Reinsberg, J. (1999). Understanding young children's behavior. *Young Children, 545*(4), 54–56.

Reynolds, E. (1996). *Guiding young children: A child-centered approach.* Mountain View, CA: Mayfield.

Riley, S. R. (1984). *How to generate values in young children.* Washington, DC: National Association for the Education of Young Children.

Rizzo, T. A. (1989). *Friendship development among children in school.* Norwood, NJ: Ablex.

Rizzo, W., & Corsaro, W. A. (1991). *Social support processes in early childhood friendships.* Paper presented at the biennial meeting of the Society for Research in Child Development, Seattle.

Robinson, C. C., Mandleco, B., Olsen, S. F., & Hart, C. H. (1995). Authoritative, authoritarian, and permissive parenting practices: Development of a new measure. *Psychological Reports, 77,* 819–830.

Rothbart, M. K., & Bates, J. E. (1998). Temperament. In Damon and Eisenberg (Eds.). *Handbook of child psychology* (pp. 105–176). New York: John Wiley & Sons, Inc.

Ruckman, A. Y., Burts, D. C., & Pierce, S. H. (1999). Observed stress behaviors of 1st grade children participating in more and less developmentally appropriate activities in a computer-based literacy laboratory. *Journal of Research in Childhood Education, 14*(1), 36–46.

Saarni, C., Mumme, D. L., & Campos, J. J. (1998). Emotional development: Action, communication, and understanding. In Damon and Eisenberg (Eds.). *Handbook of child psychology* (pp. 237–309). New York: John Wiley & Sons, Inc.

Sabatino, D. (1991). *A fine line: When discipline becomes child abuse.* Summit, PA: TAB Books/McGraw-Hill.

Sadalla, G., Holmberg, M., & Halligan, J. (1990). *Conflict resolution: An elementary school curriculum.* San Francisco: The Community Board Program, Inc.

Sansom, A. V., Smart, D. F., Prior, M., Oberklaid, F., & Pedlow, R. (1994). The structure of temperament from three to seven years: Age, sex and sociodemographic influences. *Merrill-Palmer Quarterly, 40,* 233–252.

Schmidt, F., & Friedman, A. (1992). *Peacemaking skills for little kids.* Fresno, CA: Peace Works, Inc.

Schorr, L. (1989). *Within our reach: Breaking the cycle of disadvantage.* New York: Anchor Books/Doubleday.

Schweinhart, L., Weikart, D., & Larner, M. (1986). Consequences of three preschool curriculum models through age 15. *Early Childhood Research Quarterly, 1,* 15–45.

Selman, R. L. (1980). *The growth of interpersonal understanding.* New York: Academic Press.

Selman, R., & Schultz, L. (1990). *Making a friend in youth: Developmental theory and pair therapy.* Chicago: University of Chicago Press.

Siccone, F., & Lopez, L. (2000). *Educating the heart: Lessons to build respect and responsibility.* Boston, Mass: Allyn & Bacon.

Simmons, B. J. (1991). Ban the hickory stick. *Childhood Education, 68*(2), 69.

Skinner, B. F. (1965). *Science and human behavior.* New York: Free Press.

Skinner, B. F. (1971). *Beyond freedom and dignity.* New York: Knopf.

Slaby, R. G., Roedell, W. C., Arezzo, D., & Hendrix, K. (1995). *Early violence prevention: Tools for teachers of young children.* Washington, DC: National Association for the Education of Young Children.

Smith, C. (1998). Children with "special rights" in the preprimary schools and infant-toddler centers in Reggio Emilia. *The hundred languages of children: The Reggio Emilia approach-advanced reflections* (2nd ed.). Connecticut: Ablex Publishing Corporation.

Soukhanov, A. H. (Ed.). (1992). *The American heritage dictionary of the English language*. Boston: Houghton Mifflin.

Spencer, M. B., & Markstrom-Adams, C. (1990). Identity processes among racial and ethnic minority children in America. *Child Development, 61,* 290–310.

Springen, K. (October 16, 2000). Family: On spanking. *Newsweek, CXXXVI* (16), p. 64.

Staley, L., & Portman, P. (2000). Red rover, red rover, it's time to move over! *Young Children, 55*(1), 67–72.

Straus, M. A. (1991). Discipline and deviance: Physical punishment of children and violence and other crime in adulthood. *Social Problems, 38*(2), 133–154.

Tabors, P. O. (1998). What early childhood educators need to know: Developing effective programs for linguistically and culturally diverse children and families. *Young Children, 53*(6), 20–26.

Teaching Tolerance. (1997). *Starting small: Teaching tolerance in preschool and the early grades.* Montgomery, AL: The Southern Poverty Law Center.

Teaching Tolerance. (1999). *Responding to hate at school: A guide for teachers, counselors and administrators.* Montgomery, AL: The Southern Poverty Law Center.

Thomas, A., & Chess, S. (1977). *Temperament and development.* New York: Brunner/Mazel.

Thompson, R. A. (1998). Early sociopersonality development. In Damon and Eisenberg (Eds.). *Handbook of child psychology* (pp. 25–104). New York: John Wiley & Sons, Inc.

TRUCE. (2000). *Media violence and children: A call to action!* (brochure). Sommerville, MA: Teachers Resisting Unhealthy Children's Entertainment.

Vissing, V. M., Straus, M. A., Gelles, R. J., & Harrop, J. W. (1991). Verbal aggression by parents and psychosocial problems of children. *Child Abuse and Neglect, 15,* 223–238.

Vygotsky, L. S. (1962). *Thought and language* (E. Hanfmann & G. Vokar, trans.). Cambridge, MA: MIT Press. (Original work published in 1934.)

Vygotsky, L. S. (1978). *Mind and society: The development of higher mental processes.* Cambridge, MA: Harvard University Press. (Original work published in 1933.)

Watson, M. (1999). The child development project: Building character by building community. In M. M. Williams & E. Shaps (Eds.). *Character Education: The foundation for teacher education* (pp. 24–32). Washington, DC: The Character Education Partnership.

Weaver, C. (1994). *Success at last! Helping students with attention deficit (hyperactivity) disorders achieve their potential.* Portsmouth, NH: Heinemann.

Wieder, S., & Greenspan, S. I. (1993). The emotional basis of learning. In B. Spodek (Ed.), *Handbook of research on the education of young children* (pp. 77–87). New York: Macmillan.

Williams, M. M., & Shaps, E. (Eds.). (1999). *Character Education: The foundation for teacher education.* Washington, DC: The Character Education Partnership.

Wolery, M., & Wilbers, J. S. (Eds.). (1994). *Including children with special needs in early childhood programs.* Washington, DC: National Association for the Education of Young Children.

Wolfgang, C. H., & Wolfgang, M. E. (1995). *The faces of discipline for early childhood.* Boston: Allyn & Bacon.

Children's Literature and Videos

Carle, E. (1977). *The grouchy ladybug.* New York: HarperCollins.

Carlson, N. (1990). *Arnie and the new kid.* New York: Viking.

Carson, J. (1992). *You hold me and I'll hold you.* New York: Orchard Books.

Cosby, B. (1997). *The meanest thing to say.* New York: Scholastic Inc.

Cutler, J. (1993). *Darcy and Gran don't like babies.* New York: Scholastic Inc.

dePaola, T. (1975). *Strega nona.* Upper Saddle River, NJ: Prentice Hall.

dePaola, T. (1979). *Oliver Button is a sissy.* San Diego: Voyager/Harcourt Brace Jovanovich.

Geisel, T. (Dr. Seuss). (1954). *Horton hears a who.* New York: Random House.

Grimm, Brothers. (1967). *Rumpelstiltskin.* New York: Brace and World.

Havill, J. (1995). *Jamaica's blue marker.* Boston: Houghton Mifflin.

Henkes, K. (1991). *Chrysanthemum.* New York: Greenwillow.

Hess, D. (1994). *Wilson sat alone.* New York: Simon & Schuster.

Hoffman, M. (1991). *Amazing Grace.* New York: Dial Books for Young Readers.

Lobel, A. (1972). *Frog and toad together.* New York: Harper & Row.

Milne, A. A. (1957). *The world of Pooh.* New York: E. P. Dutton.

Steig. W. (1988). *Spinky Sulks.* New York: Farrar, Straus and Giroux.

Steptoe, J. (1987). *Mufaro's beautiful daughter.* New York: Lathrop, Lee, & Shepard.

Viorst, J. (1972). *Alexander and the terrible, horrible, no good, very bad day.* New York: Antheneum.

Wade, B. (1990). *Little monster goes to school.* New York: Lothrop, Lee, & Shepard.

Williams, A. (1996). *Dragon soup.* Tiburon, CA: HJ Kramer Inc.

Wood, A. (1985). *King Bidgood's in the bathtub.* San Diego: Harcourt Brace Jovanovich.

Yashima, T. (1976). *Crow boy.* New York: Puffin/Penguin.

Curriculum for Peaceful Classrooms

Committee for Children. (1991). *Second Step: A violence-prevention curriculum.* Seattle: author.

Gibbs, J. (1995) Sausalito, CA: *Tribes: A new way of learning and being together.* CenterSource Systems, LLC.

Kriedler, W. J. (1994). *Teaching conflict resolution through children's literature.* New York: Scholastic.

Sadalla, G., Holmberg, M., & Halligan, J. *Conflict resolution: An elementary school curriculum.* San Francisco: The Community Board Program, Inc.

Schmidt, F., & Friedman, A. (1992) *Peace-making skills for little kids.* Fresno, CA: Peace Works Inc.

Siccone, F., & Lopez, L. (2000) *Educating the heart: Lessons to build respect and responsibility.* Needham Heights, MA: Allyn & Bacon.

Teaching Tolerance. (1997). *Starting small: Teaching tolerance in preschool and the early grades.* Montgomery, AL: The Southern Poverty Law Center.

Teaching Tolerance. (1999). *Responding to hate at school: A guide for teachers, counselors and administrators.* Montgomery, AL: The Southern Poverty Law Center.

Name Index

Subject Index